Oath of Office

by
C. Lee Thornton

authorHOUSE™

1663 LIBERTY DRIVE, SUITE 200
BLOOMINGTON, INDIANA 47403
(800) 839-8640
WWW.AUTHORHOUSE.COM

© 2006 C. Lee Thornton. All Rights Reserved.

No part of this book may be reproduced, stored in a retrieval system, or transmitted by any means without the written permission of the author.

First published by AuthorHouse 01/10/06

ISBN: 1-4208-9391-2 (sc)
ISBN: 1-4208-9392-0 (dj)

Library of Congress Control Number: 2005909678

Printed in the United States of America
Bloomington, Indiana

This book is printed on acid-free paper.

Table of Contents

About The Cover vii

Acknowledgments ix

Prologue xi

1 My Thanks to Him: Lessons Learned 1

2 This Is College - Can They Say That?? 59

3 Application to the FBI 95

4 First Assignment 123

5 Motown Is More Than Music… 137

6 This Ain't the Movies 161

7 Undercover Contract Hit 193

8 Operation Greylord 211

9 It's Not My Time… 239

10 The Burglars and Drug Dealers 273

11 The House of Judah 289

12 Missing From Oak Park 327

13 Terror At Metro Airport 351

14 Welcome To Puerto Rico 363

15 Bank Robbery – Puerto Rican Style 395

16 North County Task Force 411

17 You Know When It's Time… 423

Epilogue 441

ABOUT THE COVER

Highlighted on the cover is the Gateway Arch which symbolizes the gateway to the West. The arch sits on the western bank of the Mississippi River in downtown St. Louis, Missouri.

Pictured beneath the arch is the Old Courthouse where the Dred Scott trial was held in 1847 and 1850. This case concluded with a landmark Supreme Court decision in 1857.

Rising above the Old Courthouse is the badge of the Federal Bureau of Investigation.

ACKNOWLEDGMENTS

I wish to extend a sincere thank you to all my many friends and family who assisted and encouraged me in the development of this project. Without your love, dedication, and understanding this book would not have been possible. From my heart *"Mil gracias por todos."*

PROLOGUE

Oath of Office is dedicated to the memory of my father, Carey Thornton, Sr., who taught me the value of education and to never forget my history. Pop, or the Old Man as we sometimes called him, taught us to never be ashamed of our history and to pass it on from generation to generation. Pop had eight years of formal education but he had the wisdom of a tenured college professor. He knew his history and the history of our struggle inside and out. Pop was not ashamed to give a history lesson at any time to anyone who would listen. In our case we had no choice but to listen as Pop told us how things were when he was a kid and that we'd better take advantage of what he put in front of us.

Pop proclaimed our marching orders daily and constantly let us know that the lack of understanding of those orders could be the difference between a life of "freed slavery" and the good life in a house with automatic heat and cooling. I can still hear Pop's preaching, "Boy, get that education and get all you can. That's the one thing nobody can take from you." We would hear that over and over in a generation when you didn't question advice from the old people. You didn't ask them to repeat it twice, you just did what they told you to do. At a very young age Pop made sure that we understood the meaning of his marching orders.

Unlike some fathers of today, he did not shield us from the "not so nice" things in life. He would show us what happens to those who didn't have an education. Many of the unfortunate were his friends, while others were people we met on the street. Pop always emphasized it was not their fault that they missed out on a good life. He said the denial of a good formal education made life a struggle for many of them. Pop had worked hard to move north and he did his best to keep a roof over our heads. He proclaimed our job was to get a good education and to do our very best for those behind us.

Pop would often take us around his friends while they were just "shooting the bull" in the barbershop and sometimes on the street corners. During those days adults didn't curse or swear in the presence of children but they would "boast and lie" to one another like crazy. One thing they all had in common was a hell of a case of the "I wish I hadda". They all wished they had had the opportunity to travel here or there. They wished they could have driven this car or that car. They wished they could have had the means to buy their wives this coat or that appliance. Regardless of how serious the case of "I wish I hadda" turned out to be, they would always turn to me and say, "Young man, you get that education and you can get anything you want." In those days every adult we met, drove education into us. Friends and family had me repeating that I wanted to be a lawyer or doctor before I knew what I was saying. I only knew that the "grown folk" said lawyers and doctors made a lot of money and that was good enough for me.

Pop and his friends despised how they were treated in the South and they despised the people responsible. They detested being denied educational opportunities and the right to a "good life." Those old guys gave prejudice a new meaning and they preached against their oppressor's everyday. More than anyone in the world, they all detested J. Edgar Hoover and the Federal Bureau of Investigation. When I was very young I couldn't understand how they detested anyone so intently but I learned they all carried a lot of unpleasant history with Hoover and law enforcement.

Needless to say it was a shock to Pop when I told him I had been accepted to the FBI Academy in 1979. He felt the FBI was contrary to everything he had ever taught me. He preached about how Hoover had treated blacks in the South and that it would be next to impossible for any black man to get through the academy. Pop raved about how rotten and disrespectful the police had been toward people of color and that I should try another occupation. Pop told me, "You're going to throw that Master's degree right down the sewer with the FBI. Don't do that to yourself, Son."

For the first time in my life I went against Pop's covenant of obedience to his advice. One day I had to listen. I listened for hours as Pop and my mother, whom we called Moms, gave the most heart-wrenching sermon of their lives trying to convince me not to join the FBI. I just sat and looked from one parent to the other as the words poured out of their souls. My gaze suddenly fixed on my father. He saw the way I looked at him and quickly turned away. He knew what I had seen in his eyes. For the first time in my life I saw something I never wanted to see nor did I ever see again. I had seen hurt—not hurt coming from my disobedience but hurt that came from a lifetime of wanting better things for his people and at this moment thinking that it was not to be. After what seemed like an eternity, I finally spoke. "Pop," I said. "I know the history of the FBI with black folks in this country. But if we're ever going to change any of those things, I can be more effective from the inside. If I can make it in and bring in others, then the bureau will someday be better for everyone." I'm not sure Pop ever bought my logic but I let my better judgment rule my thoughts and went on with my decision to join the FBI.

My aunt, Ida Harris, got word from Moms that I was planning to go to the FBI. She was in her early seventies at the time and had been very active in the civil rights struggle in St. Louis for a number of years. She had taken part in a number of historical movements in St. Louis including the historic March on Jefferson Bank in August, 1963. This movement took place around the same time as Martin Luther King's March on Washington. However overshadowed, this march was the biggest thing to happen in St. Louis in years. Aunt Ida was one of the focal points of this historic march and led the protestors proudly. During this period, black people could deposit their money into Jefferson Bank but had little representation as employees. The march was successful and the bank agreed to open jobs to "colored" people. Aunt Ida often told us how she and my older brother took off running when the police showed up with dogs. She said, "I had made my point and I just didn't want them to let the dogs loose on me and Bruce. I had seen too much of that stuff in the South as a little girl."

Aunt Ida despised J. Edgar Hoover with a passion. As a child she would sit us down and tell the stories about growing up in the South. She told us about the hot cotton fields where she picked cotton as a little girl and the horrible conditions under which she was forced to work. She said, "Those grown white men would come out to the fields and look around for young pretty girls. They'd always grab the prettiest ones they could find and just use them all day. Those dogs would bring them back late in the afternoon after they were through with them. The little girls would be all messed up and crying to their Mamas. Those dogs would just put them back to work in the hot fields. The law or no one would ever do anything about it. Those little girls would just keep having all those mixed babies no one wanted. That's why I want y'all to get a good education so you can make things better for our people." I found the stories about the South fascinating and as a young man began to wonder what happened to all the offspring that were fathered in those hot cotton fields of Mississippi. My Aunt Ida and her twin sisters had very fair complexions and very course, dark, straight hair. I recalled asking them about their father one day. They told me to "Shut up and stay in a child's place. You don't ask grown folk about their private business." Needless to say, I never heard any of those old folks talk about their natural fathers.

When Aunt Ida got the word that I was going to the FBI Academy she said, "Boy, have you lost yo' mind?" I went through the same explanation as I did with Pop and somehow it didn't matter to her either. Joining the FBI was the first time in my life I had defied my parents and family. But I felt I could make a difference and help people.

Aunt Ida preached to us many times about her struggle to vote when she was young. She was one of St. Louis' biggest advocates for voting rights for everyone. She voiced her displeasure about Hoover and the FBI whenever she had the chance. She asked me, "How in the world can you even think about the FBI? Your daddy and granddaddy were beaten just a few years ago trying to vote." She added, "Our folks had to pass a stupid test and pay money to white people just to get a chance to vote. Hoover and them knew 'bout it and just turned their heads on your people. Boy, please get on your knees and talk to Jesus!!" I told her I understood what she was saying and that I wanted to make things better for people in this country. I said, "I'm going to make you proud. Just support my decision this time. And no, I haven't forgotten my history. In fact, I know my history well and I want to be a part of it."

After I completed training at the FBI Academy, Moms told me Pop was starting to get used to the idea of me being in the FBI. She said that Pop had actually bragged to his friends about me. The first time I showed them my FBI credentials they both actually stood proudly and smiled. Although they were still very suspicious about law enforcement and especially the FBI, they told me to be careful and not to take any unnecessary chances.

I wasn't as successful with Aunt Ida. She wasn't ready to accept me as an FBI agent. She sat me down one afternoon as I was visiting her and told me a troubling story. She said she had gotten on her knees every night and prayed to God while I was in the academy. I said, "Thank you for your prayers. I really needed all the help I could get at times." She told me, "I prayed every night that you wouldn't get through that academy and become a member of that racist FBI. I didn't want any nephew of mine to be associated with Hoover. But I guess God knows best. Be careful in those dangerous Detroit streets." Aunt Ida passed away in 1985, never really accepting the idea of blacks in the FBI. But the life she fought for and her history guided her thoughts. I decided long ago that I couldn't let others deter me from doing my best and representing my family in the FBI. I wanted to show Aunt Ida that the FBI was different from what she had known years ago.

****

The old guys always talked about their admiration for Jewish people and how they raised their children. They always said the Jewish people proclaimed that no Jewish child would ever forget his history nor would he be ashamed of it. Jewish people keep their history in front of their families' everyday. The Jewish knowledge of their history was the driving force that kept them striving to succeed as a people. The old guys would say, "Jewish kids go to school with a goal in mind. You do the same, Son." I'd always respond with the customary, "Yes sir."

They told me they were preaching to me so that I wouldn't forget to prepare for a rainy day. Moms said over and over, "Son you've gotta prepare for that rainy day because as sure as I'm sitting here, it's gonna come. Prepare yourself in school and the water will just roll off your back." Thanks to the older folks in my neighborhood and to my parents, I was taught black history long before I learned it in school. In fact, by the time I reached college, black history classes were just becoming popular. Before the early seventies the only black history taught in my school were the stories of Booker T. Washington and Eli Whitney's cotton gin. Most kids didn't know very much about Dr. Martin Luther King while he was alive. He actually became popular after he was killed in 1968. Prior to his death, many Americans viewed Dr. King as a "rabble rouser" that kept things stirred up. When the 1970's arrived he was finally starting to be revered as a hero. In other words, I learned black history at home where it was taught correctly, untainted and without negative opinions.

Pop had his own twist on U.S. history, which was much different from that taught to us in school. For example, Pop always refused to buy us fireworks on the Fourth of July. We were sometimes the only kids in the neighborhood who didn't have fireworks. He said that black people had nothing to celebrate on the Fourth of July. Pop said during the 1700s, most blacks in America were slaves and an integral part of the agricultural economy. When England had control over the United States, it was always a hope of slavery being indentured. He felt that there was always a hope that after slaves worked off their passageway, they would be freed one day. Pop said, "When the United States got loose from England, my great-great grandparents had no hope of ever being free people. For black folks, the Fourth of July is the same as a welcome to Permanent Slavery Day. I ain't celebrating my entry into permanent slavery and you ain't either." Right, wrong, or indifferent, I never heard the Fourth of July discussed in that manner in school. That's why Pop said we should know our true history.

Pop was not too fond of celebrating Thanksgiving either. He always said, "I'll take the day off and cook chitterlings but I feel sorry for the Indians. They were here first and just got tricked out of their land and culture. I won't be a part of celebrating them getting ripped off." Pop was a hell of a street corner historian and always told us he could back up his history with facts. He said, "You should get the real history in school but they won't teach it. There's more to us than Booker T. Washington and Eli Whitney's cotton gin."

One of Pop's good friends lived to be 107 years old. Jeff Kimble, whom we called Mr. Jeff, said he knew President William McKinley, personally. He said they grew up as boys in the same area of Monroe, Louisiana. I was no older than four or five years old when I heard Mr. Jeff telling my Pop, "They only killed William 'cause they found out he was a colored man." At the time, I had no idea what they were talking about. I later found out that President William McKinley was assassinated and he may have been a mulatto from Louisiana. I'm still not sure if history recorded that but Mr. Jeff talked about him all the time and said they were old friends. In reality, Mr. Jeff was my first history teacher and told stories much more interestingly than any teacher I ever had in school. He talked about things I never heard my teachers talk about and he based each story on his personal facts. Needless to say, Mr. Jeff only had three years of formal education but could match historical facts with any college professor. He just told us, "Y'all git your education and be prepared for the rain. When I was a boy, they would let us do nothing but work in those hot fields. School was only for the white and sometimes the light." (Meaning light-skinned colored folks)

Mr. Jeff's wife, Miss Corine, was our first family doctor. Although she never had formal medical training, she could whip up a potion to cure anything we developed. Her potions tasted like poison but they always seemed to work. Miss Corine was our best alternative to not having medical insurance. Whatever was in her potions, none of us were ever hospitalized as children with any serious illness. Whenever we hurt, we'd generally have to visit with Miss Corine. However archaic were her potions, she lived to be 89 years old, and we stayed fairly healthy as children. She may have lived longer had she not developed pneumonia after being burned in a fire.

Pop didn't play when it came to school. Although he didn't have the slightest idea how to help us with complex mathematics, he'd always say, "If you sit there long enough and follow the teacher's directions, you'll catch on." For whatever reason, that method always seemed to work for me. Pop's directions, as well as the constant reminders of his marching orders, were the catalyst that kept me focused in school throughout my life. His rules were the same for all of us. After high school or whenever you ceased to be a student, you had three choices as far as he was concerned. He'd say, "Boy, you're going to the Army, to college, or to work. Either way, you're going to do something." The idea of living at home and taking it easy was never an option.

In my case and that of my oldest brother, we took all three options. Besides, with only a "three room" apartment, it really wasn't conducive for entertaining company anyway. A kitchen, living room, and Pop's bedroom didn't provide space for dating or entertaining the ladies. The one television set was always on the channel that Pop wanted to watch. I now thank God that the set didn't always work and we had to read for recreation. I would sit down with a book and travel all around the world, whenever I felt like going somewhere. I'd take pride in Pop asking me what I was reading. Since he was stationed in Europe during World War II, I would always ask him to enhance my books with true accounts of Italy, Germany, and France. He would make all the books literally come true and I'd be encouraged to read more.

Once when I was young, the television set was "outta fix" for two years. We couldn't afford to get it repaired on our meager budget. So for entertainment, I just read more books. Living with Moms and Pop was just uncomfortable enough to make you want to get out and get your own place one day. Pop made sure your incentive to be a man was always present under his roof.

During those days, it was considered fatal to have a teacher call your home because you may have misbehaved in school. Parents felt as hard as they struggled to move north and to provide you a home, a child's classroom behavior was expected to be nothing less than exceptional. Those few times when my parents received calls from teachers became very memorable around my home. I remember receiving a telephone call one night at about 9:30. It was my older brother's fifth grade teacher. The ringing of the telephone was startling because during the week, the lights were out in Pop's house at 8:30.

For the telephone to ring so late at night meant something serious had happened. When Moms told Pop a teacher had called about my brother misbehaving in class, I remember Pop simply saying, "I'll handle it." At the time, the three of us slept in a fold out couch bed and I was in the center. Generally, the guy who jumps in bed first gets the warm spot in the middle.

Pop grabbed his strap, which he pronounced, "strop" and went to work on my brother's rear end. He swung that thing so wildly that I got a fair amount of his licks. When Pop was giving out punishment, your instructions were to stay put, i.e. you'd better not run, grab the strap, or try to move out of the way. As Pop swung the strap on my brother's rear end, he preached the marching orders over and over. He preached about the whippings he had to take from white people, the times he was called names, the jobs he has been denied due to a lack of education, and how he was struggling to provide for our future; and to think that one of his sons would go to school and act a fool with a teacher was unacceptable. Moms watched until she felt my brother had learned his lesson and grabbed the "strop" from Pop. My brother was ordered to dry up and go to sleep. Under normal circumstances the whipping would have been a tag team butt whipping for all of us, but the lateness of the hour saved us this time. Moreover, the drying up was only limited to a few moments. If he continued to cry, there would definitely be a round two. Needless to say, education was serious business around my home.

Pop would often say that the children of today needed a good old-fashioned whipping to start them respecting teachers and taking advantage of education. However, because of present laws, children can't be whipped any longer, thus a lot of factors that kept us in line when I was a boy, went down the toilet. If the same laws were in place thirty years ago, everyone I knew would have ex-convicts for parents. Practically all of our teachers would have been put in jail. But as Pop always preached, "Teachers loved you and you learnt' anyway. They're just preparing you for the rainy day, which will come one day. You'll need that umbrella or you'll get wet." In fact, Pop emphasized that we had to fear parents and teachers a little in order for them to keep us in line.

Not only were my teachers role models, but they also treated us like their own children. Although some of my teachers were stunningly attractive, they were still ladies and someone you respected. Looking back over the years, I'm glad I feared my parents and teachers. Thanks to that fear, I followed my marching orders a lot closer than many of my peers; many of whom are no longer living today due to straying from their teachings. Some of my peers who are still living today aren't doing so well, because they strayed from their parents and failed to plan for the rain.

One old guy told me at a very early age, "Know your history and don't be ashamed of it. One day you've got to pass it on to the young folk." Pop would always say that many so-called professional folk keep their history quiet just to get along…just to blend in. Another old guy told me, "Don't be ashamed of our history 'cause one day you've gotta write about it. We want it proud and accurate. Be as proud of our history as that Jewish guy."

As for my advice from Moms and Pop about being careful and not taking any chances. I redefined the phrase, "taking chances," over the next twenty years or so as an agent with the FBI. But my adherence to the FBI's Oath of Office, Pop's marching orders, and faith in Him never faded. That faith guided me through a successful career; having never received one scratch or injury in the line of duty. This is my story and I thank Moms and Pop for giving me a birthday.

Close friends, my family, and I reveal the perception of the Federal Bureau of Investigation as seen in this book. Throughout my career, I've found their opinions of the FBI so fascinating that I began to catalogue their questions and my responses. Because many of them were the products of urban environments, I soon realized they felt the same way about law enforcement as most of the criminals I've arrested. Over the years, after interviewing many criminals, I found their upbringing and the conditions under which they lived, were in many instances no different from my own childhood experiences. The biggest difference between them and me was the presence of Moms and Pop in my life.

Most importantly, I remembered the many lessons my parents taught me as a child. I've carried those lessons with me throughout my life and used them as a basis to guide my career with the FBI. I also examined their unique style of child rearing in the face of the poverty and racism under which we lived. Despite a multitude of obstacles and disapprovals from my family, I defied their advice and became an agent with the FBI. I realized early in my career that my FBI Oath of Office and Pop's marching orders were basically the same.

****

Chapter One

- MY THANKS TO HIM: LESSONS LEARNED -

"You are about to embark on the most fascinating career an individual could ever wish for in his life. None of you will ever have to look for a job again; you have reached the pinnacle that every person in the world should envy. You are about to enter the FBI Academy and soon you'll be FBI agents. You have been chosen from thousands seeking to join you from all around the world. You are sitting where you are because you are special, you are unique, and you are the best qualified in the nation. Look around the room ladies and gentlemen. Be proud to know that no one can match your accomplishments."

"Let it be known that your friends and family are extremely proud of you and will henceforth brag about your accomplishments, your assignments, and the contribution you're making to our country." The tall, stately agent then bellowed, "Congratulations, ladies and gentlemen, you have made it to the FBI Academy! Be proud of yourself and what you have achieved up to now."

"I want you to know that this does not automatically make you FBI agents. You have a long, grueling, sixteen weeks ahead of you. Unfortunately, the weak will not be among you on graduation day.

Look around again. Will you be among the proud to receive those credentials sixteen weeks from now?"

As I looked around, I first noticed everyone seemed to look alike or at least cut from the same mold. Every new agent recruit in the room donned the traditional dark suit, shiny dark wing tip shoes, and white dress shirts. Although it was 1979 and hairstyles were fairly long, the new agent recruits had relatively conservative hairstyles. Moreover, everyone seemed fairly studious and ready to show the next person he was there because he was the best of the best.

More than anything else, I noticed only one other person who looked like me, and he was sitting in the far corner of the auditorium. We made eye contact and exchanged the traditional, "What's up brother" greeting from across the room. Although we didn't formerly talk nor were we introduced, we knew we'd have to depend on one another before this ordeal was over. We had that unspoken, "I got you covered" conversation without ever saying one word.

The Bureau executive then swore us in to this elite organization and told us to get to know one another. He said we had a long ride to Quantico, where we'll begin our initial training in a few hours. "Gentlemen", this time without acknowledging the women present, "You have just taken the most serious oath of office any man can ever undertake. Take it to heart and understand you are the elite thirty new agent recruits in the nation. We have searched the country over and we've invited you to join our ranks." Being among the best in this elite group, I quietly counted and realized there actually were only twenty-nine of us. But I knew that the way to stay on their good side was to let them think they're right. That separated the smart from those with plain old good common sense.

I could hardly believe that I had made it through the grueling testing and screening the FBI had put me through the past six months. I couldn't help but think of the things that happened to me as a youngster that not only would have prevented me from being here, but also may have landed me in jail for a long time. By the grace of God I'm here and doing something positive.

I couldn't forget about the time when a fight in the seventh grade could have landed me in jail along with my brothers. I recalled standing in line waiting for the bus, when a tall skinny guy walked up from behind, and thumped me in the head so hard I cried. I charged that guy and cried as I went into him with both fists. But he was just too big for me to fight. Each time I moved in with lefts and rights, I caught a shot to the head. I just kept going at him but I couldn't get to him. I just kept fighting and crying as hard as I could, to no avail.

Out of nowhere came my older brother, who was still shorter than the big guy but a lot tougher. He moved in with the swiftness of Muhammad Ali and connected blow after blow to the bully's head until he went down. He beat that big guy within an inch of his life for picking on me. As he whipped him, he told him over and over not to ever hit his little brother again. He dusted me off and we boarded our bus for home. Little did we know the tall guy was a member of one of west St. Louis' most vicious street gangs, the Termites.

The Termites were comprised primarily of school-dropout street thugs. Most of them had done time in reform school and had felony juvenile records. For the most part, the only reason they weren't in prison was because they were under 18 years old. The Termites were also known to carry weapons. During those days, the weapon of choice was a switchblade knife, and they carried the reputation of cutting guys within an inch of their lives.

We thought everything was over, until a few days later, when about ten of the Termites boarded the bus we were on and got off at our stop; the corner of Clara and Ridge. We knew there was trouble because although we were bused downtown to Vashon Elementary School, the Termites all lived in the area of Hodiamont and Page and seldom attended school. Hodiamont and Page was quite a distance

C. Lee Thornton

from our neighborhood. On this particular day, they all showed up at school and hung around the building without going to class. The teacher riding our bus, Mr. Russell, was terrified and knew something bad was about to happen. He just sat and said nothing.

As we made the long ride home, they kept shouting from the rear of the bus that they were going to get the Thornton boys. It was a long ride that afternoon and Mr. Russell was more frightened than we were. We were afraid but refused to show it. We had instructions from Pop to always stick together. So despite any assistance from Mr. Russell we stayed together. When we got off the bus, Mr. Russell knew something was wrong but refused to get involved. He quickly jumped into his car, which was parked on Clara Avenue and drove off. Mr. Russell left us all alone with the huge crowd of gang members walking behind us. I was shaking like a leaf.

I walked ahead of my two brothers by a few yards as we headed home that afternoon. Bruce, my older brother and the best fighter among us, was only a few steps ahead of the Termites gang members who closely followed and taunted him. We all refused to run; we just walked fast. On this day, we took a shortcut up the alley between Clara Avenue and Temple Place. I wanted to tell Pop as soon as I could that the gang was following us home. When I got near our backyard I began screaming to Pop. Pop was down on his luck at the time and unemployed. Luckily, he was home when we arrived. I shouted, "Daddy!! That gang is after us and they are about to grab Bruce!!" Pop grabbed his pistol and threw a shotgun and a rifle down the steps to me as soon as I opened the rear door.

By this time the huge crowd was taunting my big brother from the rear of the house. They had not yet entered the yard but were just getting in a position to surround Bruce. I threw the shotgun to Harold, my middle brother, and started running toward the crowd with the rifle to help my big brother. I was so mad I was crying and I couldn't focus on anyone because of my tears. But I was determined the Termites would pay the price for following us home.

After seeing the guns, the gang ran away down the alley. I was chambering a bullet into the barrel of the Remington .22 rifle and still trying to focus. I loaded the round, got down on one knee, and aimed at the escaping gang members, but I couldn't focus through my tears. I wiped my eyes again, took aim through the rear sight, and began a slow squeeze of the trigger, anticipating a target. Although I couldn't make out a target, I could see guys running down the alley away from us. I was determined to shoot at least one of them and continued to apply pressure to the trigger. As soon as I wiped my eyes a final time and cleared my vision, the last gang member had just rounded the corner out of my sight. I was so angry that I didn't get a shot off, I started to shoot up in the air. I heard my Mom scream at me to put the gun away. I lowered my aim and walked back to the house, disgusted that the round intended for the Termites was still chambered.

If I had fired into the crowd of angry gang members, there is no way I'd be taking my oath of office for the FBI. I would probably have been sent to reform school for protecting what I thought was my honor. But for the grace of God, go I......

****

"Ladies and gentlemen, please place your tray tables in the upright position and prepare for landing. A flight attendant will make their final rounds to pick up anything you'd like disposed." At that moment, I realized I was deep in a dream, reliving events I had experienced years ago. I felt like a new recruit again on my first day at the academy. It seemed as though I could still hear that speech as I sat in the main auditorium at FBI Headquarters in September 1979. I could still see the scared faces of the new recruits as we waited in wonderment, not knowing what to expect next. I started to smile when I remembered the chiseled frames, the baby faces, and everyone seeming anxious to show he was going to be the leader. Little did they know, I was the leader, and as far as I was concerned, I was the best.

But moreover, I remember how I felt that day in west St. Louis when I was so angry I wanted to shoot into a crowd of gang members to protect my brother.

I thought to myself, what an amazing dream and how blessed I am to be here today. Now, I'm going back to my hometown to visit Pop who is gravely ill in Veteran's Hospital. For some crazy reason Pop didn't believe any hospital existed other than Veteran's Hospital. He always said he was going to get everything coming to him from his service in the military. Although some of his wounds never healed, he felt it was the government's responsibility to handle his medical care as long as he was alive.

Pop was 84 years old at the time and was suffering from a blockage of the small intestines. He always felt this condition was a result of an injury he sustained while fighting in Germany during World War II. He often told us stories about his service during the war and spoke proudly about his service to the United States. However, his proud service tour and wounds were over shadowed by the treatment he received when he returned to this country after the war. He'd often say, "As much as we did for this country, over there the colored soldiers had to ride behind German prisoners on the transport trains. We even had to eat separately from white soldiers, even though the Germans shot at all of us with the same bullets." Pop was our personal historian on World War II. He told us stories and history we'd never get from textbooks.

But now, Pop was lying in a hospital bed fighting for his life. I felt it was my job to carry on his legacy and to not let his service to this country be forgotten by our family.

Oath of Office

As we made our initial approach I could see the Gateway Arch and I recognized The University of Missouri (St. Louis) just ahead of us. I couldn't believe how it had grown since I was a student, back then it consisted of only a few buildings. I couldn't believe how much the campus had expanded in nearly 30 years. I only hoped some of the vermin that taught there back in the 1960s and 1970s were no longer around.

The day was hot and steamy as I waited for the shuttle to take me to the rental car company. I quickly realized I had overdressed and it was going to be uncomfortable. I don't know why, but I really expected to see lots of people I knew at the airport. But that wasn't realistic; I hadn't visited St. Louis in years. People move, people change, things change.

As I drove to the hospital, I traveled east on Interstate 70 through north St. Louis, past the old neighborhood. I noticed how, it too, had changed. Many of the previously gorgeous homes were in disrepair. Although it was early afternoon, there were scores of young men milling around with seemingly nothing to do. As I slowly drove through the streets, it appeared they stopped what they were doing to stare at me. I knew from years working street crime, staring was a tactic used by thugs to make you uncomfortable. Little did they know, I was use to that old street corner tactic, and it didn't work. People who didn't know any better would just identify the neighborhood as a tough area and leave. I just viewed them as lost people with nothing better to do. I returned their stares, after all I was in the neighborhood first.

I decided to drive to my old school, since I was early for visiting hours at the hospital. When I got to Penrose and Kingshighway, I parked the car and walked onto the schoolyard at Scullin School, where I once attended. Two police squad cars sat at the far end of the schoolyard. It seemed as if they were discussing the issues of the day. Both of them just stared at me. That caused me to relive how I felt about police when I was a kid.

I recalled living in the same neighborhood as a youngster with fear and hatred for the police. During those days, they used kids as their recreation. Just for kicks, the police would pick us up and put us in the rear of their police cruisers for what they called a ride. They would always tell us they were checking our records to make sure we didn't have outstanding warrants. After we sat in the cold paddy wagons until we almost froze to death, they'd say we were clean but we had to take a ride. They would take us north of Highway 70 for a few blocks and put us out to walk. They knew that part of town had white gangs who roamed the streets looking for action. They would laugh as we ran like hell to get out of the neighborhood and back south of Highway 70. If you couldn't run fast enough or got cut off, the white guys would catch you and give you a good butt kicking. The police wouldn't help—they would laugh and drive away. When I was a kid, everyone hated the police, and for good reason.

I stood and reflected on the first time I walked onto Scullin's schoolyard. It was the spring of 1963. I was twelve years old and had come to Scullin School as a seventh grade transfer student. I remembered standing in the schoolyard with my brother and no one would speak to us. We just assumed they were waiting to see if we were as tough as everybody thought we looked. We carried that "you better not try me" look. It seemed to work for us on that first day at the new school.

I saw kids playing and taking turns on the swings. We never had swings at our other schools. Playground equipment was only installed where white kids went to school. I couldn't believe I was finally going to get a chance to play on a real swing. I figured if recess lasted much longer, I'd get a chance to try out a real steel-based swing set. I inched closer, while a short, bald-headed kid sat on the chain railing waiting for his turn on the swing set.

Suddenly, a ruffian-looking guy walked up to him and pushed him backwards. This guy jumped on the little kid and started punching him like a crazy man. The little bald-headed kid cried and screamed, but no one came to help him. He was completely defenseless and the tough kid was having a ball beating him up and laughing. I couldn't take it any longer. I couldn't stand to see the little kid getting beat up by nothing more than a thug. After all, I was fresh off Easton Avenue and if I couldn't whip the thug, my brother would come to my rescue, and we'd kick his butt together.

I jumped in the middle of the fight, which was none of my business, and hit the tough kid with a series of combinations to the head and body. Although he was bigger than me, he felt the series of hard blows and knew he had more than he could handle. The tough kid surrendered without much of defense. I told him to leave the little kid alone and take off. I picked the little bald-headed guy off the ground and walked him to the swing for his turn. I told him I was new to the school and the bully wouldn't bother him anymore. That same little bald-headed kid became a lifelong friend and we have never been far apart since. That fight was one of the first times of many that I stuck my nose into something that wasn't my business. I guess that was a precursor for my motivation to join the FBI.

****

As I walked into Veteran's Hospital, it had the typical stench of most hospitals. As much as I hated the place, I had no choice because I knew Pop was waiting to see me and was depending on me to handle things. When I found Pop, he was somewhat groggy. Several of his buddies were sitting around the room. One had brought his grandson with him. It had been several years since I had seen some of Pop's buddies, two of them and the child I didn't know. I said, "Hey Mr. Thomas, how are you doing?" He said,

"Fine son, this is Bill and Joe. This is Joe's grandson, Randy." We all exchanged greetings and shook hands. Mr. Thomas then said, "This is Carey's youngest boy, the FBI agent. Son, where are you living now?" he asked. "San Juan, Puerto," I said. They all said in unison, "San Juan what?"

I later explained to them that I had lived in Puerto Rico for the past three years. Mr. Thomas said Pop told them I was out of the country, but he was very secretive about where I lived and what I was doing. Pop always felt I was working on a big secret mission and it was his job to keep it as quiet as possible. I told them I was supervising a Special Operations Squad and it was only a secret to people on the island. The kid and one of the older guys were then full of questions, which I tried my best to avoid. Luckily, Pop finally woke up and saved me from the barrage of inquires about the FBI.

He said, "Hey when did you get here? Where's Elsie?" "I just came in from the airport and she'll be here tomorrow. She's still visiting with her folks in Virginia. But how do you feel?" I could see by the way Pop was moving around in the bed that he didn't feel well. He had no less than six tubes in him. It really hurt to see him in that condition because I knew he hated hospitals. More so than hospitals, Pop hated most doctors because he felt they just wanted to experiment on poor people and practice good medicine on the rich people.

Pop said, "Moms just left before you got here. She was here all morning. They want to cut on me but I still haven't talked to the doctor but once since I got here three days ago. I just don't like it but they said my intestines have a blockage." I could see Pop getting weaker as he tried to explain his condition to me. "Just try to get some rest, I'll get with the doctor and see what they plan to do. We'll get to the bottom of this before anything happens," I said. I could see that Pop had lost a lot of weight since the last time I saw him. He was very weak and it was obvious to all of us that he needed immediate medical attention if he was going to make it. It really hurt seeing Pop in his condition. He started to slowly drift off to sleep.

Young Randy said, "Are you really an FBI agent? That sounds like a really cool job. What do you do everyday? Did you really grow up here in St. Louis?" One of Pops friends then asked, "How long have you lived down there? Can you speak that Spanish stuff like the Puerto Ricans?" I was accustomed to this line of questioning, after being an FBI agent for such a long time. Although I didn't feel important, most people treated us like celebrities. I sometimes got the treatment of an entertainer or professional athlete. Everyone wanted to know something about you. It sometimes seemed hard for the public to imagine that someone who worked for the FBI was a regular, everyday guy. But most agents, including me, enjoyed the attention. I used the attention, often as a means of getting to some of our young people, because I knew, for once, I had their undivided attention.

Randy was a typical teenager. He was about 14 years old and dressed in the typical fashion of his time. His pants were baggy and he sported a big chain around his neck. His grandfather said, "Before you answer that, please explain to him how you got to where you are. My daughter and I have been trying to talk to him, but he thinks everything comes so easy. He skips school so often we just don't know what to do. That's why I got him today. He needs a man around him. I know you remember when we used to talk to you and your brothers and it seemed y'all at least listened. This boy is different. Tell my grandson how you got in the FBI." Randy then asked, "You mean you grew up here and never been locked up?" I said, "Yes, that's exactly what I mean. In fact, let me tell you about the time when I was your age and thought I would be killed trying to acquire an education. Your education is the key to take you anywhere in life you want to go. Randy, you've got to trust your Grandpa on this one. He's 100 % right." No one said a word, just stared and waited to hear what I would say next. I saw Pop continuing to drift in and out of his sleep. I think he was alert enough to hear what I was saying. Besides, none of us wanted to leave Pop's side until we were certain he would be fine. Unfortunately, the doctors hadn't made any promises.

I told Randy that the road to the FBI Academy was not paved with gold for me because of the way I grew up. It was a difficult path to maneuver but not impossible to conquer. I said, "I'm going to explain how I made it with hard work and God's mercy.

More than anything, I listened to what the old people had to say and used what they told me."

****

I told Randy that the one advantage I had when growing up was being in a home with two parents, which unfortunately, is not very common today. My parents were poor people from the South who knew if we received a good education we could enjoy advantages later in life. I looked directly at Randy and told him that is the reason we do not play with education. We didn't try to laugh, joke, or distract anyone from receiving an education. To play with education was equivalent to committing suicide. By making a joke of education, you're giving someone the stick with which to whip you all your life. I looked at him and said, "Do you understand what I'm saying?" He shamefully nodded as if he understood. Pop's friends just listened and watched Randy. His grandpa couldn't believe the attention Randy was giving me. This time, he was totally silent and waited for my next word.

I told Randy when I was young, my Pop would sometimes put us in his car and drive us around various neighborhoods in the city. Pop was pretty popular and seemed to know people from all over town. He felt perfectly comfortable in the slums (later called the ghetto) or in the county (later called the suburbs). He would point to bums on the street and tell us we'd get a chance to stand next to them if we didn't get a good education. He would say to us, "Sure they seem happy and as far as you can tell, and they're pretty cool, too. But that coolness just serves to mask the pain of the misfortune of not having an education. Don't get an education and some rich guy will point you out to their kids one day." Although Pop only had an eighth grade education, he sometimes displayed the wisdom of a Harvard professor. He could bring a point so close to home that it didn't take a genius to understand a concept like the lack of education.

The bums would be dirty, drunk, and they staggered as they tried to walk. He would tell us to feel sorry for the bums because many of them had been denied the advantage of an education. Many had arrived from the South just like Pop, but they had been dealt a different hand to play in the game of life. He emphasized over and over we wouldn't be able to use that excuse. He was going to place that advantage of education in front of us if it killed him. Pop was serious.

Pop opened his eyes and said, "Randy, listen 'cause he's telling you the truth. You've got to quit giving your mom and grandpa such a hard time. Go ahead, son. I'm glad, for once, he's finally listening to somebody." Randy said, "So he's the one you've being telling me about, right?" Pop said, "That's him and you listen."

I told Randy Pop would sometimes take us to the homes of many of his less fortunate close friends. Pop didn't make fun of them or make light of their living condition. A few of them lived in boxcar houses near the river. I explained to Randy that boxcar houses were abandoned railroad cars that were left near a section of the Mississippi River in downtown St. Louis. Poor people would move into these boxcars for shelter because they had no other place in which to live. Most residents of these structures were entire families who had moved from the South in search of a better life.

I could see the look of amazement on Randy's face having never to imagine families lived like that in St. Louis. I told him the one thing the children living in boxcars cherished and looked forward to was the opportunity to go to school. Forget about television or the conveniences of life, the boxcars just provided a place to live for the unfortunate families.

I told them that we visited poor people so often that by the time I was five years old, I knew education was no laughing matter. Pop and his friends preached education so much that I knew not to take it lightly. Randy interrupted and asked, "You probably did good because you went to preschool and got a jump on the other kids." This time Pop laughed out loud. I was glad to see he still had his sense of humor. "Preschool? No, I didn't attend pre-school. I started learning to count by looking at the clock everyday. When I got numbers one through twelve down pretty good, I would ask my folks about the other numbers and I would write them down and remember them." I told Randy I would drill myself over and over until I learned my numbers backwards and forward. I took pride in being tested on my numbers in the presence of grown folk. During those days if grown folks labeled you as "smart", they'd give you money to showcase your skills. They would say, "Hey son, count to twenty for me. Show yo' uncle how smart you are." In fact, that was the only time you were allowed to speak in the presence of adults and I'd do my thing every time!

Because my parents often bought newspapers, I would do the best I could do to recognize numbers and letters to keep myself busy. I had heard about preschool but I honestly thought that was something for the children of rich people. Pop told us to be prepared by the time we went to school because kids who had gone to preschool would try to make you look stupid. At that time, I didn't know anyone who had gone to preschool. I recalled seeing children in preschool on television. It really seemed like they were

Oath of Office

having fun, but far as I was concerned, that was in another world. Even so, I was determined that no kid, black or white, preschool or no preschool, would ever make me look stupid.

Randy said, "Then how did you make it out of the hood? Did y'all take nice vacations in the summer?" This time everybody in the room laughed, including Pop. I said, "Randy, the few times we left town during the summer, we went south to visit relatives. We usually went to Arkansas or Mississippi and only for a few days. Pop would always drive our car and we'd leave in the evening just prior to dusk. Randy asked, "Why did you leave so late? You can't see the sights that well at night."

I explained that due to the racial climate in the United States when I was young, black people were not allowed to use many public restrooms, restaurants, or go to motels or hotels along the highways. Pop tried to shelter us from those elements by having us sleep through most of the trip at night in the rear of the car. Most of the time when we awakened in the morning, we would have arrived at the homes of our relatives. From time to time we'd be awakened if a state trooper stopped Pop along the highway. Just to be ornery, the officer would shine his flashlights in our eyes to wake us up. I can't recall Pop ever being given a speeding ticket on any of our trips. However, the state troopers would always stop out of state drivers and especially black people, for nothing at all. If we awoke in the middle of the night and had to use the restroom, we would use the side of the road. Going to most public places, including service station bathrooms, was out of the question.

I remember on one trip south, I woke up in the middle of the night so hungry I couldn't stand the growling in my stomach. Mr. Thomas said, "I remember when you was a boy you always ate more than your brothers. Your daddy said you always wanted to stop on the road to eat, but during those days you had better keep driving." I explained how I started whining for Pop to get some food. I whined until Pop couldn't take it any longer. I heard Moms ask him to just try one restaurant to see if they would sell us a couple of sandwiches. I recalled we parked on the lot of a diner in Newport, Arkansas. Pop purposely parked the car at the far corner of the parking lot, although there were plenty spaces near the building. He wouldn't have dared park too close to the diner and let the white people see him getting out of a shiny new car. He said that colored people, who appeared to be living well, might offend some of them. I heard Pop tell Moms he hoped there wouldn't be any trouble because he only wanted a couple of hamburgers and a coke. He felt if they saw him with a small child they would be less likely to start trouble. At the time, I had not yet started school. I was very young and really didn't understand the fuss over a couple of hamburgers and a coke.

We both walked into the front door of the diner. We could see plenty empty seats and tables. We just stood in one place near the front door waiting to be acknowledged. Everyone got quiet as we entered the door and stared at us. The cook walked from behind the counter and approached Pop and me. He was a big fat guy wearing a white apron and a white chef's hat. He wasn't smiling as he walked toward us but Pop didn't move and held me close to him. The guy started waving his arm as if he wanted us to get out of the restaurant. We backed out of the door as he walked toward us and walked around to the rear of the building. He motioned for us to enter the diner through the kitchen area. We went inside the back door and stood in the middle of the kitchen until the cook came back to see Pop.

I remembered Pop ordering two hamburgers with onions and mustard and two Cokes. We stood in the kitchen and moved from side to side as the workers mopped the kitchen floor. They worked as if we were invisible. None of them said one word to us as they mopped the floors around us. We just continued to move out of their way with no one having the courtesy to say "Pardon me." I

Oath of Office

thought the cook was the nicest guy in the world because he let us see where our hamburgers were being cooked. A short time later, the cook handed Pop two bags. Pop paid him, and we walked out of the rear door to our car. I was really excited as I told Moms how they let us see the hamburgers being cooked in the kitchen. Although plenty of tables in the diner were empty, we ate our food in the car as we drove down the road. My only hope was that my two brothers stayed asleep so I wouldn't have to share my hamburger and Coke with them. Mr. Thomas and his friends all laughed.

Vacationing in the South was no cakewalk for black people in the 1950s and 1960s. I told Randy to remember the path has been paved so that he can vacation in places such as Disneyland. When I was a youngster, we thought a place such as Disneyland was for the rich and was only a dream for kids like us.

During the summer of 1959, I almost didn't live to see the end of our trip to Mississippi. I had only visited Kemper County, Mississippi once before and it was not one of my favorite places. But as a kid you went where your parents took you and asked no questions. My uncle lived along a long road with few neighbors in a small frame house. Because he was an old man, the town's white people would drive by the house a couple days a week to see if he was O.K. They would drive down the road in an old pickup truck and stop in front of my uncle's house. One old white man would yell from his truck, "Hey Niggah!!" Uncle Chappy would come to the door and wave at him from the front porch. I assumed that was the signal to them that Uncle Chappy and his wife were fine. They would continue down the road, having never gotten out of their old truck.

I hated visiting Mississippi, mainly because we couldn't do anything but stay in the area of the house. We only went to town to the store and were told to stay in our place when we got there. Uncle Chappy told us, "If you get out of your place, you might get somebody lynched." Being city kids, we had a tough time understanding exactly

C. Lee Thornton

where our places should be. But the old folks told us that staying in your place meant saying "yes Ma'am" and "yes Sir" to white people. Because my older brother was getting older he was told not to gaze or whistle at white girls. They could accuse you of eye rape and that crime could get you lynched. Eye rape was a law on the books in Mississippi that meant a black man was staring at a white woman as if he wanted to rape her. It was a serious offense, and had fatal consequences for many young black men. That's how they lived in the South during those days. I didn't like it and a visit to Mississippi was no fun for me even as a small child.

Uncle Chappy had an outdoor toilet that was about 20 yards from the house. I hated using that smelly little building but we had no choice. I would sometimes hold myself most of the day until I had to finally give up. Going to the outdoor toilet meant a walk through high weeds to a little wooden building that smelled like a sewer. But that was the only place to use the bathroom because there was no indoor plumbing in Uncle Chappy's little wooden house. There was also a wasp nest in the top of the little wooden outhouse that was active all day. I recalled that one day, I had to use the bathroom so bad, that against my better judgment, I decided to walk by myself through the weeds to the outhouse. As I sat in the outdoor toilet reading what was left of the Sears catalogue, the wasps became active over my head. My toilet paper was the sheets of the latest Sears catalogue. No flushing was obviously necessary for the toilet but the next person expected to have some of the catalogue to read for his comfort.

Being a city boy, I didn't recognize the sounds of angry wasps, I just thought they were active and flying around in circles. I simply sat in the tiny, smelly, cramped little wooden structure, oblivious to the outside world. In reality, the sounds of the rural woods were quite relaxing. The humming, the buzzing, the noise of the country was soothing to my ears. The sounds were unlike those I had grown accustomed to in St. Louis.

Suddenly, and without warning, I felt a horrible pain on my neck and realized I had been stung by something while taking a soothing, relaxing bowel movement. I jumped up with my pants still around my ankles and starting running to Pop. I screamed like a madman, "Daddy!! Daddy!! Something stung me!!" I still had that big, buzzing thing trapped under my hand on my neck. The pain and buzzing was unlike any I had ever experienced during my short life.

Pop came running to me and knocked the wasp from my neck, it had stung me several times before he got it off of me and killed it. My old uncle didn't have any medicine for wasp bites and my neck began to swell. Uncle Chappy didn't make matters any better when he told Moms that people have died from reactions from wasp bites. He told us we could go to town but he didn't think there were any doctors who would treat a colored boy. Pop decided we had to find a doctor because my neck had already begun to swell and it was starting to affect my breathing.

We all piled into Pop's shiny green Buick and headed to Meridian to find a doctor to treat my wasp bite. We were careful to drive slowly and to mind our manners because, after all, we were in the South and Pop didn't want any trouble. People standing on both sides of the small streets, pointed and shouted, "Niggah" as we slowly drove past. The fact that we were driving a shiny 1953 Buick, everyone knew we were outsiders and did not belong in Mississippi. Our Missouri license plates further identified us as foreigners to Meridian. However, we knew to "stay in our places" because we had been warned by Uncle Chappy. Even in 1959, and at the age of eight years old, I knew that "colored people" were expected to act in a certain manner around white people. I knew from newspaper accounts that not to do so could be fatal. I had read the story of Emmit Till. Moms constantly reminded us of his unfortunate fate.

C. Lee Thornton

My Dad found a doctor's office and carried me in his arms to see him. We walked through a crowd of shouting, unfriendly white people. Pop ignored the taunting and kept walking with me in his arms. It was obvious we weren't welcomed in this town, but we didn't want any trouble, we only wanted some medical treatment for the wasp sting on my neck. Before we reached the top of the steps to his office, the doctor walked out of the office door. He was an older man and I clearly recalled seeing his white jacket, although I was somewhat in a daze. Upon initially seeing him, I felt a temporary sigh of relief. My neck was still swelling and burning with pain, but I felt whatever medicine he had would make it better. The doctor met us at the door and was emphatic about us not opening his office door. He made it clear to the shouting people from the street that he had nothing to do with us coming to his office. I recalled his loud voice over the crowd saying, "I'm sorry I can't treat that colored boy here. I'd lose my practice and be run outta this town." I was drowsy and my head was pressed against my Dad's chest, but I heard Pop say, "Thank you, Sir," in a sobering voice. We turned around to face the angry crowd and went back to the car. I can still see Moms crying as Pop handed me to her waiting arms from the rear seat of the car. I was struggling to breathe as the car drove away through the shouting, angry crowd. Pop drove slowly so we wouldn't be pulled over by the local police for speeding. While we were parked at the doctor's office, the local sheriff sat in his car across the street and just watched us. Pop was sure he was searching for a violation to either pull him over or to beat and arrest him for no reason.

This scene was repeated at several other doctors' offices around the small town. Each doctor told my dad the same thing: he didn't care how bad I needed help, he wasn't going to have the people in the town mad at him for treating a colored boy. Pop asked one doctor, "Well sir can you give my boy a prescription to stop the swelling and help him breathe? Can't you see he's only eight years old and he's having a hard time breathing?" The doctor told Pop, "Look I ain't doing nothing for that boy. He's colored and I don't treat colored folks. I've gotta live in this town. Now go on away from here!" Pop just dropped his head and said, "Thank you, Sir." He turned again to face an angry crowd standing near our car. Each doctor refused to give us medicine, nor did they recommend something for the swelling that had started to restrict my breathing. We were just told to get away and not to cause any trouble. Mom continued to cry as I continued my struggle to breathe.

My mom and aunt began to pray and cry as we sat in the rear seat of Pop's car. Over and over, they asked Jesus to save my life. During those days, my mom and aunt were young very attractive women. As we drove through the little town, white men would make catcalls at them, which by southern law, my dad and uncle could not to respond to. They were saying over and over, "My, my look at those fine nigger gals." Their stares and taunting let my dad and uncle know that they had better not say a word in defense of the women. We continued to drive through the little town, praying the local police nor any overly aggressive "good" citizen wouldn't stop us. I could feel my breathing getting harder and harder because of the swelling from the reaction to the wasp sting. Mom's cries and prayers got louder and louder.

Pop was being cool, although I knew he was fighting mad inside. He didn't want to do anything to get arrested or get pulled from the car and lynched. We drove to the colored section of Meridian, and asked an older black man if he knew where there might be a doctor who would treat colored people. He told my Pop there was a doctor in York, Alabama who had been known to help sick colored folk. As far as Moms was concerned, the information sounded like a Godsend. We were still quite a distance away from York, but Pop said the drive was worth the risk because we had no other choice.

C. Lee Thornton

We drove to the main interstate and headed to York as fast as Pop could drive. Moms and my aunt continued to pray to Jesus to save my life. They could see my breathing was becoming shallower and shallower. I just couldn't seem to force enough air through my windpipe. It seemed to be swelling shut as the day went on. As we drove towards Alabama, Moms and my aunt sang spirituals and prayed. Between prayers they cried. Cry and pray, pray and cry. Moms and my aunt were inconsolable.

Uncle Chappy, who had been nursing a pint of bourbon since we had left his house earlier that afternoon, suddenly realized I was in bad shape. He decided to use an old southern remedy that was used by black folk before doctors were available to us. I'm not sure if Uncle Chappy was tired of all the praying and crying or if he was drunk. Nevertheless, as we sped toward Alabama, Uncle Chappy went into action. He pulled a big wad of snuff and tobacco from his mouth that he had been chewing on all afternoon. That stuff smelled like something from a rotten sewer, masked with the strong odor of bourbon. He rolled that smelly stuff into a huge ball; the brown juice ran over his hands. As I lay in my mother's lap, without saying a word to anyone, Uncle Chappy slapped that smelly stinkball onto the side of my neck! The slap hurt as much as the sting and no one knew what the hell had gotten into my old, drunk uncle. The slap, I later learned, was his way of forcing the juice into the pores of my skin. Tobacco juice and stink rolled down my neck and chest as Uncle Chappy held his hand on my neck. Under normal circumstances my mom would have said to him, "Chappy, what the hell are you doing to that boy!!" But in this case we were reaching for straws.

Within moments, my breathing started to become stronger. Within twenty minutes my breathing had returned to normal. The swelling in my neck had all disappeared. I smelled like a whiskey soaked sewer but I could breathe again. Moms shouted out, "Thank

Oath of Office

you, Jesus" about 50 times. I couldn't say for sure, but Pop also got a little emotional. Of course he was our resident tough guy and wasn't allowed to let anyone see him tear up. But in this case, it was okay with me because I could breathe again. Pop composed himself and asked me, "Tell me what you want. You can have anything you want..." I lifted my smelly head from Moms lap and asked, "Daddy, can I have a vanilla ice cream cone?" He said, "Let's go get it."

We drove back to Meridian. Pop stood in line at a corner ice cream stand. He ignored the stares and jeering of white customers and ordered one vanilla ice cream cone for me. On that hot afternoon, I recalled that being the tastiest ice cream cone I ever had in my life. I shared it with my brothers as we drove back to Uncle Chappy's house. In exchange for the stench of whiskey and old tobacco, I was spared to live a little longer to carry out Pop's marching orders.

We later returned to Kemper County, where the ordeal had started earlier. Later that day, the old red pickup truck returned to Uncle Chappy's house out in the woods. The same old white guy drove by and shouted his daily greeting to us, "Hey Niggahs!! Y'all okay?" Uncle Chappy stood on the porch, and as always, waved until the truck drove away.

We left Mississippi the next day, just as dusk set into the horizon. My savior, Uncle Chappy passed away a few years later. He was in his late 80s when he died. He lived his entire life in the South, never having tasted the freedom experienced by citizens in the North. Throughout his entire life, he never knew the respect of being addressed as Mr. McCallum, by the white people of the town. The town's people always referred to him as "Niggah". I have not returned to Kemper County to this day.

****

I said, "So Randy, the path has been paved for you so that you don't have to endure near death experiences because of your race.

You may want to thank God you can vacation at Disneyland, rather than Kemper County, and don't tell us what you wouldn't take if you lived during that era. You would have taken it and not said a word about it." For once, the seemingly unappreciative Randy just sat and said nothing smart to his grandpa.

Mr. Thomas said, "Tell Randy how your Daddy taught y'all to work and how lucky he is he didn't have your daddy." Randy said, "How can you work when you had to go to school?" Pop lifted is head and said, "Boy, you've got a lot to learn." I told Randy that Pop was a stickler for us learning to work and understanding the meaning of hard work. The three of us were all less than ten years old when Pop introduced us to his job as a porter/handyman. Things were so tight around our house that he vowed if we didn't get a good education, we'd better have a strong back, learn how to work, and be prepared to take a lot of crap off of people in order to survive. We didn't know if Pop was teaching us to work hard or if he had so much to do that he needed three additional people to help him. However, at the age of eight I learned to use a power lawn mower on one of Pop's many jobs that summer.

Pop was laid off and by the grace of God he found a job with a rich family in St. Louis County. The rich family, the Kanes, owned an automobile dealership and had a house so large it resembled a castle. The ground surrounding the house was a small park that took the four of us two days to cut with power mowers. From time to time the lady of the house would hire Moms as her housekeeper for a few days. At one time, our entire survival depended totally upon this one rich family. We were completely at their mercy.

We handled the yard duties for about three years, but Moms only worked for them a few months. The family had eight children that ranged from an infant to teenagers. One day, some of the children complained to their mother that Moms wouldn't address them as Mister or Miss. Moms refused and was never called back to work for the family, although we stayed employed. The children in this family were our age but they very seldom spoke to us. They'd stare and watch us working in the hot sun without saying a word. Sometimes they would bring their friends to watch us. We felt we were in a sideshow, meant for their enjoyment. Pop told us to keep working and not to pay them any attention. I felt as if we were nothing more than their personal slaves.

One day the lady of the house saw us eating lunch in the garage and I got the impression she felt sorry for us. She told us, "Why Carey, you and the boys don't have to bring your lunch here. Just come on to work and I'll have your lunch ready for you tomorrow." Pop just responded by saying, "Yes ma'am, that will be fine." Of course, she never gave us the impression we could eat lunch inside the house or even use their bathroom. Whenever we had to use the bathroom, we went behind a tree in the far corner of the property. During those days, black people didn't use white people's bathrooms. We were only allowed to peek inside the house from the garage. Only Moms was allowed inside the house and that was only because she was cleaning it.

However, the next day Mrs. Kane saw us working in the hot sun. As we were finishing an area of the huge yard, she motioned for us to take a lunch break and come to the garage to eat the lunch she had prepared. As always, we each went behind a tree to relieve ourselves before lunch break. We used the garden hose to wash our hands before we sat on the milk crates in the garage that served as our chairs. I was tired and hungry from the long morning in the yard. To our surprise, Mrs. Kane had prepared two tuna fish sandwiches that she had cut in half. She had also poured four tiny cups of grape Kool Aid. The cups resembled small urine specimen cups at the doctor's office. Pop was so angry that he cursed like a sailor. He couldn't believe she prepared two sandwiches for four people and served us in the garage. He just gave the three of us his half of the sandwich and refused to eat anything.

Whenever things like that upset Pop, he would preach to us about the value of education, reminding us of the crap you have to take from people if you don't have it. He said, "I hope you guys see the mess people give you if you don't have an education. Don't you dare stop school until you can get all you can. Don't you dare! Boys, one day it's gonna rain on you. I can't stop it, but your education is gonna be your cover." We all said, "Yes sir" in unison. That afternoon, we returned to the hot sun still very hungry from the half sandwich lunch served to us in the garage. That was the last time we left home without a lunch to tackle a days work.

Pop worked for the Kane family a short time longer after that summer. Pop was later laid off because they said they didn't have any more work for him.

Later Pop got a job offer from a rich family in Kirkwood, Missouri. The family owned a huge house with a carriage house in the rear of the property. They were willing to employ Pop as the family maintenance man and Moms as the family maid. While we worked for them, they would have allowed us to live rent-free in the two-bedroom carriage house. Pop discussed the idea with us and talked about sending us to Kirkwood schools where we'd get to study with white kids. We thought that our ship had finally come in to port. We stayed up all night talking about going to school in Kirkwood and sleeping in a "real bedroom." Pop and Moms also had a lot of conversation about the possible move, but not very positive.

That next morning, Pop called the family and declined the job offer. He sat us down and told us he didn't want to put our entire future in the hands of one person. He and Moms told us the real reason was the family could get angry with us for any reason and put us in the streets. They were realistic in thinking that we'd be too beholden to the family. Pop said, "All it would take is for one of us

Oath of Office

to get into it with the family and we'd all be in the streets. Naw, I think I'll just keep looking for work and y'all just go on to school with colored. You just never know what's on white folks minds."

****

I had spoken to dozens of youngsters over the years and I know some of them are a little tougher to get motivated than others. Randy seemed to be one of the tough ones. The tough children are those that create the most trouble, or might I say the greatest challenge for the parents and teachers. Randy, Mr. Thomas' grandson, had a lot of baggage, and it was being unloaded on his grandpa. But it was not his fault. He was a victim just like many people I had arrested over the years.

Randy suddenly became more interested in what I had to say. He had given me the status and attention of a celebrity. Although Pop's illness was a sad occasion, I seized this one opportunity to reach a young man that represents the future...like it or not. By now Pop had drifted back to sleep. His medication was numbing his pain and discomfort. This caused him to sleep a lot, until the doctor's could determine a way to treat him. Randy then blurted out, "My uncle said when he was young he had to fight white boys all the time on the north side where you grew up. My uncle was a bad dude and I know he wouldn't put up with any stuff from anybody. How did you get in the FBI if you lived over there?" This time I knew I had his attention and that I had made some headway with him.

I said, "Young man, your uncle was right about north St. Louis years ago. Fighting was very common among the races but we survived and managed to go to school. We all managed to learn in spite of the disagreements and sometimes hatred.

"Let me explain life to you in the simplest terms possible. Throughout the episode of your life, you're going to face barriers that will stand in your path of success. You can fight those barriers or use them as an excuse not to do better. It's your choice. But the barriers will present themselves throughout your entire life and some form of barrier will always be in your way." Randy said, "Then tell me what stood in your way."

"I'm glad you asked that question, but let me make it even easier for you to understand. Just always remember, someone is always willing to whip you but you don't have to hand them the stick to do it." The next two hours, as we sat with Pop, would be spent explaining just how many times I refused to hand that stick to someone as they tried to beat the desire to succeed from my body.

I explained to Randy about the unofficial caste system called tracking that was prevalent at one time in the St. Louis public school system. I told him how fortunate he is that students aren't tracked or caste in his school today. Tracking was a system developed years ago that tested children in the eighth grade to determine the level they would study in high school. If you were a smart student, you'd be placed on track one. That meant you took college prep classes and everyone knew you would go to college and achieve big things.

If you were average like the majority of us, you'd take college prep classes mixed with classes that would also prepare you for trade school. Those kids were track two students. In other words, you had a 50-50 chance of making it in life. Randy asked, "What does tracking have to do with fighting white guys to survive in north St. Louis?" I explained to Randy in this case it has everything in the world to do with it. In fact it was one of the first times in my life I thought I was going to die over education. Randy then asked, "Did y'all have study sessions to prepare for the test like they do today?" I told him he had a good question but the reality was we had nothing prior to the test. In fact, many of us had parents who were barely literate and couldn't help us if they wanted. We were on our own and making a tremendous life decision at age 13 or 14.

I asked him to let me finish telling him about strife between the races and why the track test was so important at that time in our life.

Those students who didn't do well on the track test had to study on track three. That meant they only took the basic high school classes. They generally did not take college prep classes and were actually directed toward factory jobs, trade school, or if they were guys; the military. You could only imagine the fate of track three girls. Their only choices were marriage, domestic work, or manual labor.

In January 1964, Northwest High School was set to open during the final week of the month. It was located well inside the "DMZ" (imaginary demilitarized zone between blacks and whites) as far as we were concerned. In order for us to see where most of us would go to high school the following fall, the St. Louis School Board decided to let us take the track test at the new high school the week prior to its opening. We all knew we were venturing into uncharted land because "colored people" weren't really accepted in that part of town. Looking back, you would have thought our parents would have been frightened for us to go over there.

"Why did your parents let you go?" Randy asked. "Couldn't Pop drive you and pick you up after the test?" I explained the reality of growing up poor. Our family had one car that ran, sometimes. Pop was the only person in the family who could drive and at the time he was looking for work. Our parents' instructions have always been the same: "Boy, go to school and get a good education. They can't take that from ya. If you let them stand in the way of your education, you may as well be a slave." Those were our marching orders.

"You have to understand, my folks were the first generation to travel north from the south. Most blacks moving to the north were uneducated and unskilled. They moved north in search of an opportunity and to educate their kids in good schools", I said.

C. Lee Thornton

Unlike many families who were moving to the northside for better schools, we moved because the apartment we rented on the west side just became too rat infested. It got so bad, the big ones came up to the second floor where we lived and began searching for food. One daily duty, even though we were little guys, was to empty the mice traps every morning. Never mind you didn't want to touch them, just empty them—those were Pop's orders. He felt if he could bring home the bacon, we could empty the mice traps.

We knew things were getting tough when one evening we heard the mice trap spring and unlike a normal springing. The trap seemed to flip around a little more frantically than usual. It flipped and flopped around for a long time. After a while, we stopped listening, and we certainly didn't go to investigate. I recalled that we went to sleep and decided we'd empty it the next morning, as usual.

It was my oldest brother's turn to empty the mice traps that were in the pantry where we kept food. No sooner had he entered the pantry, he called out to us. "Hey look at this thing!!" We ran to the kitchen and saw the longest rattail we had ever seen. The tail had to be a foot long and had been ripped right off the rat's body. The trap was bloody and messy but the rat had gotten away. When we showed it to Moms and Pop we heard them say we had to move. We knew one of their biggest fears was one of us being bitten by a rat. It would have been devastating because rats carry all kinds of diseases and we didn't have medical insurance. We'd heard stories about children dying after being bitten by rats.

On the first day of the track test we boarded the Lee bus and got off at the corner of Riverview and Thekla. We were met by hundreds of local bigots and followed to Northwest High School. "Did they shout at you?" Randy asked. I said, "Yes, they did and not too kindly either...but I had my marching orders to do well on the test."

He then asked, "Well, how did you concentrate with all those people looking at you and making you feel unwanted in the neighborhood?"

Oath of Office

I told him I just kept remembering my marching orders. The first day of the test was interesting for all of us from my school. When we went to the bathroom, we made a pact to go in groups. Both guys and girls agreed to stay together. We went nowhere in the building alone during the turbulent two days. It certainly affected our performance, but we had no choice. When the first day ended, hundreds of "locals" taunted us while we waited for the bus at the corner of Riverview and Thekla to return us to our neighborhood.

We could hear conversations from people in the crowd. Both students and non-students were saying they were going to get the "colored kids" tomorrow. Despite the circumstances, we were more determined than ever to return to take the test. I didn't sleep well the night before the last day of the test. I kept recalling my marching orders from Pop, "Don't let 'em take your education from you."

Prior to boarding the Lee bus for Northwest High School, the next day, we stopped by our school briefly. A few students mentioned to the teachers that the white kids were not kind to us and it was hard to concentrate. The teachers told us to do the best we could because one day all the hatred will be gone. They too, told us to stay together and to stay in groups. They also emphasized the importance of education. With that, we boarded the Lee bus not knowing what to expect later in the day.

When we arrived at Riverview and Thekla, the huge crowd of teenagers and adults let us know, in no uncertain terms, that we were not welcome in north St. Louis. Just like the previous day, we were followed to the school by crowds of hecklers. We had to think about our safety and focus on one of the most important tests of our young lives as well. We adhered to our marching orders and remained together in groups everywhere we went in the building. This time I recalled hearing the "enemy" saying they were going to get the colored kids after the test today. As soon as I left the bathroom, I told my classmates what I had heard. I said to myself,

"How the heck can I concentrate on a test when I've got to worry about getting my butt kicked after school by a pack of wild white boys?" I could remember asking myself how could they hate us? We didn't do anything to them?

On that cold Friday in January 1964, 43 eighth grade students from north St. Louis left Northwest High School headed to the only way back to safety. We walked in one group to the corner of Riverview and Thekla to catch the bus for the return trip to our neighborhood. We tried to assure the weaker students and the girls that they were completely surrounded by the stronger boys. This day was different from the day earlier due to the atmosphere of the all white neighborhood. The crowd following us to the bus stop was much larger and we could clearly hear "Nigger" from the mouths of many of those following us. Some of them were driving cars, others were walking behind us, and some walked in front of us as if they were leading us to a slaughter.

I asked myself again, what could we have done to make them hate us so much? It finally came to me after looking into the eyes of one person in the crowd. It was 1964 and we were colored—nothing more, nothing less.

As I told the story to Randy I could see his young face mesmerized and fixated on every word I spoke. I knew then, that unlike his grandfather, I had the young man's attention. The older men in Pop's hospital room listened attentively as I talked. They had lived through similar ordeals many times in their lives and could understand my feelings. Their weathered faces were etched with the trials they had endured over the years. The pain hidden deep in their bowels crept to the top forcing them to remember why it was there. I paused for a moment, watched Randy's reactions, and continued the saga.

We arrived at the bus stop anxiously waiting for the bus to take us home to safety…away from the growing crowds that were forming on the street corners adjacent to us. The crowds got larger and more hostile. I knew we were in big trouble when small rocks and objects started pelting us from all directions. We didn't see any signs of the bus arriving or anyone that was going to turn the crowd away from the forty-three of us.

Automobiles loaded with angry white people began to stop in the street, people came out of their homes, and the crowds continued to grow with hostility. I saw some of my classmates crying, while others prayed out loud. I was frightened as hell, but I considered myself to be a leader and the last thing I wanted to do was to let the weaker students see my fear. As a teenager, we learned early not to show fear in the presence of the opposite gender. Although I was only 13, I felt the weight of a lot of students on my shoulders that afternoon.

As the rocks and objects started to increase in volume, we put the girls in the center of our group for better protection. The crowd was growing and getting more intense. Up to now no one had retaliated or said one word to the angry crowd confronting us. Suddenly, one girl left the center of our group and smashed a beer bottle over the curb, leaving sharp jagged edges exposed. She joined us on the outside of our group with only our fists as weapons.

One guy from our group picked up a rock and threw it in the direction of the crowd. It seemed that all hell broke loose with that one returned rock. The crowd of angry white men, women, and teenagers started moving toward us from across the street. A white teenager ran up to our group and threw a rock directly into the face of Gwen Maurey. Her face began to spurt blood over her blouse. Several students went to her rescue to stop her bleeding. Suddenly, an older Chevrolet came to a screeching stop in the bus stop and the driver went into his trunk and retrieved a tire iron. The crowd surrounding us shouted louder and louder. The crowds of teenagers and adults started moving closer toward us from across the street.

All of the boys had their fists poised to fight while the girls remained inside the circle we had formed.

Just when I thought I had seen my last day on earth, the Lee bus appeared from nowhere and cut through the middle of the angry crowd who was advancing toward us. The driver, a black man, sensed we were in trouble and opened the front and rear doors for us to hurriedly board. We quickly pushed the girls on first and by now several fist fights had broken out among angry white people and several of our boys. The angry crowd was all over us as students got onto the bus. Cletus was the biggest boy in the eighth grade and was fighting with two big white guys. He was holding them off pretty good but he was cut off from the bus and they made sure he couldn't get on with us.

By now the crowd was so large no one could get out to help him. We all said, "Run!!" Cletus ran to the side door of Walnut Park School, on the corner, well ahead of his pursuers. Luckily for him the side door was opened and they didn't follow him inside the building. We assumed the school officials saw the angry crowd and had called the St. Louis Police Department to respond.

The crowd started to hit the windows of the bus with rocks and sticks. Suddenly someone hurled a large rock through the bus driver's side window striking him on the head. In addition to the one student having a cut on her face, the bus driver was bleeding profusely from his head. The bus was blocked in by an older Chevy with the driver wielding a tire iron at us and daring anyone to get off the bus and fight him. The guy was at least twenty years old. Just when I thought we were saved from the mob, we were again trapped in the bus. I had never heard the word "Nigger" so many times from so many angry white people. I kept asking myself, what had we done to them?

However, our only goal up to now was not to let the mob on the bus because the teenagers and adults were now trying to open the doors. Someone in our group found the door release and closed both doors.

We then heard sirens from police cars coming in our direction. The cars from the angry mob were still blocking the bus as the St. Louis Police Department squad cars arrived. A police officer talked with the bleeding driver. The bus driver explained to the police that the mob was attacking the children at the bus stop. We could hear people from the angry mob still shouting, "Those niggers are causing trouble!!"

The driver could hardly get in a word when the police officer interrupted him and said, "We'll escort you outta this neighborhood." Cletus came running back to the bus from the side door of Walnut Park School. He wasn't hurt but he was exhausted from running. He got on the bus without being noticed by the angry crowd. The officer "politely" asked the crowd to disperse and no one was arrested despite our stories that we were just standing on the corner waiting for the bus. The guys blocking the bus were "politely" asked a second time so the bus could leave the area. They smiled to the officer and moved their cars. None of them were given a traffic ticket or arrested for attacking us. In light of the circumstances, we figured we came out ahead—at least we were alive and only a few students were hurt.

When we arrived back to our area in north St. Louis, we were glad to be alive. The police cars escorted us to the corner of Kingshighway Boulevard and Highway 70 and turned away. This was the unofficial border where Negroes were accepted and lived in north St. Louis. We told our neighborhood friends what had happened. We all told our parents who simply repeated their marching orders, "Boy don't let anyone take your education from you. Get that education because no one can take that from you."

Randy then said, "Dang man, that's messed up. You mean no one went to jail for jumpin' y'all?" I said, "No one. By the way, most of us made track two, which meant we could make it but we had to work. A small article appeared in the St. Louis Post Dispatch that said a group of Negro students had fistfights with whites in north St. Louis. It mentioned one student was hit with an umbrella. She was actually hit in the face with a flying rock. I was standing there and saw the entire incident."

The article also indicated that two juveniles were detained. We all knew that wasn't true. No one was arrested or detained. We were fighting for our lives at 13 and 14. In summary the article was written as if we had gone to north St. Louis to start trouble. Of course no reporters ever talked to us and nothing was done to the persons who started the riot against us.

He asked, "If things were so tough back in the day, did you hate all the white people?" I said, "That is a good question but let me tell you about a man who made it possible for me to help my family and continue going to high school."

Going to high school represented far different challenges for me than many of my peers. I felt I was forced to be a man simply because we were poor, although in reality we didn't know we were poor. I just felt things were a little tight and sooner or later Pop would get that "good job" and everything would be fine. Even at a very young age we followed the teachings of the preacher at church. He'd always tell us to "just hold on to your faith in Him." We assumed that meant if we waited just a little while longer, our ship would sail in to the port. I later realized we didn't live near water.

From time to time Pop would tell us he was going on an interview for a job that seemed to be the elusive "steady work". We would all be so excited and felt that at last our ship had come to port. Sometimes we'd even start imagining the things we were going to buy when Pop got that "good job". We'd think about having things like a house with our own rooms just like on the television show *Leave It To Beaver*. We would even imagine waking up in our house in the winter and not being able to see our breath in the air. My older brother told us that rich folk had a little dial on the wall in their house that gave you heat in the winter and cool air in the summer. Although it was hard for us to imagine not making a fire in the furnace all winter, we dreamed about the good times when Pop would get that "good job". We knew Pop was a hard worker but he just needed that one chance to prove himself. It wasn't his fault he wasn't allowed to go to school when he was a kid.

Unfortunately the results were always the same when he came home from the interviews. By the time he would make it home, he was blasted and cursing the white man. The story was always the same. It came down to Pop and a white guy—and Pop never won. He would sit us down, and even though he was in a stupor, he would preach to us, "Get that education!!! Don't you dare let 'em take that from you. That's the one thing they can't take from ya!! If some clown is trying to make noise and keeping you from learning, kick his ass and keep studying."

It seemed that our teachers during those days were as influential in our lives as our natural parents. Although some of them were as mean as snakes, they never told us to do anything that wasn't in our best interest. They looked professional, acted professional, and were the people we strived to emulate in our lives. Besides, other than preachers, teachers were the only Black professionals we ever knew. Even if we saw them in a grocery store, they demanded and received respect from us. They were bigger than life to me and were our keys to getting out of poverty.

During the initial days of my sophomore year at O'Fallon Technical High School, I had to make a decision regarding the trade I wanted to study for the next three years. Pop was realistic when it came to higher education. He encouraged me to attend the technical high school and learn a trade because he knew he didn't have the means to pay for college. Although he wanted me to go to college, he knew the funding was far beyond his reach. For that reason I signed up for the print shop to learn the graphic arts trade. I actually had no idea what the print shop was but it sounded cool at the time. Some guys chose the welding shop because the girls thought it was cool to watch the guys walk down the hall with the big welding helmets in their hands. Other guys chose the auto shop because they would be able to repair their old cars and parade around town. In summary we all chose our trades for the wrong reasons but no one ever told us any different.

The only trades most girls could study were stenography, clerical, and cosmetology. There was a cosmetology shop but they only worked on white people's hair therefore they wouldn't accept colored girls. They always told the students they didn't have the chemicals to work with colored hair and it was too difficult. Colored girls (we hadn't graduated to Black yet) had fewer choices than the colored boys.

For the first few weeks all the new printing students met in a classroom with two of the three printing teachers. One of them was a black man named Mr. John James. Mr. James was a stern, sincere man that had our best interest in mind. He was a no nonsense teacher that demanded everyone learn and excel in his shop. One afternoon he walked in the classroom and announced, "I want all the white boys to wait in the hallway and all the colored boys to stay here with me." I thought this was unprecedented. Of course, I was curious to hear what was so important that the white guys had to leave the room. Mr. James stood by the door until the last white kid walked out and closed the door behind him.

He then said, "Guys the printing trade is a fascinating field and you will learn a lot from us if you follow instructions and do your homework everyday. However the only way you'll ever make much money in this trade is to get in a union. Unfortunately the day has not come when colored men can get in unions in St. Louis. Hopefully this will happen one day but I can't see it anytime soon. Now the white boys won't have any problems 'cause they've probably got contacts with the unions already. You colored boys don't have the inside track plus your race works against you. I wouldn't be able to rest if I didn't tell you the truth, misleading you into thinking you could make a lot of money. Now if any of you want to transfer to a different department and study something with more of a future for colored boys, I'd understand."

I stood there with my mouth wide open. I couldn't believe a teacher felt such compassion for us that they told us the truth about our future. But that was the caliber of teachers' we had during the 1960s. They were more than teachers, they were our second parents, and they cared about us. I didn't make a final decision that day but I told Pop that evening about what I had learned from Mr. James. Pop simply said, "Stay right where you are. You're going to change things one day." My final decision was to stay in printing and continue on with my marching orders.

The department did receive some high-speed offset printing equipment for students to study. At the time the equipment was the latest technology in the printing trade. Needless to say, only one colored student got a chance to use the equipment. The other 20 printing students were all white guys.

One cool Fall Saturday evening in 1966, I arrived home around 9:00 p.m. Our three and one half room apartment seemed unusually strange because no one was home and Pop's car was gone. My folks never went out to parties so I wondered where they could be so late in the evening. I couldn't watch television because it hadn't worked in about six months. We didn't have the money to get it fixed so it just sat in one place and acted like a piece of furniture. When friends came to visit us we never mentioned that the television set didn't work. We just pretended we liked the quiet. I grabbed a book that night and tried not to worry about my parents.

Moms and my older brother arrived home around midnight that evening. Mom was crying and seemed to be terribly upset. Pop had suddenly gotten sick and had to be rushed to Homer G. Phillips Hospital. He was admitted and had to undergo an emergency prostate operation. Needless to say Pop was unemployed and we had no medical insurance. Moms couldn't drive and only worked a few days a week as a domestic worker for some rich folk in St. Louis County. Pop was in a ward at the public hospital with dozens of other poor, sick people, and we had no idea how long he would be there. Needless to say we had no money coming into the home. I thought the world was crashing down around us. I again heard Ray Charles singing "I'm Busted" all over again.

Because we never had medical insurance, something we always thought was reserved for rich, preventive medical care was a foreign concept around our house. Generally we'd visit a doctor when you were hurting was so bad you couldn't stand it any longer. And that was only after Miss Corrine couldn't heal you with one of her Louisiana potions. Miss Corine was our personal family doctor, at least as far as she was concerned. Sometimes her potions tasted so bad you'd wish you were dead. I'm not sure whether her potions were good or if we stayed well just to avoid going to see her. I guess in this case her potions didn't work on Pop either.

I had just made the "B" football team and was playing first team wide receiver as a sophomore. I was real excited about playing especially because we had to play the neighborhood school later in the month. I could hardly wait to showcase my talents against my friends at Northwest High School. More than anything there were a few honeys I knew would be at the game that I wanted to impress. Moms gave me the devastating news that I'd have to quit the football team and find a part-time job. I was sickened but I knew there were no other choices; we were out of money. We had to somehow amass $60.00 a month to pay the rent or we'd be put out in the streets.

I'd seen families put out on the curb and it was not a happy sight. Now we were faced with the same thing.

Once when I was about seven years old Pop and I drove through a slum neighborhood in downtown St. Louis. We saw a young mother who had just been put out of her house. She was sitting on a chair in the middle of her furniture in front of an apartment building. She was crying uncontrollably. Everything she owned had been put on the sidewalk. While she cried, her child, who was no older than three years old, played over her belongings. The child was too young to realize they had nowhere to live. Pop pulled over in his car and spoke to the lady for a few moments but she just kept crying. I saw Pop reach into his pocket and hand the lady some money. I knew he only had a few dollars but he gave her some money anyway.

He really seemed sad when he got back into the car with me because he knew it was not very much he could do for the lady. Although I was quite young I got the marching orders lecture from Pop. I understood well that if I let someone take my education, I might end up like the lady on the street corner.

I arrived at school early on Monday morning following Pop's surgery and told the coach I had to quit the team. He asked if there was any way I could stay but I told him no. I turned in my equipment and never played high school football again. I later learned I was ineligible to play because I had only been at O'Fallon Tech for one semester.

My friend Omar's father told me there might be in a position at the federal building where he worked but he had to see if I could work after school. He had heard about Pop being sick and said, "It's about time you boys learned to work anyway." But I was only 14 years old and playing football in high school. He told me he would talk to his boss who ran the janitorial team. To make a long story short, I later was hired at the minimum wage of $0.90 an hour to work after school. My job was scraping wax off of desk table legs.

The company only provided steel wool and no gloves. I practically ran home to tell Moms who was probably more excited than me. Now she knew she didn't have to give me bus and lunch money from her meager wages as a domestic worker. Her salary was generally a grand total of $5.00 per day plus bus fare. I remember borrowing $0.39 from Moms to buy a pair of work gloves for my hands. Somehow Moms scraped up the money just to get me started on my new job. During that time rich folks would normally pick up their cleaning ladies at the bus stops and return them to the same stop in the evenings. It was their problem how they got home. They felt they were too generous by providing the extra thirty cents for bus fare.

I now had to leave school by 3:30 p.m. in order to get to the federal building by 5:00 p.m. The high school was adjacent to an old junkyard located on Manchester near Kingshighway Boulevard. I could eliminate one bus ride by climbing a fence and running through the junkyard. But the yard had a vicious old "junkyard dog" they used for security. Because I was a fast runner I'd sneak up to the fence and throw a rock to the far end of the junkyard. The dog would run toward the noise to see if he had a burglar. When he was at the opposite end of the junkyard, I'd hop the fence and run across to the Manchester side. I would always hop the second fence far ahead of the junkyard dog. The dog never came close to catching me, I'm not sure if the stupid dog ever caught anyone.

The bus ride was always interesting with all the characters on the Manchester bus heading to the Southside projects. The Southside project guys were real gangsters. They too chased me sometimes but I was never caught. I made it to work on time everyday, ready to shine desk legs.

One day the boss came in and told me I had really done a great job and was working out fine. Showing respect, I simply said, "Thank you". To my surprise he told me I was being promoted to a job emptying trashcans on the fourth floor. My salary was going up to $1.10 an hour. I thought I had died and gone to heaven!! What was I going to do with all of that money?

The fourth floor was huge with hundreds of employees and trashcans. Many of them smoked cigarettes at their desk and were nasty as hell. The stuff they threw in their trashcans should have been against the law. But I was proud to be pulling my own weight at home with my $1.10 an hour job after school.

The fourth floor trash was a four-hour job that only allowed a few moments for a brief break. After work I had an eight-block walk to the bus stop and another thirty-minute ride to north St. Louis. The ride to north St. Louis went directly through the Pruitt Igoe public housing projects. The projects were about the worst place in the world to be caught after dark. The bus drivers would always turn off the lights inside the bus when we passed through the Pruitt Igoe area.

One night a bus driver was killed when the bus stopped to pick up a passenger in the Pruitt Igoe area. I was lucky to be on another bus that night. Although it was tragic, I had to say my prayers and continue riding the Lee bus at the end of my workday. I knew my marching orders and I had no choice but to keep going to school and working. I would normally arrive home after 10:00 p.m. only to get up at 6:00 a.m. the next morning and do it all over. I studied whenever and wherever I had the opportunity.

I finally got my fourth floor trash job down to a science. I now could finish the entire floor in two and one-half hours, take a snack, and study my homework until time to leave. I'd always find a desk in a far corner of the floor, turn on the desk light, and study until the end of my shift. I thought my boss assumed I was finishing just in time to punch out at 9:00 p.m. I really had it made, $1.10 an hour for a trash hauling job after school. Life could get no better!!

C. Lee Thornton

One evening I finished my work with the usual hour and a half to spare. I took a short break and began studying as usual. I had several tests coming up and I wanted to do my very best. Pop had experienced a few complications and we had no idea when he'd be released. Besides whenever he was released, he still didn't have a job.

All of a sudden I heard footsteps coming in the direction where I was sitting at an employee's desk. It was my boss, Buddy.

He shouted at me, "What the hell are you doing? You should be working!! We don't pay you to sit down and do nothing!!" All I could think about was being fired and having to break the news to Moms. I couldn't imagine finding another job that would pay me $1.10 an hour and allow me to do my homework. I knew I had to think fast or I'd be fired. I told him in a very calm voice that I was finished with the floor. He said, "Everything?" I said, "Yes Sir, everything." He said, "Then what the hell are you doing?" I said, "I'm doing my English homework, Sir. I have a test tomorrow." Buddy asked to see my book and I handed it to him.

He looked at my book for a moment without saying a word to me. It seemed he was engulfed in the details of my English grammar textbook. I figured he was now going to either fire me or give me more work to do. I kept thinking about my marching orders and that I couldn't study if he gave me more work. I just remained quiet and waited for the worse to happen. I was busted.

Buddy handed my textbook back to me and said, "Study hard, son. Do the best you can on that test tomorrow" and walked away. As he walked away I said, "Thank you Sir" and continued studying. I knew at 14, some people were different. As turbulent as the times were during the 1960s, Buddy proved to me all white people were not as those I had experienced earlier in my life. He had the opportunity to completely upset my world but he opted not to do so. He had given me a fighting chance to succeed. I thought that perhaps Buddy knew I had marching orders and he saw promise in me. Nonetheless I kept studying that night until the end of my shift.

The lessons I learned on my job at the federal building were important lessons. That job allowed me to sustain my education as a high school student and put extra drive in me to go even further. Pop eventually was released from the hospital and went home to recover. He was pretty weak but he soon gained strength and found another job.

****

As a high school student I realized that some of the same gangsters who lived on the west side had made their way to north St. Louis. The housing patterns were shifting and many white families were deserting north St. Louis for places in the suburbs. This was quite evident as I settled into adolescence and began developing my own group of friends. Everyone felt his crowd of friends was the coolest. No one wanted to be second rate. But when all the crowds got together, the egos always ran high. Generally there wouldn't be any fighting among groups from the same neighborhood but a lot of boasting and especially if the ladies were present. Testosterone was the chemical of the day in teenage boys.

I was 15 in the summer of 1966 and there was a lot of turmoil in the country including riots and unemployment. The war in Vietnam was well underway and I had a crush on a girl I had known since first grade. Her family had also migrated from the west side to north St. Louis. In my eyes Pam Ellis was the prettiest girl in the world. She was popular with everyone at her high school and she literally gave me chills every time I looked at her. I got word during that summer that Pam had broken up with her boyfriend. That news was music to my ears. At the same time she invited me to a party at her home. I couldn't imagine any reason she would invite me to her

C. Lee Thornton

party other than to entice me to be her new boyfriend. She knew how I felt about her and she was finally giving me an opportunity to ask her for a "chance".

Asking a girl for a "chance" during the 1960s was the way a boy asked a girl to be his girlfriend. When you thought the time was right, you'd say, "Would you give me a chance?" and you'd look into her eyes hoping to get a yes. I planned to ask Pam for a "chance" at her party that warm summer night. I felt the time was right.

Little did I know Pam's party that night would change the entire course of my life. I arrived at the party fashionably late with one of my boys. I figured if I got there too early I'd appear to seem anxious. It wasn't cool to be too anxious. I wore my best party rags and although I hadn't started shaving, I splashed on my Dad's aftershave so I could smell good for Pam. The party was outside on her patio and Smokey Robinson music was in the air. As far as I was concerned, Smokey would set the mood for the night.

Smokey Robinson's *Ohh Baby Baby*, one of my favorite slow dance songs, was playing on the record player when I finally mustered up the nerve to ask Pam to dance. I saw her Mom on the patio, so I knew dancing close enough to Pam to ask for a "chance" would not happen while her mom watched us. In fact, I had to stand back and dance like a gentleman although I laid down some of my best "mack lines". Pam was smiling and laughing like a schoolgirl; I was smooth with my best conversation. My plan to charm Pam seemed to be working like clockwork. I thought the mood was just right when Pam's Mom stepped away and went into the house. I said to myself, "The stars are lining up for me".

As the song cruised to a close I looked smack into Pam's eyes and said, "Pam, I've got something to ask you. Can we talk?" She smiled a beautiful smile, showing all 32 teeth and said, "Sure but let me run inside for a quick moment." I said to myself, "This is it". I assumed she was going inside to brush her teeth so that she'd be fresh to kiss me later. I felt like I was walking on clouds. At that moment I looked toward the rear alley and saw some strange guys who appeared to be marching up the alley just like soldiers. They were walking four abreast and there were dozens of them. I could plainly see they were carrying sticks and other objects in their hands. They were the Newstead Boys street gang!

Pam lived almost equal distance between Newstead Avenue and Euclid Avenue in north St. Louis. Due to the proximity of where Pam lived, she knew guys from both neighborhoods. In addition she had gone to elementary school with many of the Newstead gang members. Unfortunately, she hadn't invited the Newstead gang to the party due to their reputation but somehow they found out about the party. They were angry and had decided to invite themselves.

There must have been at least 30 of them in the alley and definitely far more of them than there were of us. They decided to come over the fence rather than to use the gate. As they entered the yard, they were swinging sticks at anyone in their path. They were out to get the Euclid Boys. Girls were screaming like crazy as the gang created havoc everywhere. These guys were kicking anyone's butt they could reach. There was a mad scramble for the rear door of Pam's house. Unfortunately for my boys and me, the girls had jammed the doors as the Newstead Boys fought everyone outside. There was an unwritten rule in the neighborhood that if you had a girl with you, you couldn't run—you had to stay with her and fight it out.

We were far outnumbered and lucky for me Pam had just gone into the house. I could see she was safe from the swinging sticks and blows of the gang. Besides they wanted Euclid Boys not the girls. I looked toward the house and saw so many heads inside my boys and I couldn't have fit in the kitchen if we wanted to. It was jammed with screaming girls and the guys who had escorted them to the party. Omar Thomas and I had come together so we decided to make a run for it. Both of us were high school sprinters and we knew if we got a start, we wouldn't be caught by the gang. The gate was only wide enough for Omar and because I was a hurdler, we both hit the street at the same time and ran like hell. Several guys tried to catch us but they were no match for the two of us.

I listened for the familiar sound of gunfire, which is common in this case, but luckily it never came. The gang members had a reputation of always traveling with at least one gun and they were known to use it. Someone must have been watching over us that warm summer night. We just ran until we were sure we had outrun the fastest gang member.

We made it about a block away before about six guys quit chasing us. As we looked back up the street, Miguel Miller, from our neighborhood, thought he could give the girls a boxing display in front of Pam's house. The Newstead Boys wasted no time getting all over him as he danced, bobbed, and weaved. Everyone kept shouting for Miguel to run but he had been drinking and the liquid courage had gotten the best of him. For every blow Miguel landed, he collected three but just kept dancing and fighting. In no time at all he was bloody as hell but too drunk to know the difference. From where we hid behind some parked cars about a block away, we knew Miguel couldn't take too much more punishment before he went down. The cheap wine made him feel invincible.

Although we were not far from hundreds of guys in our neighborhood, Omar and I were careful not to make a noise as we crouched below the hood of a parked car. We knew some of the Newstead Boys were still searching the streets for anyone that needed a good butt kicking. I was ready to take off again if necessary. I had completely forgotten about the offer I was about two minutes away from presenting to Pam Ellis. I was just hoping she hadn't looked out of her kitchen window and seen me clear her front fence like I was in the district finals. I hoped the Newstead Boys figured it was just too much trouble to try to catch me.

As we watched Miguel slow down, the crowd screamed for him to run. Suddenly against the moonlit sky we saw the unmistaken glisten of a pocketknife. A Newstead boy had pulled out a knife. Miguel was starting to get the best of two of the Newstead Boys. I guess they felt they had to end the fight as soon as possible. The first one to stab Miguel grunted as loudly as Miguel. He stepped back and passed the knife to the next guy. Like a baton it was passed to the third guy. After he had done his dirty deed Miguel went down. The Newstead Boys swarmed him like ants on a honeycomb as people screamed for them to stop. One of the guys picked up a huge tree branch and hit Miguel over and over. Just then we heard the sirens over the girls screams. Miguel lay on the ground motionless in a pool of blood groaning in pain.

As soon as they walked away from Miguel, one of them pointed down the street toward Omar and I. We only heard them say, "Get those two m.......f......rs!!" We knew that meant us and we both took off in what seemed to be an endless sprint for life. We ran until we were sure there were no more footsteps pursuing us.

Later that night everyone from the Euclid side assembled in Penrose Park near the baseball diamond. It was about 10:00 p.m. and the park had no lights but about eleven guys met there anyway. Our meeting was to decide what we should do about the Newstead Boys coming to our neighborhood. No one liked the idea they embarrassed our boys in the presence of girls. And it was unanimous that we had to avenge the stabbing of Miguel. No one knew at the time if he was dead or alive. Everyone felt our ego had been bruised and we'd be looked upon as chumps if we didn't redeem ourselves. If we didn't put something on the Newstead Boys, every neighborhood in the city would use us for punching bags. Whenever they felt like kicking some butt for fun, they would come to Euclid and get started. We didn't want to be branded punks. We had to strike back and quick.

The problem this night was no one had a car and Newstead was a bit beyond walking distance at 10:00 p.m. If we walked we'd surely be stopped by the police and no one could carry a blade if we walked because the police would search us. We needed a car to surprise them and make our escape.

While we contemplated our assault on the Newstead Boys we all shared about two fifths of "cheap liquid courage." The wine was hot and so was the temperature that summer night. Each one of us felt more united and determined to handle the Newstead Boys with every drop of the cheap wine we consumed. One guy stood up on the park bench and said, "We've got to do this for the neighborhood!!" Little did we know we were about to put our rear ends on the line for nothing more than concrete which none of us owned. But we didn't care—we were all from Euclid, united, and high on cheap warm wine.

Kevin Rollins, one of the older guys in the group, decided he would steal his Dad's Chevrolet from the front of his house on Calvin Street. We all thought that sounded like a good idea as we needed a ride. If I had been using my head, I would have thought about the company I was getting ready to join. Moms always told me to watch the company I keep. I was about to follow Kevin Rollins as he stole his Dad's car from the front of his house. Kevin was at least three years older than me, an ex-con, and a high school dropout. Every one of us knew Kevin had just gotten out of jail and he was not someone a school kid should be hanging around. He wasn't a part of my crowd but the "liquid courage" made everything all right for this evening.

We all waited in the park and consumed the last of the cheap wine while Kevin got the car. All of a sudden Kevin pulled up next to the park and honked the horn of the shiny blue Chevrolet. All ten of us piled in and were ready for action. Only two guys joined Kevin in the front seat. We felt the police would never stop us as long as only three people sat in the front seat. Our logic, as I reflect, didn't make any sense and I should have known better. The liquid courage told us they would never notice the other eight guys piled into the rear seat. We headed toward Vanderventer Boulevard for some reinforcements to help us with the Newstead Boys.

The area of Vanderventer and Natural Bridge was the hangout of the notorious Vanderventer Strips Gang. They had a reputation for kicking butt and taking names later. Kevin Rollins had met a bunch of them while he was locked down in Algoa State Reformatory. He said they told him to stop down if he ever needed any help. We felt this was a good time to cash in a favor.

As we rode down Natural Bridge toward Vanderventer our collective ego was still strong and all of us were more determined than ever to get revenge on the Newstead Boys for their assault on us earlier that evening. We were so pumped up no one thought to ask Kevin if he had a driver's license. As I think back, he probably didn't have a driver's license.

When we arrived on Vanderventer we found several of the Vanderventer Strips holding down the corner at Vanderventer and Labadie. Just like us, they had nothing to do but stand around and protect their concrete. Kevin recognized one of the gang members and said, "Hey Wilbert we need your help man. Those m.....f......rs from Newstead just rolled up on us and f....d up one of our boys. We need y'all to come help us get 'em back." Wilbert said, "Sorry man, we be cool with them. We can't roll on 'em. Why don't y'all try the Taylor and Cottage Boys."

Kevin headed over to Taylor and Cottage to again seek some street corner help. To our surprise the police still hadn't stopped us yet. The fact that it was a busy night and the traffic was heavy worked in our favor. Kevin was just as buzzed as the rest of us from the cheap wine and driving like a crazy man. But we didn't care because Kevin was upholding the honor of the neighborhood.

We searched until Kevin finally spotted a Taylor and Cottage Boy holding down a corner. Again it was a familiar face from the joint. It seemed that everyone Kevin knew had done time in Algoa reformatory, the medium security institution for guys 17–21 years old. It was the last stop before going to the maximum-security prison in Jefferson City, Missouri. Kevin and all his friends talked about the fun they had in Algoa and how they planned to run the big prison in Jefferson City one day. That night the "liquid courage" had us all thinking they were guys to look up to.

Kevin hollered at his friend and said, "Hey Tommie, where yo' boys tonight, we need help on the north side?" Tommie said, "Sorry man, the police locked up six of those m...f...rs this afternoon on a shooting. Everybody's laying low." Kevin turned around to us and shouted, "We gotta do it alone. Euclid...Euclid...Euclid!!" He had us so pumped up we could whip the Third Army Brigade. He sped off in the direction of Newstead and Farlin, determined to kick some butt.

We headed for Newstead and Farlin, Kevin driving like a madman in the heavy traffic and us in the back seat making our plans. While he told us our assignments, everyone reached to grab a knife to make sure he was ready for action. Kevin was a pro at pumping us up. We had completely lost sight of the fact that Kevin was an ex-con and not our crowd. My boys were students and athletes, not ex-cons and high school dropouts. But, for one night we somehow felt all to be in the same boat and equal.

Kevin told us the best place to surprise the Newstead Boys was to get them at the rear of the Velvet Freeze on Farlin and Newstead. There was an old garage back there where Kevin said they gambled on a regular basis. No one questioned our high school dropout/ex-con leader about how he knew this, but we followed his lead

Oath of Office

anyway. He told us they always gambled in a garage behind the Velvet Freeze and they could be caught off guard. He said, "We'd sneak up on them and kick the crap outta them before they knew what happened." We thought that sounded like a good plan. As we inched north on Newstead in bumper-to-bumper traffic, Kevin gave the order for everyone to get his knife ready. He said, "We're about to kick some a......"

I couldn't wait to get there because the two guys sitting on top of me were getting heavy. I looked out the window and saw Margaretta Avenue and said to myself, just one more block and revenge will be mine. I started thinking about how sweet Pam Ellis looked earlier that evening and the fact those bums spoiled my opportunity to ask her for a chance. I thought about the look in Miguel's face as he was stabbed over and over by the Newstead Boys. I could almost see the green and white neon sign on the front of the Velvet Freeze ice cream shop.

As we slowly drove up to the Velvet Freeze, I had made up my mind to be the first out of the car. Kevin abruptly put the car in park in the middle of the street and said, "Hit it!!" I grabbed the doorknob, opened the door, and had placed one foot on the ground when I heard a loud boom and then a crash. All around me was, "BOOM, BOOM, BOOM" and then the rear window of the car started caving in, landing on the top of the eight of us in the rear seat. Broken glass and bricks were landing all over us. Kevin's surprise plan had gone horribly wrong. The Newstead Boys knew we were coming and were hiding between parked cars on Newstead and Farlin. I was the only one who had stepped on to the ground when Kevin gunned the motor to get out of line of fire from the bricks and bottles. I had barely gotten back into the car when he took off frantically down Newstead.

Miraculously the bumper-to-bumper traffic had suddenly disappeared as soon as the first object hit the car. I thought we were trapped and we'd have to run for our life. In the midst of the booms and crashes on the car I wondered if they would start shooting. It was uncommon for gangs like this to attack a car of adversaries without a gun. Was someone looking over us and was this a sign from Him?

Kevin drove like a wild man until we heard no more objects striking the car. When he stopped everyone in the rear seat was bloody as hell from the shattered glass but no one was seriously hurt. My hair was full of glass and I was bleeding down my back. The warm feel of my blood running down my back quickly cleared the buzz I had. I didn't know if I should get on my knees and start praying for thanks or have someone pick the glass out of my back. Although the praying would have been more appropriate, it wouldn't have been cool in front of my boys. So I silently prayed to God and thanked Him for not letting me walk my dumb ass into an early death. I told Him I was going to turn my dumb behind around and never follow an ex-con anywhere again. I thanked Him for protecting me although I knew I didn't deserve His mercy. That night gave new meaning to Moms preaching to me, "Boy watch yo' crowds. You can get into a lot of trouble simply by following the wrong crowds around." At 15, I knew exactly what she meant. She would never have to tell me that again.

I thought about asking Him to help Pam say yes because I had planned to ask her for a "chance" but, He had already done too much for me. As I walked down Lee Avenue I could only imagine how lucky I was to still be alive. I almost got killed protecting the honor of concrete that I didn't own. I kept thinking how my death would disappoint my folks. Although my parents didn't have much money, I somehow felt I deserved a lot more than to die following an ex-con to a senseless gang fight.

As I walked back to the neighborhood I couldn't help but rationalize how I got into the fix that night. Would I be bleeding down my back had I not gone to the party to see Pam? Or could I blame my predicament on too much wine? Maybe I could blame everything on Kevin Rollins' bad planning. Whoever was to blame really didn't matter.

I later stopped by a friend's home whose mother was a nurse. Several of us arrived scared and bloody to be cleaned up with her medical kit. Needless to say we were a bit sore behind the stings of iodine on our backs. But that was nothing compared to the fate we could have suffered for being plain old stupid. We heard Kevin say he was going to park the car somewhere in the neighborhood and let his dad report it stolen the next day. He would just pretend he knew nothing about it or the busted windows and blood in the rear seat. The eight of us in the rear seat blocked all the flying glass from Kevin. He was completely unscratched.

The next day I called Pam Ellis to see how things went after the party. I was lucky she had no idea I had hurdled her fence to get away. Because she didn't know that I had run, I didn't have to make any excuses to keep my ego intact. She told me that Miguel Miller had multiple stab wounds and was at Barnes Hospital in intensive care. I decided to show her my sensitive side and said, "Hey, why don't we go down and see him? We can ride the bus together." When she said, "Sure, that's a good idea", I almost passed out with delight. We made arrangements to see Miguel the next day. I really didn't care about Miguel. In fact I didn't know him that well but I'd get a chance to be close to Pam Ellis. I never told her about my near brush with death the night before. I thought I'd hold that story to a time when I could use some sympathy from her.

I walked over to Pam's house the next day to pick her up for the bus ride to the hospital. She looked like an angel. She was so pretty I couldn't look at her straight. Her long brown hair and smooth caramel toned skin seemed to light up each time she smiled. We walked to Lee Avenue and took the Kingshighway bus to Barnes

Hospital. I played my caring, sympathetic role to show Pam I had compassion. I decided to wait until after we saw Miguel to pop the big question to Pam. By then she should be feeling pretty bad that her party was the reason the poor guy was in the hospital. I felt she could use some consoling and I was the guy for the special moment. I figured this special time with Pam was His was way of showing me there were better things to do with my time than following an ex-con to a gang fight.

When we got to Miguel's hospital room he looked a mess. He had tubes and machines all over him. He didn't recognize a soul and his mom was sitting next to him crying. It seemed his older brother had suffered a similar fate just two weeks earlier. Mrs. Miller was a single parent and felt this was more than she could take. I decided to come out of my sensitive bag to impress Pam and said, "Have you tried prayer?" Mrs. Miller said, "Yes and often." I said, "We need it everyday", and I peeked to see Pam's expression. She was smiling and I felt the time was near to make what I felt was the move of a lifetime.

We spent about 20 minutes in Miguel's room with his mom and then excused ourselves so she could be alone with him. I'm not sure he knew we were ever there plus he didn't know me that well anyway. Besides my goal that day was to spend some quality time with the lovely Pam Ellis and to ask her for a chance. So far everything was lining up in my favor......at least as far I could see.

We left Miguel's room and went to the cafeteria for a Coke. I knew girls liked to eat and drink so this seemed to be an ideal spot to set what I thought was the romantic mood. I continued with small talk until I finally said, "Pam do you remember what we were talking about just before the party broke up last night?" She looked at me and smiled with her big brown eyes and said, "So many things have happened I really can't remember. Is there something on your mind?"

I thought that now I really had to go ahead with my plan and it was no turning back. The stars had lined up for me, He had brought me safely from a near death experience, and what did I have to lose? I said, "Pam I'm not going to beat around the bush. I have known you since first grade and I have always liked you a lot." She smiled and said, "I've always liked you, too." I took a deep breath and paused for a moment because I knew what I said next could make it or break it for me. I kept imagining going to a football game in the fall with Pam Ellis on my arm. Every guy in the stadium would be watching me with envy. Because I went to a different high school, my boys would really wonder where I met such a pretty girl.

"Pam I really like you a lot and I want you to give me chance," I said. I held my breath and waited for Pam's next response. I felt everything that had happened to me in the last twenty-four hours had led up to this moment. Pam put on a big smile and said, "I'm really flattered. I like you a lot too but at this time I really just want to be your friend. School is going to be tough next semester and I want to be able to concentrate. Let's just stay good friends for now." I felt like crawling under the table but I had to be cool. Pam was being straight with me and I really hadn't planned a comeback for that kind of response from her. However, I knew that telling someone you just wanted to be friends was the equivalent of saying, "I'm shopping somewhere else", but in a nice way.

I couldn't help but think about all I had gone through over the past two days to impress this girl, only to get a "let's be friends" for an answer. But I knew I had to maintain my cool and act like I was glad she wanted me to be a friend, instead of a boyfriend. Football season was coming up and a friend wouldn't do it if you had a "rep" to maintain. My response to her was simply, "That sounds like fun. We'll be friends." I felt like I had been punched in the gut by Smoking Joe Frazier but I was still standing.

I later developed a hell of a case of the "what if's". What if I hadn't gone to the party to see Pam, would any of this ever have happened? What if I had been caught before I could have gotten out of Pam's yard? What if Kevin had had an accident while driving like a crazy man with a car loaded with drunken teenagers? More than anything else, what if I had jumped out of the car and been the first one in the line of fire? What if the Newstead Boys were shooting guns rather than throwing bricks at us? As I looked at Pam's bright smile and big brown eyes, I thought; after all He has done for me over the past two days, what's so wrong with having a "friend" like Pam Ellis? My ego was terribly deflated but I was glad not to be lying in the hospital bed like Miguel.

If things had lined up just a little differently for me that terrible night I wouldn't be doing a lot of things I'm doing today. A minister approached me recently and asked me, "Young man do you know your Savior?" I just smiled at him and said, "More than you can imagine! More than you can imagine!" Things actually did line up in the right order for me over the past 35 years. Pam Ellis is still my friend.

Moms had always warned me about keeping company with the wrong crowd. That was the last time she ever had to give me that warning.

****

Chapter Two

- THIS IS COLLEGE - CAN THEY SAY THAT?? -

Growing up in a poor family prepared me to handle many of life's challenges although at the time I really had no idea that I was all that poor. I thought we just had a stroke of bad luck and things would get better one day. Being poor meant you didn't have the counseling, direction, and money it took to get started on a college search like some students. No one in my family had ever gone to college and certainly no one had ever graduated from a college. In fact, we only had a few high school graduates in the family. We revered the few high school graduates like Harvard scholars. We thought they had really hit the top of the heap and were equipped to go places. Even though I had remote thoughts of attending college, I didn't have the slightest clue how I would get there, who would pay for it, how much it cost, or what to do once I got there.

I knew that Pop had rules around the house. Showing respect was not discussed, it was assumed and demanded. You showed respect or you'd have big problems. You had to go to school, go to the military, or go to work. Regardless of your decision, you had to go somewhere. Take your pick and do it in any order, but go somewhere.

C. Lee Thornton

During the latter part of my senior year in high school I went to the placement office in search of that elusive steady job. I found a company called Warson Directory that was willing to hire a student who had studied printing. The placement office told me they paid $1.90 an hour and the student could work in the afternoon while still in high school. The job sounded like the chance of a lifetime. I thought that I could use the money to help out at home and buy some sharp new clothes.

I really hadn't made any definite plans about study beyond high school but I thought the idea about trade school sounded good and hopefully one day I could get into the printers union. I knew that 1968 was not a time for a Negro kid to dream about being a union printer but things were changing.

I put on my Sunday best and scheduled an interview with Mr. Don Warson, the company owner. I told him I was a fast learner and I had trained on all the machines that were used in his factory. He told me, "You seem like a sharp kid and you can make some good money working here." He let me know that in 1968 to earn $1.90 an hour was considered good money and this was "steady work". I agreed with everything he said and he hired me a few days later.

On my first day at the plant Mr. Warson introduced me to the foreman who told me what my duties would be during the afternoon shift. He told me Mr. Warson had worked closely with a trade school in Iowa that trained workers in the printing trades. He said the school was unique because the students were all deaf and mute.

After I met a group of the deaf and mute guys I realized they were really very nice people...they just couldn't talk or hear. We worked fine together and soon we started to learn about each other's world. They had never worked around a black guy and I had never worked around deaf guys.

After I graduated from high school in the spring of 1968, I really got into the routine of the operation at the printing plant. Because the equipment was so loud, using sign language was sort of a natural means to communicate for everyone. Within a short time I became fairly proficient communicating with sign language and I learned to have good conversations with the deaf workers.

I had graduated from high school and I thought life couldn't get any better. I was 17 years old at the time and I had at least six months before I had to think about the military draft. I thought by January 1969 I'd enroll in a trade school and apply for a draft deferment. Even though that was six months away, when you're 17 years old, it seemed to be a lifetime. I was earning over $66.00 a week after taxes, driving my Dad's old second car, and as far as I was concerned I was living large.

One day as I was having a conversation with one of the guys, the topic of salary came up. The deaf guy told be me he was making $2.40 an hour. I couldn't believe as nice as Mr. Warson had been to me that he would pay me less than those guys. After all, I had a high school diploma and could talk. I had placed Mr. Warson in another category but I realized he was no different from the rest of them. I told one of my friends that weekend that I was going to march into Mr. Warson's office on Monday and get him straight.

The following Monday I arrived at work a little early and went directly to Mr. Warson's office. His secretary told me he was in the plant but she would give him the message that I would like to speak with him. I later found him walking through the plant and I asked him if we could talk. I said to him, "Mr. Warson, I'm upset over some information I recently received. I found out you're paying the deaf guys $2.40 an hour but you're only paying me $1.90 an hour." I paused and saw he was still busy with some papers he was reading in his hands. He looked up and said, "I'm sorry, so what do you want?" It was obvious to me that he didn't consider my complaint very important. I said, "I want $2.40 an hour, too." He glanced up from the papers and politely said, "O.K., now go back to work."

C. Lee Thornton

    I remember walking happily away and saying to myself that I really got him straight and now I'm really rolling in the dough. I'm a high school graduate and earning $2.40 an hour. I didn't think life could get any better and now I knew I had been blessed. I had finally got that "steady job" that Pop had talked about for years. Later, after talking to my boys, I realized I should have asked for more money. But I was just glad to be working and helping out at home. It really made me feel good to buy groceries and give Moms some money at the end of the week. I thought I knew how it felt to be a man.

    As the summer of 1968 moved on, the job was fine, I was fine, everything was going my way. There was a lot of racial turmoil in this country and the war in Vietnam was hot. However, I was the last one of the three of us at home and I felt I was handling life the best I could under the circumstances. I had both bunk beds to myself and I could sleep up or down, wherever I pleased when I got tired—life was good. The folks didn't sweat me and gave me lots of freedom, since I was helping out with the bills.

    My parents were really proud of me and bragged to their friends about their son, the high school graduate, who had a "steady job". I had achieved what I felt was the pinnacle of success by graduating from high school and landing that so-called "steady job". It was considered a good job, at least by 1968 standards. My normal shift at the plant was 1 p.m. until 9 p.m., Monday through Friday. Payday was every Thursday evening for the afternoon shift. It really made a teenage boy feel like a man when the clerk came through the department and handed you an envelope with your paycheck. The payroll clerk was a blond white lady with clothes about two sizes too small. She'd come bouncing into the plant area and knew she had the attention of all the men. Even the deaf guys, in their own way, would make catcalls. She would be sure to reach over machines and desks with the checks so everyone would get a free peek at her super-sized chest. It somehow made me work a little harder that night. I knew that there was absolutely no chance in hell of me getting with a woman like that, for a number of reasons. The main reasons were she was a white woman and it was 1968. Most of all, I knew that you never put your "pen" in "company ink." I needed my steady job too much to jeopardize it over a white woman. Besides, I already had a girlfriend.

On one particularly humid July night, all I could think about was finishing early and having fun like any teenager. After all, I didn't have to return to work until 1 p.m. the next day. Staying up late after my shift ended at the plant was no problem for me. On that evening I was operating the large flatbed press and handling it like a pro. The large flatbed press was used to print the pages of a directory for our primary customer. I recalled the shop was as noisy as ever but we were communicating with sign language as usual.

On that hot night in July 1968 we had most of our assignments completed and we were finished for the night. If we completed our shift early, we could leave and still get paid for the full eight-hour shift. It was somewhat of a record-breaking night for my shift, something that we hadn't accomplished up to that date. Everyone was looking forward to finishing early with a new record and a chance to enjoy the rest of the warm summer night.

I had one more plate of type to fasten into the press bed, lock it down, and I'd be ready to run the last page for that evening. I took two metal slugs over to the table saw that we used for trimming type set slugs. I had to trim them to a common size in order for the slugs to fit on the bed of the press. I had problems in the past with the table saw because the locking arm was not holding properly. To compensate for the broken locking arm, we had to hold the metal slug down with our thumb as it passed through the saw blade. I had done it dozens of other times and this night was no different.

Earlier I had asked Mr. Warson to have the locking arm on the table saw repaired. He told me a number of times that he'd do it later. On this night I had used the table saw at least four to five other times and realized the slugs were getting increasingly harder to hold down with my thumb. But I was a strong young man; I could do anything.

I placed the final plate of type onto the press and realized one more lead slug had to be trimmed before I finished the final runoff for the evening. I ran to the table saw, turned it on, and the saw blade started to turn in the normal rapid manner. The single lead slug moved into the blade with the full strength of the saw motor, just as it had done dozens of other times in the past. This time seemed just a little different because the slug started moving toward the saw blade with unusual pressure. My left thumb followed the slug as I tried desperately to hold the metal slug steady. My thumb suddenly moved into the saw blade and came to a rest on the sharp, rapidly spinning saw blade. The blade had ripped through the top of my left thumb so fast that I initially didn't feel any pain at all.

I suddenly realized the top of my left thumb was practically severed by the sharp saw blade. I stepped back, turned off the machine, while my mangled and bleeding thumb dangled in front of me. I waved to the foreman and got his attention. He saw my bloody hand and ran over with towels and covered my bloody left hand. I was losing blood so fast that within a few seconds I was very dizzy.

The shop foreman decided to drive me to the Jewish Hospital emergency room rather than wait for an ambulance. I quickly started feeling really weak due to the heavy loss of blood rushing from my left hand. We were at the end of the shift, I was dirty and had ink all over me.....I really looked a mess. I remember walking down the second floor stairwell toward the foreman's car when the lights went out for me. I guess he just threw me over his shoulder and into the rear seat of his car. I can only image the blood I left in his rear seat that hot night.

Jewish Hospital was less than three miles away, but the drive seemed to take forever. As we drove to the hospital my mind started wandering in order to mask the excruciating pain in my left hand. I remembered dreaming about things that had happened to me years earlier as a small child. Even though I felt I had gotten a good handle on life with my "good job", I wondered how I ended up hurt and being rushed to the emergency room with a mangled hand? I started to dream about the old four-family flat where we lived in on Temple on the city's west side. For some reason I could clearly hear Moms voice calling, "Cary Lee!! What are you doing boy?" Unlike today, when your mother calls you, you answer her right away. My answer was always the same when we played in the basement of the old apartment building. I said, "Nothing, we're just down here playing with our bb guns."

When I awoke that night, I was lying on a gurney with about six medical students and a surgeon standing over me. Although my eyes were still closed, I could hear them talking and I felt like a lab specimen. The surgeon was explaining to the students the various nerves in my hand and how he was going to surgically reattach the top of my left thumb. They all asked the normal student type questions as the surgeon explained the surgical procedure.

I knew I looked like hell because I was sweaty, inky, and dirty as hell from my shift at the plant that night. But I didn't care. I wanted to keep the top of my left thumb.

I then felt strong enough to open my eyes and look around the emergency room. I first looked down and saw my left thumb in a bloody jar. The liquid was so dark I could hardly see it and I was afraid to pull my hand out to see how much of my thumb was left. Nonetheless it hurt like hell and there was nothing I could do about it. I recalled seeing several baby faced, young medical students, and the surgeon standing over me. The students didn't look much older than me. They were all so young and seemed eager to learn, while using me as their lab rat. I knew they had to be in their twenties but they looked so young and all so eager to learn and to really be someone important.

I said to myself, "I can do that, I can do that. They are just young guys like me." As I lay on the operating table, the times Pop had talked to me about going to school and being someone important really started to make sense to me. I finally realized that this is what he was talking about—be someone important.

It was embarrassing to be a lab specimen for the young students and I hated that my unfortunate injury was a cause to further their education. The surgeon then began working to reattach my left thumb. I couldn't help but feel uneducated compared to the young medical students. I felt like a hopeless lab rat.

As the anesthesia wore off and I slowly came out of my sleep, I told myself, "I'm not getting my hands dirty anymore. To hell with the $2.40 an hour steady job. I'm going to college, get an education, and become just as important as the medical students who used me as their lab practice. Those young guys aren't going to experiment on me anymore."

That was the day I decided to go to college. I made up my mind that this would be the last time some young college student would use me to further his education. I stayed away from the plant for two weeks. As soon as I returned, I told Mr. Warson about my decision. He didn't try to change my mind or offer me anything to keep me working for him. He gave me the necessary time off to apply to community college and to take the placement tests. Mr. Warson really was an honest man and a good man. He knew I had made the right decision and supported me in doing so.

July 1968 was too late to apply to the University of Missouri but it was not too late for community college. I tried to be the first person in line for registration at Florissant Valley Community College in August 1968. My plans were to attend community college for one semester and to transfer to the University of Missouri in January 1969. And that's exactly what I did, but not without hurdles to overcome. I never looked back or regretted my decision.

My first semester at Florissant Valley Community College was somewhat of a challenge. It was the first time in my life I really felt tested academically. I soon realized that in college there was no one to tell you to do homework or to study everyday. I had heard about college from older friends but now I was faced with doing everything all on my own. Just as with my first job, I was ready for the challenge.

I really got a funny feeling to see what it was like to speak in class while all the white students got quiet to see if you really split verbs or used horrible ghetto English. I got a kick out of literally surprising the hell out of all of them. Nonetheless, Florissant Valley Community College was much different from my old high school in the city. I knew my job was to make my family proud by doing my best in class. Now Pop's could really brag to his friends that his son was a college student.

I got right into the swing of college life by going to parties and pledging a fraternity during my first semester in school. I recalled one Friday, a friend and I found our way to a college party that was being held near St. Louis University. The hall was loaded with fine ladies and everyone seemed to be having a good time. There were college students from everywhere and for the first time I felt I was attending a big gathering and didn't have to worry about a fight breaking out. There were no gang members in attendance to start fights with the students. As I listened to the partygoers it didn't seem like anyone was ready to fight at all. This was a real college party.

C. Lee Thornton

I was having a good time and said to my buddy, "Hey man, I think this college thing is going to be all right." He said, "And look at the honeys I'm getting to work." Just then we heard the music stop and all we could hear was noise and stomping coming from the area of the main door. I knew then that I was home, it sounded like a fight was starting at the door. We both got in a defensive position and got ready to rumble. We could see the ladies screaming and running toward the door. We just assumed if we protected a few ladies from the commotion, we'd be their protectors for the rest of the night.

But we didn't hear any police, we only heard screaming coming from the ladies. We could hear what sounded like guys dancing and singing as they entered the door area. I was totally confused and so was my friend Cletus. I came up from my karate stance and asked Cletus, "Hey what the hell is going on?" By now we could see the ladies pushing and screaming to get close to the group of guys singing and dancing in the center of the floor. Cletus said, "Man, I don't know but somebody said they're called a fraternity, and if you join you get a lot of the girls." I said, "Girls?? Are you sure?"

Cletus said, "Man, look at the chicks fighting to get to those guys." I said, "Well hell man, where do we sign up?" I later pledged and have been a member of Alpha Phi Alpha Fraternity, Incorporated, since March 1969. It all happened quite by accident. I just happened to be at a party that seemed to be fun. But pledging in college was still not without challenges.

Randy then said, "Man that sounds like a good reason to stay in college, right?" I said, "Randy, it helps that the scenery is nice and the parties are fun but let me explain some of the challenges we faced during the sixties in college."

Mr. Thomas said, "Son you really had your work cut out for you. It seems you're a fighter just like the old man." I explained to them that pledging a fraternity could be fun but it was full of pranks that the new pledges had to endure. Sometimes the same pranks that would be normal and part of the college experience for white students could be nearly disastrous for black college students. One evening the fraternity brothers took ten of us to the track at Florissant Valley Community College for a hazing meeting. It was about 6:00 p.m. on a Sunday in the fall of 1968 and our assignment was to run around the track a few times and recite fraternity history. As a former high school sprinter, running didn't bother me at all. In fact I thought the ten or so laps around the track was a nice warm up. The meeting took about an hour and after we finished, our instructions were to walk back to the city from the Florissant Valley Community College campus. We were told to wait for further instructions on the corner of North Kingshighway and Penrose, at the entrance of Penrose Park. The fraternity brothers took our cars and all of our money. They left us with only our driver's licenses for identification and nothing else.

After they drove away from campus, the ten of us started walking from the college campus, which was in a secluded wooded area of Ferguson, Missouri. We finally made our way to West Florissant Road and began walking east toward the city of St. Louis. Because we didn't have any money, taking a bus or a taxi was out of the question. We had only walked along West Florissant Road about twenty minutes when we saw police cars coming our way from two directions. As they neared us they were blocking traffic as if there was a serious problem. We just kept walking, unaware that we were the problem until they all converged on us with flashing lights, loudspeakers blaring, and pistols drawn pointing at us. We heard one of the officers shout on the loud speaker, "Drop whatever you have in your hands and get against the wall!! Now drop to your knees and raise your hands and you won't be shot!!"

John said to us, "Do what he says so there won't be any accidents." Traffic had stopped on both sides of the busy street and we could hear people calling us criminals and young hoodlums.

C. Lee Thornton

As fast as we dropped to our knees cops were on us like flies. They were shouting at us and calling us all sorts of names. We knew it was wise to just be quiet, not to resist, and follow their instructions. The cops went into our pockets, took our identification, and went back to their squad cars.

After about ten minutes the sergeant in charge walked over and said, "None of you have any warrants. Now what the hell are you doing out here at night?" John Parks, being the spokesman for us said, "Officer, we are college students from Florissant Valley and The University of Missouri. We're pledge members of Alpha Phi Alpha Fraternity. We just finished a pledge meeting at the college and are walking home. Did we do something wrong?" The officer said, "Fraternity? Students? We got a call that a colored gang was looking for someone to beat up and rob." He motioned for two cars to come over and said, "Take these boys back to the city limits and get'em the hell outta Ferguson. Look, don't y'all bring your black asses out here at night again, scaring my citizens. You understand?" We all said, "Yes Sir," and piled into the two squad cars. The comments repeated by the white citizens in the crowd were horrible, but at least the police was there to protect us from them. We were called everything from black dogs to hoodlums looking for white women to rape. We were only black college students stopped by mean, racist cops.

Within minutes, the Ferguson Police Officers had whisked us to the corner of West Florissant and Riverview Boulevard. Our final instructions from the officers were, "And don't bring yo' black asses out here again." Both patrol cars then sped north on West Florissant toward Ferguson, Missouri with the ten Black students in their rear view mirrors. The only thought in my mind was how I was going to attend classes with those instructions from the cops. I said to my friends, "I'm staying in school and I'll just leave the campus before

Oath of Office

sunset." I remained at Florissant Valley until the end of the fall semester, successfully completing my freshman classes.

In December of 1968, I received a letter from the University of Missouri. I could hardly sleep, anticipating attending a big university. I knew that my plans were now on track and I would soon get away from racist Ferguson, Missouri. I had only planned to attend Florissant Valley Community College for one semester and to only take the first semester of the business curriculum at the junior college. Since I had received the threats from the Ferguson Police, for nothing more than being a black student, I had no great desire to stay at the campus any longer. Everything appeared to be working out on schedule for me at that time.

The letter instructed me to meet with Miss Dora Zackman on January 18, 1969 at 2:00 p.m. It stated she was my assigned freshman counselor. According to the letter they had received all of my test scores and I was instructed to bring my paperwork from Florissant Valley to verify my grades and classes I had taken during the first semester. I knew a few students who attended the University of Missouri and felt my Dad could finally say his son was attending a big university. I literally couldn't sleep anticipating the meeting with Miss Zackman.

January 18, 1969 could not come fast enough, as far I was concerned. Although the semester was not quite over at Florissant Valley, I knew I should have pretty good grades in Accounting, English Composition, Introduction to Business Administration, and Algebra. My final grade point average was 3.25 for that first semester. I thought that was fairly respectable for a kid who hadn't planned to attend college six months earlier.

I arrived at Miss Zackman's office at approximately 1:45 p.m. The last thing I wanted to do was to give the counselor the impression that I couldn't arrive for an appointment on time. She was waiting and ready for me when I walked into her office. I first noticed she appeared to be a tall white lady with blonde hair and heavy make-up. Frankly, I had never seen anyone with blue and green stuff all over their eyes, combined with a tall beehive hairdo. To complete her attire she wore blue, horn rimmed, pointed eyeglasses. In my eyes, she looked a mess....but she was my counselor and I knew I had to show her respect despite her ridiculous costume attire. By today's standards she would resemble Marge Simpson, Homer's wife.

Miss Zackman had been reading my paperwork prior to my arrival and as I walked in her office she stared at me without saying a word. I was only eighteen years old and I simply thought that was the way adults treated young people. I introduced myself and told her I was there for a counseling appointment. She just sat at her desk and stared at me as if I was the one wearing the costume.

Miss Zackman spoke to me saying, "Young man, why are you here and why are you in my office? What do you want?" I thought that was a strange comment coming from a university official painted like a clown. But I had been taught to be respectful to adults and Miss Zackman was in that category. I politely said, "Ma'am, I'm here for my counseling appointment. I was a Business Administration major at Florissant Valley Community College and I want to continue my education here."

Miss Zackman looked at me and stared at me as if I had two heads. She sat back in her chair, pushed all the paperwork in my direction, and continued to stare at me. To say the least, I was totally confused and thought the costume was starting to affect this woman. After a long silence she said, "Young man, it says here you come from one of those inner city schools." I said, "Yes Ma'am." Then she said, "From the looks of your paperwork your family does not have very much money. In fact what does your father do?"

I was still confused and had no idea why a counselor had to ask about my father's job because I was applying to the school, not my father. But I kept in mind my upbringing about respecting adults. I told her, "My father is a porter at an apartment complex in Creve Coeur." I didn't know how much longer he would be working because he had talked about possibly being laid off. But I wasn't going to mention that at this time. She then asked me, "Then what does your mother do for a living?" Now I was really hot but I was not going to let this ignorant clown-painted lady stand in the way of my education. I again recalled my marching orders and the lessons I had been taught by Moms and Pop.

I now felt she was making fun of Moms, who worked two to four days a week for $5.00 a day plus bus fare. I recalled how angry Mom was once when she was fired for not addressing the children of a family as Mister and Miss. Moms told us about the time when her employers would leave nickels and dimes around their homes as traps for the "colored cleaning women". They would accuse the cleaning women of taking the small change as an excuse to fire them and not pay them for work they had done that day. Moms was a proud lady and did what she had to do to provide a living for us. Her goal was to one day see us get a good education and live a good life.

I felt that Miss Zackman was making fun of some real tough times I had endured to get to her office. I started to think about the first time I heard the song "I'm Busted", by Ray Charles in the summer of 1963. I remembered the words, ".....a big stack of bills that get bigger each day. The county is gonna haul my belongings away. 'Cause I'm busted." The day I first heard that song I thought Ray Charles made that song for my family. Pop was laid off. The car was barely working and Moms had a cleaning job that day at a home in University City. She was paid a grand total of $5.00 a day plus bus fare. I remember on that day, we had one half block of government cheese in the refrigerator and a half loaf of day old bread. That afternoon Pop gave us the longest speech about the value of education. He was so mad at white people that I thought he was going to cry. The longer he preached, the more I listened to Ray Charles sing his song. That same day Pop took us to the social security office in downtown St. Louis to apply for our social security cards.

Now Miss Zackman was making a joke about all I had endured to get to her office. She was not going to deny me anything simply because I was poor and black. She was not going to hinder me with her snide remarks. What Miss Zackman didn't know was that my marching orders were stronger than any racial putdown she could make. I looked directly at Miss Zackman and said, "My mother performs domestic housework for a living, Ma'am." I insured Miss Zackman the respect she was obviously denying me. There was a silence for more than a minute, while she stared at me through her horn-rimmed glasses.

Miss Zackman looked at me over the top of her glasses and said, "Young man, you don't belong here. You come from one of those inner city schools, your parents are poor, and you're just wasting my time and yours trying to enroll here. Why don't you enroll in one of those junior colleges where you can be around your people? I think there are a lot of colored students at Forest Park Community College." I refused to show my anger or any form of emotion. I was going to maintain my dignity and respect but I also was going to get my point across. Despite what she said, I was not going to let her stand in the path of my education. I knew my marching orders and I planned to follow them.

I gathered my composure and said, "Ma'am, yes I do come from a poor family and I'm the first in my family to attend college. Last semester I was a business major at Florissant Valley Community College and I intend to continue that course of study at this institution. I have successfully completed the first level of business courses with no problems. I have a 3.2 grade point average and my SAT and

Oath of Office

Missouri Placement test scores are good. I think you should have those in front of you."

Miss Zackman looked surprised that I could construct a complete sentence and actually make an argument for enrolling at the university. After all, I was a "colored" eighteen year old, poor, inner city teenager. She then panted and puffed and said, "The only way I will admit you to this University is for you change your mind about the business curriculum and convince me you can make it here at this university. You need to try something easy and not Business Administration. I'm going to erase Accounting 2, Algebra 2, and College level English. Here, look through the catalog and find something easy like Sociology or Basic Writing and maybe History. Perhaps that way you won't waste your money and my time like so many of you people do every year." She made it clear she was through discussing the matter with me and stood up from her desk.

I politely gathered all the papers that she pushed toward me without showing any anger, disgust or any emotion. I was an eighteen-year-old teenager and my parents had taught me to respect adults even if they are ignorant bigots. I was not going to ruin my chance to get into the University of Missouri by cursing out a bigot. Besides, whom would I go to and what could they do to help me anyway?

I thought about calling my folks but they were "poor colored people" who had given me marching orders when I left home that morning. I could still hear Pop saying, "Boy, don't let anyone or anything stand in the way of your education. When you get that education, no one can take that away from you." I had never experienced that level of overt bigotry in quite awhile and I was a little unsure how I would resolve the ordeal.

As I gathered my paperwork and course catalog, I turned to Miss Zackman and said, "Thank you." Little did Miss Zackman know she was not going to keep me out of the University of Missouri because my parents were poor and because I had graduated from an inner city high school. She had to give me a much better reason than that to stand in the path of my education. Miss Zackman had the nerve to smile at me as I walked out of her office.

I had dealt with people like Miss Zackman all of my life. She was no different from the bigots that attacked me in north St. Louis when I was thirteen years old. She was no different from the doctors that refused to treat me in Mississippi in 1959. Miss Zackman had given me reason to fight harder and to find a way around her ignorance.

Among the papers Miss Zackman returned to me was her counseling appointment letter that contained her signature. It was the original letter asking me to come to her office for my counseling appointment. She also gave me my course card on which she had erased a number of classes that I had intended to take during the semester. In those days the course card was written in pencil just in case you didn't get into a particular section and had to change your classes.

As I sat outside her office I saw white students going into her office and appearing to have the grandest of times. They were laughing and joking and bonding like old chums. From what I could hear, no one went through any of the humiliation I had just endured. They were filing in and out a few minutes at a time with no problem. I knew this meant if they were enrolling, classes were filling up fast......especially the Business Administration classes that were popular at the university. I knew what I had to do...I found a quiet place to sit. I rewrote my courses on the course card, Accounting 2, College Algebra 2, College English Composition, and U.S. History.

My next hurdle was finding a way to get Miss Zackman's signature on the course card in order to officially be admitted to the University of Missouri. I knew she would not admit me to the university if I insisted on taking the Business Administration curriculum. In fact,

Oath of Office

she was against me attending the university simply because I was colored (that was before Black was popularized.....colored or Negro was still being used in those days). I looked at her signature at the end of my counseling letter and took out a separate sheet of paper and began to practice.

I began to write Dora Zackman, Dora Zackman, Dora Zackman, over and over and over again. I must have written her signature a hundred times that afternoon. I had accumulated a huge stack of paper in front of me that no one seemed to notice. After all, the white students just assumed I was practicing how to write in order to fill out my application for the school. I was not perceived as a threat so no one paid me any attention. I finally got Dora Zackman's signature down to near exact. I wrote her name in the counselor's approval section of my enrollment card. From the looks of that forgery, the FBI couldn't tell the difference.

I politely walked past her office as she was having a laugh with a young blonde, white student. I walked to the enrollment office, presented my paperwork, and the enrollment card, complete with Miss Zackman's signature in the approval column. The university officer stamped my packet, smiled, and told me go to the bursar's office to pay my fees. I only said, "Thank you."

In January 1969 I officially became a student at the University of Missouri. I had forged Miss Zackman's signature on my enrollment card and I was proud of it. That was the last encounter I had with Miss Zackman while I was a student at the university. In fact, I kept a copy of her signature for use whenever I needed it. I refused to go to her office for any further counseling or degrading of my family.

My decision to finally go to college was one I would not change for anything in the world. Although the reason I decided to attend and the time applied was more of an accident than anything else. I thank God for all the elements that lined up in order for me to finally see what was best in my life. But the most challenging days were still ahead of me. The manner in which I dealt with those days was nothing more than fate, a blessing from Him, and good old fashioned home training at work.

I've always felt that it was a blessing growing up poor rather than having rich parents. Poor kids learn to struggle and overcome obstacles early in life in spite of it all. Pop once said, "Poor folks don't jump outta the window when the stock market crashes. They just go out to apply for the job of the guy who jumped." I had demonstrated my desire to struggle over and over by the time I was eighteen years old. However after entering the University of Missouri and despite the obstacles placed in my path by Miss Zackman, my next major obstacle was not passing the classes but keeping enough money in my pocket to stay in school.

By the beginning of my first fall semester at the university, I would have had to borrow money to qualify as broke. I was completely out of money and I had no idea how I was going to pay my next semester's tuition. Although I had a part-time job, I only earned enough money to pay for my bus pass, lunch, and a few extras on the weekend. Asking my parents for money was senseless because they didn't have any money to spare, in fact they didn't have any money. There was barely enough money in the house to pay the living expenses and the rent. Rent was about $60.00 a month yet it was a major obstacle. With only Pop working from time to time, I may as well have asked for a million dollars. We just didn't have the cash.

One day I had the nerve to ask Pop for $180.00 for tuition during my second year in college. I was completely out of money and felt I had no other person to seek a loan for tuition. One Saturday I sat around all day trying to muster up enough nerves to ask Pop for money for tuition. Pop walked in the door; as usual he was tired and dirty. I knew this would be tough but I turned to him and said, "Pop I really need $180.00 for tuition next semester." I waited for the silence to pass and waited for the worse. He looked at Moms and slowly turned to look at me with a weird look on his face. He said to Moms, "That boy's gone out to that white folk's school and done gone crazy." He looked at me and walked away without saying one more word. A question like that around my house didn't deserve a response. To ask for $180.00 when we could hardly pay our $60.00 rent was like asking for a million dollars. Pop and I never had another discussion about college tuition.

I later told my folks that I would try to get a loan in order to stay in school. I had to listen to the lecture about someone Moms knew who signed for a student loan for her son. She said the youngster didn't graduate or make an attempt to repay the loan. According to Moms the family had their home taken by the bank as repayment for the loan. Pop said to me, "Boy those white folks will take our home and everything we own if you don't graduate". I said, "Pop we don't own anything, we're renting this place and I don't think they want this old furniture." He looked at me without saying a word but his eyes told me, "Boy, you're getting' outta line. You're boarding on talking back." I knew I should shut up and stay in a child's place. I was teetering on talking smart, which was fatal around my house.

However during my early years at the University of Missouri, I became an expert at finding available funds. Since I was out of money that fall semester, I didn't think it would hurt to call my aunt in Arkansas to beg for a loan. Aunt Aray was Pop's sister and had been a domestic worker all of her life. However she had also managed her money very well. She believed in saving for a rainy day and not buying anything she didn't absolutely need. Aunt Aray had the money skills of a Wall Street banker and a bank account to prove it. No matter how tough times were, Aunt Aray always had money to spare.

I figured the worse I could get from my aunt was another no and I'd just keep looking for a source to keep me in school. I wouldn't have cared about going to the military but at the time too many guys my age were dying in a place called South Vietnam. A few guys in my neighborhood were returning from the military but they looked like zombies and some of them gave the term "junkie" a new meaning. I wasn't quite ready to deal with the military style of life because it was a little too dangerous.

I called my aunt and explained to her that I was the first in the family to go to college. I told her I really needed $180.00 for tuition to enroll for the upcoming semester. After my long explanation and begging she said, "Why sho baby, I'm gonna send you my bankbook to put your name on it. Then I want you to call Mr. Turner and tell him what you need for that college." I couldn't believe my ears. I had been saved again from dropping out of school.

Aunt Aray's bankbook arrived in the mail a few days later. I signed it without really looking at the balance and enclosed a thank you note with the return envelope. Even at the age of eighteen years, I was taught to be honest and if I was promised tuition, I was entitled to nothing else. In other words the balance in her bank account was not my business. I returned the bankbook and called Mr. Turner later the next week. He told me he was glad to hear from me and was waiting for my call. He said, "Your auntie is a fine lady I've known her for years. She told me she had a nephew that was making the family proud by going to a big college up north."

I asked him to send me $180.00 from the bank account but my aunt had already told him exactly what to send me. I'm not sure but I thought I was being tested to see if I would ask for more than the $180.00. He told me he would send me a check for my tuition right away and to call if I needed anything more. By the grace of God and Aunt Aray, I paid my fall semester tuition on time.

Throughout my entire remaining college career, I never called Aunt Aray or Mr. Turner again for a loan. In fact to this day, my name is still on her bank account in North Little Rock, Arkansas.

One fall evening as I was leaving class, I walked from Benton Hall toward the student center where students would gather after class. At that time the student center was a temporary metal building with a jukebox and vending machines. I guess the university felt the importance should be placed on classrooms and laboratories, not recreation. However, it gave students a place to congregate between classes.

I remember pondering over where I was going to get $180.00 to register for the following semester. One cool fall evening as I walked from class at Benton Hall, I found myself walking behind two white guys and eavesdropping on their conversation. I overheard one of them mention to the other in a low tone the words "money" and "grants". My ears perked up and I walked a little faster to hear what they had to say. One of them said the university had received a huge grant to be used for tuition and scholarships for anyone willing to study policing and corrections. That was enough eavesdropping for me.

I immediately detoured from the student center and walked to the administration building. I went into the financial aid office and asked to see the chief officer. He was not in the office but I made an appointment to see him the next day. I could hardly sleep that night because I knew I had to get in on this new money source early. Hopefully no one else had eavesdropped on those two guys and beat me to the bank. Their whispering fortunately was just a little too loud to keep me out of their conversation.

As soon as I arrived on campus the next day, I went to the financial aid office to see the director. I told him I was there to inquire about the grant recently received by the university for students studying policing and corrections. He told me that they had received a large grant and students were beginning to apply for the next semester. Without showing emotion, I was now excited as heck to finally see a way out for myself. He asked me about my major and my present grade point average. As soon as I said proudly, "Business Administration, Sir", he stood up and said, "Sorry, the money can only be given to Administration of Justice majors. But thank you for your interest." He didn't give me a chance to say another word and walked away.

I said to myself, he's not getting off that easy. I stopped him and asked him to explain the requirements of an Administration of Justice major and what were the requirements of the grant. He told me the grant recipients had to major in Administration of Justice, which had a core course requirement of thirty-nine credit hours. He said there were ample electives to take courses in other departments but the focus was on police administration and corrections. I asked him if I could still take my Business Administration courses if I majored in Administration of Justice and to my surprise he said, "Yes, that's no problem and the department encourages outside course study." I thanked him, shook his hand, and left his office. I think he thought he had seen the last of me that morning.

I left his office and immediately walked to the School of Business Administration Office in Clark Hall. I asked the secretary for a form to declare Business Administration as a minor and to drop it as a major course of study. A counselor signed the card with no questions asked. I think the counselor signed it because they really didn't take "colored" students serious anyway. In 1969 we still hadn't graduated to black nor were we taken as serious students. At the university we were considered either Negro or colored and our official records reflected that in the race column.

I then asked the secretary for directions to the Administration of Justice Office. It was a new department and most students had not yet heard of the department. I located the office and asked to see a counselor in that department. I was introduced to the new department chairman, Dr. Gordon Miller. He was a very stoic and reserved man with a keen interest in reforming the criminal justice system. In our first conversation he told me he had been involved in a number of movements and demonstrations during the turbulent 1960's. He told me a story about sustaining a broken rib during the 1968 riots at the Democratic National Convention in Chicago.

The story was fascinating but my goal was to get a department major card signed and to get some money to stay in school. Dr. Miller was a sharp guy and I think he knew why I was visiting with him. I was in front of a long line of students changing their majors that week. Everyone needed money and would go to any length to get it. After he signed my card, he said, "Now go to the financial aid office and inquire about available scholarships and grants". I tried to act surprised and said, "Scholarships? Grants? Maybe I'll stop over after I go over the curriculum list at the library. Thanks anyway".

I left his office and practically ran to the financial aid office. I again asked to see the financial aid officer. I could see him in his office and he gave me one of those, "I thought I got rid of you" looks. I was still breathing deep from my excited run to his office. I couldn't believe my money troubles may soon be solved.

When I walked into his office I could see the disgust on his face. He said, "I thought I told you earlier you had to have a major in Administration of Justice to qualify for the scholarship program?" I told him, "I took care of that" and I handed him my department major card signed by Dr. Miller. His eyes showed both surprise and disgust but I didn't care. I also handed him the card from the Business Administration department listing that department as a minor.

I think he reluctantly called his secretary and asked her to give me the forms to apply for the funding from the U.S. Department of Justice. Little did he know he was stuck with me until the money landed in my bank account. The secretary resembled a younger version of Ms. Zackman, she was painted with heavy blue and green make-up, dyed blonde hair, clothes a size too small, and she had a bad attitude. I assumed someone told her she was cute and that she shouldn't be seen speaking to a "colored student" for the sake of her reputation.

However cute she thought she was at the time, I was going to adhere to my marching orders, and do nothing to cause her to lose my application for tuition money. I vowed to be the most polite student she would work with that day. Although she was not much older than me, I addressed her as, "Ma'am" and showed the painted lady the utmost respect. She explained to me that scholarship recipients had to agree to work in state or federal law enforcement or corrections for four years or agree to repay the money with interest.

She read out loud the stipulations of the loan and said, "Can you agree to that?" Her demeanor was very condescending and disrespectful toward me. I said to her, "I sure can, maybe I'll graduate and work for the FBI." She looked at me through the costume makeup and said, "Yeah, right. Take these and fill'em out" and walked away leaving me in the office.

More than thirty years later, I can still see the smug look on her face as she threw the application forms at me. And the rest is history...

****

I must admit I was very naïve when I finally was admitted to the University of Missouri. For some crazy reason, I thought that once I was admitted as a regular student, I would have the same equal chance to pursue my education as any other student. I thought the last obstacle that I would have to overcome was Miss Zackman, whom I would never have to face again. I found out that there were other obstacles worse than Miss Zackman. As my personal motivation to succeed, I'd repeat my marching orders from Pop to myself over and over. Those marching orders would be the prayers

Oath of Office

to keep me going. Sometimes I'd play a James Brown's song over and over in my head, "I don't want nobody to give me nothing, open up the door, I'll get it myself. I don't want nobody to give me nothing, open up the door, I'll get it myself." The song was not one of James Brown biggest hits but it was a hit with me. It was the fuel to keep me going during tough times. Sometimes as I sat in the library tapping my foot and smiling, I'm sure some students thought I had lost my mind. In reality, I was trying to keep from losing it.

That James Brown song was my personal national anthem. Unfortunately, when I was a student, I couldn't afford to buy the record. Even if had the money to buy it; I didn't have a stereo to play it. So I just recited it over and over in my head. Somehow I just didn't think every student at the University had to live with the same bigotry as myself. But I had my marching orders and my favorite James Brown song as motivation to keep me going.

When I entered my sophomore year at the university, I had a professor that made Miss Zackman seem like a civil rights activist. The Administration of Justice program required several sociology classes to be completed by all majors in the department. I could only take Sociology 101 at 11:15 a.m. on Tuesday and Thursday due to my work schedule. This allowed me ample time to get to my part-time job by 2:00 p.m., after class ended.

The class was held in a large lecture hall that had approximately 200 seats. I recalled on the first day of class, about ten students were left standing, due to a lack of seats in the lecture hall. The professor walked on to the stage and announced, "My name is Dr. Henry Bish and this is Sociology 101. This section can only hold 200 students because we only have 200 seats. We have to have about ten of you to pick up another class or go to another section." The crowd got quiet and no one moved.

Dr. Bish then explained his testing method. He said, "I can make this a difficult class to pass. I give two tests and a comprehensive final." He looked around the room and two students walked out. He then said, "My tests are multiple choice. I give choices ranging from A, B, C, D, E, F, G, H, and I". He looked around and four more students walked out. As bad as I wanted to leave, I had to keep the class because it was required and I had to get to work in the afternoon after class. This class was in a perfect time slot in order for me to get to work on time. My plan was to sit in the center isle of the lecture hall in order to have a straight shot at the door when class ended.

Dr. Bish then announced he still needed a few more people to move to another class or section. He repeated what he had just announced about the difficulty of his class and his testing method. He then said, "I can be your worse nightmare because I'm unreasonable, set in my ways, and in general I can be a rotten son of a bitch!!" That did it, students poured out the room by the dozen. Dr. Bish had achieved his objective. Unfortunately for me, I had to stay and endure his wrath. Little did I know the worse was yet to come from Dr. Bish.

I looked around the huge lecture hall and realized there was only one other person in the class who looked like me. From the texture of his hair, I assumed he was not African-American but probably from some Latin American country. I tried to make eye contact but he confirmed he was not a brother. When I looked in his direction and gave the "what's up brother" nod, he looked at me as if to say, "What the hell is that, some type of gang symbol?" He turned away toward some white guys as if to say, "That colored guy is nuts".

I knew then I was alone in this class. I noticed he was pretty chummy with some white guys in the back of the lecture hall. They laughed and backslapped like old friends. Of course, they left me out which was no different than any other class I'd ever taken at the university. As with most classes, my study group would have the usual one student. He would never be late for the study group and

Oath of Office

he would always have his assigned work on time. The lone group member would always do his fair share of the group project.

Dr. Bish knew he had me captive but I was not going to be had by him or any other professor at the university. He went on to say how he was going to weed out the slackers and he was known for being a tough S.O.B. around the campus. I just listened without a whimper and took good notes. Unlike many of my colleagues, I didn't have the choice to drop the class or maybe to change sections if the class got to be a little too much work.

I had to stay in the section because my job was important and I had to stay in school. I viewed dropping a class as a defeat and I didn't have the money to waste. In my home, college was as much of an investment as the stock market. Around our house, Pop was Dow Jones and you'd better not lose value. In other words, education was serious stuff that was not to be tampered with. Dr. Bish may have had the power, but I wasn't going to let him use it over me. He was going to have a hell of a fight on his hands if he thought I was going to be defeated by his boasting.

The last point Dr. Bish made during his opening lecture was for us to form study groups to prepare for his tests. He'd already told us they were more than tough and he intended to flunk as many students as he could in this class. As he covered the course syllabus, I knew he had to be joking about a study group. Who did he think was going to invite the only black guy in the class to join a study group? Each time I looked around the class and tried to make eye contact, I got one of those, "You gotta be joking" looks from another student. Just like any other class, I'd pass it with my usual, dependable study group of one.

I arrived at every lecture early in order to get a seat in the center of the lecture hall, directly on the main isle. This would allow me a quick exit at the door so that I could get to work by 2:00 p.m. Besides, my seat in the center made it easy for me to keep my eye on Dr. Bish and take good notes during his lectures. My dark skinned friend made sure he sat far enough away from me so he wouldn't have to speak. After all, what good international student wanted to be associated with an African-American student? I'm certain he didn't want to be mistaken for African-American and lose all of his friends.

The semester was well underway when Dr. Bish began covering a section involving problems and factors associated with urban cities. Whenever he would mention inner city issues that seemed foreign to my white colleagues, I could feel nearly 200 heads turning to look for my response. Sometimes I felt Dr. Bish was directing certain stereotypical comments in my direction as a means of harassment. I was not too difficult to locate, due to my seat in the center of the lecture hall on the main isle.

I initially thought I was being overly sensitive and imagining his over emphasis on words such as ghetto and poverty. However, one day he let his true colors show and they spilled all over the floor. In the middle of one of his more direct lectures on the inner city, he said, "When you drive down some of those inner city streets at night, smart white people will hit that little button on their door. You have to take precautions to keep the niggers out." I thought I was hearing things because I knew a university professor wouldn't say that in a crowded lecture hall. Then Dr. Bish said, "Niggers in certain cities can be dangerous creatures." I felt like diving under my seat. I felt the wrath of everyone in that lecture hall staring in my direction, waiting to get my reaction. I just sat in my seat and continued taking notes.

In addition to my white colleagues glaring in my direction with their mouths open, so was my dark friend from Latin America. He looked at me as if to say, "He ain't talking 'bout me. I'm not from here." I was all alone with this one and embarrassed as hell.

Oath of Office

Dr. Bish made a point to use this degrading word no less than a half dozen times during each subsequent lecture during the semester. It finally got to the point where I just waited for one of my white colleagues to use it in one of their responses to Dr. Bish. Lucky for me, I never had to endure that embarrassment or knock one of them out. I finally decided I wasn't going to take it any longer, so one Tuesday afternoon I took off from work. I made an appointment to speak to Dr. Bish in his office about his use of the word "nigger" so flagrantly in his lectures. I knew I couldn't afford to take off work but I felt this was important and I wanted him to show me respect.

I marched into Dr. Bish's office and sat down in his lobby. I was summoned into his office, and in a very polite but demanding manner, I made my displeasure known about the "word" in his class. I told him it was embarrassing to me and disrespectful to an entire race of people, as well as every Black student at the university. I emphasized to him that I was the only Black student in the section of almost 200 students. I told him that every time he used that word, everyone in the lecture hall looked at me for my response or reaction.

Dr. Bish sat back in his office chair, looked me in the eye and said, "I can say whatever I want in my lectures. I use the word 'nigger' in a sociological context and it is helpful to emphasize the points in my lectures. Besides, I know all about you people, my wife is Black." I couldn't believe my ears, that at 18, I had to confront a racist professor, proclaiming his superiority in my presence. I repeated my displeasure to him, and he repeated, "I'll teach my class in any manner I want and if you don't like it, you can drop my class." I said to myself, he's not getting off that easy. I stood up and said, "Thank you" and left his office.

Since I was off work anyway, I decided to take my complaint to the Dean of Academic Affairs. I asked the secretary outside the dean's office if I could briefly meet with Dean Dennis Gones. She called him and within a few minutes I was sitting at the foot of Dean Gones' desk, voicing my complaint about Dr. Bish.

Dean Gones listened intently about my embarrassment and the difficulty I had concentrating when Dr. Bish spews his racist ideology. From the looks on his face I thought I finally had someone to come to my rescue. Dean Gones stood up and said, "Dr. Bish can teach his class in any manner he desires. If you don't like it, then transfer somewhere else. Thank you." His standing and thank you was equivalent to saying, "Git yo' Black behind outta my office" and I promptly left.

I was angrier than the time Miss Zackman refused to sign my registration card. But I knew after going through all the crap I had endured to get into the university, I was not going to be beat down by a bigot like Dr. Bish. I thought about rounding up a group of Black students and heading back to the administration building to raise some hell. With the turbulent times of the 1960's, it wouldn't have taken too much to get a demonstration started. As I walked to the student union and looked around for some of the more radical Black students, I convinced myself to talk to Pop before I made any rash decisions.

Pop was home that evening and although working, he wasn't making much money as a porter at an apartment complex. I knew I was his pride and joy because I was a college student at a big university. I knew he didn't want me to do anything to interrupt my education or to cause him embarrassment.

Pop listened while I complained about Dr. Bish and the refusal of the dean to do anything about his behavior. I could see Pop was struggling to give me the right advice. He said, "Well as I see it you've got a couple choices. You can get some of your boys and march on the college and raise some hell. You might even wanna burn it down. But you'd get kicked outta school and you can't stay here. Or you might just go back to Dr. Bish's class, pass it, and tell him to kiss your ass at graduation."

I took Pop's second suggestion and went back to Dr. Bish's class. I never told the radicals about Dr. Bish because I didn't want to be the reason anyone was kicked out of school. Many students were willing to raise hell over much less than racist comments in class. But they didn't have the marching orders that I had from Pop. My consequences, coming from a poor family, were much greater than most of them. In other words I had a lot more to lose. I returned to his class and despite studying all alone, despite his crazy testing methods, I passed his class and moved on through the curriculum.

In fact, before I graduated I took a class taught by Dr. Bish on one other occasion. He never stopped his bigot tactics and I passed Criminology 200 just as I had passed Sociology 101. Just as before, "nigger" was a regular part of his vocabulary.

Graduation day on May 18, 1972 could not come soon enough for me. For several years I had rehearsed in my mind the cussing out I was going to give Dr. Bish and Miss Zackman on graduation day. I had finally made it and my speech to both of them was already prepared. That afternoon the new student gymnasium was loaded with proud parents from all over the country. I sat next to students whom I had never seen before and others who had never spoken to me although we had classes together. The gymnasium was so crowded that I never saw Moms or Pop that afternoon. Nonetheless the ordeal of University of Missouri was finally history for me.

Following graduation the faculty stood outside the gymnasium to congratulate students. I couldn't believe I actually saw some of them shaking hands with Black students. I searched the crowd and couldn't find Miss Zackman. I had planned to politely go "north side" on her and really give her a bit of what I had experienced several years earlier. Since I couldn't find her, I decided to look for Dr. Bish. I saw him smiling and grinning with a group of white students and their parents. He glanced over and saw me waiting to speak to him next and actually acknowledged me standing and waiting. I had my "you dirty bigot" speech all prepared for him. I had planned to quietly let him know a bigot like him could not and would not deter me from my goals. I was going to tell him that he was lucky I never went "north side" on his short racist behind. I had planned to also tell him about his friend the racist dean. I waited because he knew I would be next on his list of "skinning and grinning".

Dr. Bish finished with a group and their parents and walked over smiling in my direction with an outstretched right hand. I thought to myself, "How in the hell can he reach to shake my hand after all the obstacles he's placed in front of me? How dare he reach to shake my hand after calling me nigger dozens of times in front of hundreds of white students? He must be crazy, after dozens of times placing me in the most embarrassing positions I've ever been in my life. Is he nuts? He really has some nerves of steel."

Although Dr. Bish was standing less than twenty feet from me, his walk in my direction made me reflect over the past three years and dozens of lectures. Now I was faced with the moment I've contemplated for years. I was about to get my revenge on the worst bigot I'd ever known. As he put his right hand in a position for me to shake it, I briefly thought about my great aunt that passed at age eighty-five in 1958. Aunt Bicky was the youngest child of two former Tennessee slaves. Her father was run out of town by an angry mob shortly after she was born and was never heard from again. She used to sit me down as a child and talk to me about showing my character and representing the family. She would say, you can win a fight by not throwing one blow if you're a real man. She'd say, "Show'em you're a bigger man than him." She was full of wisdom acquired over the years. I reflected on Aunt Bicky as I looked at Dr. Bish's outstretched right hand.

As he handed me his right hand, he said, "Congratulations Mr. Thornton." I returned a firm handshake and said, "Thank you, Dr. Bish." I knew then, at the age of twenty-one years that I was much bigger than Dr. Bish. I felt I had defeated a university trained, Ph.D. bigot.

Little did I know, Pop had witnessed the entire event unfold. He later told me that I did exactly what he would have expected me to do—to be a bigger man than Dr. Bish. He said, "Dr. Bish had the power, but you didn't let him use it over you."

****

Chapter Three

- APPLICATION TO THE FBI -

Pop's friend Mr. Thomas was pretty involved in my stories about my experiences at The University of Missouri. By now Pop had drifted off to sleep and we decided to continue talking until he woke up again. Mr. Thomas asked, "Once you got your college degree was it easy to get through the FBI process? Were you able to move right through the application process with no problems with all that education behind you?" I told them that when you graduate from college you do not have the ticket to a guaranteed good life in the suburbs or with the FBI. In fact that degree only means you have endured a particular college program and have passed the classes. It means nothing more and nothing less. Randy looked at me as if to say, "Then why are you telling me to go to school?"

I told them that joining the FBI is a long arduous journey for anyone, black or white. I explained in addition to taking the right classes in college, your associates, and conduct might also keep you out of the bureau or furthermore a job with any company.

"Let me tell you about my long road through the job process that served as experience for me when I applied to the bureau. I had several experiences that challenged my faith in my college degree and tested my endurance." I explained to them that after

C. Lee Thornton

The University of Missouri I attended Southern Illinois University in Carbondale, Illinois to pursue a Master's in Business Administration. After all, I was advised to go back to college, get another degree, and to gain more work experience before applying for the bureau. A graduate degree was my rode in the right direction.

While a graduate student at Southern Illinois University in Carbondale, I worked at a large retail store at the local mall. I had managed to get a job in a management-training program and the salary for a college graduate was not too bad. However this was not the job I desired to make a permanent career. However southern Illinois was still the South and many attitudes had not changed from the days of the early civil rights struggles.

Many employers hired college students who worked part-time while the local residents worked the full-time positions. At the time, I had two full-time local residents working in the six departments I managed at the store. One lady was a very nice middle-aged lady and the other lady was a younger woman. The older lady was very responsible and was a pleasure to work around. However, the younger woman was a chore to manage and had a difficult personality.

The younger woman's husband would often visit the store and would seldom speak to me or acknowledge that I was in the area. I simply wrote him off as ignorant. He was about six feet tall, 250 pounds, and wore a long scraggly beard, which reached down to his chest. His normal attire was bib overalls and a wrinkled hat. I always thought he dressed strange for a guy less than thirty years old. To say he was ignorant was being very kind to him.

I began to notice that the younger lady was leaving assignments undone and wasn't cooperating with the older lady. I'd ask her to do various assignments and she'd refuse to do anything that I had assigned to her. One day, I called her into my office to see if there was a problem with her following my instructions. She listened as

I spoke to her and was cordial and respectful as I talked to her. As she listened she showed no emotion, just as she always had done when listening to my instructions. When I finished speaking, she looked me in the eye and said, "Mr. Thornton, my husband told me I didn't have to do anything a colored man said, and that was whether he was my boss or not." The woman made this statement to me without one spark of emotion. I couldn't believe she had the nerve to say those words to me. I refused to lose my temper or show any emotion, which would let her know she was in control of me. I held my temper with the ignorant little woman and told her to leave the department. She politely walked out. I could see her walking upstairs toward the personnel manager's office.

As soon as she left the office, I called the personnel manager and explained what the woman had just told me. I knew this would be her last day in the store and I was relieved to see her go. To my surprise, later in the day I found she had been reassigned to another department and was working for another manager. The personnel manager's rationale was the worker would simply be happier in another department.

I later attended a job fair and began interviewing with some large corporations while I was studying for my M.B.A. I assumed my management background and degrees would put me in contention for a good position with a large company. I interviewed with a company I'll only refer to as JPC, who produced baby products. It was a large fortune 500 company and seemed to offer a lot of potential for growth.

The managers' at this company reviewed my résumé and asked me to meet with them in Carbondale for my first follow-up interview. I was pretty excited because I knew this company was on the breaking edge of hiring minorities in key management positions. I hoped I would find a position that I could pave the way for people like myself. I met with some key management officials who seemed to be impressed with my background and the fact I was pursuing an M.B.A.

The managers indicated there might be a second interview scheduled soon as a follow-up. I was encouraged after the first interview concluded. About three weeks later, a top marketing manager had scheduled an interview for me in Clayton, Missouri. I accepted the invitation and could hardly wait to display my talents to another group at JPC Corporation. I rehearsed my presentation during the entire two-hour drive to Clayton. I arrived early, which is an essential selling point when interviewing.

I walked into an office and met three young white men who told me they would be conducting my interview. Although I was twenty-five years old, I doubt if any of the young executives were more than 30 years old. I figured at least by being about the same age, we might have something in common and perhaps this could be a crucial stepping-stone for me. The interview seemed to be going well and I was returning all the right answers, as far as I could determine. In the middle of the interview one of the young guys stood up from his seat and looked down at me. This caused the rest of them to walk over and stand in front of me, too. It seemed that their actions had been rehearsed since they all moved at the same time.

The senior of them looked at me and said, "That's it, this interview is over. No one is going to make us hire anymore blacks, we've got enough." The three of them said nothing else and motioned for me to leave the room. Still stunned beyond belief, I stood up without saying a word and left the office. Time seemed to move in slow motion with the abrupt end to my interview by the three young executives. As the elevator doors closed, they stood in the doorway of the office and watched me disappear onto the elevator. It seemed that the walk to my 1970 Volkswagen took a lifetime as I internally reflected on lessons taught by Pop and Mr. Jeff years earlier. Reflecting on lessons learned always seemed to console me when things got too tough to bear.

Pop and Mr. Jeff had taught me years ago that I would encounter people like the three JPC executives and I was to remember, that although they sat in a position of authority, I possessed several things they could never take from me. I was armed with my education, dignity, and knowledge of my history. I was never so naive to think that although I was young and educated, I would not have to confront racism in its purest form. I recalled Mr. Jeff telling me as a young child, "Boy when it hits you, don't be surprised, don't kick their butts, just keep yo' head up, and pray for 'em. Remember you have something they can never take from you and right is on yo' side." As I drove toward Carbondale that afternoon I went over those lessons over and over in my head and I let those lessons replace the hate that I could have felt for the three young men.

I continued to expand on my earlier history lessons from the old people as solace to replace my anger experienced during the interview. At the time, I was taking a graduate class in historical economics, which focused on the development of the agricultural economy in the United States. During the time I took the class, I waited for the professor to emphasize or give credit for the free labor provided by the slaves in the construction of this country. However, he provided praise and accolades to everyone except the slaves themselves. He talked about the slave owners who supplied the labor and capital to build the United States into the vast machine, which it had become today. I knew to open a debate about the economic value of the slaves would do nothing more than to place the spotlight on me for the balance of the semester and perhaps earn myself a failing grade. I was the only minority student in the class and I had the usual study group of one.

But I was taught my history lessons as early as four or five years old, and I knew why the professor only mentioned the names of Washington and Jefferson as builders of this country rather than as slave owners. Years ago, Mr. Jeff and one of his friends gave my brothers and me a history lesson on slave trade as was taught by their grand parent's years earlier. At the time of our lesson, Mr. Jeff and his friend were in their late eighties and were as sharp as ever on the subject of agricultural economics. Mr. Jeff said, "Boys let me tell you what my granddaddy told me when I was 'bout yo' age. You see, my granddaddy was a slave in the south and his last name was Kimble. Kimble was the last name of the owner of the plantation where they all lived and worked. On the next plantation over, all the slaves were given the last name of Washington. The George Washington family owned all those slaves. Once he became president, his relatives and people with the last name of Washington were ashamed to be associated with that last name. All those white people with the name of Washington changed their last names. Even today, you can't find a white person with the last name of Washington and you won't find any with Jefferson, for the same reason. And boys, that's y'all real history." I said to myself, "No wonder my professor never brought up the subject of who owned the slaves. After all he knew everything else about the agricultural economy." But I know my real history.

As a struggling college student I had no money for a lawsuit against JPC Corporation and there were very few agencies handling that type of discrimination activity in the 1970's. I simply reverted back to my upbringing and recalled Pop's marching orders. After that interview, I figured the best way to get back at them was to never buy any JPC products again. In today's environment, that company could have been sued out of business but in the mid-1970s they just kept up their practices.

****

The road for me was still not smoothly paved to the FBI Academy, despite my preparation and lessons learned. A key factor to getting into the FBI and with most big corporations is a satisfactory background investigation. That process takes a look at the applicant and the people around you to determine if you're a person who can be trusted.

Randy, still unusually attentive asked, "You mean if my brother or somebody has been in trouble, then I can't join the FBI? What if I run into few problems paying my bills from time to time? Does that mean I can never join the FBI?" I told him that a background investigation takes a close look at you and the people you let influence your life. In today's environment, everyone's got someone in his family who has been in trouble with the law. Some may have gone to prison and others may just be shady. An important factor to judge your creditability is your credit rating. Sometimes an FBI agent may be trusted with millions of dollars in cash and often highly sensitive information.

Just ask yourself if you'd give your money to someone who can't manage his own money? Or how about giving your money to someone who has a ton of overdue bills? That's not wise for you and not wise for the FBI either. I told Randy to get in the habit of paying your obligations on time in order to show your trustworthiness. Your credit rating is nothing more than a gauge the FBI uses to determine whether you can be trusted.

An example of how associations can derail your pursuit of an FBI career was an old classmate I ran into whom I hadn't seen since high school. We met at a club in west St. Louis County completely by accident. The guy was Tee McRae. As we talked I told Tee I was in the process of applying for the FBI Academy. He suddenly became very reserved and told me not to tell anyone in the club but he was an FBI agent working undercover. I couldn't believe I was talking to an actual undercover FBI agent.

Tee told me he was stationed in the Denver FBI office and had been tracking a group of high-level drug dealers across the country. He said they were inside the club and he was watching them to see who they were meeting. I asked him if he wanted me to do anything to help him because he made his job sound so interesting. He hesitated for a moment and said to tell his office I saw him if anything happened to him. I assured him I'd watch his back. The last thing he said before he disappeared in the crowded club was that he could make my final processing move faster. He told me to list his name on my FBI application as a personal reference and to tell them we're friends and old high school classmates. He said to me again, "Don't tell anyone I'm in here...it could be dangerous." The guy made the FBI seem like a dream job.

I assured him his secret was safe with me. I never saw him again after that night. I really couldn't wait to tell our old classmates that I had seen Tee and he was doing big things for the FBI. But I didn't tell anyone he was working a big undercover drug case right out of St. Louis.

On the following Monday I called the St. Louis FBI office to update my application. I told the applicant coordinator I was including Tee McRae as a personal reference on my bureau application. He said they would be in touch with me later after my background investigation was completed. My background investigation was being conducted at that time and I knew my connection with Tee would seal my acceptance.

To make a long story short, prior to being assigned an academy slot, the new recruit has to be interviewed by the processing agent at a field office to insure all of his paperwork is in order. The applicant coordinator told me that everything in my background investigation went smoothly despite the fact I had a few people in my family who had problems with the law. The agent explained that as long as they aren't people who are close to me or that influence my life, the processing could proceed.

The processing agent went through my application package and then said, "Everything is fine with your background up to here," and pointed to the name Tee McRae. He said, "Who is this guy?" I said proudly, "He's one of your guy's. He works undercover drug cases out of the Denver office. I saw him a few weeks ago." The agent looked at me and said, "No he doesn't. We've never employed a Tee McRae." I was so embarrassed you could have bought me for a dime. He told me to be careful of people masquerading as FBI agents, scams like that happen all the time. He said they'd check him out but they would finish my processing.

I had been assigned to the Detroit Division for about two years when Moms sent me a newspaper article about Tee McRae. McRae had been convicted of molesting a twenty-two year old retarded boy. He had worked for the Missouri Special Olympics and had apparently been taking advantage of the clients for quite a while. According to the article he was caught in the act and confessed. He pled guilty and was given a long prison sentence to think about his actions.

In my case, bad associates weren't fatal but some scam artists make a living off of unsuspecting victims. Mr. Thomas then asked, "Son, how did you finally decide to join the FBI? Did you wake up one day and just decide you would join? I know how your daddy grew up and I know he didn't like police from years back." I said, "That's a very good question and let me give you some background on my decision to apply to the bureau. It was by no means anything I had dreamed about or the result of any grand plan."

I told them that we all know that some situations we find ourselves in are by accident, rather than planned. My decision to join the FBI was no different although it was more of a blessing than anything else. Two people were very influential to me at the time I decided to apply to the FBI. I had spent a short tour in the active military and in the Army Reserves during the 1970s. The Vietnam War didn't make the military an attractive place to go because hundreds of young people were dying during the war. I decided to take my chances and hoped my decision to join the Army Reserves wouldn't prove fatal for me as it had for thousands of others.

In August 1970, at the beginning of my junior year in college, I received a draft notice that caught me completely by surprise. At the time I was nineteen years old and doing very well in my classes. On the day I reported for my physical examination, I took with me all of my school records in order to prove I was a full-time student. I saw guys that day that looked like death being inducted in the military. Some guys seemed to be in poor physical condition but the military was interested in live bodies at the time. One guy failed the hearing and vision exams, he couldn't bend over, but he was still put on the bus for basic training. To say the military was desperate for live bodies was an understatement. These guys became known as "round blockers" for obvious reasons.

Another guy was so certain he would beat the draft that he took a huge stack of medical papers to the induction station. He said he told his wife he would be home for dinner that evening. However he was also put on the bus and sent to basic training. I was the only one in the group given a delay and told to report back in June 1972, immediately after my scheduled graduation date.

I enrolled in school that semester and began a quest to beat the short trip to South Vietnam in less than two years away. I located an Army Reserve Unit that I heard was in need of men for a personnel detachment. The day I walked into the recruiting office to inquire about joining the Army Reserves, I really had no idea I'd ever be called by the recruitment sergeant. In fact, the day I filled out the paperwork as a potential recruit, my application was one of hundreds on the sergeant's desk.

Oath of Office

I was called to begin reporting to training meetings a short time later. I was sworn into the U.S. Army Reserves during September 1970. However I was told I might be called to training and active duty at almost any time and I'd have to drop everything and report to duty. I was also told I may be called for active duty in Vietnam if the unit was needed. I decided to take my chances since I figured I might end up in South Vietnam anyway. To my surprise I was called to active duty in the middle of my junior year in the spring of 1971. I was in the middle of the semester when I had to drop most of my classes.

On the morning I left home to report to active duty Moms cried uncontrollably. She was afraid I would be hurt or killed and that my unit would be called to South Vietnam. Hundreds of young men were dying everyday in the war on the other side of the world. Pop got up at his usual time that morning and headed for work. He couldn't control Moms crying and said nothing to me until it was time for him to walk out of the door. As Pop opened the door to leave he turned around to me and only said, "Keep your head down," and walked out of the door. He had told us many times in the past that a lot of soldiers die because they don't know how to stay low. That was his way of saying stay low and stay alive.

My brother arrived a few minutes later to take me to the airport for my first airplane trip to Fort Knox for boot camp. He had recently gotten out of the Air Force and was glad to be away from the military. I hugged Moms goodbye and Bruce and I left for the airport. Bruce didn't say much during the ride to the airport because he knew what I'd soon be facing. When he dropped me off at the front of the terminal, we shook hands, and he said to me, "Keep your head down," and drove off.

I went to basic training at Fort Knox, Kentucky and then to advanced training. I had a stroke of luck while waiting to be assigned a job at Fort McClelland, Alabama. After my advanced individual

C. Lee Thornton

training was completed, I was assigned to the post funeral detail. My job for the next several weeks was performing military funerals for guys who had been killed in Vietnam. I figured that was a much better duty than being stationed in Vietnam and dodging bullets.

In August 1971, I was released from active duty to return to St. Louis but I was told my unit might be activated at a later date. The last thing they told me was not to get too comfortable at home because I may not be there long. I decided to take my chances and enrolled in school for my final two semesters. I had attended summer school every year and had always taken a larger load of classes. For that reason the semester and summer I lost in the military didn't alter my schedule for graduation.

I decided to go to a veteran's job fair at the old St. Louis Arena to see what the job market may look like when I graduated the following spring. I walked in and immediately saw a tall black guy with a big afro. He was standing in front of the FBI booth with a white guy and appearing to be passing out brochures and information. I knew the FBI was tricky and I assumed the black guy was a plant to spy on black folks coming through the job fair. I had heard all the stories about Hoover from Pop and the tricks that had been pulled on the black community over the years. I figured this was one of the rottenest tricks Hoover could pull on black people. I figured the black guy was hired for the job fair in order to get black people to fill out job applications. I assumed the FBI would use the information to spy on the black community later. I didn't trust Hoover or anyone associated with him.

I walked up to the black guy and introduced myself. I asked him, "Hey brother, how much are they paying you to spy on us? Everyone knows Hoover is tricky." To my surprise he said, "I'm really an FBI agent and I'm here to recruit FBI agents from the local community." He showed me his FBI credentials and I still didn't believe him. I knew Hoover was known to cover all the bases when he went after

Oath of Office

black folks. The agent told me he was one of only a few black FBI agents on board and he was hoping to attract new recruits. I still could not believe my ears that Hoover was changing after all the years of pulling tricks on black people.

Special Agent Ron Jones gave me some material and asked me to follow-up after I graduate from college the following spring. I stood there and waited for him to yell, "Surprise!!" but he didn't. He actually was a black FBI agent.

Following graduation I followed up with the application procedure but I was told the minimum recruitment age was twenty-three years old. At the time I was barely twenty-one but I had my B.S. degree. Special Agent Jones advised me to go back to school, get a Masters Degree, and acquire some work experience. He told me to reapply in a few years. I've always been known to follow instructions so I returned to school, got a Masters Degree, some work experience, and applied later. However I soon found out it was not that simple.

One cold winter day in March 1979 two FBI agents arrived at the manufacturing plant where I worked in Illinois to interview one of the workers. I asked them to stop by my office when they finished speaking to the worker. The two guys came to my office about an hour later and we all sat down. They answered my questions about the FBI and I told them I had applied a few years earlier. The younger of the two gave me a telephone number to the St. Louis field office and encouraged me to call the applicant recruiter. I then remembered Agent Jones' name and called the office to speak to him. I was gambling he would still be working in the same office after over eight years. After all Hoover would have found a reason to get rid of a black guy after all that time. But I found out he was still assigned in St. Louis but he was away from the office that afternoon. I asked to speak to any FBI agent about answering some questions about recruiting.

An FBI agent answered the telephone and told me the FBI was recruiting but they were only looking for accountants and lawyers. I read the material I had in front of me and it indicated all backgrounds were being recruited. Besides I had been told several years ago to get a Masters Degree to become more competitive. I told the FBI agent thank you and hung up the telephone.

I immediately called back and asked the operator again for any FBI agent who could provide me some information about recruitment for the FBI. This time I spoke to another FBI agent and I gave him some information about my academic, military, and work background. He told me, "A Masters Degree is fine but in order to qualify for the FBI you really needed a law degree or some experience as a police officer. I'm sorry but you really don't qualify for the FBI. I suggest you might want to try another federal agency." He also suggested I apply to the St. Louis Police Department. I told him, "Thank you for your time and concern" and I hung up the telephone.

Later in the day I decided to call again because no one had told me what I had read in the recruitment brochure. I still couldn't understand why two different FBI agents had given me two different sets of requirements for the FBI. But I was determined to either speak to Agent Jones or someone who could tell me I was qualified. I wanted to speak to someone who could tell me how to begin the application process.

I again telephoned the St. Louis FBI office and was told Special Agent Jones was still away from the office and probably wouldn't return that afternoon. I asked the operator if there was anyone who could tell me the entry requirements for the FBI Academy. The operator told me there was one gentleman working in the office who was going to the academy in a few weeks. She said she would check to see if he was in the office.

A short time later she connected me to John Samuels. He was very polite and said, "Yes I'd be glad to help you get started on the application process." He told me he was scheduled for new agents' classes in a few weeks. Mr. Samuels said he was presently working as a clerk in the office and was excited about leaving soon for new agents' school. I could tell from his voice that Mr. Samuels was a black guy. I explained to Mr. Samuels that I had spoken to Agent Ron Jones several years earlier about the FBI. I told him that I had a Masters Degree, several years of manufacturing experience in safety engineering, a veteran, and I had management experience.

He said, "Young man your background is perfect. Get that application over here as soon as you can." Mr. Samuels told me to send the application to the St. Louis office and to direct it to the applicant coordinator. He said the FBI is on a recruitment campaign to add quite a large number of new agents. This was the first time I was told I was qualified for the FBI and that I should begin the application process. He also told me he would mention to Agent Jones that I had followed up after so many years. Mr. Samuels wished me good luck and I forwarded my application to the St. Louis field office that same week.

Randy asked me, "Why did those guys tell you that you weren't qualified? Do all FBI agents try to discourage black people to keep them out?" I said, "Absolutely not but there are some people with mean hearts that will discourage you if you aren't persistent." But I have always wondered how many young, qualified recruits were turned away by bad information provided by agents for no reason. I took the new agents entrance exam in April, 1979, the oral exam in May, 1979, and physical in July, 1979, and I was sworn into the FBI in September 1979.

My timing was perfect because the firm where I worked in Illinois was in the process of divesture during early 1979. The firm started the rumors of selling the operation during the spring of 1979. The divesture was completed by late August 1979 and workers were beginning to lose jobs by the time I was ready to leave the company. A final decision was being made about the jobs of the plant management when I got my notice of assignment to the FBI. I made their decision a lot easier when I left the company in September, 1979. My last day at the plant was Thursday, September 13, 1979. I was later told the owner's son-in-law moved into my office the week after I left the company. One of the older workers told me that my fate would have been sealed had I stayed any longer. After all, the new owner would have had to make a choice between his son-in-law and me. I'm not sure if he would have chosen me or not.......

I formally met Mr. Samuels when I was sent to the St. Louis field office for my first assignment in December 1979. He was still as helpful and cordial as he was on that cold day in March 1979. Agent Jones was also still in the St. Louis Division and also still active in the recruitment process when I arrived there for my first assignment. Both of them have always been role models for all of the new recruits assigned to the St. Louis Division. Again, this was perfect because my youngest daughter Christy Marie was born ten days after I completed the new agents academy, on December 31, 1979.

The road for me was still not smoothly paved to the FBI Academy, even though I had qualified and passed the initial entry tests in the spring 1979 and had successfully passed the background check. Randy then said, "Tell us about the training program you had to go through at the FBI Academy. Was it hard to keep up with the guys in your class?" I began by explaining to him that the physical training doesn't start when you arrive at the academy. Your physical training starts long before you arrive at the academy with proper eating, exercise, and rest. I told him the FBI Academy is only where you're tested to see how you compare with other recruits from around the country. You've got to be ready and in good condition on the day you arrive at the facility. Unlike in your school, you can't go there to get in shape.

After we were sworn in, I rode on the bus enroute to the FBI Academy. I knew I had prepared well for the academic and physical aspect of the training. When the group of us got off the bus, we were met by our class counselor who told us to drop our things in our dorm rooms and meet him at the gym in thirty minutes for our first physical training examination. There was no time to get accustomed to our new surroundings or to get acquainted with one another.

No one really talked that much as we dressed for the physical training test. Those of us who read and studied the literature knew the test consisted of push-ups, sit-ups, pull-ups, a shuttle run, and a two-mile run. As I listened, I could hear a few people asking others what the test consisted of and what the standards would be in order to pass. I knew that I was at least ahead of many of them because some hadn't read the material.

While in the locker room, I finally got a chance to meet the other black guy in my class. His name was Pablo Ramirez and he was from Naples, Florida. I was surprised to learn that for the past nine years, he had been a clerk for the bureau. I had assumed everyone had at least a Masters Degree and backgrounds similar to mine. I soon found out that was not the case. To me, my first big hurdle was showing my twenty-eight classmates that I deserved to be at the academy. I made a vow to myself to be in the top ten percent in push-ups, sit-ups, and pull-ups for the class or I'd do them over again. I wasn't the fastest runner but my goal was to stay in the front of the pack.

The class counselor informed us we had to make at least 21 points on the physical training test before we could graduate from the academy. The test on the first day was the first of three required physical training tests that we had to pass. For some new recruits, the thought of not passing various portions of the physical training test was the first stressor they would undergo during our sixteen weeks.

Ramirez and I let everyone know the first day that we belonged in the class by our physical training performance. We both made twenty-nine out of the maximum thirty points. Although there were some good athletes in the class, we stood in the top ranks. We began to earn our respect in the gym right away.

After our physical training test, the entire class finally got an opportunity to formerly meet one another in a classroom setting. We all met our class counselor and staff counselor in room 310 in the classroom building. When everyone was assembled, our class counselor introduced himself and gave us a summary of his background and previous FBI experience. His background sounded exciting and we all envied him and wished we could someday wear his shoes and stand before new agent recruits with the same beaming pride. He then said, "Now let's go around the room and I want each of you to take a few moments and formerly introduce yourself to your classmates. Tell us some things about yourself and I'd like to know what your family and friends think about you joining the FBI. Let's start up front, right here." The counselor pointed to the guy sitting up front. I said to my self, "You've got to be kidding. I can't tell anyone what I just went through to get here."

One by one the proud trainees stood up and gave a synopsis of their academic, military, and family backgrounds. Everyone had tremendously impressive backgrounds. One new agent was a Medal of Honor recipient during the Vietnam conflict. As they presented their backgrounds, I realized there were only a very small number of new recruits that were attorneys or accountants. Two new agents were former police officers. This only served to confirm to me that had I listened to the first agent, whom I spoke with at the St. Louis field office; I wouldn't be sitting in this classroom. I knew, since my name started with the letter "T", I had plenty time to structure my brief presentation and hold my own at boasting with the best of them.

However, each person in the group summed up his presentation by telling us how proud his family was of them for making it to the FBI academy. These guys were all apple pie and flag waving Americans. Each one summed up his statement with something to effect of, "My family is overjoyed and proud I've become an FBI agent." Everyone's motivation to join the FBI was strikingly similar. They had sought the position since elementary school or their families had known FBI agents all of their lives. One guy said his entire neighborhood was comprised of police officers and FBI agents and he's always revered and respected them as professionals. Another new recruit told the group that he was inspired to join the FBI in elementary school when he met an FBI agent during a career day. Everyone had a truly inspiring testimony about his quest to join the FBI. As a group they all loved police officers and most had very pleasurable experiences with law enforcement as youngsters. No one had ever been harassed, beaten, or disrespected by the police for any reason. None of them had ever had a negative encounter with law enforcement, and most of all...they seemed to love and revere Hoover. One guy was so "gung ho" about J. Edgar Hoover, he was later nicknamed J. Edgar Wheeling by his classmates. Throughout our training school period he smiled whenever someone addressed him with that title and wore the name proudly.

I knew I had to fabricate a believable story for my classmates by the time I had the floor. In reality, my family and most of friends still thought I had lost my mind, even though I had made it to the academy. The only persons on my side who hadn't called me crazy were my wife, kids, and just a few friends. My kids were probably too young to know any better. My parents and most of my friends survived such negative experiences with law enforcement, that they hated cops and federal agents with a passion. My father did his best to talk me out of joining the FBI due to the history J. Edgar Hoover had with black people in the South. However, there was no way

I was going to say my family was proud of me because in reality, they were ashamed of my decision. My Aunt Ida got on her knees and prayed to Jesus that He would "pump some sense into my hard head" and turn me away from the bureau.

I had never personally known an FBI agent and my elementary school definitely never had an FBI agent to visit us for a career day. In fact, we never had a career day the entire time I attended elementary school. The only police officers we saw in our neighborhoods were harassing us or taking someone away in handcuffs. Moms always told us to say, "Yes sir and no sir" to the police and to never run from them even if you haven't done anything. She always said, "Don't run from them 'cause they'll shoot you in the back. I don't wanna lose one of y'all to one of those bad cops." She told us as a little girl she saw that happen too many times. Needless to say, Moms had no love for cops and now her youngest son wanted to be an FBI agent. She just assumed I'd lost my mind and sooner or later I would come to my senses.

When it was my turn to introduce myself, I did and eloquent job displaying my academic, military, and work experience for my classmates, but it was obvious I had left out the part about my family's opinion about my decision to join the FBI. Before I got a chance to sit down my class counselor asked, "Agent Thornton, how does your family and friends feel about you joining the FBI? I know they must be proud of you." I looked around and I could see everyone sitting on the edge of his or her seats waiting for my next response. I think many of them were stunned to witness me speaking the kings English and that I had a non-criminal background prior to the FBI. I looked around and said, "My family and friends support my decision." I then sat down without saying another word. I was smart enough to know any negative statement would cause my next sixteen weeks to be miserable and place the spotlight directly on me. On this one occasion, I surmised a little lie was quite appropriate. I wasn't giving anyone ammunition to fire in my direction over the next sixteen weeks.

Early in our physical training regimen the class was introduced to the combat boxing phase of training. Ramirez and I knew we could use our fists from our days growing up days back home. Many of our classmates had never been in a fistfight in their lives. This aspect of training was important because often criminals will attack the weakest or smallest person first. If the officers aren't small in stature, the person who appears to be in the poorest physical condition is frequently the target. Many of our classmates had a tough time with this segment of training. Although I didn't talk about it to anyone other than Ramirez, I hoped that I'd never have to take some of them in a tight spot with me. Most of my classmates were smart as whips in the books but some seemed to be a little too timid for the streets. I just didn't think some of them had what it took to make it on urban streets. Most urban streets in large cities would be tough for a person not prepared physically and often fatal for law enforcement officers. I didn't plan to become a victim because of a weak partner.

We had one exercise that required everyone to box in one big group. Ramirez always took one end of the gym and I took the other end. We bobbed and weaved like professional middleweight fighters. Many of our classmates had never seen that style of boxing in their lives, although it was quite common in our neighborhoods. But it was just street corner shadow boxing. I thought to myself, "Thank God for Muhammad Ali and Sugar Ray Leonard." By the time we finished displaying our street corner boxing skills to everyone in the class, they all knew the two brothers could handle themselves if things got tight. We never sparred with one another although our classmates asked us many times. They weren't going to get that show.

The physical phase of the training academy involved more than being able to overpower an adversary. One point the seasoned instructors always emphasized was stamina. One of them would always say, "After you chase a subject and catch him, you've got to have something left to handcuff and subdue him. That's when street corner grappling skills become important." We were given dozens of examples where the cop won the foot race but lost his life because he had nothing left to fight with and his gun was taken.

Needless to say, the physical training was not as much of a challenge if you're in good physical condition when you arrive at the training academy. The second big hurdle at the FBI Academy was the academic phase.

On the first day we arrived at the academy the counselor stood in front of the class and invited anyone to leave who couldn't maintain an 85 academic average for the next 16 weeks. I could see the shocked looks on a lot of faces in that room. Now I knew why I was quizzed so much on my academic preparation while I was applying for the FBI. I soon realized that everyone didn't have a Master's Degree, a military background, or had engineering experience as I did. I was different from the rest of this crowd and I planned to make academics my advantage over my classmates. I knew from my days at the University of Missouri that some people don't take "us" serious when it comes to academics. I explained to Randy, "Young man, you've got to beat them in the gym and the classroom. And beat them even worse in the classroom."

The class counselor told us that we'd have eight academic tests covering behavioral science, legal studies, field office administration, fingerprint techniques, white-collar crime, and interviewing and interrogation techniques. I continued to glance around and I saw confused faces. I think many of my classmates thought once they were recruited for the FBI, the badge and gun was automatic. The counselor explained if you score 84 or less, you would be placed on academic probation. You would have one more chance to pass the test on a second attempt. If the candidate scored less than 85 the second time, he would be dismissed from the academy and sent home.

I felt that would have to be the most humiliating experience a person could ever go through in his life. I made up my mind the first day that I had come to graduate. The room had a hush over it. Many really thought that graduation from the FBI Academy was automatic after you passed the entry phase. My marching orders from Pop became more important than ever during my early days at the FBI Academy.

Everyday in class was similar to finals day in college. You didn't allow yourself to miss anything in class and you studied every night to stay up on the material. Unlike at The University of Missouri, we studied in groups until late at night and quizzed one another constantly. No one wanted to be left behind.

During the first week no one got personally too close. I think we didn't want to get too close to someone who may not be around after the first test a few days away. The first academic test was behavioral science and was given on the Friday of the first week. It was considered the test used to weed out those who can't cut it academically. The instructor was a genius in the subject matter of behavioral science and always provided excellent lectures. His lectures were so interesting students sometimes found themselves listening and sometimes falling short on note taking. The instructor later became one the FBI premier criminal profilers.

Throughout that first tense week, we saw agents standing in the circle in front of the cafeteria with a glum look on their faces and their luggage next to them. We soon learned that was the familiar sight of a recruit flunking out of the academy. Everyone in the academy cafeteria could see them waiting for the long taxi ride back to Washington National Airport.

We'd only hear that the person was in class and was tapped on the shoulder by his class counselor. The class would never see him again. The recruit's room would be cleaned out completely by the time his class got back to the dorm. There were rarely any signs that the poor guy was ever at the academy. This was probably more dreaded for his roommate who would now be in the room all alone. From the way his dorm room appeared, the poor guy was never there. We always shuddered when our class counselor walked into our classroom after a major test. Academic tests always caused the stress level to go up among the class.

Many of us had families and had left good jobs back at home to pursue becoming an FBI agent. Bombing out of the academy was not an option. Graduation was a must because my youngest daughter was due to be born the month after my scheduled graduation. There was no way I was going to return home flunked out and jobless.

Leading up to the first major exam in behavioral science, it was unusually stressful for all of us. We were told we'd have a good idea if we belonged at the Academy after the first test. The entire class stayed up practically all night studying and quizzing one another in preparation. At the conclusion of the test, the air was thick with stress. No one talked about how he thought he had done out of fear of being wrong. All of our conversation during lunch was about something other than the behavioral science test we had completed a few hours earlier.

As we sat in the bleachers at the firing range on that afternoon, we saw our class counselor to give us the news about the results of the first exam. Our class counselor walked across the field toward us. Everyone held his breath waiting for the news. He stood for a minute, listened to the firearms instructor, and quietly called Ramirez to come with him. The counselor and Ramirez walked away in a hurry. Ramirez would be our first casualty but luckily for him it was his first test. He was scheduled to repeat the exam on the following Monday morning. I personally took it upon myself to pump up Ramirez's ego, which had been seriously deflated. We studied like hell all weekend to make sure Ramirez would be ready on Monday morning. He couldn't afford to be tossed out of the academy for academic deficiency because he also had wife and several children at home in Florida. I wasn't going to let the only other minority in the class leave me all alone. No way.

Monday morning couldn't arrive fast enough for everyone in the entire class. Ramirez took the behavioral science re-exam prior to our first scheduled class on Monday morning. Halfway through our morning, the class counselor peeped in the classroom and gave thumbs up to Ramirez and the rest of the class. Cheers broke out all over the place. Ramirez was still with us and we could go on to the next academic segment. However, Ramirez was not allowed any more scores less than eighty-five in anything or he would be dismissed from the training academy for academic deficiency.

The balance of the new agent recruit classes was equally as stressed as we had been during the first week. Ramirez never failed another academic test and we only lost one other classmate during our entire stay at the academy. The released agent was my roommate and a very nice family man from Utah. I noticed during our training that he seemed troubled from time to time after watching films of shootings. The films depicted situations where law enforcement officers would sometimes find themselves. He was a very religious man who would spend hours in his room praying and reading the Bible. After viewing a number of videos one afternoon, involving police shootings and dead bodies, he told me that he really didn't feel he could ever shoot a man. After six weeks, he tendered his resignation.

In the final training phase of the academy, we had to endure firearms qualifications. Many recruits had never fired a gun in their lives. Some of us had an advantage by being prior military or law enforcement and had a familiarity with firearms. However, pistol and shotgun qualification was a little different from firing an automatic rifle while lying on the ground. Those with the prior skills had to help those who were new to firearms. Just as with the physical training and academic tests, we had minimum scores to achieve in order to graduate from the academy.

After shotgun training, many recruits returned to the dorm rooms to ice down their shoulders. We were given specific instructions how we should hold the shotgun. It had to be held firmly against your shoulder or you'd pay the price. If you weren't strong enough to hold the shotgun up or failed to hold it firmly, the gun could knock you to the ground, bruise your shoulder, or both. It was important to be physically strong as well as to follow the instructions closely. Some recruits didn't follow the instructions or were not physically strong and sustained shoulder injuries.

Our final firearms qualifications test was taken on a cool fall morning, and this time we didn't have the luxury of being nervous. Nervousness did nothing but make the target harder to hit, thus you flunk the test. As I looked down the range, I could see a few of my classmates struggling to keep up with the group. The pistol qualifications course involved shooting from the fifty-yard line and moving in as close as the seven-yard line. As we moved from station to station, we had to focus on our targets, reload, move quickly, and fire within a certain number of seconds. I knew my eyes weren't the best but if I remained calm I knew I could hit from the fifty-yard line and be near perfect from the twenty-five yard line.

My scores were excellent, but several of my classmates were put in the stress seat again. As a class, we had to work in shifts all night with several class members to get them ready to retake their final firearms test. Whether or not you liked a person, or whether you had personality clashes with him was unimportant. Getting the entire class through the academy was our goal. We had seen dozens of new recruits on the circle waiting for the taxi and we made a vow our class was not going to add to the numbers.

Oath of Office

    The class counselor came to visit us after the two members retook their final test for firearms test. He again gave us the thumbs up, indicating we had no more class casualties. We had passed the final hurdle and would be graduating in a few days. Unfortunately, throughout my tenure at the FBI Academy, minority recruits were very few in numbers, but comprised a high percentage of the washouts in many classes. I made a personal goal to insure I helped as many minorities as I could to finish the academy successfully. Throughout my career, I put myself in the forefront of the FBI recruitment effort and assisted dozens of new agent candidates.

    I told Randy, "The proudest I'd ever been in my life was the day I was handed my FBI credentials and badge on graduation day. I felt like a celebrity." I explained to him, that the key to finishing the FBI Academy successfully is no different from your key to finishing any school successfully. You've got to study everyday, work together, and listen to your teachers. Those factors are important, whether you're an FBI recruit or a student in high school.

Chapter Four

- FIRST ASSIGNMENT -

My first assignment in the St. Louis field office was everything I ever thought it would be and more. I got an opportunity to do everything I had always dreamed an FBI agent does for a living, in addition to working along with seasoned veterans. However, I met my first challenge much earlier than I had expected. When I was a new agent, the vehicle budgets for FBI offices were very skimpy. For that reason, most new agents had to share or borrow cars in order to cover leads around the city and to complete their assignments. We would have to beg the veteran guys for their cars and promise to have them back within a certain amount of time. We all knew it was sometimes impossible to predict the time some interviews would end but we told them whatever it took to get the cars.

One time I was told by one of the veteran agents to get his car back in an hour because he had "p.b." to handle. I didn't have a clue what he had to do but another agent later told me it just meant he had personal business to handle and he needed his car back as soon as possible. The agent probably just had scheduled lunch with someone and he didn't want to be late.

I had been assigned to the office for less than a week when a veteran agent introduced himself to me. He was a tall imposing man who was assigned to the fugitive squad. All new agents wanted to work on that squad because those agents were always involved in the action. They worked the most active informants and if there was butt to be kicked, they kicked it. Fugitives were always running to get away and since we were young and fresh out of the academy, we were often called to assist. New agents were always ready to prove they could get the job done and earn their way on to the fugitive squad.

The guy told me he had a fugitive he couldn't seem to locate and asked my help because I was originally from the St. Louis area. He told me the fugitive had raped and assaulted a 72-year-old woman in Wellston, Missouri. He told me the story of the assault as he searched for the guy's wanted poster. I thought to myself, "How the hell was I supposed to know someone who had done something so horrible?" However I listened as he described this vicious assault in detail. It seemed that the old lady didn't have a chance as the guy broke into her home while she was in bed asleep. I had gone to school with some crazy people but this had to be the worse, most vicious person on Earth.

When he opened the wanted poster I couldn't believe my eyes. I recognized the picture before I read the name. I had gone to high school with this wild man and had hit on his sister a time or two. I told him, "That's Mark Marlowe, we were in the same high school class at O'Fallon Technical High School." I couldn't believe someone I'd known for so long could have his face plastered on an FBI wanted poster. Marlowe had been kicked out of school during our senior year and didn't graduate with our class. We immediately went to work to locate this vicious animal to make the streets of St. Louis safer.

I looked through my high school yearbook and located Marlowe's address when he was in high school. Although it was several years prior, it provided us a good starting point to find him. We did some background investigation in his old neighborhood but no one had seen the guy in several months. His mother still lived at his old address so we decided to interview her. She told us that she didn't know what had gotten into her son. She told us he had left town several weeks ago heading to Milwaukee, Wisconsin to visit some relatives. She provided us no more information as she cried when she saw his picture on the wanted poster. She asked us not to hurt Mark when we found him. We asked her to tell him to turn himself in to our office to avoid any confrontation. We thanked her for the information as she showed us out of the home.

We provided all the information we had compiled to the Milwaukee Division who immediately enlisted the services of the best informants in the Milwaukee area. Within two days of sending the information, Mark Marlowe was arrested while hiding at a cousin's home in Milwaukee. Thanks to our coordination, another vicious fugitive had been removed from the streets.

****

On a particularly cold January morning in January, 1980, I rode the bus to work. I walked toward the federal building to begin my workday just as any other normal day. We had been warned earlier to be particularly alert due to a number of assaults and robberies in downtown St. Louis. On this day I had left home in such a hurry that I had forgotten to take my gloves. I realized I didn't have them when I got off the bus that cold morning. I just put my hands in the pockets of my topcoat and started the six-block walk to the federal building.

On most mornings I'd walk across a small tree lined park directly across the street from the federal building. This morning was no different other than it was unusually cold and I had my ungloved hands in my pockets. As I approached the dark tree lined area I noticed a male figure walking rapidly in my direction and quickly looking left and right. I assumed it was someone on the way to work like myself. As he moved closer to me, I saw the figure of a man remove his hands from his pockets to his skullcap. The skullcap suddenly became a ski mask, which now covered his face. I continued to walk toward this person but instantly I decided to remove my hands from my pockets as the figure moved closer to me.

I sensed something was a little unusual about this person who was now looking rapidly from left to right as if he was getting ready to strike at any moment. I reached up with my left hand and unsnapped the two buttons on the front of my coat. I completely opened my topcoat in two quick motions. The figure continued to move toward me and put his hand inside his jacket pocket as if he was reaching for something, all the while nervously looking around from left to right as he moved in my direction.

By now I knew this guy had chosen me for his next victim. When he got about 15 feet from me I threw my coat open and let him see I was reaching for my service revolver. The guy saw it, stopped, looked around, and quickly ran in the opposite direction. I could clearly see a shiny object in his hand as he ran away from me. The object seemed to be small, similar to a knife or pipe. I didn't chase him but I got a good description of him to alert the employees in the building since a number of my co-workers also walked across that same park every morning and evening.

I started to reflect how fortunate I was to have forgotten my gloves that morning. If I had worn gloves that morning, I would not have been able to open my topcoat and draw my revolver that quick, I may have become his next victim. To this day I don't own a pair of dress gloves and refuse to wear anything that restricts my hands in the winter, regardless of the temperature.

****

Oath of Office

As a new agent you find investigations you thought looked simple on paper really aren't simple at all. In fact, you realize that some investigations will probably never be solved and may remain open for years without being resolved. But new agents are tenacious and believe even the toughest cases can be closed.

My first supervisor was from the old school of thought. He held the position that agents should be out of the office by 8:00 a.m., developing informants, and solving crime on the streets. He would sometimes walk through the squad room at 9:00 a.m. shouting, "Get the hell out to the streets! There are no criminals in here, they're all out there!" For that reason we had to get to the office early in the morning to do our paperwork and get out of the office long before 9:00 a.m.

I was probably spoiled with some successes early in my career. Although I was assigned to the white-collar crime squad, we really focused on con men that made their living swindling unsuspecting citizens. Most of these criminals moved counterfeit checks and all over the country. These criminals were the forerunners of identity theft. One of the most notorious con men I investigated was Stu Goodson, the king of con men. He hit St. Louis during early 1980 and left his mark on several unsuspecting ladies.

Goodson didn't have roots and seemed to travel all over the country swindling lonely ladies. He once said his specialty was lonely ladies and he made a living out of their plight. Goodson fancied himself as a pretty boy; a ladies man who felt women only existed to dress him in fine clothes and keep money in his pocket. He was a better than average looking guy and used his looks and charm to his advantage. I was given a lead to track down Goodson and arrest him when I was still a green new agent. He had just emptied the bank accounts of two ladies in the St. Louis area and left both of them lonely and devastated. After talking to them I wasn't sure if they really missed the money as much as the soothing charm of Goodson.

My new partner and I went to the meet one of the unfortunate ladies to interview her in an attempt to develop leads where this guy may strike next. To say she was ashamed of herself for being so naive was being kind. She simply called herself Goodson's sucker.

We located Ms. Dianne Petry, the first victim, working as a waitress at a hotel restaurant near St. Louis International Airport. She was a fairly attractive lady, in her early thirties, divorced and lonely. She was almost too embarrassed to tell us what she had allowed Goodson to do. She explained to us she met Goodson in the hotel bar one evening in January 1980. She said he was well dressed and told her he was a businessman handling investments. He was a very charming man who really showed a lot of attention.

The lady said Goodson told her he was staying at a nearby hotel that did not have a restaurant and bar. She said she saw him eating in her diner every evening and, although he was always busy, he was very cordial and friendly to her. She continued with her story and said, "He seemed to be so busy with papers in front of him all the time. I just assumed he was a salesman or something. He always had time to speak to me and he had the biggest smile. One day we had a conversation and he asked me out after I got off work. I told him sure, "I had nothing else to do."

The story got sadder as she went on and it appeared to follow the same pattern that Goodson had used all over the country. She said she had confided in Goodson that she was divorced and was trying to piece her life back together. She said Goodson had really showed her a good time and he spent lots of money on her during the short time they dated.

Goodson later told her the investment project he was working on was going well and he would soon come into a large sum of money. She said Goodson promised to help her with her bills as soon as a big deal closed. Ms. Petry said they became close and she soon let him move into her apartment with her. I asked her why she decided to let him move in with her when he was staying at the hotel. She said the big business deal was taking longer than he had anticipated and as soon as it was completed he would have a large sum of money. Ms. Petry said his story seemed so believable and Goodson was so attentive to her. She said she knew Goodson was "the one" by the way he continued to give her attention and make her feel special. She said, "I was drunk with Stu, he could do no wrong. I must have really been a fool."

Ms. Petry told us that Goodson had lived with her for about a month when he asked to borrow some money until his expense money arrived and the big deal closed. She felt they had gotten along so well that he had become her best friend. She said she wrote him a check for three hundred dollars with the promise he would repay her later in the week. She told us she left him at her home and went to work on the morning she gave him the money. She never saw Goodson again. Somehow Goodson found her bankbook and completely emptied her account, which included her life savings. Ms. Petry said although she only had $2,100.00 in the account, it was the only money she had saved. In addition she told us Goodson wrote over $600.00 in bad checks against her account that bounced. Ms. Petry was devastated but also embarrassed over the entire incident.

Goodson had struck another unsuspecting victim. Again he completely emptied the victim's back account with his charm and moved on to the next person. Ms. Petry had a difficult time with the interview because she frequently stopped to cry. I think the crying was more out of embarrassment than anything else. She kept saying she didn't know how she could have been so foolish and open her home to a complete stranger. She said loneliness had overcome her and Goodson's charm got the best of her.

When we finished with her interview we told her about the true background of Goodson. We told her he had traveled the entire Midwest and had swindled dozens of women out of their life savings. The lady began to cry uncontrollably. She allowed us to search the room where she and Goodson had slept for about two weeks. Unfortunately for Goodson he had left several dry cleaning receipts in a dresser drawer. They indicated an address in Madison, Wisconsin that we had not previously associated with him before. The victim had no idea where he was from but she indicated he had mentioned Madison several times in the past.

Ms. Petry went through her bank statement and realized not only had Goodson withdrawn all of her money from her bank account but also her checking account was continuing to be over drawn. She realized her loneliness had cost her all of her money, which would take a very long time to replace. She was one of six Missouri victims that fell prey to Stu Goodson.

Before we left her home she asked us, "Do you guys think you can find him and get my money back from him?" "Unfortunately Ma'am, I wouldn't hold out a lot of hope. Generally guys like Goodson spend money fast," I said. Ms. Petry cried as we left her apartment.

When I returned to the office that later that afternoon, I immediately summarized my interview notes and sent all the information I could assemble to the Milwaukee Division. I followed up communication with a telephone call to the Milwaukee office and let them know my information was on the way to them. To my surprise I received a call a week later informing me the cleaning ticket was the key to arresting Goodson in Madison, Wisconsin.

The address on the cleaning ticket was that of a lady whom he lived with on one occasion in Wisconsin. Goodson had returned to Madison to visit a lady whom he had swindled earlier. This time his story was he had reconsidered his life and really wanted to be with her. He told her he loved her and his big deal had finally come through.

Oath of Office

He said and he was going to pay her every dime with interest as soon as the check cleared in the bank. By the time the agents from the Madison Resident Agency Office arrived at the home, Goodson was sitting in her living room while she was considering if she could trust him for the last time. The Madison victim was similar to all of Goodson's prey. She was lonely, desperate, and taken by Goodson's charm. When he was taken away she cried and begged the agents to let him go. She said they had planned to marry soon.

At the time he was arrested, Goodson had no visible means of support and less than $20.00 in cash in his pocket. Goodson was arrested and charged with federal mail fraud and numerous local theft charges in several jurisdictions including St. Louis. He was sentenced to 12 years for his crimes. I was given an "ataboy" by my supervisor and another case to solve.

****

My next case big case involved assisting the fugitive squad with an arrest of a murder suspect whom we thought was living in an apartment in Maplewood, Missouri. As a new agent we always looked forward to fugitive hunts because the young guys got a chance to showcase their skills if the criminal got out of line. The older agents were smart enough to know if any running or fighting was going to take place, the young guys were better suited for that stuff.

From the information we received from an informant, the Maplewood address seemed to be on target for our subject. The informant told us the subject had been hanging around downtown Maplewood trying to buy drugs to support his habit. The teletype on the guy had the dreaded caption "WARNING: ARMED AND DANGEROUS" at the top and bottom as a caution. FBI agents are always particularly cautious whenever that caption is added to a fugitive.

One of the senior agents gathered us and made plans to hit the apartment around 7:00 a.m. one Friday in April, 1980. It was still a little chilly but we felt we could surprise the guy by surprising him early in the morning. From the information we had on him, he was living alone in a second floor apartment. His mode was to walk the streets all day hustling and stealing to survive.

In this case the senior agent gave two of us new guys the point (first agents through the door). When we arrived at the location that cold morning, it was still a bit dark outside. We all wore our ballistics vests with gold FBI letters on the front of our jackets. Agents were stationed at the rear of the building just in case the guy tried to run. The senior agents made sure to put two good runners at the rear. We crept up the front steps, making sure we made as little noise as possible to draw no unnecessary attention.

I was one of two agents leading the charge and as always I said my silent prayer as I approached the front door. I recalled in training that I shouldn't stand directly in front of the door in the event the bad guy fired a shot through the door. I checked my vest to see if it clearly covered my entire left and right sides as well as my front section. I patted my bullet pouch to make sure it was full and secured. On one early arrest I patted my bullet pouch and realized it was loose and all six rounds fell on the dark ground.

I thought about my family and regardless of how tough the guy might turn out to be, I was going to win the fight and return home that evening. I thought about Pop and Aunt Ida hating the fact that I had joined the FBI and that I had to prove to them that I had made the right choice. My last thought prior to knocking on the door was my silent prayer, "Father, watch over us and keep everyone safe. Amen." Using split second precision we hit the front door with a battering ram and it popped open. The apartment was dark with the exception of a half dozen our flash lights. I shouted, "FBI don't move!" as I entered the living room area. Immediately we saw one guy lying on the floor of what seemed to be an empty apartment. The guy was groggy and sleepy and moved slightly as I moved toward him. To maintain our surprise assault, I immediately grabbed him and handcuffed his arms behind his back. He remained face down while the rest of the team cleared the remaining rooms in the apartment. My only concern was this guy's hands and insuring he had no fight in his system. We had the smelly, stinking guy cuffed on the floor, and his hands behind him within seconds. One at a time guys shouted, "Clear!!" indicating the rooms had been secured and there were no threats to any of us. As they shouted, lights were turned on in several of the empty rooms.

The first thing I noticed was the guy we had handcuffed smelled like an old wet dog. He was only wearing a dirty t-shirt and stained under shorts. His hair was a mess and it was obvious he was still somewhat incoherent. He literally had no idea what had hit him, which is exactly the surprise we had intended. The apartment was practically empty of furniture. The only item we could see was a stained brown bag in the corner of the apartment, which appeared to be the subject's personal belongings. One of the agents on the team emptied the bag on the floor of the apartment to check the contents. The bag contained two snickers candy bars, a half bar of soap, some wrinkled clothes, and an old newspaper.

After the agents cleared the apartment, the case agent turned the guy around to see if he was our fugitive from Chicago. I couldn't believe my eyes when I saw his face. He was equally as surprised to see me, too. To my surprise it was my old eighth grade class cut-up, Jimmie Pierce. I hadn't seen him since eighth grade. Jimmie was so cool that he decided very early in life that high school was only for "squares" as he sometimes called his classmates. I recalled how he used to laugh at us as we read aloud in class. He did his best to disrupt those students who were listening. The better I read, the more Jimmie would laugh and try to distract me.

Ms. Henson, my eight-grade teacher, encouraged us to read all the time but by the eighth grade it was second nature in my home. Although neither of my parents graduated from high school, they could read and made us read all the time. We were told by Pop, "Dancing ain't gonna feed you, read, read, read." My first reading lessons came from my Pop who would buy a newspaper and tell me to look through the "For Rent For Colored" section. The "For Rent For Colored" section of the St. Louis Post Dispatch newspaper was a classified section for apartment and housing rental. This section was where blacks could find a place to live in St. Louis. We often would look through this section to find a better place to live when things just got too bad. During those days you never knew when the landlord would just call and say, "Get out by the end of the week." They didn't need a reason to evict poor black people and there were no housing rights or agencies to help you.

If your family was somewhat well off and you had the money, you could look through the "For Sale To Colored" section of the classified section. When I was a kid I didn't know many families who owned their homes but a good place to start looking if you could afford it was in the "For Sale To Colored" section. One time when Pop had a steady job he had the nerve to tell us to look for a home in the "For Sale For Colored" section of the newspaper. I really felt things were going good with us because Pop always tried his best.

I overheard a conversation he had with Mom about a house he was trying to buy. The house was on Rowan Avenue and the mortgage payment would have been $108.00 a month. They debated and debated and finally came to the realization that $108.00 was just a bit beyond their meager budget. Lucky for us Pop decided against the purchase because he was laid off shortly after that day.

But we learned early that practice of steering people of color to the worse, rat infested areas continued. Pop always preached to us

Oath of Office

that the way to get around poverty was through education. That was preached everyday and reading was no laughing matter.

Thus, kids like Jimmie Pierce had little to no effect on me. We had class clowns but I knew to ignore them because they weren't going to stand in the path of my new car and fine suburban home one day.

I remember Jimmie told us he was going to drive a sleek automobile and pass by us while we stood on the bus stop. I clearly recalled him saying, "I'm going to have all the pretty ladies and I'll just leave a few scraps for you school boy squares." He would just walk away with a couple ladies on his arms and laugh at us. Now I have Jimmie Pierce, naked, dirty, smelling, and in handcuffs on the floor of a vacant apartment which he obviously hadn't rented. There was absolutely no furniture in the entire apartment and he was sleeping underneath a nasty, smelly, cotton blanket on the floor. I couldn't imagine one of my early FBI arrests would be an old schoolmate, a former class cut up.

As I shined my flashlight in his face, he looked at me and said, "Is that you Thornton?" I said, "Yes it is. What are you doing here?" My supervisor asked me if he was Jay Willis, our fugitive. I said, "No, this is Jimmie Pierce. I went to school with him in north St. Louis a few years ago." Pierce said, "Willis moved last week and I'm just sleeping here until I get myself together." We looked at the photograph and confirmed Pierce was not our fugitive.

After the team leader confirmed Pierce had no outstanding warrants, I recalled the team leader's last words to Pierce was, "Get the hell out of here and don't come back." Pierce said nothing but put on some nasty, dirty clothes he had in a plastic bag and I last saw him walking south on Big Bend Boulevard. I'm not sure whether he was more ashamed of looking like a bum, smelling so bad, or because he thought I might tell some of our old classmates about him. Nonetheless it was no longer funny watching a class clown because he no longer had a class to disrupt. Pierce had trained to be a bum, practiced his trade, and had turned out to be pretty successful at it.

I said, "Randy one day you'll meet the class clown and bully and it won't be so funny anymore." As I looked at him he appeared to be spellbound and stared at me, as he hadn't earlier. His grandpa said, "Are you going to say something Randy? I know your friend Romero is just like the guy he told you about. What have you got to say?" Randy just sat and stared without saying a word. It seemed for once, he was speechless.

****

Chapter Five

- MOTOWN IS MORE THAN MUSIC... -

I was transferred to the Detroit Field Office in August, 1980. At the time I had no idea how I ended up in Detroit. During those days offices such as Detroit were considered disciplinary offices. When an agent screwed up a case or got into trouble, as his punishment he would be sent to an undesirable place like Detroit, New York, or Newark. I couldn't understand my transfer to Detroit because I hadn't been around long enough to tick off anyone. I later realized it was just a routine transfer and I was glad to see no one was mad at me. In fact, the guys who really fell between the cracks had drawn the New York and Newark assignments.

Pop and Moms had a long conversation with me before I left for Detroit. Pop talked about the tough streets of Detroit during the old days and how I'd really have to watch the kids up there. He said, "Make sure you keep a close eye on the kids 'cause Detroit can be a tough place to raise 'em."

It seemed that Pop's friend, Mr. Thomas, was as inquisitive as Randy. He had talked to Pop about me many times but now Mr. Thomas wanted some answers for himself. Mr. Thomas was in his sixties and had lived through turmoil as a young man growing up in the south. I had heard Mr. Thomas and Pop swap stories but for once he wanted to see how it was to really talk to an FBI agent and get the real scoop. He said, "I've seen a few movies but they've always been about some guy sitting in an office and not really about the guys doing the real work. Tell us the real deal son. What actually goes on when you work in a big city? Have you ever seen anything happen and not been able to do anything about it?"

I explained to Mr. Thomas that living and working in an urban environment is hazardous and certainly can be very dangerous. Things happen in your presence and you do everything you can to help those involved but sometimes it just is not possible. Unfortunately while working undercover you have to balance the value of the information you're attempting to obtain with the seriousness of the offense being committed in your presence. Obviously the safety of yourself and the citizens you serve is a major factor to consider.

I said, "Keep in mind that while working in an urban environment, many crimes you might face may occur outside normal working hours." I began telling them about something that happened to me one Sunday as I left church with my son.

My son, Cary III was about seven years old when one Sunday after church; we had a street corner encounter with a criminal. Because of the heavy attendance that Sunday we decided to leave a few minutes early to avoid the rush of other departing worshippers. Because there were more cars than usual, we were forced to park on the opposite side of the highway, several blocks away from the church. As we walked across the Lodge Freeway overpass, we were virtually alone.

As an FBI agent I'm always looking around in order to spot trouble before it sees me first. This time I spotted trouble clearly by accident and I was forced to confront it. I looked across the highway on the south side away from the church and I saw a man with what appeared to be a long metal object in his hand. He was looking around nervously as he walked toward a late model Cadillac.

Oath of Office

I assumed the car belonged to one of the members of the church who had parked there. I took my son by the hand and hurriedly got into my vehicle that was parked in the opposite direction. As he climbed into the rear seat I told him to stay down because there might be trouble when we get around the corner.

I circled the block and as I approached the location of the Cadillac, the guy was leaning inside the driver's window that had been broken completely out. I again told my son to stay inside the car. He said, "O.K. daddy", very nervously. I sensed he understood I was about to do something.

I stopped my car directly behind this guy, less than a few inches from his backside. I quickly exited my car and told him to come out and show me his hands. I held my credential case and badge in one hand and my revolver in the other. The guy turned around, looked at me, and ran down the street. I chased after him and shouted, "Hold it, FBI!!" He had run about twenty yards then suddenly stopped and turned around in my direction. He began walking slowly toward me with a fifteen-inch screwdriver raised in the air. I knew that I had to act quickly in order to protect my son who was inside my car. I said to him, "Drop the screwdriver or you're a dead man!" My five-shot revolver was pointed at his chest area. He looked from left to right and continued walking in my direction. He was now about 20 feet away. My only thoughts were, what if he gets past me and gets to my son, who was nervously watching everything happen? The guy continued to walk in my direction with the raised screwdriver until he was about 10 feet away. I then raised the aim of my pistol directly between his eyes and said, "You've had it!" He stopped walking, looked around, and slowly began to lower the screwdriver. I can only assume that he really didn't think my revolver was real until he was close enough to see it. My Smith and Wesson Model 49 is a small frame, five-shot pistol. I carried the small revolver because I was assigned to an undercover case on the east side of Detroit. Small frame pistols are easy to conceal when you're wearing jeans and climbing under cars. When the guy finally stopped walking, he was close enough to clearly see that the pistol was real, my finger was on the trigger, and I was aiming dead center between his eyes.

The moment he glanced away from me, I moved toward him, hit him hard on the left side of his head, which caused him to drop the screwdriver and fall to the ground. As I rolled him over on his stomach, I let him feel the barrel of the pistol behind his neck. I then said, "Go ahead, make your momma cry, go ahead!!" I ordered him to spread his arms apart and dared him to move a muscle as I moved away from him. I shouted to my son, "Quick!! Knock on any door and ask whoever answers to call the police right away!!" He jumped out of the car and did exactly as I asked him. He knocked at one door and shouted until a lady answered the door. I held my badge in the air and shouted for her to dial 911 right away. I told my son to stay on the porch until the police arrived. Again he obeyed me with no questions.

It was cold that Sunday morning and there was a light dusting of snow on the ground. By now I had moved away from the guy and kicked the screwdriver far away from his reach. I dared him to move under threat of a bullet in his head. It seemed that the Detroit Police was taking forever to show up. It was cold on the ground and I could see the thief getting restless and attempting to move around. I let him know if he tried to get up it was over. I said, "If you try to get up, I'm booking your funeral!!" He said nothing in response to my threats.

Just when I thought I had my bluff over this guy, a strange looking guy walked up the street in my direction from the south. I saw my guy acknowledge him as if he knew him. He tried to do it quietly but I could see they knew one another. The guy got about ten feet from me I pointed my revolver on him and said, "Make one more step and you're a dead man! Don't take another step in this

Oath of Office

direction!" I ordered him on the ground next to the thief, even though he swore he didn't know the guy. I told him if his hand moved anywhere near his body I was shooting both of them in the nuts. Their arms were spread wide on the ground in the light snow. I'm sure they didn't want to give me any reason to put a bullet in them. I could hear them talking and I was then convinced the second guy thought he was coming to his rescue.

Because of my alertness, the second guy didn't get a chance to help his accomplice. My son and the helpful neighbor watched the entire event unfold in front of them from the porch. If things had gone bad they would not have been able to help me. Within a few more minutes, I finally heard sirens coming in my direction.

I knew that the discipline I had instilled in my son paid off. I only told him one time to stay inside the car and not to come near me. I could only imagine if I had to tell him four or five times to run to the neighbor's home for help. I shudder to imagine the results if I had had to repeat my instructions to him a dozen times before he moved or responded. If he had come near me, he may have easily become a hostage of either of the two thieves on the ground. As frightened as my son was that day, he remained on the neighbor's porch just as I asked him and stayed out of harms way. I became his hero that afternoon but in reality he was my hero for obeying me without any questions. I was proud of my son that cold, Sunday afternoon in Detroit. I will always be proud of him for being an obedient son. I hope that one day he will instill the same discipline into his children. On that cold Sunday afternoon, my son was my hero.

The Detroit Police responded with three squad cars. They quickly secured and searched my two suspects. My son came running when the police finally put the two suspects in the squad cars. Luckily this arrest turned out to my advantage. Two against one is not a fair fight but Smith and Wesson put the odds on my side. The Detroit Police had arrived on time as always……

C. Lee Thornton

****

On one cold winter afternoon my partner Ken Kirkland and I were driving west on Grand River Boulevard in the downtown Detroit. Ken was a family man with two kids and was destined for great things in the bureau from the day he stepped off the stage at his new agent graduation. We had been partners for a short time but we just seemed to click from our first meeting. Ken was the case agent on our undercover operation and I was the primary undercover agent. This simply meant I had the majority of the direct contact with our subjects. Ken was smart enough to know at an early stage in the project, that sometimes it wasn't very healthy working too close to the street bums. He was the case agent because he was simply smarter than John, the other undercover agent, and myself. One afternoon Ken and I were going to meet an informant that had promised to give us some auto theft information. It was about 2:00 p.m. and Grand River Blvd. was heavy with traffic and pedestrians just as any midday afternoon. People were going about their business as any normal day in Detroit. We glanced toward the doorway of an abandoned warehouse and I thought I saw two people standing too close for comfort. Because we were on the opposite side of the street driving west, we could barely see if the second person was male or female.

Ken, a former Detroit police officer, swung a wide U-turn in the middle of traffic and we jumped out of our car to investigate this unusual sighting. We quickly walked to the doorway where the two images were standing face to face. One of them was a short, very heavy, black guy whom we had startled when we approached him. He quickly turned around and pulled up his pants, which were below his knees. We both drew our revolvers and Ken said, "Move your hands away from your body and step away from the door!" Ken carried a chrome plated Smith and Wesson magnum which made his revolver easy to see in the darkened doorway. Our drawn revolvers had frightened the guy who reluctantly followed our directions. He slowly stepped away from the doorway of the warehouse and revealed a teenage, white female. She also began readjusting her clothes and pulled up her panties. She looked at us and started mumbling and waving her hands—it was obvious she was deaf and mute. Although her panties and dress were in disarray, she continued mumbling and began walking east on Grand River Boulevard. We were certain we had interrupted what appeared to be a rape in progress.

Ken went after the lady and tried to make her understand we were FBI agents. Even though he showed her his gold badge and credentials, she did not seem to understand him. I searched the man and handcuffed him as he stood in the doorway of the building. He kept telling us he she was his girlfriend and she was letting him do it to her. The guy was smelly, dirty, and about 30–35 years old. I felt like slapping his disgusting face with the butt of my revolver.

I couldn't believe a sane human being would rape or even have sex with a retarded teenager, in the doorway of a building, and at 2:00 in the afternoon. The lady seemed no older than 16 or 17 years old. There was a shelter home located near this building that we thought the teenager had apparently walked away. She appeared to be walking in that direction when Ken caught her and detained her.

We radioed for the Detroit Police to respond and they arrived in the next few minutes. The disgusting man was arrested and the police took the lady away to be identified. Unfortunately we had no way to communicate with the retarded teenager but we provided the responding officers with our statements. We never heard from the arresting officers after that day. We only hoped things worked out for the unfortunate retarded teenager. Urban streets are dangerous and sometimes disgusting.

****

FBI agents often find themselves faced with street incidents and sometimes we aren't always in a position to respond. Often while working undercover we simply have to take good notes and follow-up later with our office or the local police later. Sometimes a law enforcement response on our part could compromise months of investigation. The proper response can be difficult to make when someone is being harmed or injured in your presence. This was the case when Ken and I worked a long-term undercover operation based in Detroit called Operation Steamclean.

One morning Ken and I found ourselves on the west side of Detroit around 6:30 a.m. As usual we were chasing an informant lead. This guy was one of our tested informants who had proven to be fairly reliable in the past with the information about car chop shops. We knew he was sending us to a rough area of Detroit but we were accustomed to the neighborhood and we felt we'd be fairly safe during the early hours. We had been seen in that area so many times we blended in with the locals.

On that particular morning we had planned to meet a guy to make a deal on a stolen car. This was one of the cases when we planned to buy a straight steal to get closer to the dealers and chop shops in the area. By buying locally stolen cars that were being fenced, we'd buy creditability with the car thieves. They would see our operation had money to spend and they would want to deal with us in larger quantities later. Our main goal was to determine where stolen cars were being shipped after they left the Detroit area. We also wanted to determine who was ordering the stolen cars in Detroit.

Ken and I drove two separate cars that morning because I was the one planning to meet the guy. Ken had another undercover agent with him to act as the driver if the deal worked out. We sat in our cars waiting for a seller that we had never met. We were only

Oath of Office

provided his description by our informant and as the clock ticked, the guy was late. We didn't have cellular telephones during those days so we had to rely on our last communication with our informant. I sat close to the meeting location which was in a residential neighbor near Davison. I noticed a guy walking across the street in front of me with a plastic bag which seemed to be heavy with objects inside it. Ken and the other undercover agent could barely see the guy from where they sat about three cars behind me. The plastic bag seemed fairly heavy based on its obvious weight.

The strange looking guy walked to a home several doors from us without paying us any attention. The house was on the corner and was a two family unit that seemed to be in horrible disrepair. He knocked on the door several times and started shouting at someone inside the house. A lady came to the door and was mad as hell at the guy. They immediately became involved in a shouting match which drew the attention of everyone in the area. The two of them became involved in a hell of a fistfight. She was swinging at him with her fists and he was swinging the bag with what appeared to be canned goods. She was a small woman but she was holding her own against the guy with the plastic bag. She was landing lefts and rights to his head and body like a professional boxer. He continued to strike all over the body with the heavy plastic bag. There were a few neighbors on their porch that had heard the commotion but no one was going to intervene in the fight. One neighbor shouted at them from across the street to stop fighting or he was calling the police. They ignored his shouts and continued fighting like wild people.

We were on a time schedule and didn't know if our guy would show up in any moment so we just blew our car horn to get their attention and hopefully make them stop fighting. They just kept fighting uncontrollably on the porch. She was really landing some hard blows to his head. The man had taken all the punishment he could and jumped off the porch while she retreated to the house.

It looked as if the guy was looking for something to help him win the fight. He looked around the front yard but didn't appear to be leaving the property.

We thought the fight had ended until the woman reappeared at the front door with a long kitchen knife. The guy ran back on to the porch and started swinging the bag at her again. She resumed fighting and cursing like a sailor at him. Each time he would swing and missed, she would stick him in the side with the knife. Each time she'd stick him, he'd let out an "Uggh!!" and continued swinging at her head. He swung a second time and missed and he blurted out, "Uggh!!" but kept fighting. We continued to blow our horn at them just as several other passing motorists. By now neighbors had come out on their front porches and were shouting at them to stop fighting. The vicious fight continued and they refused to let up.

We held our positions and waited for our guy to meet us to discuss the stolen car. A neighbor shouted that he had called the police and they were on the way. The two fighters kept going at it like wild animals. The guy continued landing blows to her head with the bag however he paid for every missed attempt. The lady hung in the fight well, stabbing the guy no less than four times in his side. He just kept fighting and swinging the bag at her. Although he was landing blows to her head and body with the bag, it didn't seem to be affecting her at all. We assumed the guy had taken all the whipping and stabbing he could and he just quit fighting. He again jumped off the porch, this time bloody as hell all over his chest and both sides. The lady continued to curse and tell him what she was going to do to him. He now appeared to be looking for something larger than the bag of weighted goods in his bloody hand. He was looking on the ground around the building but couldn't find whatever he was looking for. He was now bloody as a stuck pig but still mad as hell and cursing the woman. It seemed that he just gave up and decided he'd better go while he could still walk away.

The poor guy walked back across the street carrying the plastic bag in somewhat of a hurry. This time he was defeated and looked as if he had run into a meat cleaver. His clothes were ripped and bloody and he retreated down the same street from where he had walked earlier that morning. The lady shouted as he walked away and said, "M.....f..... Don't come back here f.....g with me again. Get away from here!!" She went back into the house with the dripping bloody knife. Our guy never showed up so we left before the Detroit Police arrived. By now we could hear sirens coming in our direction. There were plenty neighbors and eyewitnesses around to tell the police what had happened if they asked. The poor defeated guy was nowhere to be found. The poor guy had just received the whipping of his life and had barely gotten away alive. In this case for the sake of our cover, he was on his own.

We could only assume the flashing lights and police cars kept our guy away from us that morning.

****

To say the streets of an urban city can be dangerous is a gross understatement. We often found ourselves moving about at the direction of informants and sometimes not sure what to expect next. On another occasion we found ourselves on the eastside of Detroit, again waiting for something to happen. It was the middle of July and the temperature was in the upper 80's. Ken and I sat in front of an informant's house debriefing him about an auto theft ring operating near his neighborhood. A lady walked hurriedly past the house where we waited and toward a vacant lot about a half block away. The lady was dressed in jeans and old clothes and seemed to be upset about something. But she wasn't saying a word to anyone. She just kept walking and mumbling to herself. It was obvious she was either high or mentally unstable or both. We were both dressed in old clothes and blended into the neighborhood as we watched the lady go through her gyrations. We then noticed the woman, who was small in stature, become involved in a loud argument with another woman who was standing on the vacant lot.

Both women shouted louder and louder to a point everyone on the block could hear them. Suddenly, the shorter of the two ladies went into a boxer's stance and began swinging at the taller lady. They both started swinging and landing hard punches to the face of the other. They were only throwing and connecting headshots, they threw nothing to the body. After receiving several headshots in a row and dancing like Muhammad Ali, the shorter lady went down on one knee and quit fighting. She seemed to be taking an official eight count. The taller lady quit fighting and continued to curse and dance around the parking lot. Everyone could still hear the commotion from the parking lot and dozens of onlookers stood on their porches to watch the fight.

By now the neighborhood had become involved in the fight but only from a distance. We thought someone would have pulled the two apart but no one was getting close to them out of fear of receiving some of the whipping being given out. The smaller woman rose from one knee and found a new burst of energy to resume the fight. She began swinging and connecting blows again to the head of her opponent again. Just as we thought we'd have to run down and break up the fight, a guy came running from nowhere with a large empty trashcan toward the fighters. We assumed he was going to throw the trashcan between them to separate the dueling pair. When he got about ten feet from them, he turned the trashcan on its bottom, sat on it, and took a close ringside seat to better view the action. He watched intently, with his head in his hands, from his perch, while the two women continued to swing and curse at one another.

By now the two had fought and sparred around the vacant lot for at least five minutes. As we walked toward the two to break up the

Oath of Office

fight, along with several other people from the neighborhood, the shorter woman suddenly quit fighting and stepped back again. The taller woman turned and walked in the opposite direction. Although the shorter lady cursed and had resumed landing some solid punches, she had clearly lost the fight and looked like it. Her clothes were torn but she surprisingly had not lost any blood. The only sign she showed of a fight was a severely red face. She walked down the street as fast as she walked up. It seemed the only person upset was the guy who sat on the trashcan. He began to curse and to beg for more action out of the two of them, but the fight was over and the combatants were gone. We managed to maintain our cover in the neighborhood and finished debriefing our informant.

****

Mother's Day, 1991 was an unusually beautiful day in Detroit. I had attended church that morning and had received my weekly dose of fire and brimstone. The minister was an eloquent speaker that never let you down. It was as if I had just attended a concert and got my money's worth and more. Life was good. I was in good health, and had just filled my spiritual gas tank to get me through the week. Little did I know I would soon meet a challenge later in the day to test my endurance, faith, and make me question my own sanity.

After church I decided I would go to visit a family friend. That afternoon my friend Elsie, who later became my wife, and I had planned to visit with Mama Mabel. Ms. Mabel Horn was a good friend of the family and was all of 95 years young. She was a very wise older lady. Even at 95, her mind was sharp as a tack. She would sit and talk for hours about things that occurred 50 years ago and recall events as if they had occurred yesterday. Her accounts would be remarkable and it was as if you were watching a historical movie rather than listening to her. I figured that an afternoon with Mama

C. Lee Thornton

Mabel, gathering wisdom, would be well spent and after all, it was Mother's Day.

As I exited the John Lodge Freeway and prepared to turn south on Livernois, I noticed a large crowd had gathered across the street on the opposite corner. I could barely see through the crowd of people but I saw someone with a large object appearing to be swinging and hitting a person on the ground. It seemed that the recipient of the blows was in trouble.

This was shortly after the Rodney King beating which was clearly on everyone's mind during this time. King was beaten unmercifully on a public street by a group of police officers, while citizens stood by and watched the events unfold. The trial had not yet occurred but no one knew why the officers continued to beat the defenseless man. I was a sworn law enforcement officer and no one was going to be beaten like Rodney King in my presence—cops or not.

I immediately made a quick right turn and a U-turn directly into the front of the crowd. I could recall Elsie telling me not to get involved and to let the police handle it. I turned a deaf ear to her because by now I could see the guy on the ground was being beaten unmercifully by a man standing over him. Every time he struck the guy with the baseball bat, the crowd of onlookers would shout and cheer. I told her to stay in the car near the steering wheel just in case we had to get out fast.

I jumped out of my car and reached for my credentials and revolver in the same motion. The last word I heard from her was, "No, don't get involved!!" I pushed my way through the large crowd of onlookers and saw the guy with a baseball bat in the middle of the crowd. He was swinging and hitting the guy like a dead animal. The guy on the ground was screaming each time he landed a blow from the baseball bat. Each time he struck the guy, the crowd shouted as if he was hitting a home run. It was a mob action in process.

Oath of Office

    Without realizing the position I had put myself in, I stepped in front of the crowd and pointed my five shot revolver at the face of the guy with the bat. I held my gold badge up and shouted, "FBI, drop the bat!!" The crowd briefly stepped back. They kept shouting, "Kill the m.....f.....!! Kick his ass!!" By now I'm not sure if they meant the guy on the ground or me. But I didn't back off and repeated my demand to the guy with the bat.

    He looked directly at me and hesitated momentarily. He saw my revolver pointed at him, as I demanded that he lower the baseball bat. The crowd continued to urge him to hit the guy again. He stared down the barrel of my pistol for a moment, which seemed to be an eternity, although it was actually only a few seconds. Someone in the crowd said the guy had just caught him breaking into his car. I could see a vehicle parked at the curb with the passenger side window broken out. Shattered glass was all over the ground.

    I repeated, "FBI, drop the bat or you're a dead man!!" The guy slowly lowered the bat. He took his eyes off of me for just a moment and I grabbed him and spun him over the hood of my car. As I wrestled with the 250 pound, baseball bat wielding, crazy man, I could still see Elsie inside the car. The crowd continued to agitate while I struggled with the guy who didn't want to hold still.

    This was before cellular telephones were commonplace, so I had no way to contact the Detroit Police other than to wave at passing motorists. I found myself all alone with an angry crowd of no less than 20 people who were all demanding to see some more action. I glanced over to the guy on the ground who was a bloody mess. His clothes were dirty and he was bloody especially from the waist down. His right pant leg was ripped and bloody to the bottom. The bone in right thigh was protruding through his pants and bleeding profusely. He was trying to crawl away but the crowd stood in his path. I told him to stay still and not to move. He only mumbled but I could tell he was grateful he was not receiving any more blows from the baseball bat.

There was no sign of anyone willing to give me assistance with the huge guy I was holding against the hood of my car in the midst of an angry crowd. The crowd got louder and louder and had apparently given the huge guy an added dose of street corner courage. I was determined he was not going anywhere but he had other thoughts in mind. This guy was at least six inches taller than me but I made up the difference with Mr. Smith and Wesson. In one big push, he used his massive stomach and pushed himself off the hood of my car. This time I knew I'd have to shoot him or pay the price for not doing so. I thrust my revolver into his crotch and said, "Your next move, you're dead. Don't move!!" He looked into my eyes, felt the barrel of my pistol in his groin, and lay back on the hood of my car. When he turned over on the hood of my car, I stuck the barrel of my pistol into his rear end where he could feel it. I couldn't believe that with all the commotion, no one had called the police.

The crowd continued to grow and it didn't seem that anyone was on my side. The poor guy on the ground was virtually passed out and starting to lose consciousness. Just when I thought I had to make a drastic decision and try to throw that big massive guy on the ground, a guy came running through the crowd with a badge and a gun drawn. The crowd now started to step back. Now they saw two crazy guys who looked like they were ready to start shooting. No one wanted to be next. The guy told me he was a Wayne County Sheriff and I thanked him. I told him to hold the crowd back and I'll handle the huge, baseball bat-wielding guy. Suddenly, I heard sirens and it sounded like the cavalry coming to our rescue. It seemed like it took the local police days to arrive, time seemed to move so slowly since I had jumped out of my car to risk my life for a car thief.

The first to arrive was an EMS van that immediately went to the guy on the ground. He was in bad shape but still alive. Several

Oath of Office

moments later two Detroit Police squad cars arrived and took the suspect giant off the hood of my car. I was certain to hold my gold badge in clear view as they approached me. I didn't want to be mistaken for some thug with a gun and become another victim. The sheriff deputy kept his badge in plain view, too. We had both been in Detroit long enough to know that an accident can happen and we weren't going to cause any that day.

After I was relieved of the big guy, I explained to the officer in charge what I had just witnessed. I thanked them for showing up before this thing got too far out of control. The sheriff deputy and I exchanged cards although we never got together again to talk about our near miss with disaster.

Needless to say, it took several hours to calm my friend. She said she thought the crowd would have taken me if the police hadn't arrived in time. However, we went on to visit Mama Mabel that afternoon. After telling her the more dramatic account of what had just occurred she calmly said, "Baby, you know you didn't have to worry 'bout nothing. God was watchin' over you." Although I tried not to show it, my heart was still beating pretty fast but somehow her words of wisdom calmed me. I suppose that's how Mama Mabel lived to be 95 years old—she had always put her trust in God.

****

From time to time as an FBI agent you might find yourself reaching out to people whom you would generally never have contact. Sometimes I found myself extending a hand simply because it was the right thing to do and that was how I was raised. I was always taught to never be so content or high and mighty that I couldn't bend over to help a man that's down on his luck. I realized I could have been in his position had it not been for Pop and Him. I met a guy in that stage of life one afternoon early in my tour in Detroit.

Once I was assigned to investigate a case when the facts took us to a home to interview a man about his knowledge of a major property theft ring. Although the man was not a subject in the case, we felt, because of some of his associations, he could provide us valuable information that could close the investigation for us.

We went to his address several times and found the home empty. We returned one afternoon and found his wife at home in the middle of the day. We earlier assumed everyone worked but since we were in the neighborhood thought we'd try another time. She seemed startled that someone would come to her door in the middle of a hot day in July looking for her husband. She immediately noticed we wore suits and were well dressed for the hot day. Ms. Jackson was probably a very pretty lady. She was of medium height, well built and appeared to be extremely intelligent. On this particular day though, she didn't look attractive with her unkempt hair. When she answered the door, she stood next to a man whom we did not recognize as her husband according to the photograph we had with us. They were holding one another fairly close at the time. It was obvious they were still in the dating stages of the relationship because they were just too happy and clinging close to one another. The man was well over six feet tall, approximately 250 pounds, bulging muscles under a tank top, and wearing casual shorts as if he was lounging around the house. The guy had a scar across his face as if he had been in a fight. Frankly, the guy looked like someone who may have just been released from prison.

Mrs. Jackson immediately told us she was Lenny Jackson's estranged wife and the man next to her was her new boyfriend. She provided the boyfriend portion of her explanation voluntarily. Mrs. Jackson told us that Lenny Jackson was no longer allowed at the home and her new boyfriend was going to make sure he didn't come back again. She was extremely hostile at the mention of the

Oath of Office

name Lenny Jackson. Whatever Jackson had done to the lady, she was mad and had an enforcer to carry out her will.

Mrs. Jackson said she no longer wanted to see Lenny nor did his five-year old daughter. The boyfriend kept interrupting her statements by saying he was not allowed in his house anymore. We didn't ask, but we couldn't understand why the boyfriend was so concerned about a lady who was obviously still married to another man. Throughout the time we talked to Mrs. Jackson, the little girl hugged the leg of the new boyfriend. She had apparently grown very fond of the new boyfriend and fancied him as her protector and her "new daddy".

After Mrs. Jackson and her boyfriend made their point perfectly clear, we asked if she knew where her estranged husband was living. She said, "I have no idea nor do I care where he is living as long as he doesn't bother us." She said the last she heard he was working for the city of Detroit in the Refuge Department near the Davison Freeway. She told us that if we saw him, he owed her money for child support and she wanted it right away. The boyfriend said, "Yeah, he hasn't brought us any money lately and we need it." We didn't respond to him or address anything he said in the midst of our conversation. The boyfriend seemed to be running the house in the absence of Lenny Jackson. Whatever Jackson had done, his wife and her boyfriend were angry with him. She was so angry that she had a huge bouncer to enforce her rules. We thanked her for the information and left the home. I really felt sorry for the poor guy who no longer had a home to return. As we left, the child and Jackson's estranged wife seemed to be fairly content with the way things were going.

That same afternoon we drove to the Detroit City Refuge Department located near Highland Park, Michigan where Mrs. Jackson had directed us. It was a bright, hot, sunny day and the sun was cooking the garbage and refuge that had been spilled over the waste yard. The refuge yard was full of flies and we knew that as soon as we got home our clothes were destined for the cleaners. We never received a clothing allowance although we argued for one on a regular basis. The bureau felt they paid us enough money to clean our own clothes.

No one seemed to notice that we were lost and needed help. We went to what appeared to be the main office and asked a secretary if we could to speak to the manager. The secretary smoked a long filtered cigarette and wore heavy makeup. She was an over-weight, middle-aged woman who wore a pair of what appeared to be "kiddie" jeans judging from the size and style. They were too small and ten years too youthful for her. She took a long puff off her cigarette, blew the smoke in our direction and asked, "Who are you guys?" Neither of us spoke as we showed her our FBI credentials. She looked over her wire-rimmed glasses and shouted, "Tommy! Some FBI guys wanna talk to ya!" A few moments later a large smelly guy came out of the rear office and introduced himself as, Tommy, the man in charge. We could see he was really proud of his position as the boss. He seemed to be proud of the fine operation he was running.

He told us Lenny Jackson was a temporary worker whom he uses when regular guys don't show up for work. He said, "Since Lenny is a temp, we have few if any personnel records on the guy. He asked, "Donna have you got any records on that temp guy, Lenny Jackson?" She got up from the desk as if she was going to hunt for the records but not until she took one more puff off her cigarette. She then took a big stretch so that everyone could see her over sized chest and undersized jeans. The manager said Lenny Jackson was a good worker who would show up early every morning anxious to work. Tommy said he wished that he could keep Lenny full-time but he only had so much payroll and other workers took all the available routes.

Oath of Office

After the secretary checked her records she said that Lenny Jackson was not working on that hot, July afternoon. It may have been good for him with the sun cooking everything outside to a crisp. But unfortunately Jackson needed to work in the worse way. She shouted from the rear room, "You guys might just find him hangin' 'round the scrap yard. I saw him earlier this afternoon." The boss told us he heard the guy was having trouble at home and really didn't have anywhere to sleep. He said he assumed he slept in the trucks at night, although it was against company policy. He told us, "More than anything, it is dangerous sleeping in the trucks out here 'cause a rat or something might bite him." I wondered after seeing Jackson's state in life, if he had a secret death wish. Jackson had run into a streak of bad luck and we certainly didn't want to make it any worse.

We thanked them for the information and walked through the hot, smelly, scrap yard looking for Jackson. My partner had talked to Jackson several times so he knew him if he saw him out there. The 85 degree plus heat and the hot sun really was doing a job with the garbage that had spilled all over the scrap yard. The flies were literally having a picnic feasting on everything from garbage to dead carcasses. I could not imagine how anyone could work at that place all day, and heaven help him if he had to sleep there at night. We hunted all over the scrap yard and finally walked up on a guy eating a vending machine sandwich and sitting on a barrel. Ken recognized the guy as Lenny Jackson.

Jackson was dirty and smelled like his surroundings. He chewed the sandwich like it was filet mignon. He did his best to keep the wrapper against the smelly cold cut sandwich but it kept sliding down. Next to him set a can of Coke that had attracted its share of flies. Jackson continued to dine in possibly the only shaded spot in the refuge yard. He looked up and seemed happy to see a familiar face but kept eating as if it was his last meal. Ken said, "Hey Lenny, how is it going man?" He said, "Look at me man. Does it look like I'm doing good? Man, life is tough but I try to handle things day by day."

Jackson immediately went into the story about his wife, whom he said he still loved although they had some problems. He knew all about the boyfriend who had moved into his house and took his family. He couldn't understand why his wife didn't want to work things out because he still loved her. We listened and he started to cry while telling us how he lost his truck drivers job due to a work slow down. Jackson said, "I was on top of the world one day and the next thing I knew I was walking the streets, homeless, and just happened to walk into this city refuge yard. I literally begged Tom to let me fill in whenever guys don't show up in the mornings. Man, I even hit on that old woman to get her to talk to Tom for me. I had to swallow my pride but I did what I had to do to survive." Jackson said the guy felt sorry for him and told him to hang around one day to see if anyone calls off. Jackson said Tom pays him under the table so he could get a couple days work a week.

Jackson told us when he was not working; he hung around the yard because he couldn't go home. He cried when he told us he only had the clothes on his back when his wife's boyfriend threw him out of his own house. Jackson said, "I wanted to shoot him but I didn't want to go to jail and be away from my wife and daughter. He beat me half to death in front of my wife and kid. She used to go with the guy before he went to prison but I thought that was all over." The poor guy continued to cry and tell us he has no reason to live if he can't get his family back.

We told Jackson we wanted to talk to him about some guys he worked with as a truck driver. He explained he hadn't seen any of them in several months and had no idea where they lived. He just continued to cry and talk about his pretty wife and daughter. I didn't have the heart to tell him we had spoken to his wife and she seemed pretty happy with her new life with the ex-con; and there was no way I was going to tell this guy she wanted money from him. Jackson was by far the saddest person I have ever seen in my life. The poor guy repeated over and over that he wanted to end his life. I did my best to convince him that although life was tough, it was worth living. I told Jackson, "Look man, sometimes you've got to move on and do what you have to in order to move on. Just like you had one family, you can get another. You're a young man with a lot more good life to live. But you've got to look ahead." For some strange reason, Jackson suddenly quit crying and looked up at me.

Jackson went on to tell us he usually hangs around the scrap yard at night and hides inside the cab of trucks in order to have a place to sleep. He described the dozens of rats who feast on garbage spilled over the yard after dark. He said a rat has never bitten him but he has been lucky so far.

We told Jackson good luck and I handed him a twenty-dollar bill from my money clip. I told him, "Look, I know this won't do a lot for you, but go over on Woodward to a restaurant and get a decent meal." I suggested to him while he was on Woodward, to knock on the door of the biggest church he could find and ask to see the minister. I told him to explain his story to one of the preachers and ask him for help. I said, "Lenny there are as many churches in this neighborhood as there are liquor stores and both of them are all supported by poor people. They give their hard earned money and public assistance money to the churches every week and liquor stores everyday. I'm not too sure the same folks don't own all of them. After all, most preachers boast about helping the community all the time. Hell, man most of the churches have living quarters where the preachers live like kings when they are away from their suburban homes. Ask one of them if you can sleep in the basement and clean the place until you can get on your feet. Tell the preacher you need the help he talks about that Jesus gave to the poor."

Jackson said he would do that as soon as he got a good meal but he was going to make sure the yard wasn't locked before he got back that evening. He said, "Man, that's a good idea, but I really don't trust preachers, they're all talk. But I'll try your suggestion anyway. I've gotta get started somewhere."

Before we left, Jackson asked us to do him a favor; if we see his wife and daughter, he said, "Tell them I love them and I want to make our lives work." All I could think about was the big, bald headed, ex-con hugging his wife and kid—poor guy. I just said O.K. and left him standing in the rubbish yard, still savoring a luke warm cold cut sandwich. I know its always three sides to every story. There's her side, his side, and the truth somewhere in the middle. We wondered how the truth would sound after listening to both of them.

****

Chapter Six

- THIS AIN'T THE MOVIES -

More than any other question, inquisitive people have always asked me if I've ever shot anyone. Most people think an actual shooting is like it is in the movies. The person spins around and makes a dying declaration while the cops stop by the donut shop to brag with their buddies. Many citizens have never really seen anyone shot in real life. A shooting incident is definitely not as portrayed on television or in the movies. Most people never see a real shooting victim as he reels around in pain on the hot ground and cries out for Jesus to help him. None of them has ever seen the poor guy lying in the hot sun while he waits motionless for EMS. Most people never see the flies accumulate on the body as the motionless body waits for EMS to arrive.

My first shooting when I returned fire was nothing at all like it is in the movies. I was so busy trying to survive I didn't have time to be afraid. It was all completely by instinct and all of my training somehow kicked in automatically.

I recalled watching the Monday Night Football game in the rear bedroom of my home. The kids had relinquished their room to me since Monday night was my time and the game was televised fairly late. Somehow prior to the end of the game I had fallen asleep on my son's bed and I was lying beneath an open window. I had fallen asleep during the football game and I had left the television set on. It has always been said that God wakes you when he's ready. For some reason I was awakened before my normal time of 5:00 a.m. when I started my regular day. When I was awakened it somehow seemed terribly early because it was still dark outside and the curtains were blowing in the brisk wind. I found myself awake for some reason and staring at the blowing curtains, although it was still at least an hour before my normal rising time. I recalled the curtains were standing up, blowing in the wind, and seemed to be my message that morning.

As I stared at the blowing curtains, I suddenly heard a loud knocking noise at the rear door of my house. I first thought it was only the wind but the noise continued and was unusually loud. I knew then I was not asleep and dreaming. I sat up in the small bed and realized there really was a knocking noise at the rear door of my house. While still somewhat dazed from being awakened so early, I slowly walked to the rear door all the while trying to clear my eyes and groggy head. I opened the curtain at the rear door window to expose the small opening in the door. I looked out and saw a man staring through the door at me. He had practically ripped my storm door off the hinges and was working on the last line of defense to my house.

I yelled at him, "Get the hell away from here!!" He looked at me and said, "Open up!" I ran through the house to my dark bedroom, reached in the far corner of the closet top shelf, and grabbed my loaded service revolver. I knew exactly where to reach because I always kept my service revolver where the kids couldn't reach the shelf. I assumed since the guy knew I had seen him, I'd see him run past the front of the house and I'd get a look at him. I looked out of the front door but didn't see anyone running. Somehow I still heard the noise continuing at the rear door and getting louder.

I knew now this guy was still trying to come through my rear door and enter the house.

With my service revolver drawn, I ran to the rear of the house: a thousand thoughts going through my mind. I told myself I had to stop this crazy man because I was the last line of defense for my family. If that guy got past me, he's inside and could hurt my family. My only thought then became, he is not getting past me without a fight. When I returned to the rear door, the crazy man was still pulling against my rear door lock, attempting to tear the door off. I shouted, "FBI, back up and show me your hands!!" The guy slowly moved back and started to walk off my small rear porch. I threw the door open, pointed my revolver in his direction, and insured I was shielded by the inside of the door well. By now the guy was staggering and was about ten feet away from me. I again shouted, "Show me your hands!!"

The guy slowly spun around in my direction, while reaching from his waist, and began to lift his right arm in a drawing motion. My instinct and training instantly flashed in my mind. My training had taught me to get in a defensive position and prepare for the worse in a situation like this one. By now I was kneeling and partially bladed by the door, which was my only cover. I knew his next motion would be facing my direction while he appeared to be drawing an object from his waist area. In an instant I thought about what would happen if this guy got past me or shot me. My wife and kids were inside the house and defenseless against this crazy man. I told myself that I was not going to wait for him to fire at me first. I didn't want him to be lucky enough to hit his target and find his way into my home. I thought to myself, "If I was about to make the wrong move, then let me be judged. This guy was not going to fire first." From a slightly kneeling position, I fired one round from my revolver in his direction and it seemed the bullet left my revolver in slow motion. I literally saw the bullet spiraling from my revolver and landing in the man's rear end.

At that point everything appeared to happen in slow motion. I saw his feet slowly leave the ground as if an NFL lineman had hit him. He appeared to slowly rise into the air about four feet and land on his shoulders to momentarily lay motionless. Almost in an instant, I could hear sirens coming in my direction. I peeked from my bladed position behind my door and watched the guy start to slowly wiggle on the ground. I shouted, "Show me your hands!" I knew then he had been hit by my one shot somewhere in his lower body, as evidence of the squirting blood he was leaving on the ground. He sat up and fell from left to right as he staggered onto his feet. He staggered through my driveway, where my two cars were parked. The driveway was completely dark which, allowed him plenty cover to escape from me.

Again instinct and training began to guide my judgment. I could see the guy falling over my cars as he staggered through my driveway. He had obviously been wounded but still moving away from me. I felt if I followed directly behind him he might have someone with him who was hiding in the dark and waiting to attack me. I knew I had no choice but to win this fight and on my terms. I shouted to my wife and kids not to come outside. Although it was a greater distance, I ran around the opposite side of my house in order to get to the front of the house. I was attempting to see if I could spot the wounded guy and get a description of him if he was trying to escape. I didn't see anyone and I assumed he was still hiding in my driveway possibly between my cars. The sirens seemed to get closer and closer to my home as I looked for cover and peered into the driveway. Unfortunately the Oak Park Police still hadn't arrived nor did I see the suspect in the dark.

I kneeled behind my car and with my revolver drawn, I aimed into the driveway. With five rounds remaining in my service revolver,

Oath of Office

I moved closer to the front of the driveway. As I approached the darkened driveway I saw movement in my next-door neighbor's hedges. Although it was dark, I pointed my revolver in the direction of the noise and ordered the person to come out and to show me his hands. As I kneeled down and without warning, the guy dove out through the hedges directly at me. He landed just a few feet away from me with his outstretched arms reaching toward me. I fired low in front of him while moving out of his reach. The single round landed in the ground and kicked dirt high into the air. This time my shot clearly missed him although I did not fire to hit him. Contrary to my training, I didn't fire a second shot in the direction of my target. I'm certain I could have hit him with the second shot but since he was retreating, he didn't pose an immediate threat to me. He jumped back into the hedges without saying a word. He had landed close enough for me to fire directly into his skull.....but I didn't shoot the second round to hit him.

By this time the Oak Park Police had arrived. I waved my gold badge in the air in their direction. It was dark and I didn't want the police officers to make any mistakes that might cause them to think I was the burglar. I realized there was an advantage to having gold badges at night, with very little light, they can still be seen. Still kneeling behind my car, I shouted to the officers that the guy was wounded and hiding in the hedges in front of my next door neighbor's home. The officers converged on the area after we all ordered the guy out several times. They had completely surrounded him. They pulled him out and cuffed him as he bled from his leg.

I finally got a look at the person who interrupted my sleep early that morning. He was grimy, bloody, and I had never seen him before in my life. His eyes looked like those of a crazed maniac. I still couldn't understand why he chose my house at 4:00 in the morning. I looked toward my house as the ambulance took the guy away and realized my family was still terrified and in a daze. My youngest daughter was very young at the time but she had the look of horror on her face after the shooting. The only comfort I could give my tiny daughter was a long hug.

The guy was taken to the local hospital with a bullet wound to the side of his right leg. Although no weapons were found on him, a hypodermic syringe was found in his sock. According to the police officers the guy was apparently under the influence of some type of drug.

In about thirty minutes my house was swarming with FBI agents from the Detroit field office. We were trying to determine if this guy had any connections with any cases that I had investigated. We later determined the intruder was a heroin addict who actually lived about a block away from me with his family. He may have lost his way home and decided to break into a home to get drug money. Unfortunately, he tried the wrong house and could have been killed.

The one thing you never see on the movies is a true account of what happens after a shooting. After my shooting the Oak Park Police seized my service revolver for a ballistics test. This was probably the most venerable I had ever felt in my life. I felt completely naked with no firearm at my disposal to protect my family. Thank goodness, Ben Roberts, one of my co-workers arrived and handed me his service revolver. My FBI family stayed with my family for several hours to calm us down after the police left our house that morning.

Another thing you never see on the movies is the local police who immediately request a statement about the shooting that had just occurred. Later that morning my office legal staff also ordered me to provide a statement about the same events. In reality, my recollection of the event at 4:00 a.m. and 11:00 a.m. may have been slightly different. I was forced within a very short time to get all my facts straight and to provide them in writing to the authorities.

I was put on administrative leave for three days following the shooting. It didn't take long to realize that three days was a lot of time to be home alone and to ponder over a shooting. I also had to think about whether my office was going to determine my act to be a "good shooting" or a "bad shooting". The bureau psychiatrist, Dr. John Suskin, called me about 10:00 a.m. the next day after the shooting at my home. He asked me a lot of questions to basically determine if I appeared to be crazy or stable. He also tried to assist me with any apparent problems that I may have been experiencing as a result of the shooting. With the exception of the "what if's" I felt I was just fine. I still worried about my family and especially my youngest daughter who seemed to suddenly have problems sleeping. I had no choice in the matter; I had to be the strong one for my family.

An interim director headed the FBI during the fall of 1984. Judge William Webster had recently left the leadership of the FBI and John Otto had been appointed the interim acting director. I never had any idea that anyone in upper management ever knew I was alive until later the day when John Otto called me at home. That was a good gesture from FBI headquarters; I really didn't think upper level managers cared about the real agents until that day. He was cordial and seemed to show genuine concern for my family and me. After two days off work, I couldn't take being away from the office any longer, although I was allotted three days off. I went back to work on the third day for my own sanity and just to be around my co-workers again.

Psychologically, I played the shooting scene over and over in my mind. Unlike the macho gunslingers on television, I started to developed a hell of a case of the "what if's". What if I had missed my first shot at the burglar? What if he had fired first and hit me? Who would have stood in the door to protect my family? What if someone had jumped me when I ran outside after the guy? But I reflected back to how everything I did was by instinct and training. I surmised that my FBI training had kicked in and I did everything right. That's why I won the fight and lived to tell about it.

My family never had another restful night sleep in our Oak Park, Michigan home after that dreadful day. My youngest daughter, Christy, frequently cried and couldn't sleep alone in her bed any longer. The kids constantly talked about what would have happened if the bad guy got past Daddy. The possible outcomes were too horrible to ponder and were best left alone. We bought another home and we moved from Oak Park, Michigan about six weeks later. That was our way of putting that awful night behind us and attempting to forget September 1984.

The intruder was later prosecuted in local court for attempted burglary of a home.

****

In the world of law enforcement the primary source of information and intelligence is a good informant base. However any police officer or federal agent knows you can live or die by the actions of your informants. They can get you into deep trouble or make you look like a hero depending upon how you control them. I realized early in my career it was always good to keep informants beholding to you. I always kept a carrot dangling in front of my informants to make them work just a little harder and to keep them honest.

As a rule you never get to close to an informant or his family regardless of how tough things were going in their lives. I never let them think I gave a damn about them or anyone related to them. An experienced federal agent or police officer never dealt with an informant while alone and especially with informants of the opposite sex. In fact I tried to make it a policy to never deal with female informants, especially the pretty ones....that was the best way in the world to get in trouble. Many police officers and federal agents paid a big price for violating these basic rules. Most of these rules aren't taught in the academy, they're taught on the streets. After all, most informants are accustomed to trouble and finding a way out of it.

I tried to live by those rules and they saved my rear more than enough times over the years. I learned my best lesson when I recruited Glenn Parks as an informant in Detroit during the early eighties. When I met him he was out of control, he was a federal agent's worse nightmare. Although when he was under control, you couldn't operate without him. Controlling Glenn was the problem the majority of the time.

I met Glenn Parks when he was about to be arrested by the Detroit Police on a drug possession charge. The charges were marijuana possession, which due to the small quantity of drugs, he was more of a nuisance than anything else. I spoke to the officers involved and they agreed to give Glenn a ticket rather than adding to his long list of arrests. In this case a ticket was their option and a lot less paperwork for an offense that would probably never be heard in court anyway. The officers took his marijuana roach, gave him a stern lecture, and turned him over to me that afternoon. I managed to convince Glenn that I went through a lot of crap to spring him from jail and he owed me for my effort.

Glenn had two small children and a wife, who for whatever reason, wanted him at home. I just couldn't understand their logic because Glenn was nothing more than a hype anyway. A hype is a hard-core drug user who travels with dealers as they go about their days work selling drugs. Glenn's dealer sold heroin and cocaine on the west side of Detroit, Michigan. Glenn would travel with the guy and allowed himself to be used to test the strength of the dope for the buyers. The dealer would allow Glenn shoot heroin into his arm in order to show the buyer the dope was a good strength. The hype would normally inject the drugs wherever he could find a vein that wasn't already collapsed. The buyer would watch Glenn nod out, symbolizing a good high. In order to show the buyer he had good cocaine, the dealer would let Glenn inhale a spoon of coke into his nasty little nostrils. Glenn would pump up immediately and start jumping around.

The buyer would then decide on cocaine or heroin based on how Glenn reacted or what he planned to buy. The dealer would get a sale, the customer would have confidence, and Glenn would get a free high. Everyone was happy and went his own way. From time to time Glenn would get a few dollars for his trouble, which he would normally use to buy more drugs from the same dealer. Glenn performed this service for several dealers including his dad who was also a noted drug dealer in Detroit.

Based on Glenn's profile we knew he could probably give us a large shipment from time to time. Although we weren't sure and could never prove it, we always thought Glenn kept a shipment for himself from time to time just to help his suppliers. We always suspected it but we could never prove it, so we watched him closely. Sometimes a hype would try to sell information to the fed's and sell other information to the local police. We later found out Glenn was selling information to the FBI, DEA, the Detroit Police, and anyone who'd buy it from him. Like any slick informant he would sell his information to the highest paying agency. Generally the fed's paid better and faster. When I met Glenn I had planned to give new meaning to "slow and no pay".

However Glenn was one of the best informants in town for making federal and local cases on local drug dealers. I knew I was taking a chance with him but I felt I could control him since he was indebted to me. After I sprung him on the first day I met him, I let Glenn know that he owed me big. He agreed to work for me by keeping his ears open for incoming shipments of heroin and cocaine to Detroit. He swore to me everyone was dry at the time I met him. He swore to me he was working hard to stay clean but always

Oath of Office

said, "Man, staying clean ain't like talkin' about it." I gave Glenn my business card that Friday afternoon and told him to call me on the following Monday. When I last saw him he was walking home to his apartment on Schaffer in Detroit. That turned out to be an unwise gesture on my part and a good learning experience.

Early the very next morning, which was Saturday, I received a call from the Schaefer District of the Detroit Police Department. The police officer told me Glenn Parks had been arrested early that morning. The Detroit Police Department had been called as Glenn Parks was casing homes for burglaries in his neighborhood. A citizen was alerted when Glenn knocked on her door and introduced himself as FBI Agent Cary L. Thornton, Jr. The lady saw him holding my business card to her window as his identification. Glenn told her he was doing security surveys for the FBI and he was there to inspect her home. Glenn was dressed in old clothes, his nose was running, and it was about 6:30 a.m. The lady went along with Glenn and delayed him as long as she could while she called the Detroit Police Department.

When the police officers arrived at the home Glenn was still standing on the front porch waiting for the lady to open the door. Glenn saw the arriving police officers and said, "Hello officers, I'm FBI Agent Cary L. Thornton, Jr. from the Detroit Division." He gave them a wide smile as he held up my business card as identification. One of the responding officers knew Glenn as a local hype. He said, "Glenn turn around and keep your hands in sight. You're under arrest." Glenn said, "Aw man..." and turned around with his head down. This time Glenn had to stand for his own charges of attempted burglary. He was released on the following Monday morning pending trial in Detroit Recorders Court. I made sure that Glenn saw me shortly after his release so I could take credit for springing him from jail again. Glenn didn't know he would have been released anyway pending trial so I just let him think I was the reason for his release.

I knew the Detroit court system was so bogged down that charges like attempted burglary would take forever to be heard in court. I thought I'd take advantage of the delay and put Glenn to work making cases for us. As far as he knew, I got him out of jail and he owed me twice.

When I took Glenn aside that morning, my partner and I let Glenn have our wrath. He swore it would never happen again and begged us not to beat him. Glenn had received a few whippings in the past and quite frankly he was so nasty and smelly, we didn't want to touch him anyway. He promised to work extra hard for us later in the week and apologized over and over.

Since we had him in the rear of our car, we told him we were taking him to the east side of Detroit to drop him off in front of his friends. I said, "When we put you out of the car, we'll just say thanks for the information, so your friends can hear it." Glenn screamed, "Man please don't do that! You'll get me killed!" I said, "Hell Glenn, that's the idea." He continued to beg us not to take him for "the ride". He promised to stay out of trouble and to deliver for us if we didn't take him for "the ride". Glenn knew "the ride" was tantamount to a street corner execution and that fact alone kept him fairly honest with us. We knew Glenn could only be trusted as far as we could see him and that wasn't too far......

I said to Glenn, "This time and only this time you're off the hook. Next time we'll go for a ride, understand?" Glenn replied, "Thanks man, you won't be sorry. You'll see what I can do." We let Glenn out of the car in front of his house on Schaffer and Plymouth in Detroit. He thanked us all the way to his door, turning around and bowing in appreciation.

However we always kept Glenn at an arms distance and he knew from then on not to "b.s." us. To keep him honest we always promised him if he ever lied to us or tried something stupid again, he would be dropped off in front of his friends. Glenn's worse nightmare was letting his friends find out he was a federal snitch. The thought of "the ride" seemed to keep him fairly straight with the FBI anyway. Glenn continued to give us information on drug shipments entering Detroit but we only paid him a minimal amount of money because we knew he'd shoot it up in his arm. As a payment we sometimes bought him groceries and pampers for his kids from our pockets cash. That way his family benefited from his services and we didn't have to fill out long complex vouchers to give him a few dollars.

Unfortunately the drugs got the best of Glenn and we had to discontinue contact with him. In fact his wife later became hooked on heroin, too. She was once a very attractive lady but the last time I saw her, she looked like an old sea hag. Heaven only knows where his children are today.

****

One of my other earliest close encounters caused by an informant happened also on the west side of Detroit. This informant considered himself an expert at locating stolen cars. He owed me like any good source and always needed help. And like any other informant, he was paid little to nothing for his services. This guy was always working off a debt of gratitude to the government. In addition the paperwork necessary to pay an informant was never quite worth the hassle. I never wanted the government reviewing my vouchers with a fine toothcomb over a few hundred bucks. I always got more mileage by buying the guy a box of pampers and a six-pack out of my pocket. At least I knew his kids would get something.

Anthony "Jazz" Taylor held himself out to be the premier when it came to locating stolen cars. He always stayed one step ahead of the car theft rings and always knew when they were ready to move loads of hot cars out of Detroit. He felt the dealers could trust him because he made them believe he had connections inside the police department. In reality, he was just a mediocre snitch with zero contacts.

The truth of the matter was he was wired into a few theft rings but would try to play us against the local police for information. He had so few stolen property contacts that he would do his best to sell information to the highest bidder. Sometimes the highest bidder turned out to be the stolen car ring itself. The informant didn't care; he was all about the money. Eventually that's what sent him back to the penitentiary. I always told him if I caught him selling information to the highest bidder his rump would be grass. Jazz always liked to contact the fed's because he heard we paid better and faster than the Detroit Police Department.

We were working several stolen car rings in Detroit when we decided to drop by Jazz's place one afternoon. My partner and I had received information from Jazz that the house next door to him had stored some hot cars, ready to be stripped, in the rear garage. We really didn't believe him but we thought we'd check it out anyway. We figured if we dropped by unannounced from time to time, we could keep him on his toes. That way he never knew when to try something illegal. In other words we were the guardians that kept him honest.

One Friday afternoon we decided to swing by Jazz's place after a surveillance and get an update from him. No one was home so we decided to look around the back of his house. The place was completely empty. Since Jazz didn't have regular job we just assumed he was out doing whatever an unemployed informant normally does. However he told us several days earlier the house next door to him on the alley had been used to store hot cars. According to Jazz the cars were waiting in the rear garage to be stripped and sold for parts in Detroit. Jazz really hadn't proven himself so we couldn't put a lot of creditability in anything he told us.

Oath of Office

Before we left the area, we decided to just peek around the rear of the house that Jazz had given us a few days earlier. We really didn't expect to see anything but any good federal agent would check out all leads. Ken and I walked into the alley to take a look into the rear door of the garage. As we walked toward the garage we noticed the rear door was open onto the alley. As we got closer we heard the noises of several men. To our surprise we found ourselves standing face to face with nine guys stripping two luxury cars....we drew our revolvers and shouted, "FBI, put your hands in sight!!"

Everyone in the garage was holding some type of tool or large wrench in his hand and looking directly at the two of us. We knew that we startled them as much as they did us but we weren't backing down. Ken shouted again, "Drop your tools and put your hands in sight, now!!" All of them just stood in one place as if they were waiting to make a move on us. One guy dropped his large wrench and took off running up the alley. Ken, being the fastest runner, ran after the guy. As Ken ran after the guy he shouted to me, "The first one who tries something, shoot him in the head!!" That left me with eight guys with tools who hadn't decided if they were going to surrender.

I knew I had to come out of my crazy man bag just to get the jump on them. I shouted, "Everybody drop everything or I'll shoot this guy first!!" I pointed my revolver directly at the youngest guy in the garage, aiming directly at his face. He was only about sixteen years old and he stood nearest me. He was shaking like a leaf on a tree. I started sniffling as if my nose was running when the young guy started pleading for me not to shoot him. I let him see my hand shaking as I held my revolver in his face. He said, "Don't shoot me I'm doing what you want man. Please don't shoot me officer!" I told him I was going to shoot him because the rest of them wouldn't lie down on the ground as instructed. The young guy started crying and begging his friends to sprawl out on the ground with him. They followed him into the hot alley one at a time and laid on the hot pavement. I had my bluff over them by playing crazy but I kept my revolver pointed directly at the young guy.

By the time Ken returned with the runner they were all complaining how hot the pavement had become. It was no less that eighty-five degrees that afternoon and the sun was bright. I knew I had to keep them on the ground because it was just too many of them to control while standing up. Ken started a pat down of each one of them to make sure there were no guns among them. These were the days before cellular telephones and we knew our bureau radios were generally worthless when we needed them most.

Ken pulled the car into to the alley and called to our radio operator. He called over and over but did not get a response. After ten minutes or so he finally reached the operator and asked her to call for backup. We could hear her calling and calling but she received no responses. It was getting hotter and hotter on the ground and the "peanut gallery" started to show up. Everyone in the neighborhood had something to say about our suspects on the ground. Before we knew it, no less than ten people had gathered behind our bureau car and all of them had an opinion about police.

Ken finally reached the operator and told her to call a Detroit Police unit to assist us. To our surprise it was almost 3:00 p.m., on Friday, and we knew that was shift change for the local police. The peanut gallery got larger and larger and at least one alley dog had shown up. It was all we could do to keep our prisoners on the ground and to keep the "peanut gallery" back away from our prisoners. The crowd started cursing us for holding the guys on the hot ground with our guns drawn. They were shouting police brutality and all type of foul names at us. Soon the crowd swelled to over twenty angry residents. It seemed the shift change would never end and the operator continued to call for agents to assist us but she got no responses.

Oath of Office

    Ken went back to the radio and told the operator that the crowd was getting out of hand and we needed help right away. By now the temperature seemed to be rising and the sun was beaming hot on the guys sprawled in the alley. Now our prisoners had started to talk among themselves, which we stopped right away. This really made the crowd angrier. One peanut gallery member shouted, "Hey man, they can't tell y'all not to talk! That's police brutality! Y'all don't have to take that!" One prisoner got up and started to run up the alley. Ken again went after him with a full sprint. I had to go back into my crazy bag and I promised to shoot the young guy if anyone tried anything. The young guy helped me keep order by swearing he didn't want to be shot for them. I grabbed the young guy off the ground, stood him up, and held the barrel of my revolver up his rear end. He shouted to his friends, "Hey man, don't nobody move. This guy is nervous and he's gonna shoot me up my ass!! Y'all please don't move!!" The crowd got larger and angrier at us for detaining the car thieves.

    Just when Ken and I didn't think we could hold our prisoners any longer, two Detroit Police squad cars appeared and split the crowd in half. We felt like the cavalry had arrived that afternoon. The crowd was still angry at us for holding the nine young men on the hot ground in the midst of the hot summer heat. But after all we didn't tell them to strip the stolen cars. That really didn't matter to the crowd that was still growing as the police officers arrived. The prisoners were all placed in handcuffs and taken to jail. The two recovered cars were from Ohio and had been stripped to the core. Luckily all the parts were still inside the garage.

    As for Jazz, he became a hero because he finally had delivered on a promise. He simply bought himself an "I'll spring you from jail" card. We all knew he'd have to cash it in some time soon. None of the nine young men had any idea they were given up by Jazz. It was lucky for us the young guy in the group was afraid he might be shot and kept the others under control.

The delayed Detroit Police response was a result of the day and afternoon shifts changing at the time we called. Most of their squad cars in the district hadn't hit the streets when we called for help. The delayed response from the FBI was a result of nothing more than our crappy radio systems. The poor radio quality almost cost us a street corner whipping from the mob that had formed around our prisoners. Thank goodness agents today have much better radios and they all have reliable cellular telephones.

****

One of the questions I've been asked often by citizen groups are whether all agents are treated the same? I've also been asked if I've ever experienced any prejudice treatment as an FBI agent. My response has always been yes. But the treatments I've received in those isolated instances were the results of ignorance which no law enforcement agency or company is immune. Some of the perpetrators would probably have done the same thing whether they were in law enforcement or working for IBM. It really didn't matter—they were ignorant.

I once worked an investigation with a guy by the name of Johnny Morgan and you can determine if he was ignorant, prejudiced, or both. Keep in mind law enforcement officers are a cross section of society and as a black person I have experienced a multitude of interesting responses. But the great majority of the officers and federal agents I've worked with from around the world are fair and honest people. The ignorant ones have always been in the minority and rare.

Johnny Morgan was an officer from the Norfolk and Western Railroad Police, in Tennessee. Johnny told us when we first made contact with him, "All my friends call me Junior Morgan. You guys just call me Junior, O.K.?" Of course we just assumed he wanted my partner Ken and I to be his friend so I just said, "No problem, Junior."

I first met Junior on the telephone while we were investigating a major railroad theft ring that was operating in the southwest section of Detroit. It seemed the Detroit Police had gotten so close to this ring that was operating in Detroit, that they moved their operation to a small town in middle Tennessee. This group of young thieves had hit the railroad yards in Detroit so hard they had interrupted production in some local manufacturing plants. The thieves were stealing everything from automobile taillights to bolts and screws.

The group of thieves were all related and called the Taylor Boys. The Taylor Boys had an elaborate network that could fence anything they stole in almost any city in the country. These guys specialized in moving car parts and they were good at their craft. With the car theft market booming in Detroit, they felt the market was ripe elsewhere.

The Taylor Boys had some relatives near Memphis, Tennessee, who decided to continue their business and expand over the state. The Tennessee relatives also specialized in stealing automobile parts and fencing them with local chop shops. They felt the small town police departments would have a tough time keeping up with big city thieves. The group never counted on meeting detectives from the Norfolk and Western Railroad. Junior Morgan soon became their worse nightmare. His tactic was similar to the one we used in Detroit. Junior set up surveillance and paid an elaborate network of informants to provide information.

Junior took advantage of the low employment and the local desire to make quick money. Within about five months after flooding the small town of Dexter, Tennessee with informant money, Junior had identified all the local fences and the ringleader of the Taylor

Boys. Needless to say Harley Taylor was arrested and was shipped back to Detroit to be prosecuted federally for his crimes.

Junior Morgan was as happy as a lark that his months of hard work had finally yielded him a big Detroit thief. At the time he had never met Ken or me because we worked our portion of the case from Detroit. We had spoken to him dozens of times while we jointly investigated the Taylor Boys. We had had talked over weekends and dozens of times during the week while we exchanged information. Sometimes we exchanged information several times a day. Finally a series of arrests were made and we were going to federal court on the Taylor Boys.

We realized how very happy Junior was to clean up crime in middle Tennessee. He called Ken shortly after the first arrest and said, "Hey Ken!! We finally got one of them. We got the first of them "coons" and we're gonna get the rest of them soon." Ken said he couldn't believe his ears that this guy felt the liberty to use that language with him. Then we realized the issue. We had never physically met Junior and because we didn't split verbs and use what he considered ghetto English, he thought we were white guys. Ken never gave Junior a response to his statement of ignorance.

We decided to let him continue to stick his foot in his mouth. Over the next four weeks we had dozens of conversations with Junior while we prepared for trial. In every conversation Junior became more and more relaxed with his ignorance. Our conversations were like, "Hey Junior how are things going?" Junior would respond, "Man I can't wait to get to court to hang those coons out to dry. I really hope we get a judge who hates coons. What do ya think are our chances?" I would say, "We'll do just fine in federal court. Just be prepared and don't worry." Junior was so stupid he never realized we never responded to his racial insults. Not once did he ask us if we were white guys nor if we minded his references to the suspects. It seemed the longer we knew Junior, the more ignorance he displayed to us.

Conversations were no different when he talked to Ken. We made a pact to let him continue to display his true colors until we met him at trial time. The trial was scheduled for June 10th and we couldn't wait to see his face when he finally got a chance to meet us. Finally trial time arrived and we had to meet Junior in the lobby of the Pontchartrain Hotel in downtown Detroit. We figured the Pontchartrain Hotel was a good location for Junior to get a room because it was a short walk to the federal courthouse. Besides we assumed after Junior met us he wouldn't want to depend on us to get him around town. He would probably elect to just walk around downtown with his ignorant head down.

We got a call from Junior on the day prior to the trial that he was arriving at approximately 1:00 p.m. on June 9th. His first order of business was to meet with us and the United States Attorney to handle the final details of the trial. Ken and I decided to meet Junior at noon and offer to take him to lunch. We figured if we were lucky he would choke while he tried to pretend he was enjoying himself with us.

Ken spoke to Junior on the telephone before he left the Memphis Airport. Junior said, "You know Ken I've been talking to you fellers for over six months and I still don't know what you federal boys look like." Ken responded, "Awe Junior you'll recognize us. We'll be the two guys standing in the lobby with the dark suits. You know all FBI agents have to wear dark suits to court." Junior said, "You know you're right, we southern boys just wear regular clothes and our good boots. I just can't wait to face those coons in court." Ken just listened and hung up the telephone.

Ken and I arrived at the hotel lobby early and were sure to be crisp and dapper as we waited in the Pontchartrain Hotel lobby. He told us he was going to grab a taxi from the airport and meet us just before noon. Reflecting back, I only wished we had a camera to capture his face in print.

At exactly 11:54 a.m. we saw a taxi pull up to the front of the Pontchartrain Hotel. A short, dumpy guy with a beige western sport coat got out of the taxicab. He looked around like this was his first trip to the big city. He seemed taken with the size of the tall buildings. He just stared toward the huge Renaissance Center and scratched his crotch. He was probably saying to himself, "Buildings just ain't that big in Dexter." Junior quit gazing and walked toward the lobby to find the two guys in dark suits. As he walked into the lobby he seemed confused because there were no white guys in dark suits in the lobby. We decided to frighten the hell out of ol' Junior. I said, "Hey Junior, over here!!"

He turned around and saw my face and became white as a sheet. He said, "Ken? Cary?" We said, "In the flesh. How was your trip, Junior?" He swallowed and almost choked as he said, "Fine guys. Y'all know how we make fun down South. We really don't mean much by running our mouth. We just like to have fun." We just stood and stared at the short dumpy little hillbilly who called himself Junior. We just let the moment of silence eat him up. He could clearly see it was no laughing matter. Ken then said, "Hey Junior, we got a few minutes. Let's go over on the eastside to grab some lunch." He started to hesitate when I said, "Aw come on Junior. We just want to be friendly. Besides, the lunch will do you good."

Junior knew from his investigations that certain areas of the Eastside probably wouldn't be his favorite place in Detroit. But to save face he said, "If you guys say so, you sure it's OK with y'all?" I said, "No problem buddy, let's go."

In order to welcome Junior to Detroit, we took him to Greens Barbeque on the eastside of Detroit. It was one of those "stand at the window and order places." Junior was as nervous as a housefly as he stood at the window. He looked around every few seconds to see if anyone was approaching him. He stuck to us like glue because this time he didn't have his gun.

Ken said, "Relax Junior, you're among friends." Several local street guys just stared at Junior without saying a word. We delighted in hearing Junior apologize every few minutes for his multitude of bigoted statements over the past six months. Junior told us about 60 times he wasn't a bigot and he had lots of black friends back home. I said, "No kidding Junior, so do I." When we finally got tired of listening to Junior choke, Ken said, "O.K. Junior, enough." I told him, "Let's get the trial over so you can get back to Tennessee." Junior hung his head and said, "Right." He didn't apologize any more because he knew it wouldn't do him any good. We sat on the bench outside the barbeque joint and watched Junior choke down his sandwich and Coke.

Over the next few days Junior was probably the most uncomfortable person in Detroit. He stayed in his hotel room at night and kept everything above board as he talked with us. The trial was fairly routine and uncomplicated since we had prepared so well. The jury was only out for one hour and quickly convicted two of the Taylor Boys. Shortly after the jury returned the guilty verdict, the Detroit ordeal was over for Junior. Junior apologized to us for the last time and packed his bags in his hotel room. We offered him a ride to the airport but he declined our offer and took a taxi. Junior wanted to get his ignorant rump away from us as soon as he possibly could. I think we were fortunate to give Junior four of the worse days in his life and a good dose of Detroit culture. We never heard from Junior after that trial. I just supposed Junior had been eaten alive with embarrassment or maybe he just didn't like Detroit.

****

Some criminals are sinister by nature and nothing you do to them or for them is going to change their thinking or way of life. Many criminals enjoy what they do and enjoy the thrill of getting away with their thieving acts. Needless to say, most of them are seldom caught the first time they commit a crime. Some of them are never caught at all. With so many criminals walking our urban streets and the scarcity of law enforcement officers, catching and convicting criminals is tough to do. Those few that are caught and convicted can generally be viewed as "plain old unlucky" and should probably find another occupation. Such was the case of Lee Johnston, thief extraordinaire.

Johnston viewed his occupation of thief to be as noble an occupation as any resident of any urban city. Just as your neighbor might make his living as a banker, Johnston made his living as a thief. He took pride in his occupation, just as any accountant took pride in his chosen profession. Just as the CPA attends professional development training to stay abreast of his profession, Johnston honed his skills by stealing to the limit of his ability and taking pride as he got away with it. He graded himself by how easy it was to get away and the amount of money his ill-gotten goods produced. Johnston fancied himself a professional at the top of his trade. He stole well and lived well. He was so good at what he did that he was seldom a customer of the Wayne County penal system. After all, Johnston knew the cops were just too busy on more serious crimes to worry about him. Unfortunately for us, Johnston was exactly right in his assessment.

He knew as long as he was in Detroit, he could live and eat well while he practiced his trade. What Johnston didn't know was the FBI had different priorities than the Detroit Police. In fact, the Detroit FBI had an entire squad dedicated to removing people like him off the streets, so honest hardworking citizens could sleep at night and not have to worry. For the FBI, Johnston was nothing more than another project waiting to be prosecuted and hauled away to jail.

Just like most of our subjects, Johnston was a product of a broken home and poverty. The only stability Johnston experienced in his life was the few times he was locked up in jail. Johnston's incarceration was a time when he could sit with other professionals and hone his thieving skills to a fine science. Johnston was not a big guy so he refrained from fighting. He told us he'd rather use his head to make a living. He told us he always kept the other prisoners entertained with his knowledge of the streets, so they protected him. In this respect, he was fairly smart.

The Detroit FBI came in contact with Johnston one Saturday afternoon, by way of the Gibraltar Trade Center in Taylor, Michigan. Generally, FBI agents could count on most Saturday's in the fall of the year as a time to watch Michigan football or just enjoying the spectacular colors change. As with most major investigations, they always start with a tip by an informant or concerned citizen. In this case, a concerned citizen decided people like Johnston had pillaged their neighborhood enough and decided to alert the FBI.

The concerned citizen who called the Detroit field office said he was sick and tired of vermin pedaling stolen goods at the Gibraltar Trade Center. He said thieves make it tough for honest vendors to make a living and he wasn't going to stand for anyone ruining the reputation of the trade center. The bureau clerk quizzed the caller as to how he knew someone was selling stolen goods.

The caller said he was a machinist with a local trade union and used MATCO tools everyday. He knew MATCO only sold their brand of tools through approved vendors from MATCO tool vans. According to the caller, a man was selling MATCO tools from trays on a table at the Gibraltar Trade Center for discount prices. The guy seemed upset and hung up the telephone after providing the limited information. The caller didn't provide a return telephone number therefore the weekend clerk didn't have an opportunity to question him any further about his allegations.

C. Lee Thornton

We were not so sure why the caller was angry. It could have been because this guy saw items selling for less than he had previously paid full price. Or he may have been a hard working union guy who was tired of some guys making an easy living while he had to work overtime to make ends meet. Whatever his reason, it was enough to tear me away from a Michigan–Ohio State football game to go to work and investigate the allegation. I found myself equally as steamed as the caller but for another reason. University of Michigan was just about to take the lead but the information provided was too timely to let it wait until the game ended. As I reluctantly tore myself away from the football game, I called two of my partners to screw up their afternoon as well. I told them I was on the way to pick them up.

The Gibraltar Trade Center was as busy as any other Saturday afternoon. The gigantic parking lot was loaded with everything from pickup trucks to luxury cars. As always, finding a parking spot close to the building was not the easiest thing to do. But we were the FBI. We simply made a parking spot in front of the main entrance and put our blue bubble on the dashboard. The blue bubble told the cops to try another car; we're on official business. On this day we weren't taking for any grief from "part-time guards". We had just missed the end of a Michigan–Ohio State football game and none of us were happy to be there.

We walked into the main entrance of the trade center and began the hunt for the thief. Generally, finding someone in the trade center on a Saturday afternoon was like finding the proverbial needle in a haystack. The gigantic swap meet had hundreds of vendors and nothing was in any particular order. The few of us fanned out over the area to find anyone selling MATCO tools. The caller had provided some limited information, which we decided to follow before we began our witch-hunt. To our surprise, the caller's information was fairly accurate and we walked right up to a booth advertising MATCO

Oath of Office

tools for sale. We couldn't believe it, our guy stood right in front of us just as the caller had reported to the weekend clerk. Johnston was a black guy, about six feet tall, wearing an Ike Turner type wig on his head. From a casual glance he looked like a throw back to the 1970s.

We had already done our homework and had contacted the local MATCO tool distributor prior to driving to the Trade Center. The distributor told us only licensed distributors sold their products from MATCO tool vans. We also knew that a van was recently stolen from a distributor who lived in Kokomo, Indiana. His entire inventory had been taken. The Indiana State Police told us the theft was still outstanding and the van was listed in NCIC as stolen. We couldn't believe the solution to our theft was standing directly in front of us, trying to sell us tools. We looked like good targets because we were dressed as if we had just cleaned a garage. Johnston was polite and asked if he could interest us in some tools.

I decided to draw on my engineering background and ask him if he had a small set of Allen wrenches. The vendor (Johnston) said, "Of course, I've got anything you need." He handed me a small packet containing eight small wrenches. He said, "I can give you a good deal on them if you buy two sets." I could sense this guy was either a good salesman or he just wanted to get rid of the stolen goods as soon as he could. I told him I wanted to check the packet. He handed me the wrenches and went to wait on another customer at the end of the table.

There were no serial numbers on the wrench set but I noticed he was selling drill bits out of a drawer placed on the table in front of us. This guy was either very stupid or he just didn't know the drawers came directly out of the van that was stolen. By now, my two partners had arrived at the booth. Business was brisk and Johnston was taking advantage of every customer.

After we examined the trays on the table, we decided to look under the table where his supplies and displays were stored. Under the table, Johnston had no less than five large boxes with labels that read, "Herman Jones, 1245 Kentucky Street, Kokomo, Indiana 32321." According to the information we had received from the Indiana State Police, Herman Jones was the victim that reported the theft two days earlier. After Johnston waited on his final customer, we told him we were from the FBI. We told the rest of his customers the booth was closed for the day.

Johnston was as casual with us as he was with his last customer. Although we were prepared for a fight, Johnston let us know he was only upset because so many customers had to be turned away. We really could have used a scuffle because we could have let out our frustration over the Michigan–Ohio State game—Michigan had lost. One wrong move from Johnston and we'd let him know how bad we wanted that win. But Johnston was calm and caused us no trouble at all. He calmly submitted as we placed him under arrest and put handcuffs on him. As I searched Johnston, I felt his head to insure he had nothing hidden beneath his wig that could be used as a weapon. Apparently Johnston hadn't tacked down the wig too tight because when I felt through it, it moved to one side. As he was marched out to our car in handcuffs, he drew a few stares from patrons, as he peeked around his side saddled wig. I just told him, "Sorry buddy, I'm not a beautician. You can handle your wig later, we've got to get downtown." Each time he moved, the wig laid a little further in the "ace deuce" direction. Ike would have been proud of him.

We used the two remaining bureau cars to collect Johnston's stolen goods. We had to show our identification no less than a dozen times to finally convince the Taylor Police and the Gibraltar Trade Center building security we actually were FBI agents. Most of them had never dealt with the Bureau and because three of us were black, they probably suspected we were stealing, just like Johnston. I'm not sure they believed us after we showed identification, but we were carrying guns and no one wanted any trouble.

We registered Johnston as a customer of the Wayne County Jail system with a check out date of the following Monday morning, when he would appear in federal district court. We called our supervisor and let him know we had missed the Michigan game and that Johnston was in custody. He only said, "Good job guys. See you on Monday morning. Be sure to log in the property." We weren't sure exactly what he meant by good job, but we all went home to enjoy the rest of the weekend.

Over the next several weeks, Johnston was appointed a federal defender and despite all the evidence against him, he insisted on going to trial. Because Johnston had a long record of assorted felony charges, he was given a high bail, which really seemed to tick him off. To tick us off, he decided to take the case to the limit and go to trial. Despite the overwhelming evidence against him and being caught with the stolen goods in his possession, he refused to plead guilty to interstate transportation of stolen property (ITSP). For once, a charge that Johnston thought was only a local theft became a federal case—major interstate theft matters—a case that was the specialty of my squad. Johnston's federal public defender decided he was going to make us prove our case in court. During the trial, the federal prosecutor laid out our case against Johnston like a pro. He covered the timetable from the theft in Indiana, to the time the caller notified the FBI, until we walked to Johnston's booth and actually saw the boxes under the table with the victim's name on them. The assistant United States Attorney demonstrated to the jury how Johnston was in the process of selling stolen goods when we arrived and how he tried to sell us stolen wrenches. Quite frankly, it was what most prosecutors call a slam-dunk.

Johnston's public defender was defenseless and still puzzled as to why he decided to go to trial. Johnston's defense was hopeless and his public defender was completely humiliated. Needless to say, the jury was out about 30 minutes and returned with a guilty verdict against Johnston. We think the jury took that long because they wanted to eat the free meal that had been delivered to the jury room. Sentencing for Johnston was set for later in the month, before the same federal judge.

On the sentencing date, I sat in the courtroom because I really wanted to hear Johnston's motivation for going to trial. I refused to believe he had a death wish. A guilty plea would have been faster and less costly for the government. I could tell from where I sat, the judge was angry with Johnston.

Johnston stood before the judge and listened as the judge reamed him and his attorney for wasting federal dollars on a case that was clearly a plea situation. The judge chastised Johnston for not providing accurate information to pretrial services, which made his pre-sentence report much more difficult to prepare. Johnston told the pre-sentence officer he had a Bachelor Degree in Business Administration but investigation proved, that too, was false. The judge continued to list the false statements Johnston had provided and the money he had cost the government with the senseless trial. Throughout the lecture, Johnston stood silent before the court.

Before his sentencing, the judge asked Johnston if he had anything to say for himself and to explain to him his justification for wasting government money on the trial. I also wanted to hear Johnston's explanation. Johnston paused, looked around, and said, "Judge the FBI caught me as I was selling my goods. That part I admit, they got me. My profession is a thief, and up to now, I have been very successful at it. These guys are FBI agents and I assume they are good at what they do, too. Judge, you may beat me down and the FBI may beat me. One thing I'm not going to do, is give you

Oath of Office

the stick to whip me with. If you whip me, you're going to have to bring your own stick. I'm not going to help y'all do it. If you think I'm guilty, then prove it in your court."

Johnston was sentenced to 36 months in federal prison. He proudly accepted his time and nodded to us as he was led out of the courtroom. For some strange reason, we agreed that Johnston deserved respect for speaking his mind. To this day, I still remember his declaration to the federal judge, prior to the sentencing. Somehow, you've got to respect a man who refuses to lie down and be beaten. From the words of Lee Johnston, "I'm not going to give you the stick to whip me." Don't give up. Don't give in. That attitude should be an axiom for life for all people.

Working the case involving Lee Johnston reminded me of some of the lessons taught to me by my dad. He told us everyday, that we shouldn't be surprised if we don't always get those things, which we were qualified. Pop always said, "Education will get you most of the way there but, not all the way. But, if you don't have that good solid education, you're giving the Man the power over you." Pop was saying the same thing as Lee Johnston. Johnston said he may be guilty but, he wasn't going to lie down. We had to prove he was guilty. Using Pop's logic, a high school dropout is doing nothing more than giving society the stick to whip him. Pop said, "That young person who drops out of school wouldn't be any worse off if he climbed to the top of a skyscraper and dove off. Either way, he's dead. Either way, he's hopeless. An uneducated man in this country is nothing more than a slave."

Pop's rule was always to "never go in half stepping". If you go after a goal, be ready, be prepared, and in your mind be the best. If you don't look like you're the best there is, you're not. If you don't look like you're ready to take on the world, you aren't. Johnston felt he was the best there was in his field. I was the best in mine. That's why Johnston was on his way to federal prison.

Johnston and I really weren't that much different from one another based on our backgrounds. Johnston grew up in poverty, just as I had grown up. Johnston told me his father worked odd jobs all his life, just as my dad had worked. But, Johnston decided to use his drive to make a living out of stealing. I used my drive to stay in school and become an FBI agent. We both reached the fork in the road. We simply took different paths.

****

Chapter Seven

- UNDERCOVER CONTRACT HIT -

The FBI provides tremendous rewards for those of us involved in successful undercover operations—an opportunity to do the next one. Your name and exploits travel around the Bureau and you soon get a reputation for playing the role that gets the big one. Too often, successful undercover agents realize that with the exception of a few cash incentive awards and a ton of "ataboy's", there really isn't a career path in undercover work. Some agents get the undercover life style in their system and can't get away from it. Some agents like the idea of driving the fancy cars, the parties, wearing flashy clothes, and running around strange towns with the aura of a rock star.

Your fellow agents envy you because you get lots of attention and often, a few nice perks. Perks, such as fine jewelry and a fat bankroll are enough to attract the average agent to the mysterious roles played by the seasoned undercover agent. The new agent sometimes finds themselves envying the undercover agent because they have all the glamour.

One of the curses I possessed early in my career was success playing a number of roles as an undercover FBI agent. Assuming different identities, playing the different roles, and becoming someone else came natural for me. Although the Bureau sent us to undercover school and certified us to do the work, a true undercover agent has to have a natural knack to assume the different identities. It is absolutely nothing the FBI can do to teach an agent true undercover skills, it has to be natural or it seems phony when applied to the streets. It might also prove fatal for the unprepared agent. The greatest skill has to be the ability to think on one's feet and to stay within the bounds of federal law. One blunder or misstep, an entire operation can fall in the sewer and the undercover agent might find himself going to jail along with the subject. It is a delicate balance and a renegade agent does not fit the role. Undercover work is nothing at all like Hollywood.

Early in my career, I became a veteran of several successful undercover assignments, including Operation Steamclean, Greylord, Barleycorn, Snatchback, and dozens of others that didn't have official titles. Despite the varied circumstances and identities I assumed, I was successful getting the job done each time. When I received a call from the Toledo Resident Agency in 1987, I viewed the new assignment as another challenge in a long line of assignments. As always, I met with the case agent and the supervisor in charge at a remote location far away from the FBI office for security reasons.

I had previously worked several undercover assignments in Toledo, Ohio and I was familiar with the majority of the FBI agents in that division. This particular briefing was no different from many others in the past; and just as many times before, I was ready for the new challenge.

Supervisory Special Agent Henry James told me the warden at the state prison in Wood County, Ohio had recently contacted their office. A prisoner had contacted the warden and told him two recently arriving prisoners approached him with a proposition. The two had received long sentences for narcotics charges in northern Ohio. They expected one of their accomplices to follow them within the next few months after he went to trial. The accomplice had his

Oath of Office

trial delayed due to several evidentiary matters that arose between the prosecutor's office and the assigned defense attorneys.

The two prisoner's had recently arrived at the institution and were soliciting for someone to put a hit on the sheriff deputy who convicted them and was about to convict their accomplice. The prisoner who contacted the warden told him he took the contract. He told him he could get the job done on the outside through some of his boys. The prisoners told him he could make a lot of money if the hit was pulled off successfully. Their goal was to have the deputy killed before he got to court to testify against the narcotics suspect.

The supervisor in charge told me I was contacted because the prisoners offering the contract were Hispanic and the people he'd have to contact on the outside were also Hispanic. They had the reputation of being some real bad people. They wanted to know if I felt comfortable playing the part of a contract hit man. The supervisor and prosecutor told me I had to get enough information to convict the group arranging for the hit. Of course I told them, "No problem, when do we meet the informant?"

I had assisted the Toledo Resident Agency several times in the past with some Spanish translation. About a year earlier, I assisted the office with a case involving a Mexican national, whom we thought was being held against her will. She only spoke Spanish and worked as a maid for a family in Toledo. After interviewing her, she said she was as happy as she had ever been in her life. She told me she was living in the United States and living what she deemed, a dream life. She said she had no desire to learn English as long as she had her job, her room, and friends from Mexico. The lady said she couldn't imagine anyone believing she was being held against her will. From that time on, the Toledo Resident Agency knew I could be counted on to assist them with anything involving Spanish subjects or victims.

I got the impression this assignment would be a real challenge and I was ready to go to work.

The fact that I could operate in Spanish was an advantage for me that many agents didn't enjoy. It made me slightly more valuable as an undercover agent. I was also slightly more desirable because I was a black agent. After all, who'd ever suspect a black guy could speak Spanish? The better you are at what you do, the more you'll get to do it.

About a week later, the informant was sprung free from the prison to meet with the Toledo FBI agents and myself. In order to not draw any attention, his fellow prison mates only knew he had a doctor's appointment and the prison doctor couldn't handle his problem. This ruse bought him about four hours away from the facility, without drawing any attention to himself. The prisoner's name was James Wilson and he hated prison life with a passion.

Wilson and several prison officials met us at a small restaurant near Toledo. Wilson was as happy as he could be to breathe free air, after being locked up more than two years. The prison officials told us if this operation was pulled off successfully, the warden has promised Wilson's time served would be reduced. Wilson would also be moved to another institution to do the balance of his time. Wilson told us he really wanted this case to work, probably as much as the FBI.

Wilson said, "Two Mexican guys arrived in the joint and on their first day, they started looking for someone to do a hit on a Wood County Sheriff Deputy. Man, these guys were desperate. They hit on white guys, Mexican guys, old guys, everyone. They were desperate. One of them worked in the laundry and even asked me. I told him I could handle it with my cousin in Michigan. I went straight to my case worker." According to Wilson, he jumped on the deal as soon as he heard about it because he wanted to get something out

Oath of Office

of it. He said it took him two weeks to get the information to the warden through his caseworker.

The prison official said he didn't know for sure, but he thought the warden tried to get an undercover agent from the Ohio Department of Corrections to work with him, but they didn't have any guys who spoke Spanish. Wilson said, "I told the Mexican guy I have a cousin in Flint who could take the contract for $5,000.00. I told them he had been locked up for popping a cop." He said the guy gave him the contract right away but told him to work fast. Wilson said they were going to give him the telephone number of the people to contact and they would handle everything from there.

As with most informants, I only trust them as far as I can see them. Wilson looked shaky and I had to decide if I thought he could be trusted or was he trying to cut a deal to get out of prison. We decided to deal with him, but only at a distance. He had to prove himself. I gave Wilson my undercover telephone number and told him to give it to the guys on the inside. Wilson's instructions were to return to the cellblock and not to be too anxious to get with them for a few days. I told him, "Look, you're supposed to be at the doctor's office. If you get back right away and seem too anxious to get with them, they might think you met someone out here. Wait a few days and just tell them you finally caught up with your cousin in Flint."

I told Wilson, "Don't seem too quick to want to pull it off right away. Remember to tell them your cousin is on paper for a hit and he only got pinched because someone snitched on him. Don't give them any names and just tell them to call this number I'm giving you. Tell them to use the phrase, 'Hey Carl' and I'll know what they want. They should know to be cool while they talk. You don't have anything else to do. We'll be in touch with you later."

Wilson had his marching orders and we decided to give him a few days to make his contacts. He knew he was not supposed to write anything down except the telephone number. Wilson got the best meal he had in a year and returned to the prison that afternoon. Over the next two weeks, I remained in contact with the assistant United States attorney and we made all the plans we'd have to have in case the call came through for our contract.

The Toledo Resident Agency and I planned our surveillances to cover me when the contacts were made with the subjects. We spent the next two weeks drawing up the paperwork for the court orders for my consensual recorders and audio wires.

Exactly three weeks later, one afternoon, I received a call at my undercover site from someone beginning the conversation with, "Hey Carl...." The caller sounded Hispanic and I knew the contact from Wilson had been handled. The guy on the other end of the line spoke very slow and seemed to be cautious. I could tell he was guarded with what he was saying. He told me he got my number from Raul. Raul was one of the guys locked up in the Ohio prison. I told him, "You gotta be cool on the telephone but let's meet to handle our business a little later."

During the brief conversation I taped the call. The guy told me his name was Jose and we should meet on Thursday at the diner off Highway 75, just outside of Toledo. He said, "I'll be with one other guy and I'll be driving a red pickup truck. We go to that diner all the time, so nobody will pay us much attention." Since the call came in on Tuesday, I had two days to set up my surveillance and to get things underway. The conversation was brief but from the flow, we both knew what we had to do. Before the conversation ended, I told him he would recognize me by a blue baseball cap. We agreed that 3:00 p.m. would be a good time to meet. Jose said, "We don't want the diner loaded with the lunch crowd, while we handle our business. Man, we gotta move fast, you know what I mean?" I said, "Straight up."

The next call I made was to the case agent in the Toledo Resident Agency. I told them we had two days to survey the area and to be

Oath of Office

ready when Jose and his partner showed up at the diner. I planned to head to Ohio the next day to give myself a head start on the meeting. From experience, I knew that sometimes these meetings are setups to snuff out a guy. I always expect the bad guy to arrive at the meeting location early and do his surveillance on us. I figured this time we'd get a one-day jump on our caller, and I'd be there first.

The first point of business was to contact Wilson's caseworker at the prison to see if he had a line on who we would be meeting. But according to the caseworker, Wilson has never met the guys either. He didn't want to ask too many questions, so he let the plan flow as they had requested. The best intelligence we had was the guys I was to meet were Mexican, just like the guys ordering the hit from the prison. Wilson had followed our instructions and was careful not to ask too many questions after he agreed to take the contract. The less Wilson knew about the Bureau and our plans, the better for him.

I arrived at the Toledo Resident Agency early the following afternoon and briefed the case agent and supervisor on the arrangements I had made with Jose. Since my conversation with Jose had been brief, I didn't have too many details to provide. After my briefing, I played the tape to see if anyone recognized the voice from any of their prior cases. We drew a blank. No one recognized the caller. We were on our own. One of the agents had gone to the diner and had lunch earlier. While Special Agent Taylor was in the diner he sketched a diagram of the restaurant to add to our undercover plans. By the time our briefing was finished, Taylor was busy putting a final touch on the drawing. We didn't want to leave anything to guess work when our Thursday afternoon meeting took place.

Unfortunately for us, no one had ever heard of Jose, and surveillance in northern Ohio still hadn't located a red pickup truck driven by two Hispanics. To be on the safe side, every reasonably trustworthy informant was contacted for any worthwhile intelligence on this group. Again, we drew a blank and had to rely on our own intelligence network and surveillance by the Toledo Resident Agency.

Thursday morning was filled with last minute preparations for our 3:00 p.m. meeting with Jose and his partner. Our surveillance team moved into the area of the diner area around noon to locate a red pickup truck with our two subjects. As the meeting time drew near, I sat about a mile away from the diner in my car with the case agent. We listened intently for surveillance to place the two subjects inside the diner, if they had arrived early. We planned to be fashionably late for the meeting and to purposely make them wait. About 2:55 p.m., our surveillance team located a red pickup truck with two Hispanic males moving north on Interstate 75, in the direction of the diner.

Immediately, two FBI agents entered the diner, sat in separate locations, and ordered lunch. Both of them wore wires in order for our surveillance team to monitor inside activity. They soon reported the two Hispanic males were inside the diner and had ordered lunch. The inside surveillance team provided us a complete description of the two men. Outside surveillance ran the license plates on the trucks and we soon had a full background on the driver of the vehicle.

NCIC indicated the driver didn't have any outstanding warrants but he was an ex-convict from Texas. His description fit the driver, but we still had nothing on his accomplice. I was given a full description of both of them and was ready to go. For our first meeting, I decided not to wear an audio wire or recording device. Electronic equipment is normally not a good idea on first meetings. In fact, I knew from prior meetings with Hispanics, that during initial meetings they customarily embrace or hug. I knew this was their custom to pat down guys to see if they're wearing a wire or carrying a firearm. I had been pat down too many times in the past and had as yet to be caught wearing a wire.

I purposely didn't wear a blue ball cap like I told Jose, but a black hat. I figured, why should they be able to spot me? If they ask later about my blue ball cap, I'd just tell them I forgot it when I left in a hurry.

I decided to be one step ahead of my Hispanic friends and let the agents inside the diner wear the wires. I also put my five shot revolver inside the top of my left boot. If I had to get to it in a hurry, I had practiced over and over how to pull up my pant leg and reach my five shot friend. I examined every possible scenario in my head, before I entered the diner.

I walked in the diner, fashionably late, at 3:22 p.m. Although I knew exactly whom I was going to meet, I pretended to be confused as I walked into the main door. I purposely looked away from where the two Hispanic guys were sitting so that they would have to call me. Suddenly, I heard one of them say, "Hey, Carl". I acted surprised and walked past one of my surveillance agents who sat drinking a cup of coffee.

I tried to appear as suspicious as I could toward the two Hispanic men. I said, "Jose?" and he said, "Yeah". I sat down and looked around in all directions. I knew the way to get with them was to start off being inquisitive. I started quizzing them about whether or not they could be trusted. I figured I'd put them on the defensive and throw the questions into their lap. I asked them, "How did you get here? Was anyone following you? Who is the guy in the corner?" I told them I don't deal with a lot of people because I'm on paper and I don't trust a lot of people. I knew that would make them ask me why I was on paper. My questions to them set me up to go on stage again.

When they started asking me question after question, I said, "Hey man, why you askin' all the questions? Are you dudes working for the police? I can't stand police". I started wiping my nose, as if it was running, and scratching my arm, like a junkie. They started apologizing and swore to me they hated police, too. They said that's why they wanted to meet me. I started to calm down and they could see it.

This time they gave me center stage again. I had them exactly where I wanted them—in the palm of my hand. I told them, "My man couldn't talk much on the telephone but he told me I'd meet some dudes who wanted some smokin' handled. That's all they told me and 'cause that's my bag." I waited and they both started letting it all out on the table. I wished I had my tape on but I just gathered the facts in my head. From there I went back into my junkie act.

I looked around and could see our surveillance agents all around the diner. One of them was cracking up as I went through my gyrations with the guys. My signal to them, if something went seriously wrong, was to take my hat off and put it back on a number of times. I was far from sensing anything going wrong, so I just kept playing my role. I said, "Tell me what you want, man..." Jose said, "Smoke him and dispose of the carcass." The guys told me Hector and Raul had been to court and was convicted by the big hillbilly deputy. They never gave me his name, but said he was scheduled to go to court in a few weeks against Hector's younger brother. I told him, "Straight up, as long as it's worth my time. What's it worth to ya?"

They told me, "Look man, if you pop him, the money ain't no problem." That's when the guy with Jose held up five fingers. I told him, "That's cool as long as we see zeros." He said, "Grand my man, I'm talkin' about five grand." In the conversation that followed, they hovered over the table and described the guy to me in detail. They told me they wanted the body to disappear so it would never be found. They were emphatic that he was not supposed to appear in court any more. Jose then looked around and slowly pulled

Oath of Office

out a picture of Deputy James Taylor of the Wood County Sheriff Department. Jose said, "Smoke him, and soon".

The two guys went back and forth in Spanish, and I pretended not to have a clue about what they were saying. They spoke very low but I kept hearing *"confiar"* over and over. I knew then they were trying to decide if I could be trusted... I spoke a good grade of Spanish but I planned to keep it a secret for the time being. I decided to go along with them for a while to see if I could play them and get as much information as I needed to seal the case. After all, I was the FBI agent, and I'm supposed to be smarter than street bums hunting for a hit man. They weren't that smart—just desperate.

The deputy was a big imposing man who had handled some good narcotics cases in Wood County. I gathered the deputy was on a mission to clean up Wood County's drug problem. My job was to convince the two of them that I was their man, and to get all the evidence I could to send them to prison. By now, I had convinced them I was the toughest dude in town and, by the end of our meeting, I had convinced them their money would be well spent.

We agreed to meet the next week, when they would tell me where the deputy could be found in the small town. They also told me they'd let me know where to dump the body. They told me everything would be laid out for me at our next meeting. I told them my PO (parole officer) was on my case and I was going to clean myself before I drove back to Michigan. I pointed to an old Pontiac on the parking lot. Of course, it wasn't my car, but I figured as long as they thought I was a hood from Flint, why not let them think I was driving an old car. I figured I'd let them think I was desperate and needed the money pretty bad. The more in need I appeared to them, the less likely they would think I'm a fed or any type of undercover agent, and the more they would trust me.

I told them, "Hey man, I gotta be cool down here. I ain't supposed to be outta Michigan. I'm on paper for three more years.

Look, you guys leave first 'cause I don't trust that guy sitting in the corner. You know, sometimes your p.o. send guys around to follow you." I told them to leave separately also. I told them I would leave later, after I was sure it was safe. I even told the second guy to leave last because I didn't trust another guy sitting in the far corner of the diner. He was just a straight arrow looking businessman who was having lunch. He could care less about us and never looked in our direction. My motive was to keep them on the defensive and to keep the attention away from me. By the time they left, I had them both convinced the guy in the corner worked for the Michigan Department of Probation and Parole and he had been sent to follow me.

As soon as Jose left the diner and got into the red truck to wait for his friend, I figured I'd play the second guy. I quizzed him about how long he had known Jose and if he thought I could trust him. I told him, "Man, I don't wanna be tricked back into the joint by anyone. You follow me?" This guy was dumber than Jose. He said, "Hey man, Jose is cool. All he wants to do is see the cop dead, man. That's it. I know him pretty well, man. We gotta get this done and fast." He said Jose could be trusted because they had pulled some good jobs off in the past and they were still walking as free men. I convinced him we all wanted the same thing and the money was our best friend. He told me when we meet the next time, they would have everything lined up and I could get started on my job. We slapped hands and he left the diner.

After the second guy was gone, I ordered a coke to drink until I could see the red pickup truck had left the area. I nodded to my cover agents who were stationed around the diner and taking notes.

Our surveillance team took them south on Interstate 75, to a bar about 10 miles away. I knew then, I could leave and meet our agents back at our rendezvous location in Toledo. I always knew that street bums traveled with their own surveillance, too. So when

Oath of Office

I left the diner, I made sure I spoke to no one but the waitress and acknowledged no one. As I drove back to our meeting spot in Toledo, I took great pains to clean myself. I went through some fairly sleazy neighborhoods and drove the wrong way on a one-way street just to see if anyone was following me. By the time I got back to our spot, I was convinced I was not being followed by anyone but the FBI surveillance team.

We had a brief meeting and I told the Toledo agents everything went well, as far as I was concerned. My two comrades were clearly on the defensive and I was fairly certain I could wear a wire during my next meeting with the two men. I headed back to Detroit to complete my paperwork and to wait for my next telephone call from Jose. I still didn't know the other guy's name. I purposely didn't ask for it. By not asking him his name, they had no reason to ask me anything else about myself.

About a week later, the undercover telephone rang again at my Michigan offsite location. It was Jose. He told me he wanted to meet again because they thought they had found where the big hillbilly lived with his family. I tried to act like I was tired of waiting but cautioned Jose about being too specific on the telephone. I told them, "Hey man, you gotta remember the cops listen on telephones and my p.o. is still on my ass." Jose apologized and we agreed to meet at the same location the next day. I again alerted the Toledo RA who had the two guys under surveillance for the past several days.

The meeting the next day was the same except, this time, I placed a wire under the diner table where I would be sitting. Since surveillance had them covered, I decided I would arrive at the diner first. So they wouldn't get suspicious and want to change tables, I made sure I was in eating when they arrived. I also spread a few things on the table and put my jacket in a chair, so they would have to sit in specific seats, convenient to the microphones. As before, the inside and outside of the diner was loaded with agents. We kept the Wood County Sheriff deputies outside, just in case one of them was recognized.

When Jose and his friend arrived, I pretended I had just slipped my parole officer and would be in a hurry. The conversation between the two of them went right into speaking Spanish. I listened to their conversation and heard them say, I was *perfecto para el trabaja* (perfect for the job) and we needed to get started *ensiguida* (right away without delay). This time, I felt I could let them in on my secret. I answered them in Spanish and joined in the conversation, just as if I was Mexican. They were surprised as hell that I could converse in Spanish.

I knew the next question would be where did I pick up Spanish? I told them in Spanish, *"Estaba en carcel en Texas hace dos anos."* (I was locked up for two years in a prison in Texas.) We swapped stories about a couple gangs and some names I had picked up from an informant. I made sure I mentioned names and gangs they hadn't heard of in Texas. I made them think I knew more prison gang members than them. Now, I was really on their good side. I was a hit man, a felon on parole, and I could speak Spanish. I was perfect for the job.

Jose gave me the address where the sheriff deputy lived and showed me his picture again. I was insistent on getting him to tell me what he wanted done in order to get his statement on the tape recorder. He fell right into my trap. He told me, "This time, Man, I'm gonna pay you in *pulvo* and *chavo* (cocaine and cash)." As always, I told him, "Straight up". I told him to call me in a few days, after I get the guy's schedule together and we'd meet to get my down payment before I got started. I told him I had some people that could let me know when he was ready to be hit, but they wanted to be paid first. We agreed to a meeting sometime later and parted company, one at a time, as before. This time, the tape was rolling with good information, but a lot of it was Spanish slang. My plan was to get a portion of the pay up front and to show Jose a Polaroid of the dead body in order to get the rest of the money.

The next call to the undercover line was the crucial call from Jose. The call came about four days after my last meeting with the two of them. I recognized Jose's voice right away, and he told me he was ready to roll, which meant he had my cash ready. Jose did not know the officer and his family had been relocated to northern Michigan, until after an arrest had been made. The relocation caused the Wood County Sheriff Department to be short two officers and several thousand dollars for expense money. The officer, his department, and his family were as anxious to get these guys as the FBI. We felt the next meeting would finally pull the undercover operation together and hopefully conclude successfully for the FBI.

Shortly before our final briefing, we covered every possible scenario and placed about ten agents all over the small diner. We only let the diner manager know that something may go down, but ten FBI agents and a score of deputies were around the restaurant to insure the public safety. We made him swear not to mention our presence to any of the workers until the arrests were completed. To insure his honesty, he was only made aware of the operation by the case agent who talked to him outside the restaurant the entire time. The manager was never told that most of his customers that afternoon would be undercover federal agents.

Jose was surveiled from his hangout as in the past. He drove his red pickup truck to the diner and appeared to be taking all precautions as he neared the meeting location. Surveillance reported Jose had two guys with him in the red pickup truck, which meant there were now three of them. Nonetheless, we were prepared because we assumed he was rolling with drugs, cash, and most likely a gun. I arrived early and set my wires in strategic locations at the table. The three men entered the diner as usual, and I immediately jumped into both of them, using the worse Spanish slang I could muster up. The guy with them was a long skinny white guy who looked like a junkie. He sniffled and constantly rubbed his arms. They assured me he could be trusted and he was only their cocaine supplier. I tried to pretend I didn't want to do business around him, but they insisted he was cool. I told them in Spanish to never bring anyone else into the plan, or everything was off. Temperaments finally calmed down and I let them move on to the business at hand.

Jose said they had the down payment on the body and he was ready for me to get to work. I told them, "I will get you a photo of the carcass and I want the balance of my money....no questions asked." They all said it was a deal. I also told them not to bring this guy with them again because three was too many. They agreed. The tall skinny white guy pushed a small plastic bag under the table toward me. It contained about three ounces of a white powder, i.e. pulvo. Jose handed me a brown paper bag with a stack of bills inside. I knew it wasn't cool to count money during a transaction, but he said it was $2500.00. I told him, "I believe you and we'll settle up the rest after the work is done." I placed the bags inside my shirt and took my hat off and on twice for the signal to the agents that the deal was sealed.

We had very little conversation after the exchange and I took great pains not to address the white guy. I wanted to appear not to trust him, although he tried several times to engage me in conversation. With each question, I'd address Jose in Spanish and let him know I didn't want anything to do with the guy. This time, I told them I had to meet my guys in Flint, in order to get things moving. The three of them left the diner together, but not before we agreed to talk later in the week with the details of the hit. For some reason, they seemed to be in a hurry but I didn't ask them why they were moving so fast. Besides, I wanted to get this ordeal over, so I just let them go. By now, I could see several agents were in position to block the exits of the diner if they tried to get away

Oath of Office

from the parking lot. Several others were staged around their truck in case they tried to run on foot. Several teams of Wood County Sheriff deputies were all over the streets, just in case they escaped and tried to get to the interstate.

As they all climbed into the red pickup truck, FBI agents, dressed in SWAT gear, converged on the three of them like flies. All three men slowly got out of the truck with their hands high in the air and surrendered without a fight. Only Jose had a pistol in his waist but was quickly disarmed as he was placed on the ground of the diner's parking lot.

I immediately ran outside, now they knew the guy they thought was a Flint, Michigan street corner felon, was an FBI agent. They went into Spanish, but I told them, *"Quieto Y no hablando en Espanol!!"* (Quiet and don't speak in Spanish) The next word from Jose's mouth was, "Mother something..." All conversation ceased immediately, as they were handcuffed and searched.

The Wood County Sheriff Department quickly rolled onto the lot and the tall sergeant said, "Thanks a lot guys, good job." Our Toledo senior agent in charge released the prisoners to the Wood County Sheriff's Department and we turned north on Interstate 75, enroute to the Toledo Resident Agency office. I waited until I got to the office to unwind and duplicate the audiotapes from my recorders. I knew they might come in handy later, if this case ever went to trial. The case agent and supervisor of the Toledo FBI office congratulated us for a job well done! Once again I had done a job fitting enough for me to merit my next undercover assignment.

Due to the complexity of this case and my skilled use of Spanish, I was later given a cash incentive award from the Cleveland Division. The cash was accompanied by the usual "ataboy" from the Special Agent in Charge from Cleveland.

This contract-hit case ran in the local newspaper and on the evening news for three days. This investigation was the biggest case to ever happen in Wood County in quite a long time. Everyone praised the FBI for the assistance we provided in bringing the contract hit men to justice.

However, the worse was yet to come. About two months later, my legal counsel in Detroit presented me with my first job-related lawsuit. I was named in a lawsuit along with the Director of the FBI, the Cleveland Division Special Agent in Charge, the Toledo Resident Agency, and the entire Wood County Sheriff Department. The suit stated that as the FBI undercover agent, I was the catalyst and the integral part of the beating of our three prisoners that were arrested that afternoon. This was the first I had ever heard about the beating of the prisoners.

I was summoned to court a few days later and heard the entire story. The plaintiffs' attorneys were not disputing their attempts to hire me as a hit man for the sheriff's deputy. They alleged the Wood County officers detoured while returning to the county jail and gave the three prisoners a terrible whipping in an open cornfield. They were asking for millions of dollars in actual damages. The government attorney provided evidence the FBI agents turned the prisoners over to Wood County at the time of the arrest and drove back to Toledo.

Everyone was eventually cleared of all charges and the lawsuit was dismissed. Thus, my career was salvaged and I no longer needed to hire my own attorney to stay out of jail. I was later selected for numerous other undercover assignments as a reward for my effort.

Chapter Eight

- OPERATION GREYLORD -

Pop seemed to be drifting in and out of consciousness, after being on so much medication. I was trying to take advantage of his waking hours just to visit with him that afternoon, but it was clear to me, he was struggling to stay awake. His friends were also glad to hear him talking and alert for the short time. Pop and I had briefly talked about some of my undercover work on the telephone. I purposely avoided the subject, in order not to worry him and Moms. For some strange reason, he always seemed to enjoy my stories about the drug dealers and car thieves on the streets of Detroit and New York. He asked me to tell them about the big case I was involved in during the mid 1980's in Chicago. He wanted to hear about the one that had drawn quite a lot of attention in the newspapers. I had only talked about certain aspects of the case because I didn't want to worry them about my safety.

For once Randy seemed to be listening to me and not creating any problems for his grandfather. Pop once told me that Randy thought he might want to be an FBI agent one day. I thought this was as good occasion as any to give him the real story about Operation Greylord.

Randy asked me, "Well exactly what did you do when you were working undercover in Chicago? Some stuff on television is hard to believe." Pop said, "Tell him about working undercover inside that jail in Chicago." Randy said, "Have you ever been undercover inside a jail and survived? Man that's the kind of job I want..." I said, "No you really don't. It's not like the movies, this is the real world."

I began my story by explaining to Randy that undercover work is unlike episodes that you see on television or at the movies. I said, "As an FBI agent working undercover, you are more than a person on stage playing a role. Every move you make, every statement you make, may someday end up in federal court. If you do something stupid or unethical, you may find yourself out on a limb all alone. You can even compromise and destroy many months of good investigation, just because you didn't use your head at the right time. You also might get fired for your unwise actions and sometimes may be sent to jail along with the bad guy. And cops don't fare well in jail."

During the mid 1980s, it came to the attention of the FBI that the judicial system in Chicago was corrupt. According to information gathered by the U.S. Department of Justice, there were sitting judges and court officials demanding money in order to drop felony cases brought before the court. This was a tremendous slap in the face for the tax paying citizens in Cook County, Illinois. The FBI was tasked with gathering evidence to prosecute the rogue judges and court officials.

The FBI sent out a request for the sharpest, streetwise agents it had on board. They told us that the assignment could be potentially dangerous because the agents selected, would have to enter the Cook County court system as arrested subjects and be processed through the criminal justice system. After being arrested, the undercover agent would be placed in the general inmate population and while in jail, would no longer have the coverage and protection of the FBI. Those with street sense would have to use it in order to survive.

During the briefing, there were several of us young crazy undercover agents that felt there was nothing we couldn't do and do well. Many of us had participated in numerous undercover operations, in many cities. Some of us had spent time inside local lockups and survived to talk about it. Chicago was just another stop along the way. Although we attended the briefing meeting with the Chicago case agents, we still had to be chosen and placed in a specific assignment.

By the time the Chicago team came to Detroit to recruit undercover agents, the case was well underway. They included in their briefing the fact that there had been some problems with the undercover assignments since the case began. We were told several agents had been beaten up by local police officers while being arrested. Unfortunately, in order to preserve the case, the FBI surveillance teams couldn't intervene. On several other occasions, while in lockup, some FBI agents had gotten into fights. Undercover agents had to fight alone, because there was no backup available inside the jail. No one could say they didn't know the perils if they were selected and if things went bad during the assignment. Nonetheless, many of us were still willing take on the new assignment.

After the briefing, a normal FBI agent would leave examining his psyche. Although we were sworn to silence, we quietly discussed the assignment among ourselves. The phrase, "Are you crazy?" was common among us at that time. Any FBI agent that was willing to go inside the Cook County Jail, without the benefit of cover had to be strange, to say the least, but all of us, for some reason, were willing to accept the challenge. The Chicago management team, although somewhat reserved, examined each of us for our ability to succeed in this unprecedented assignment. When the meeting concluded, we were told those accepted would be contacted later with instructions.

About two weeks after the briefing, the Chicago Division management team contacted me. I was one of only a small number of Detroit undercover agents selected for the unprecedented undercover assignment. I was given a limited amount of information on the telephone about my first assignment, but was told to meet my team two days later at a location about twenty miles outside of Chicago for more instructions. I recalled the Special Agent in Charge called me to his office and asked, "Are you sure you want to do this?" I pulled out my credentials, looked at them, and simply told him, "I've taken an oath of office that I intend to uphold, Sir." He smiled, shook my hand, and said, "Good luck Agent."

I was registered at a plush resort using my undercover name. I had my first briefing at 4:00 p.m., in a remote hotel room. When I arrived at the meeting, I met an agent whom I knew from my days in training school. Seeing L.T. Wilson made my assignment a little easier because I was familiar with some of the other undercover agents on my team. This assignment was an attempt to infiltrate the drug court in the Cook County Judicial system. An informant had presented evidence that a presiding judge and his staff had a regular practice of taking bribes to drop criminal narcotics cases. According to the informant, the bribe would normally be solicited after formal charges are filed against the suspect.

Our scenario would involve the two of us loitering in a local park where drug deals were known to be transacted. I was to leave my partner in the park with a package under a park bench. The package was to contain a small amount of marijuana. An anonymous call would be placed to the Chicago Police that someone was selling drugs from a paper sack setting beneath the park bench. The officers would respond, search the undercover agent, and seize the bag of marijuana setting below his seat. The undercover agent was

Oath of Office

instructed not to resist arrest and would be arrested and taken to jail.

The undercover agent in this case would probably remain in a local lockup for several hours. My role was to appear and post his bail at a magistrate's court hearing. While the arrest was occurring I would be a part of the surveillance team recording as much of the transaction as possible. I would also be looking out for any signs of police brutality, which had been alleged against several police officers.

We decided to wait until the traffic died down later in the evening and the sun had gone down before we moved into our location. The surveillance squad set up and moved into the area to roust the local dealers. The true drug dealers were soon chased out and moved to another area of town. The last thing we needed was to have the wrong dealers arrested or to have our undercover dealers hassled by the local pushers. When our agents gave the signal, we moved into a clear area and set up shop. As soon as we set up, customers started hitting on us by the dozen. Suburban Whites and locals all came to us seeking to purchase various assortments of street corner drugs. In order to keep them away, whenever we were approached, one of our cars would drive up and the buyer would leave.

When all the props were in place, a call was made to the local police that a tall Black guy was selling drugs in the park. The caller told the police the guy was selling from a paper bag that was beneath the park bench. Our undercover agent was to sit directly over the brown paper bag. I moved around the corner and was picked up in a surveillance van. Within a few minutes the local police rolled in and began questioning our undercover agent. He allowed himself to be searched and carried nothing more than his undercover driver's license and a few dollars. Obviously he denied selling drugs and continued to glance at the brown paper bag sitting beneath the park bench.

One of the officers asked if the bag belonged to him and of course he said, "What bag?" The officers quickly discovered a small amount of marijuana in the bag and arrested the undercover agent. Up to this time everything had gone according to plans. Another agent remained close to the magistrate courtroom so that I wouldn't have to hang around too long and become noticed. His role was to monitor the magistrates call list and to let me know when it was almost time for me to appear to post bail for my fellow agent.

I received the call at approximately 1:00 a.m. Our undercover agent was coming up for his hearing in a short time. I showed up in court just as he appeared before the judge. His bail was set at $3000.00, which meant I had to post a bail of $300.00. Unfortunately in this case, no one asked for additional money to make the case disappear. I just assumed that would happen later when our agent had to reappear for a court appearance.

When we left the courthouse, we walked several blocks out of the way until a surveillance van picked us up on a dark corner in downtown Chicago. As far as this segment was concerned, my role was completed in this portion of the case. Any bribes would have to be handled by the undercover agent when he reappeared for court later in the month. I headed back to Detroit the next morning to await my next assignment.

I received a call several days later from the Chicago case agent requesting me to return for a different role and to be ready for a briefing. I didn't mind the minor role of handling bail money during the last trip. I must admit it was safer than going inside a jail cell. I was told my next role would be different from the last.

I arrived in Chicago and met my team at the same location, and the briefing meeting began as soon as I arrived. The same agent was on my team, but I'd have the starring role inside the jail cell. The focus this time was the auto theft court in Cook County, Illinois. Automobile theft was a big problem in Chicago and according to our

Oath of Office

intelligence base, the entire court and the judicial officers regularly took bribes from prisoners and defense attorneys. Although I had never had an undercover assignment inside a lockup, I felt my street corner days in north St. Louis was all the training I needed to get me through the assignment.

We were told about a problem that occurred a few weeks ago; an undercover agent, arrested in this sting, forgot to remove his credentials from his pocket. They were discovered when he was searched and almost blew the covert portion of this investigation. The one factor that has changed was now all prisoners were being transported to downtown central to be processed. Local police were careful not to do anything contrary to normal procedures and to move all arrestees to the magistrate court as soon as possible. For the undercover agent, that meant he would now be exposed to a larger, crowded, and a more dangerous facility. I was given the option to back out prior to the assignment. I accepted, after all I was from north St. Louis.

The next morning I was driven to a small market on the corner of 57th and California in Chicago, to see where the next scenario was going to be staged. The plan was for me to be driving a vehicle that had been placed into the NCIC system and reported stolen. My undercover partner was going to call the police after I entered the market. He would the tell police that I had just parked a stolen car on the parking lot of the market. If things went as planned, I'd be arrested as I left the store. The case agent, a young guy from Vermont was always very cautious, he told me, "Just let them arrest you, and please, please don't resist." I looked at him and said, "Hell man, I'm from north St. Louis. Don't you think I know better than to give cops a reason to whip up on me?" I'm not sure if he knew what that meant but I knew what to do.

At approximately 10:00 a.m. the next day, everything was in place and I drove to the small market as planned. It was a warm morning with the birds chirping and traffic extremely light in the neighborhood. Many patrons were elderly and walked to the neighborhood market. The day was rather uneventful. I entered the market, walked around for a few minutes, then purchased a bag of potato chips and a six-pack of beer. In order to fit into my undercover role, I was dressed as any everyday street bum. My clothes were wrinkled and my baseball cap was turned backwards. I had several days of growth on my face in order to lose the clean-shaven FBI look I had become accustomed to wearing. I paid for the items in cash, stuffed the receipt in my pocket, and walked out of the store as if I owned the world.

As I neared the car I heard, "Hold it!! Put your hands in the air!!" By this time the parking lot was full of cars and several customers heard the commotion. I dropped my packages and put my hands up as I was told to do. I found myself starring down the barrels of two .38 caliber service revolvers held by two police officers. One officer grabbed me around the chest and threw me to the ground. I went through the normal "What's going on?" routine to draw attention to myself. I knew the more attention I attracted from onlookers, the less likely they would be to use their batons on a person who wasn't resisting arrest. I knew from my days in St. Louis that many guys had been beaten to a pulp by police who claimed the prisoner had resisted arrest. I didn't want any accidental slips of a baton or a pistol butt in my direction. I could see my surveillance team from the corner of my eye but their assignment was to stay in place and not to intervene regardless of the circumstances. I could hear the little old ladies on the parking lot saying, "Someone said he stole that car. I wish those people wouldn't come out here with their crime. This is nice neighborhood."

One officer read me my rights as I sat handcuffed in the rear of the police squad car. The crowd who watched me get rousted and cuffed had now started to disperse. I saw the little old ladies picking up my potato chips and my six-pack of beer that I had dropped on the ground. They were walking away with my stuff as the squad car pulled off the parking lot with me sitting in the rear seat.

Within a few minutes I found myself sitting at the local precinct station where I was processed for possession of a stolen automobile. I knew that I would have to be taken downtown to Central Chicago Lockup and held for a magistrates hearing. It was almost noon and I hadn't eaten anything all morning. My stomach was growling like mad and I was thirsty. I was hoping to get some food before I went downtown because I had heard rumors about the quality of food in the lockups. It was always a delicate balance whether or not to eat anything before an assignment of this nature. If you eat a meal, you might find yourself in a position where the cops won't let you use the bathroom. If you don't eat, you might find yourself hungry for hours if they decide not to feed. Either way, you'll have problems in the lockup.

I knew I would be searched close to the body so sometime earlier I hid a small three-inch pocketknife underneath my heavy sweat socks. I knew from my street corner days that cops don't always search you close to the body. Most of them don't really want to touch prisoners and especially if they smell. Unfortunately that has caused the death of many cops. I thought I'd use their apathy to my advantage, in this case. I knew my knife might come in handy where I was going if things got a little tight. The arresting officers later searched me and my street sense paid off—the cops missed my pocketknife.

I was placed in an empty room and handcuffed, when a tall, hillbilly detective walked in holding a blackjack in his hand. As he chewed tobacco, he stood directly over me and began pounding the blackjack into his left hand, which was placed against my head. The hillbilly then said in a loud country voice, "What da' boy done done now?" As he spoke, he laughed out loud while spitting tobacco juice in my direction.

This scenario is a black, handcuffed prisoner's worse nightmare. I knew many prisoners had been beaten while handcuffed in jail lockups and from his demeanor, I was about to become this guy's next victim. I knew that when the prisoner appeared at their court hearing the story was always, "He was resisting arrest your honor and we had to subdue him." In the meantime, the defenseless prisoner would be nursing a concussion. Nothing is ever done about it and often the poor guy wouldn't receive any medical attention for his injury. When the prisoner is finally released, he is just glad to be alive and his injuries are seldom treated. I didn't want to become a statistic so I said nothing to the cop to antagonize him. Soon the big hillbilly walked away laughing, knowing he'd put something on my mind. He knew he had me at his mercy and I could do nothing about it.

A police officer walked in the holding area and told me to sign a statement admitting to automobile theft. I hadn't spoken to an attorney or anyone but he insisted they needed my signature on the form right away. The cop just assumed I couldn't read and shoved the paper and a pen in my face. I refused to sign it and was told I'd be transported to Chicago Central Lockup for holding. He said that I'd go before a judge later. This was the same tactic I heard had been used on some prisoners in order to get confessions out of them. Some poor guys just signed the forms because they didn't know it's not required and many couldn't read and write. For some reason, one of the officers brought me a McDonald hamburger and a coke. That was a lifesaver, because that turned out to be the only food I'd have over the next fifteen hours. By now, there were two of us in the lockup and we were told to eat in a hurry because they all had things to do. We obliged the officer with no question.

Oath of Office

Shortly after noon that day, I arrived in shackles and handcuffs at the rear of the Cook County Courthouse. It was a typical, stinking, hot July afternoon at the rear of the jail. Dust, trash, and old newspapers were blowing and the alley had the distinct aroma of cooked urine. I was cuffed to the other prisoner and we were immediately placed into a small 20 by 20 holding cage that contained no less than 30 prisoners. To say it was crowded is a gross understatement. There were guys cursing, some guys praying, some belching, and guys like me who thought they were the meanest dudes in the holding cell. I knew by now that I had no backup from the bureau, although I had been warned about this part of the undercover assignment earlier. My only help, if something went terribly wrong was Jesus and my north St. Louis street sense. It was all about to be tested over the next 20 or so hours.

The prisoner-processing officer called us out to his desk one at a time for booking and to verify our personal property. Everyone was locked up for something different but no one was going to act like a chump in front of the other prisoners. Every ten minutes they brought two more guys to join us in the small cramped cage. Some guys smelled like they hadn't taken a shower in weeks. Others coughed like they had contracted a rare disease that couldn't be cured. Some prisoners just farted like they had eaten a dozen White Castle hamburgers and enjoyed releasing the gas. One guy farted repeatedly and laughed out loud each time he let it out. To top off his disgusting behavior, he constantly picked his nose and thumped the waste in the air. Whether or not it was a tactic to keep guys away from him, it worked. No one approached him or said one word to him.

The cage had a few young white guys who looked frightened as hell and hated they ended up in such a disgusting environment. They probably would have given their right arms to get out of the crowded cage of dangerous, smelly black guys but they were stuck there just like me. Unfortunately for them, they were up a creek without a paddle, just like the rest of us. Suddenly, the jailer called out, "Carl Taylor!!" It was my turn to be processed and booked at the front desk.

The prisoner booking process used in Cook County is an interesting ordeal. The booking officer calls out your name, your charges, your social security account number, and then he counts out loud the amount of money you have in your property. They do it loud enough so that everyone in the holding cage who has an interest in your personal business and cash only has to listen. After you're processed, they loudly shout out, "You keep your money, we don't want to be responsible for it!" The officer then pushes your money across the counter toward you and sends you back to the holding cage with all the heathens. All the processing is done in plain view of the other prisoners who are waiting for you to return to the holding cage with your cash in your pocket.

The jailer counted my money out loud saying, "Ten, twenty, thirty, forty, fifty, sixty, seventy, eighty, ninety, one hundred, one hundred five, six, seven, and eight. You have one hundred eight dollars. Take it. We don't want it!" Without turning around I took my money and placed it in my front pant pocket. I could feel my pocketknife next to my right ankle and I thought I'd have to use it soon, but I had more street corner tricks to pull first.

I was led back to the crowded cage feeling like a pig going to slaughter. The jailer laughed because he thought he would get a chance to see a jailhouse stickup. What he didn't know was, I was from north St. Louis and I had been trained well on the streets, long before the FBI. As I walked back I somewhat staggered as if I was having the effects of a drug high. But all the time I stood at the counter being processed, I had my back to the cage where the other prisoners were being held. I had discreetly rubbed my right eye until I was sure it was deep red. As I staggered back to the cage, the other prisoners could all see one clear eye and one red eye. One red eye and one clear eye are commonly indicative of a heroin user. I looked as wild as any of them and I acted like I wasn't taking any crap.

As soon as the next guy was led out of the cage, the door was slammed behind me. Just then a tall, very dark complexioned, stinking guy walked up to me and said, "Hey man, loan me a dollar" and held out his hand. By now I had blown my nose until my nostrils began to run and I just let it drip all over me and to the floor. I looked at the huge stinking bum and I started breathing as deeply as I could without saying a word. My one red eye and dripping nostril had really kicked into gear and I looked as if I was ready to explode. I just kept breathing deeper and deeper, puffing, and blowing snot bubbles from my nose. By now this big huge guy knew something wasn't right with me and backed up to give me a little room. I began to mumble out loud.

All of a sudden I went into a karate stance and shouted, "Mother f----r!!" I started to slowly move in his direction while swinging and kicking in the air with choreographed karate movements. Some of the guys in the cage had moved back to give me room to work on this huge man. The big guy also backed away from me. Someone behind me said, "Hey that little motherf----r is crazy!!" The big guy backed up and said, "Hey I'm sorry man. I didn't mean anything," and threw his hands up and walked to the other side of the cage. My bluff had worked like a charm. If I had had to fight that big monster, I would have had to use my knife. That would have caused more problems than it was worth, but I'd still be around. Pop always taught me to never back down from anyone regardless of his size. He once told me, "Look son, most guys don't wanna fight. They just want you to be afraid of them." I guess Pop was right again, as usual.

C. Lee Thornton

I knew from my street corner days that no one wants to fight a crazy man, whether he is big or small. That works in the jail as well as on the street corner. For the balance of my time in the cage, no one bothered me because I had the reputation of a crazy man. In addition, I refused to wipe my nose, I just let the snot run down the front of my shirt until I was sure I looked a mess. Some of the other prisoners weren't as lucky as me. I saw several of them get some pretty bad butt whippings over the next several hours in the lockup.

One poor soul was about 18 years old and was one of two white guys in the cage. The guy arrived handcuffed, crying and begging the jailers not to put him in the cage with us. He made the fatal mistake of letting the others see him begging not to join us. He knew before he landed in the cage that he was "dead meat". As soon as he was processed, several big, tall, black guys took his cigarettes and "borrowed" all of his money. One at a time they'd walk up to him and say, "Hey man, gimme a cigarette and loan me a dollar". This happened over and over. One time he told a guy he couldn't give him a cigarette. That was a mistake he should not have made, especially after giving other prisoners money and cigarettes. The prisoner got angry and had to be restrained by several guys. He accused the white guy of calling him a punk in front of the rest of us. He said, "You gave everybody in here cigarettes and money and I try to be nice to you and you treat me like a m.......f.....n punk. I'm sorry man but I gotta f—k you up!" The poor little white guy definitely didn't want to fight so he just gave the guy his last cigarette and the last dollar he had to his name.

Before the white guy left the cage, a big, tall, 250-pound, black guy was leaning over his shoulder and calling him baby. Everyone just looked on because now the young white guy had a protector/boyfriend. From the conversation I heard during his processing, he was a runaway from home and had been picked up by the police.

Oath of Office

I would imagine he'd never run away from home again. The next time he'll stay in his room like his mommy tells him and go to school. Next time, running away will be the last thing on his mind, or at least he will never run away in Chicago again.

Another poor guy was a pickpocket with a wooden leg. When he was arrested, the police walked him into the cage wearing his prosthetic leg. After he was booked at the desk, the jailer took his leg off and packaged it for evidence. It seemed the guy was picking pockets and hiding the wallets inside his wooden leg. The guy had to hop back to the cage on one leg. He was mad as hell and cursing uncontrollably. He really wanted his leg back and everyone within earshot heard his opinion of the jail and the jailers. He said, "Those low down m.....f......s took my m.....f..... leg off!! I need my m.....f..... leg to walk!" When the guy was put back inside the cage, prisoners started pushing him around from left to right. He couldn't fight or do anything. He was a little "Jiminy Cricket" looking guy with a baldhead. By the time we were placed into the cellblock area, his new name among the prisoners was Hoppy. Each time someone called out "Hoppy" someone would push him from side to side and disappear in the crowd. Hoppy swore he was going to kill the first guy he could catch pushing him. He just kept hopping and swearing like a sailor.

By now the cage was so smelly you could hardly breathe. Guys were belching and farting like they had lost their minds. It was as if it there was a farting contest and some guys were doing all they could to win first place. At 3:00 p.m. that afternoon, the jailers separated us and placed us in individual holding cells. The jailers told us we'd have a cell alone until it got crowded. By 5:00 p.m. the cellblock had gotten crowded and the jailers started doubling up guys in the single cells. It just seemed that there was an open season on criminals in Chicago that day.

I was sure I'd go before a judge at least by 4:00 p.m. because I only had a first time auto theft charge. We had earlier planned that my bail undercover agent would be inside the courtroom no later than 4:00 p.m. to post my bail. Something had gone wrong with the system and I was still being held. By 6:00 p.m., I began to wonder if my undercover partner had given up and left the courtroom. He was the only person that would be available to post my bail to get me out.

Late in the evening I could see the jailer was loading three to four guys to a cell and starting to fill up the cells in my direction. I could see the young white guy about a dozen cells away from me, wiping tears from his face. He was standing and holding on to the steel bars of his small cell. There must have been six guys in the cell with him. One big huge guy stood close behind him and leaned over his shoulder. He was either whispering in his ear or kissing his neck. I couldn't really see from my cell but they were close and the young white guy was not in a position to resist any advances.

The cell next to me had just been loaded with four more guys who all arrived at the same time. I could hear them discussing their arrest and were putting their stories together. The four of them had raped a lady and beat her boyfriend in a nearby park. They were organizing their stories for their appearance before the judge. I couldn't understand why all four of them would be placed in the same cell after being arrested for the same offense. That was one of the reasons the FBI was investigating the court system, it seemed terribly corrupt and out of order.

As they put their story together, I overheard one of them say that another guy was being processed as they were coming into the lockup. They said a guy had stabbed a man near the courthouse in downtown Chicago. They described over and over how the guy had brutally stabbed the other one with a large knife. From the way they described the stabbing, at least two of them saw it occur. Just then I saw three deputies wrestling with a prisoner who looked like one mass of muscle and coming in my direction. Up to this time I was alone in my cell. The two deputies wrestled on each side of the prisoner and the third deputy had the cell keys in his hand. The deputy opened my cell door and told me to step back to the far corner of the tiny cell. In one big push, the prisoner was thrown into my cell while everyone watched in awe. The cell door was slammed behind him and the three of them walked away.

When the guy was thrown into the cell with me, he went all the way to the rear of the tiny cellblock and his head landed inside the nasty, smelly, commode. He was so high he just kept his head inside the toilet for several seconds. No one from the nearby cell or me said a word to him. I felt against my ankle for my hidden pocketknife, which I thought would have to be used to defend myself. The huge man slowly lifted his head, looked at me and said, "What the f---k are you looking at?" I knew I had to again come out of my crazy bag. I said, "F---k you, whaddaya think I'm looking at?" I think I startled this guy as much as he did me coming in to my cell. He stared, backed away, and sat on his side of the cell on the cold concrete slab. This crazy man then started bragging and raving about the guy he had just stabbed near the park. He preached on and on about how the guy had f....d with him for a long time and he just got tired of it. He said, "I caught the m.....f.....r and I stabbed the m.....f....r and stabbed the m.....f....r until I got tired." While he preached he went through the motions how he was stabbing the man. He continued on and said, "The only thing I hate 'bout it, I had to use my new knife." The guy went on to describe the beautiful hunting knife he had just bought but had to use to stab the guy who was bothering him. This crazy guy summed his story up by saying, "God knows my heart." His head fell backwards and he went to sleep on the cold concrete slab.

The entire time he preached about his conquest, I had my knife open and in the ready position. I never closed my eyes; I listened to the noises created by the prisoners around me. I could still see the young white guy. He was probably wishing he had never run away from home. After all, he could never explain his huge, new friend to his family. He just stood in one place gripping the steel bars and shyly fighting off the advances of his new friend, who was lurking over his shoulder.

Around 10:00 p.m. my stomach had started growling as loudly as the other guys were farting. I hadn't eaten a thing since early in the day. I could drink some water but the water fountain in the cellblock looked like it was breeding some sort of green fungus. In addition to being horribly corroded, it smelled like a dirty toilet. After all it was only a foot or so away from the commode that didn't flush very well. Prisoners were beginning to raise hell about not being fed, but the turnkey officers paid them no attention.

One guy called out to the deputy for something to eat. He said, "Hey dep, we ain't had nuthin' ta eat!" The deputy's response was, "F... you, this ain't Holiday Inn!!" After hearing that, I knew there was no need for me to say a word about food. I was long past doubting my sanity for taking this undercover assignment. This jail cell ordeal had moved far beyond Advanced Street Survival 101. No one ever told me I'd have to starve while sitting in a jail cell waiting for a judge to hear my case. I should have been taken before the judge and released no later than 5:00 p.m. that afternoon. I didn't want to start raising hell about getting out because I knew it wouldn't do any good and that was a sign of weakness in the cellblock. I knew that any excess noise would probably wake the crazy guy in my cell. I didn't want to seem weak to the other prisoners so I just went along with things as they were for the meantime. I had to show them I could do time, just like them with no sweat. In fact, most of my comrades seemed to be fairly comfortable in jail and

Oath of Office

they appeared to like the surroundings. They had plenty friends and most of them seemed fairly content. Reverting back to street sense, I just sat there and waited to be called to see the judge. I only hoped my paperwork was not lost in the system and that my undercover partner was still in the courtroom.

In order to remain sane, I started to recall Pop's marching orders and my oath of office. Fidelity, bravery, and integrity started to really come to light. I never questioned whether I could uphold the oath. Each time I thought about the oath made me stronger. In recalling Pop's marching orders, I started to feel sorry for many of those surrounding me in the cellblock. I wondered how many of them would be in the cellblock if they'd had my Pop to drive them and kick their butts when they got out of line. I wondered if any of them would be in jail if they'd had the history lessons that I had from Pop and his friends. It was sad that so many of them were content with the discomforts of the downtown lockup. It was obvious to me that none of them knew their history and their dad's weren't like Pop. Had any of them been raised by a real dad, the cellblock would probably have been empty. I was no different than most of them except I had my oath of office, Pop, and Him on my side.

By 2:00 a.m., my stomach was growling louder and louder. My cellmate was loudly alternating between snoring and farting. I knew the night court magistrate only heard cases up to 3:30 a.m., which made it tough to think about staying for another day in this cesspool called jail. There were probably 10 guys who had come to jail ahead of me, and still had not been called to see the judge. The hearings would not resume until 9:00 a.m., which could be a long day for a first time auto theft case. Just like all the seasoned prisoners in the cellblock, I sat and pretended to enjoy my surroundings.

Shortly after 2:00 a.m., two deputies walked toward my cell. I silently rejoiced and assumed it was finally time for me to see the judge. I sat up on my concrete slab and tried desperately not to appear too anxious. They had a paper form in their hand and shouted, "Williams!" The crazy man sat up and said, "What?" They told him they had to rebook him on murder charges. He looked at me and said, "You see, the m.....f.....died. The m.....f...... died." The crazy guy was lead out of the cell in handcuffs to be booked again. He didn't seem happy, although he tried to show a tough outer image to the rest of us.

Even though the crazy guy was gone for about an hour, I still refused to close my eyes, I assumed he was returning later. About an hour later, Williams returned and was in his usual rare form. I kept my knife open and my bluff well intact. He stayed on his side of the cell and I stayed on my side. This time I had to listen to the crazy guy preach about the goodness of Jesus. I guess since Williams had been taken out and booked for murder, he had really gotten tight with Jesus. Just to keep him going, I gave him the occasional "Amen, I know that's right."

I knew if he quit preaching and decided to act a fool with me, I had a plan to send him to Jesus by special delivery. I kept my blade open and one eye on Williams the entire time he preached, until he finally passed out on the cold concrete slab. His last words were again, "God knows my heart." I said, "Amen and amen again, my brother." Williams now seemed to be out for the rest of the night.

The time was just about 3:30 a.m. and it was a few minutes prior to the final magistrates call. One of the deputies walked back to my cellblock and shouted, "Carl Taylor!" I rose slowly and pretended I hated to leave the comforts of the cold, stinking, jail cell. I turned around slowly as if I knew the drill from experience. The deputy tightened my handcuffs and led me to the magistrate's courtroom, which was adjacent to the lockup area. I apparently was the last case to be called that morning because the courtroom was practically empty of prisoners. As I walked into the courtroom, I assumed my undercover partner would not have been waiting in the courtroom since early the previous afternoon. I had mentally prepared myself to spend another day in the jail with my new friends.

To my surprise, when the courtroom door opened, the first person I saw sitting in the rear of the room resembled a smelly, dirty looking bum. His hair was a mess and he generally looked like hell. That guy was my undercover partner who had been there all night since the day earlier. Although he looked like crap, I was glad to see him. We glanced at one another but we knew not to seem too happy to see each other. I just slowly walked to the bench like any veteran prisoner. The jailer released my handcuffs and positioned me in front of the judge's bench. A guy walked to my right side and said, "I'm your public defender and be quiet. Don't say a word. The guy on the other side wants to keep you in jail, he's the prosecutor and his job is to keep you jailed as long as he can." He pointed to the magistrate and told me he was going to read my charges to me and tell me how I was being charged. He again told me not to say anything and show no emotion. I pretended I didn't know what was going on and played the typical prisoner role, I said nothing but "Yes sir."

The magistrate leaned over the edge of the bench and motioned for the prosecutor to come over to the side bar. The bailiff and my public defender also joined the informal meeting. The judge called me over and said to me, "How much money you got boy?" I thought I would be hit on for money much later but I went along with them like a common criminal. I said, "I don't have much but my cousin brought some bail money," and I pointed to my undercover partner in the rear of the courtroom.

The judge motioned for him to come up and asked him who he was and if he had money for bail. My partner played the game well, telling them he was my cousin and he had some bail money he had gotten from my grandmother. The four then met alone at the side bar for a few moments longer. The judge pounded his gavel and brought the hearing into session.

After reading my charges he said, "Your bail is $5,000.00 and you need ten percent." I turned and asked my undercover partner if he had it and he gave me a thumbs up. I really wanted to get something to eat and I knew it wasn't going to happen anytime soon if I remained in the lockup. I was released to the front steps of the jail about thirty minutes later, where I met my undercover partner. He told me I was the luckiest man on earth. He said, "Man you don't know how lucky you are. The bureau gave me $500.00 for bail money and I have $29.00 of my own money in my pocket. Had the bail been any higher, you would still be sitting in jail." We laughed when I told him the judge had already hit on me for money as soon as I went before him.

The first thing we did was find an all night diner to get something to eat. I still had my original $108.00 in my pocket from earlier in the day. I was scheduled to appear in court at 9:00 a.m. that morning and I hadn't gotten any sleep that night, thanks to my jail cell surroundings. After we ate at the diner, I had just enough time to return to the hotel near the airport, shower, and head back to downtown Chicago. My court hearing was 9:00 a.m. and I was on a tight schedule.

My partner dropped me off about four blocks from the courthouse in downtown Chicago at 8:30 a.m. that morning. As always, I walked over several blocks out of the way to insure I wasn't being followed. I arrived at the courthouse and located my name on the court docket. From the position on the docket, I felt I should be called prior to noon. My stomach was finally full but I wore the same cruddy, dirty clothes I had in jail. I didn't want to appear too comfortable or that I was doing too well. I was much more fortunate than the guys who had been inside the lockup all night without a meal, but I didn't want to flaunt it.

Oath of Office

About 9:10 a.m. that morning, I saw the first meal of the day being delivered to the guys in the lockup. The jailer had a large tankard of juice and two plastic crates filled with plain sandwiches wrapped in plastic. From where I sat I could see the guys in the lockup being held in a room behind the courtroom. The jailer opened the door, rolled in the tankard of juice, and threw the sandwiches on the floor. A huge fight broke out in the holding room over the food. The prisoners were fighting for the sandwiches and juice like wild men.

After the guys fought for a few minutes about six huge Chicago police officers went inside the room and started swinging their clubs. They quit swinging after all the prisoners in the room were on the floor. Everyone in the court could hear the moaning from the holdover room. I continued to thank God for getting me out of the lockup a few hours earlier.

My case was called before the judge several hours later and I was formerly charged in Cook County, Illinois. Someone whom I had never seen before walked up to me and told me he was my public defender and to shut up. The judge told me I was being charged with felony auto theft and asked for my plea. My attorney had already told me to plead not guilty. I simply said, "Not guilty". He told me my case would be scheduled on a date in October and to talk to my attorney. The guy who stood next to me told me he'd call me later. He never asked me a thing because I knew this case would most likely disappear. The attorney standing with me was my undercover attorney who had been assigned to this investigation. My partner picked me up a few blocks from the courthouse. I returned to the hotel and packed my bags; I had seen enough of Chicago for a while. I arrived back in Detroit about 8:00 p.m. that evening. I received my usual heroes welcome from my kids. Little did they know, I felt like I had been to hell and back over the past several days.

I returned to Chicago several weeks later for a hearing regarding my auto theft charges. The Chicago case agent had already told me negotiations with the court to drop the case were still being handled and the final price had not yet been determined. On the date I returned to court in October, I was told the case was going to be continued by the presiding judge. I pretended to be upset, as I walked out of the courtroom with my undercover attorney.

I was ordered to return to Chicago for hearings on three other occasions and each time, the case was continued. Our undercover attorneys told us the cases were being bought off, but it was going slow. Finally, by January of the following year, I was told that my case had disappeared into the Cook County Court system. We had successfully bought our case out of the Chicago judicial system.

My case was similar to dozens of others the FBI put through the Cook County Court system. The majority of these cases were bought off by payments to the Cook County court officials. The undercover case was brought to a conclusion the following year and resulted in indictments and prison sentences for seven Chicago court officials. To this day, my auto theft case has never surfaced in the Cook County court system.

As for my first undercover experience inside a jail with actual prisoners, my street corner training from north St. Louis was far more valuable than any training the FBI Academy could ever have offered. An undercover agent has to always be aware that any action by them could ultimately wind up in a court of law. An FBI agent does not have the option to say, "He made me angry or I wasn't thinking."

I can honestly say that someone was watching over me because my acting didn't have to work each time. Things could have turned out disastrous but they didn't. The guys in the lockup weren't actors, just desperate, unfortunate people. As I reflect on them, many were not that different from me. We just made different choices in life

Oath of Office

and had different people directing our actions. To say I earned every dollar of my salary during my time in jail is an understatement.

****

Mr. Thomas said, "Man that's really something, that you went undercover inside a jail in Chicago. That's really a tough place. Your daddy said you were doing some wild stuff with the FBI but we had no idea you were undercover in a Chicago jail." I said to Randy, "That's why it's not good for you to run with the wrong crowds. Jail is no fun for youngsters like you." I could see that Randy was not sold on the jail story and said to me, "Aw that's just how it works in adult jail. Me and my boys are still juvies. We'll get rich running the game by the time we're eighteen. They can't lock us up anyway."

As a practice, I never respond to ignorance right away. My method is to stare at the source and let them think about how stupid they sound. Randy was waiting for my response and I let the future felon stew for a few moments more. I said to him, "So you think you'll just stroll in and run the juvenile center? Have you ever been locked in the juvenile center?" He said, "Naw man, not yet, but my cousin been there." I said to him, "Listen, and let me tell you about my experience in the juvie jail and don't interrupt me." Mr. Thomas said that's why his mother needs a man around to teach him he's not as smart as he thinks. This time Randy shut his smart mouth and just sat there.

I told Randy when I was a student at the University of Missouri one of my required classes was criminology. One of the class requirements was to complete an internship at a local detention facility. I was the only Black student in class and I elected to perform my internship at the juvenile detention facility in the city of St. Louis.

I reported to the detention facility not really knowing what to expect. I was assigned to the 15–16 year old dangerous offender

C. Lee Thornton

cellblock. I just imagined I was assigned there because I stood a better chance of surviving than the two white guys who also were in my class. I really didn't mind because I felt, as someone who survived numerous near death events in my short life, a group of so-called tough kids would present no problems for me. I soon found out I was wrong about that assumption.

Although the offenders in this cellblock were pretty large guys, I had no problems interacting and controlling the groups most of the time. I worked along with a former Vietnam Marine who didn't joke or take any horseplay from them. There were young guys incarcerated for rape, assault, drug distribution, and car theft. None of the young guys were choirboys; they were hard-core criminals. Sadly, because of over crowdedness in the less serious offender's wards, from time to time a runaway would be placed with these hard-core criminals. That almost proved fatal for one young white kid from South St. Louis one afternoon.

The kid found himself in the dangerous offender ward. According to the information we received, the kid was sixteen years old and had been brought to the juvenile court by his mother who said she could no longer control him. She said he disrespected her constantly and she wanted to make him a ward of the juvenile court. Although there were other white kids in the ward, they were all certified gangsters and from tough neighborhoods all over the city.

One afternoon the ward counselor asked me to watch the group while he went up front to handle some paper work. He said he'd only be away for a few minutes. Before he left he gave me his key ring, in the event of an emergency and I could lock myself inside the control booth. I assured him I would be just fine. After he left the floor, I stood around and talked to the guys about baseball. I decided to walk inside the control booth to check the camera console. The camera console had about six cameras, which were placed inside several cellblocks to watch the kids placed in confinement. I noticed nothing was unusual and the one guy in the confinement cell was staring at the wall.

The only place the cameras didn't monitor was the bathroom for obvious reasons. As I monitored the cameras I suddenly noticed the main area of the felony ward had only about 10 guys walking around. The ward had at least 30 boys assigned to it and I thought it was strange that 20 guys all went to the bathroom at once in the middle of the afternoon. I thought I'd just walk around the ward to see if everything was okay. The first place I looked was the three isolation cells and saw nothing out of the ordinary. I then looked down the hall toward the bathroom and saw several guys milling around the doorway. They looked at me and seemed unusually quick to walk away. I immediately walked toward the bathroom.

When I opened the doorway I was stunned to see what was going on. Seven felons were standing in a line and one of them was on his knees with his business in his hand. He was shaking it like there was no tomorrow. He was kneeling behind the young white kid who was the runaway. The kid was bent over the commode with his pants down and crying. The little gangster who decided he would be first was just about ready for action when I stepped into the bathroom. I knew I couldn't let them rape that kid, so I said, "Hey, what's going on? Let the guy go!!"

The little gangster turned toward me, still holding his business in his hand. All of these guys knew I had just interrupted a party and they probably wouldn't get their turn at the young boy. The group looked at Bohand, the ring leader, and waited for his instructions to move. Bohand hesitated and said, "That's Thornton. He's OK man. Let him go." Inside I breathed a sigh of relief. I helped the young kid up from the floor and took him with me to the control booth. He was still crying and thanked me over and over for saving him from the felons.

The kid told me they hadn't touched him but in another moment it would have been too late. He said he would never run away again and was going to call his mom as soon as he could get to a telephone. The kid said jail was not what he thought it would be and if he got out, he was never coming back. The group counselor returned in a few minutes and I told him what had just happened. They soon broke up the ringleaders by sending them to different wards around the building. The young runaway was placed in isolation until he was released. The move to isolation was at his request and for his own safety.

I looked at Randy and said, "No, juvie hall ain't so nice either." This time he had nothing to say, but just stared at me.

****

Chapter Nine

IT'S NOT MY TIME.....

By this time it was fairly obvious that Pop was out for the afternoon but I had become so involved in my conversation with Randy that I couldn't make myself leave the hospital. While Randy was on a roll, I felt obligated to maintain his attention. Mr. Thomas and his friend also seemed pretty interested in my talk with Randy. Mr. Thomas said, "Tell us 'bout the closes call you ever had in the streets. Your daddy really used to worry about you when you were in Detroit. He didn't know for sure but he thought you were working with some real tough drug dealers. Did you ever think you was gonna die?" I could have given them a half dozen examples but one near miss on the east side of Detroit during a car theft investigation was about as close as it gets.

Every case begins with an informant who thinks he's going to make a living off of the government coffers. We developed an east side connection who we called Jet. He was one of my partner Ken's informants. Jet was connected with the Detroit east side car theft movement and virtually made his living off of it before he went to prison. He could tell us when a certain model was hot for parts and who was looking for that particular model. He knew the people who made a living switching VIN numbers and after the switch, where the cars could be found around town. Jet was wired to the car theft trade because he had a repair shop and an old junkyard in the heart of the east side of Detroit. Like most good informants he had done time for auto theft so he felt his jail time made him an authority on the trade. For Jet, hot cars and stolen parts were a way of life.

Jet was so good at stealing cars that we used him as a test model for a new General Motors security system. The GM engineers had spent months developing a new collar to combat the smash and trip system that made auto theft famous in Detroit. The old collars on the steering system were fragile and allowed the amateur thief to crack the steering collar and virtually start the car with his finger. GM engineers finally thought they had it all figured out and were willing to test the new system with the best, no other than our boy, Jet.

The Harvard trained engineers knew they finally had the auto theft enthusiasts figured out. So we found Jet and took him to the pristine GM laboratory to apply his trade. The test lab was complete with a video camera and a timer. Old Jet just laughed as we entered the test lab area. He knew he was on display and planned to earn every dollar he thought we were going to pay him for his services. This time General Motors had the till open and Jet had planned to tap into it.

The young engineer walked out in his lab coat and said, "Hello gentlemen, I'm glad you came today. We've developed a prototype and we think we finally can offer the consumer some real protection against car theft." Jet broke out into a big laugh. Ken told him, "Buckle it up, you want to be paid don't you?" Jet dried up.

The engineer told us he had a timer and the video would be running while they watched Jet work. He said he was going to equip Jet with only the basic street corner burglary tools. Jet laughed and said, "What type of tools are those, Man?" He said, "Just a screwdriver and a hammer." Jet just continued to laugh and said, "Start the clock and do I get any extra for ripping it under five minutes?" We told him, "Just rip it and don't worry about a bonus, after all we haven't called your probation officer." Jet then got to work on the locked door. Within thirty seconds he had defeated the locked door of the new Buick and decided he would sing a Temptation song since the audio was also running. Jet decided he would light a cigarette before he started on the steering column. Ken shouted at him, "Start the car, the rollers are on the way." "Rollers" is the street corner term for the local police squad cars. Jet said, "I got plenty time, they're all on a donut break."

Jet went from singing a Temptations song to one of the Spinners while he delicately operated on the fragile, re-engineered steering column. The engineers watched closely because they were curious if their months of work was going to pay off for them. As the clock struck exactly three minutes, Jet said, "You folks wasted your money," and started the engine with his finger. We looked at the GM engineer and he was still in shock. Jet smiled and said, "You play me, pay me." General Motors went back to the drawing board.

In criminal work, your informant base is your bread and butter. Jet was our bread and butter for making interstate auto theft cases. The FBI has a tendency to rate everything you do on how well your informants perform for you. Those FBI agents who are street savvy work well within this environment. The ex-cop or inner city school teacher turned FBI agent is right at home dealing with street scum. However, the agents that are "green" to the streets, such as the former accountant from the suburbs of New Hampshire, can find himself walking up a tough road... or alley, if it's Detroit.

Sometimes our informant base may be too good. Informants can get you into big trouble and if you're lucky, just a butt whipping. For that reason a good hip pocket source is what you need to keep your caseload rolling and supervisors off your back.

My informants were no different than the norm; they would get you in trouble if you put too much in writing. Sometimes you'd wonder if they were trying to get you fired or killed. We never knew which one they were aiming to accomplish. Such was the case one morning on Detroit's lower east side.

We had worked with Jet for about a year and our Group I undercover project had made some inroads into Detroit's auto theft trade. A Group I undercover project was one that had a shelf life of greater than six months. It generally had significant FBI headquarters funding and the blessing of the United States Attorney's Office to prosecute. So when Jet told us he had a line on some straight steals, we thought it was routine work. After all, he had never led us into a pit in the past and we had no reason to think this time was any different. He always hooked us up with guys we could control and arrest without a lot of fanfare.

Jet knew that we specialized in interstate insurance jobs, i.e., stolen cars that were leaving the state for sale by an organized ring. Our undercover project prosecuted those criminals under a broad mail fraud statute. We generally took in cars that people were tired of paying for and wanted to report them stolen. After reporting the car stolen, they would make a lucrative insurance claim and start over again. These crooks were particularly costly to Detroit because they were the primary reason for rising insurance rates in the city. But every now and then we had to grab a straight steal to keep our name in the street game. We generally got nothing from buying a straight steal from a thief but creditability on the streets.

As far as we were concerned, S & C Auto Brokers was getting to be a household name in the stolen car business in Detroit. Jet knew his job was to keep us in business and he hoped to cash in on the government cheese. We all knew Jet would be calling us from 1300 Beaubein one day soon, because he stayed in a jam. One hot summer morning, we received the "I got business" call from Jet. He told us he had a group of guys in his shop looking to unload a new Thunderbird for some quick cash. According to the guys in his shop,

Oath of Office

the wheels were still hot and they only wanted $500.00. They were in bad need of cash and Jet said they were willing to make a deal. Jet knew we were what they needed and he aimed to please.

Jet said he played dumb, but gave them our pager numbers. Jet just said we had been into his shop a few days earlier looking to buy some fresh cars for VIN switching. He thought he'd do the guys a favor and hook them up. Jet played his part well by saying he didn't know us, but would pass the information to the street. The sellers fell for the ploy hook, line, and sinker. A few days later, we got a call from the street corner dealers.

The caller only gave us his street name and told us they had a white Thunderbird they had to unload and fast. Jet had really done his homework on this one. While they were at his shop he had copied the Vehicle Identification Number and the license plate and gave it to us. By the time we got the call, we knew the true owner, the insurance company, and the place and time the car had been stolen. But we went along with the thief to keep the bait out there for them. We also knew they were desperate and wanted $500.00 for the car but we played naive. We figured if they wanted $500.00 on Tuesday, we could get it for much less by Thursday. Straight steals clogged up our yard, even if we knew the true owners and had a sure arrest on the subjects.

In order to get a full background on the new east side car thieves, we decided to string them along for a few days, just to see what type of volume they were moving. The longer we strung them along, the farther Jet got out of the picture. We wanted them to be sure that Jet had no connection with us. To farther distance Jet, we told them not to tell him we were putting a deal together because we really didn't know him that well. Throughout the numerous recorded telephone conversations, the dealer, known only as Ron, assured us he would stay away from Jet. Ron became greedier and greedier because he knew the Detroit Police would be out to spot the shiny white Ford Thunderbird on the streets. Ron told us the car was stashed in a garage on the east side and no one knew the location except him.

By Monday of the next week, we had more than six recorded conversations with Ron. We were convinced he was a small time dealer because he bargained with us for more than a week and for one car. Our business was slow so we decided to offer him $350.00 for the stolen Ford Thunderbird. Just as we expected, the novice car thieves jumped at the deal. We figured we would hold it in our yard for a few days until we made the necessary contacts with the insurance company involved. As for the novice dealer and his crew, we thought it would be best to devise a scheme to get them off the streets as soon as possible. They were so green to the game that they were more of a nuisance to the Detroit auto theft trade.

We made our connections with the Jefferson Avenue precinct and told them we had a few customers lined up for 10:00 a.m. the next day. We let the squad commanders know we would be driving a burgundy Ford Thunderbird and the subjects would be driving in a white Ford Thunderbird. We only knew one guy as Ron and didn't have a good description of him. The description we had was from Jet and he wasn't sure who was who at the time he met them. The precinct told us to be sure to contact them before we set things up the next day.

Our plan was simple. When the two Thunderbirds met, the squad cars would pull up and treat us all as suspects. They would question us, then they would run the plates on the white Thunderbird. After determining that it was stolen, they would arrest Ron and anyone with him. The plan seemed simple enough, but even simple plans go astray. We had gone over the arrest scenario several times with the police officers, including telling them what we'd be wearing etc. The plan seemed simple enough.

Oath of Office

The next morning we got the call from Ron; he was ready to get the $350.00 in the worse way. We assumed he must have been a drug user because he seemed jumpy and pretty anxious to get the money as soon as he could get it. If he wasn't a junkie, he was as close as it gets. We told him to meet us at 10:00 at the corner near the Farmer Jack on the east side of Detroit. This gave the squad cars a good look from down the street at us and we wouldn't have to call them or give any signals. They could just roll down to us when they saw the white car meet the burgundy car.

We spent about 20 minutes briefing our comrades from the Detroit Police, while insuring them we had covered all the possibilities. The last thing we needed in this undercover investigation was a slip up. The four officers got a good look at us so there wouldn't be any mistakes later that morning. There were only the three of us working the east side of the city that morning. We went over everything again and again until we knew there were no holes in the plan. We let them know that all they had to do was to frisk everyone just as any routine harassment and to keep the ones with the keys to the stolen white Thunderbird—nothing more.

At about 9:55, we rolled into the area and signaled to the squad cars as we passed them. They were so far up the street they could hardly be seen from the corner we were operating on. We figured they could easily see the white car meet us from where they were parked. Our desperate comrades pulled the white Thunderbird around the corner very slowly at about 10:10, fashionably late. They pulled directly behind us at our direction. The cruddy abandoned neighborhood was a typical car thief's playground. It had plenty of old buildings and people were so use to seeing drug deals on the street, no one really paid any attention or called the police.

The car was so shiny, we were certain the squad cars saw them pull up behind us. We all got out of our cars and checked one another out. The guy we assumed was Ron was cautious as hell and looking around like he was expecting company. He had one young jitterbug with him who was also nervous as hell and acting as if this was the first time he was brokering a car deal. Ron was probably about 20 years old, dressed like a typical street thief. The two of them were the worse types of criminals to do business with: young, nervous, and definitely inexperienced. Young thieves are especially dangerous because they don't seem to mind dying. They are quick to shoot, just to see if it hurts and to build their street corner reputation. Besides a bullet hole is a badge of courage to them, an honor in the street game, which many young boys look forward to achieving some time in their lives. They really think that getting shot is just like in the movies.

We started our greetings off with small talk to feel one another out. We were all strapped and had the police down the street waiting to move in. After about two minutes of small talk and checking out the white Thunderbird, we thought the squad cars would be rolling in our direction at any second. So we continued the small talk and asking questions about the car. We could see our young thieves getting jumpier and jumpier. It seemed as if they were waiting for someone to join them.

Suddenly Ron gave what we thought was a signal with his hand and out of both sides of the street walked nine more young gangsters from between the abandoned houses. It didn't take a genius to see we had run into a setup. Ron and his boys were planning to get the money and the cars with little to no work. As they surrounded us, Ken and I looked at each other with a look that said, "Oh sh—t, where in hell are the squad cars?" Did they see the white T-Bird pull up? How the hell can we draw and shoot all those m-----r f-----'s with three six shot revolvers and live to tell about it? We knew we were in for a fight.

Within a few seconds, the young street thieves had completely surrounded us and had started to move in closer as they checked out every passing car. They stared down the passing motorist, which is a form of their street corner intimidation. Obviously no one stopped their car or even looked at them twice, they just hurriedly drove through the neighborhood as if they were lost. Ron hadn't as yet handed me the keys to the car but I had decided he was going to be the first one to get my bullet, if the shooting started. I let him know in no uncertain terms he was mine if things got hot. I kept him close to me as Ken and John continued to stall and talk crap to two separate groups of young gangsters. We knew not to get cut off from one another and to keep one another in sight. We figured we could only b.s. them for a few more minutes before something serious had to happen. By now, we had given up on the squad cars and just assumed they couldn't see us. The three of us were all alone with our eleven opponents who seemed to be ready to make a move at any moment. By now, each of them had reached toward their waistbands and was waiting for the opportune moment to grab us. The only thing that seemed to delay their next move was a constant stream of cars passing us on the street and drivers noticing the crowd of young men gathering.

Ken was normally our leader, and we were just waiting for his signal to draw down on the gang. We had rehearsed a thousand times: how to salvage situations like this one, and it seemed we were finally going to have to implement our plan. I kept watching Ken for our signal to move, but he hadn't moved yet. I kept nodding and he held fast, without giving our pre-arranged signal. Ken was waiting for John to position himself away from the crowd of gang members that had assembled around him. If we drew our firearms on them, John would certainly have been in a position to be taken hostage by the group in front of him. Ron was a little guy and I had already rehearsed in my mind my move to keep him contained.

Because I was the closer to Ron, I had planned to grab him and spin him around with his back to me. I was going to shove my revolver barrel directly up his narrow ass until he hollered. I was going to use him as a shield until they all backed off Ken and John. By this time Ken was in a good position to grab his guy but John was completely surrounded and was not getting away from the crowd. Every direction he walked, they followed closely and continued to surround him. The only bluff he could use was to let them know we were FBI agents and hopefully they would take off running. Hopefully Ron would be in a better position to bargain for John, the only white guy in the group. If we lost John in this stick up attempt, that really wouldn't look good in the Detroit news. Everyone would second guess our plans and question our motives for being on the east side of Detroit dealing with young stick up men. So Ken cautiously waited for John to move to a better position away from the four guys that had surrounded him.

Just when Ken started to talk faster and make his move away from the advancing crowd of gang members, two Detroit Police Squad cars pulled up to us. The officers pulled the usual "What are you guys doing?" routine. The young gangsters scattered like roaches but I had blocked in Ron and pretended we would play the police officers off and pretend nothing was going on. I said to him, "Hey man just be cool. They'll leave and we can get back to business." The cops walked up and like champs, went through their "harassing the brothers" routine. We were pushed and pulled and thrown over the cars like common felons. We gave them some lip to make the stop seem authentic.

While I was being searched I whispered to the officer, "That guy dropped the keys to the car down the rear of his pants." By now the officers had run the plates and confirmed the car was stolen. Ron was twisted and turned and finally the keys to the stolen car fell down his leg to the ground. The officer said to him, "Well what do we have here?" He went to the trunk of the stolen car, put in the key that had fallen from Ron's pant leg and it popped open with no problem. Ron was cuffed and placed in the rear of the squad car. In order to keep the routine going, they looked at us and said, "Get outta this neighborhood." By now all the roaches had scattered but we could see them peeking from the windows and doors of the abandoned buildings on both side of the street. As we slowly drove away we could see the disgust on the faces of the young thieves that we got away with their $350.00. We counted them before we drove away from the area. The numbers had swelled to about fifteen of them against the three of us. They had multiplied like real house roaches. To make sure we got ripped properly, they had recruited reinforcements that were hiding in the empty buildings. That $350.00 almost cost us dearly, but again we won. Too bad we didn't have several cans of Raid to exterminate each one of them.

We were lucky they were all green to the stick up game. They may have been more successful if they only had moved a little faster. They spent most of their time looking around and waiting for someone to move first. The younger, less experienced stick up men stayed hidden and frightened, just in case somebody got arrested or shot, it wouldn't be one of them. Thank God for the cowards among them.

However, one squad car remained there until we were clearly out of sight. A tow truck was later called to haul the stolen car to the precinct for inventory.

One of the officers had already been briefed as to where we would meet him later in the day. After the car was turned over to the Detroit Police, the true owner was contacted to claim his car. Nonetheless, we later had a discussion with the officers as to why the hell it took so long for them to come to our rescue. They told us from where they were parked, they only saw a white car turn the corner; they said an eighteen-wheel truck that turned behind the car obstructed them. By the time the truck passed, they thought the white car continued on down the street. They said with the bright sun and from the distance the squad cars set away from us, it was difficult to see a light colored car behind us.

The officer told us they only moved up because they thought the guys had changed their mind and decided not to show up. They said at the same time, they had another trouble call and was preparing to roll on it. We then knew how lucky we were. We almost became the victims of an east side Detroit stickup.

Again, Jet did his job and distanced himself from the crime scene. Ken paid Jet handsomely for his services. I stuck to my guns and only provided him with help when he was locked up. Once again, we were lucky to come out unscathed. No one had to tell me who had His eye on us that morning.

Ken and I had become experts at reading one another's thoughts and instincts. He normally knew my next move as much as I knew his. We always made a habit of anticipating our subjects so that we never got caught with "our pants down". For the life of me, I don't know how we slipped, one cold day in March in Dearborn, Michigan.

****

We were investigating the theft of 30 cases of automatic rifle rounds from the Selfridge Air Force Base Armory in Mt. Clemens, Michigan. This amounted to well over 6,000 rounds of automatic weapon rounds. We had interviewed people all over Detroit because we knew the streets could absorb the ammunition in no time at all. With the number of shootings Detroit experienced every day, we knew it wouldn't be long before the rounds turned up for sale.

We got a tip from an informant that a computer technician who worked in Oak Park, Michigan had purchased a large amount of the ammunition over the past weekend. It was not clear what this guy's intention was but we knew we had to track him down soon. The best description we could get from the informant was the buyer was a survivalist White guy who worked at an Oak Park computer firm. We had very little to go on but we started hunting for our subject.

We found a computer firm located on Greenfield Road that specialized in software for personal computers. We knew it was a long shot but we decided to talk to the owner to determine if he had an employee who matched the description we got from the informant. The informant said the guy was pretty distinctive because he was so big. The description was vague but it couldn't be too many people matching the description: a huge, bearded White guy, computer specialist, and survivalist. The owner of the firm told us he had a lot of workers but he would let us talk with a few supervisors who have closer contact with the employees. Again, any help we could get might take the stolen ammunition off the streets.

After speaking to three supervisors, we finally hit the jackpot. We gave the description to the supervisor who told us the description sounded like Jim Golden who had recently been hired by the firm as a programmer. He didn't have a photograph, but sent us to the personnel manager for more information. The personnel manager and the owner were extremely helpful. They found a picture that matched the description provided by the informant. According to the informant, he had never formally met the guy. He had only seen him from a distance. He added that the guy drove a green Chevy pickup truck. The personnel manager told us Golden drove a green pickup, which he generally parked on the rear parking lot. Unfortunately, Golden had been absent from work for the past two days. Golden hadn't been to work since last Friday.

The personnel manager provided Golden's address and all the background information we needed to run a full criminal check. He had no felony convictions and only a few minor traffic infractions on his record. His past history showed no violence or acts of aggression. Our database did not indicate he was a member of any survivalist groups or movements. We could not understand his need to purchase such a large stash of ammunition. We still only had the limited information provided by the informant. It wasn't enough to get a search warrant or to assume he had a tendency for violence. Ken and I decided we would attempt to interview Golden at his home and hope we could bluff the information we needed from him.

Armed with only a little information, we went to visit Golden at his home in Dearborn, Michigan. As we drove to the home we saw a green Chevy pickup truck parked in the front of the house. The truck was muddy and had Confederate stickers on the rear bumper. The stickers seemed to set the tone for what we might later encounter.

Ken knocked on the door and I took my normal position at the side of the door. Within a few knocks a guy came to the door and asked if he could help us. Dearborn was practically an all White community and two black guys dressed in suits would generally draw attention. We introduced ourselves and the door opened. The guy was about 6'4", well over 300 pounds, and resembled a huge Viking. He had a big bushy beard but seemed to be rather mild mannered. He introduced himself as Jim Golden and invited us inside to talk.

Once we were inside, I did most of the talking. I tried to make Golden feel we had the goods on him and all he needed to do was to come clean to avoid any trouble from the FBI. I told him the Selfridge Air Base Armory had been under surveillance and we knew he had knowledge about the sale of stolen ammunition. In order to keep the informant out of the picture we told him we photographed his truck leaving the area where we had surveillance last weekend. We described the number of people that were there and the color of the vehicles involved so he could know we had good information. We even described the weather that evening. Ken told Golden that if he came clean there would be no charges against him, we just wanted the ammunition off the streets.

Golden stood up and said he bought the bullets from a guy who called him on the phone, but the guy didn't say the stuff was stolen.

Oath of Office

Golden said he had never been arrested and didn't want any trouble from the FBI. He told us he legally owned a number of automatic rifles and often went target shooting for a hobby. Golden explained he had the ammunition upstairs in his room, so his mom wouldn't be upset if she found it. He said if the stuff were stolen he would gladly return it to the FBI. He then started walking upstairs. He was talking and walking so fast that before we knew it, Golden had disappeared upstairs to get the case of ammunition he had bought a week ago. After he was out of sight, Ken and I started to think about Golden being out of our sight. We waited a couple of minutes contemplating on the fact that he had no history of violence and seemed fairly mild mannered. We thought; "He was just a big guy who liked guns".

We then realized Golden had been upstairs too long for our comfort. We called upstairs to him and he said he was coming right down. I looked at Ken and he said, "I think we've screwed up." I said, "I think you're right, but it's too late now."

When Ken and I saw Golden's feet coming down the stairs, we moved apart and stood at opposite ends of the room. Right away we noticed that he was not wearing the same pants he had on when he walked upstairs. When he got into full view, we saw that he had changed into camouflage clothes: shirt, pants, and hat. He stood and looked at us with two bandoliers of automatic bullets wrapped around his body. He was carrying what appeared to be an M-16 in his arms. Ken and I both drew our revolvers and kneeled in a defensive position in the living room. There was absolutely nowhere to take cover as Ken shouted to Golden, "Drop the rifle, now!!" Our hearts beat in unison at twice their normal rate. Golden smiled and while looking at us, slowly set the gun on the floor. It didn't seem that he had planned to do anything, but he made a terribly stupid move that could have been fatal for him.

Golden stared at us and smiled with a peculiar grin on his face. He said, "I just wanted to show you guys how I look when I go into the woods." Ken shouted, "Step back and keep your hands in sight!!" Golden complied and began describing how many rounds his bandolier could hold and how many rounds his Browning, not an M-16, could hold and fire. As Ken covered me with his revolver pointed at Golden, I took the rifle and withdrew a full magazine of live high caliber rounds from the loaded Browning automatic. He may not have been dangerous but he was certainly crazy as hell.

When things finally settled down, Golden said, "The rest of the ammunition is upstairs in my closet. I keep it there so my Mom won't find it." He again gave us a wide grin. I said, "We're going upstairs with you. All you have to do is point to where you keep it." Golden led us to his closet where he had a full case of military automatic weapon's rounds. Despite the military markings on the box, Golden insisted he had no idea the bullets were stolen from a military base.

We took the ammunition, including that in his bandolier and placed it in our bureau vehicle. Prior to leaving his house, we ran the serial numbers on every gun in the house. To our surprise, everything was legal and registered to Golden. We left him standing at his door still dressed in full camouflage gear and displaying his wide grin.

Ken and I finally settled down as we drove back to the office. We realized we had violated one of the most basic rules of law enforcement. The violation of that rule could have been fatal for both of us. We let our guards down for a moment and let a subject get out of our sight. Thanks to the Man upstairs, we lived to tell about it...

****

Shortly after we completed Operation Steamclean, which had bagged over one hundred subjects, I was one of three undercover agents who were still flying high and getting more requests for my undercover expertise. In order to keep our undercover operations short, we refused to give any new operations a formal name. We just named the investigations by the case file number, thus keeping attention away from us. By the mid-1980s we felt we were the hottest undercover team the FBI had to offer; our arrests and recoveries statistics proved it. We had the record to back up our reputation.

Our next operation request came to us clearly as a result of having good informants still willing to keep S & C Auto Brokers in business. Our business front had become a household name in the hot car game. Surprisingly, even though scores of people had been prosecuted, our company name had not been tarnished. Scooter, an informant, operated primarily in downtown Detroit and had his hands in everything from stolen cars to hot government checks. A normal person would think that hot government checks were too risky and exposed the handlers to federal jail time. However, some people were willing to do anything to make a quick buck. We're never too sure how deeply involved our informants are with the criminal act itself so we had to handle them carefully. We never let him forget if he gets caught dirty, he gets the most time we can convince a judge to give him. We also told him that we'd visit him in jail on a regular basis and let all his cellmates know he's got FBI agents as friends. That should make him pretty popular during his long stretch on the yard.

Scooter made his living hustling information and hot goods wherever he could find them in Detroit. He stayed one step ahead of an arrest and his pay was an assurance from us that we might come to his rescue in a pinch. He got very few dollars from us...... primarily Pampers for his kids from our pocket cash. Our motto was "If it's not in writing, it doesn't exist", and you can never get in trouble with the Bureau. He called us one afternoon and we decided to meet Scooter to see what he had for us. We met Scooter at the

McDonald's on Grand River in downtown Detroit. He always liked McDonald's because we would let him eat until he was about to pop open. He'd always make a stop at the McDonald's because it had a clean toilet for his after meal comfort. His routine was always the same: eat, crap, and be ready to provide good information—in that order.

Scooter showed us three government issued social security checks with random names. He said he could get plenty more where those came from if we wanted to do business with someone. Scooter told us he had a source inside the Post Office that had a route on Grand Boulevard on the eastside. He said the source worked on a route that had dozens of retirement homes. He said his source told him that every month many of the people in the senior citizen homes get government retirement checks. When they die, the government continues sending the checks month after month. He said his source just collects the checks and sells them for a few pennies on the dollar. Scooter said the guy has hundreds of them every month for sale.

We examined the checks and they looked like authentic government benefit checks. We had to be skeptical of Scooter because he'd play you if you let him. We asked Scooter how the buyer could cash the checks without running into problems with the bank, since all of the checks had different names on them, both male and female names. He told us that cashing the hot checks was the easiest part of the scheme. He said, "Y'all may not know it but the government is pretty stupid. They send the checks to dead people for four to six months before they finally realize the person is dead. When the checks are delivered, the nursing home would just hand them right back to my boy every month." Scooter said his boy had several markets on the east side that cashed the checks with no questions asked.

Scooter said the storeowners knew the buyers only paid a few pennies on the dollar for the checks. They would cash a five hundred dollar check for two hundred and make a three hundred dollar profit. The stores would return the checks to the bank for deposit and make a huge profit. From time to time investigators might show up at the store and ask about the person cashing the checks. The stores would just tell them the guy showed all the identification necessary when they asked to see it. Scooter said, "Since the checks generally had a social security number on it, the store owner would have the guy write it on the check and list it as a driver's license number. As far as the government was concerned, the guy showed a driver's license as identification. What better identification can he provide? Everybody got paid."

Scooter said he could introduce an undercover agent to his guy for the right price. I reminded Scooter that he had a trial pending and he may need a word, in the event things don't go his direction. We also let him know his child support was overdue and warrants may be right around the corner. I said, "In other words we need one another and let's just keep it that way for now."

Scooter said his guy worked out of the main post office station on Fort Street and he had a route that covered the Grand Boulevard area on the eastside. The Grand Boulevard area housed a large percentage of the senior citizen nursing homes in Detroit. According to Scooter, the senior residents died at the rate of 20 to 30 a month. He said he only knew the guy as Don but he's been hooked up with him for about a year. He said Don works a day shift and is finished by 2:00 in the afternoon. He said when they're ready to do business, they always meet near a store on the eastside. We told Scooter to let his man know he had a cousin in town from Cleveland and give him no more information. Ken said, "After he agrees to a meeting with your cousin, tell him we'll get back to him later. Don't volunteer any more information."

We didn't let Scooter know we had contacts inside the post office that could narrow down Don's identity and give us a full background on him. We later contacted the United States Postal Inspectors in Detroit and determined Don was actually Donald C. Weeks and he had worked for the post office for eight years. We didn't reveal Don's full name to Scooter, we let him continue to refer to him as Don. Weeks had been working the eastside route most of his time with the post office. We suspected he had a number of outlets to sell deceased checks. He lived on the eastside of Detroit with his wife and one daughter.

Weeks' police record appeared clean on the surface, but he had an excellent scheme selling the deceased checks. We decided to surveil Weeks and plant a few checks in the system of residents who we knew were deceased. We had to call in our contacts with the Social Security Administration to pull this scheme off. We were careful not to alert Scooter of our plans to check out his story. We knew the best time to insert the checks into the system was the first of the month.

We maintained contact with Scooter until the 30th of June and told him his only instructions were to get a few checks from Weeks at whatever price he could release them. We told him we wanted the checks in our hands immediately. If we found out he was holding anything, we were calling in all of our chips and he was going to jail. Scooter told us that he understood the plan and said, "Man I swear I ain't fooling with those checks any more. I can't afford to go back to the joint."

We didn't tell Scooter that both he and Weeks were being followed by surveillance the entire day. We wanted to see how honest he was going to be with us.

Our surveillance teams got busy early the next day beginning when Weeks first hit his route in the Grand Boulevard area. The second team followed Scooter the entire day on the east side of

Oath of Office

Detroit. However Scooter's day was the most interesting to follow of the two of them. He hit the streets around 9:00 a.m. and seemed to just look for something to do. Job hunting was not an activity he put on his long list of things to do that day. He hit the streets and hung around with his boys until they could find someplace comfortable to hang out. The group of them sat in the local park and talked stuff, made catcalls to passing ladies, and argued about what they used to own.

Both Scooter and Weeks fell into our traps around 3:00 that afternoon. They met at the same park where Scooter had hung out all day. It was as if they had planned the meeting. And just like clockwork, we saw Weeks hand Scooter three brown envelopes. From where we sat, they appeared to be government checks. Our next task was to wait and see if Scooter turned over all three envelops to us as he was instructed. We got our page call from him around 4:00 p.m. that afternoon, after Weeks left him at the park. Scooter told us from the pay telephone that he was ready to give us the checks he had gotten from Weeks.

We met at Scooter's favorite spot on Grand River, the McDonald's restaurant. As always we let him order whatever he wanted on us. As far as Scooter was concerned, this was his afternoon feast. When he sat down he pushed two envelopes toward us. They were unopened and addressed to two different residents at one of the Grand Boulevard nursing homes. Neither of us said a word to Scooter but just stared at him for a moment. He got the hint and said, "What?" I said, "Don't make us get in your ass." Ken and I just stared at him for a moment and took the sandwiches away from him. Scooter then said, "I was just seeing if y'all was on the case" and pushed the third envelope to us. No one said a word, it was as if Scooter was checking to see if we were really covering him and knew what he had been doing all day. We still said nothing more to him but stared. Again he said, "What? Man I swear I don't have any more. I swear!"

Although we knew he only had three envelopes, we couldn't let him know we had followed him and he was right. We looked him in the eye and demanded the last envelope. Scooter swore again that there were no more envelopes and he was being straight with us. He said, "I swear guys, I ain't lying!! I swear there ain't no more!!" We could see he was having trouble enjoying his cola but that was exactly our intention. We finally convinced him he was being followed and we were on top of every one of his moves all day. Only then did we give him his sandwiches back.

We jumped him again about trying to play us for stupid and trying to stiff us on the one check. He swore and swore again that he had given us all the checks he had and there was absolutely nothing else. Scooter continued to swear and eat. We promised him we were going to call the court that night and turn him in for child support delinquency if we got anything more on him. He continued, "I swear to y'all, I'm not stiffing ya...I swear that's it." We told him we were going to review our surveillance tapes and he'd better not be lying to us. He gobbled the sandwiches like he hadn't eaten all day.

Scooter told us he had told Weeks that his cousin was in town from Cleveland. This was a perfect set up, so he wouldn't be surprised when he sees an undercover agent with Scooter the next day. We had the undercover agent all lined up. He was coming to town from the Chicago Division and was still at the hotel. We just told Scooter to meet us on the corner, near Tiger Stadium, on Friday at 2:00 p.m. and we'll do the rest. Scooter was still wondering how much our surveillance team caught because he hadn't seen anyone all day. Our ruse kept Scooter on his toes and kept him honest with us.

Oath of Office

By Friday afternoon, we had our undercover agent work with the surveillance team in order to get a look at Scooter and his boys. He still had no idea who was watching him, which was fine with us. We later met Scooter on the corner as we had planned, but we forgot there was a Tiger's baseball game that afternoon and there were lots of people around. After awhile, we spotted Scooter in the crowd. This time we put him in the car and went for a ride to the east side of Detroit. Scooter was introduced to the undercover agent and only had to let his boys know the undercover agent was his cousin from Cleveland. Our undercover agent only gave Scooter his assumed name, Dave, because he needed no more information about him.

We then headed for Scooter and Weeks normal meeting spot later that afternoon. Scooter got a real treat because the undercover agent bought a couple of "forty's". They just appeared to be shooting the breeze in the park and drinking when Weeks arrived for their meeting and immediately hit on Scooter for a taste of the forty he was drinking. He was introduced to Dave, Scooter's cousin from Cleveland. Dave wore an old shirt and dirty jeans. He fit into the neighborhood like an old veteran. However he still was more presentable than Scooter who always dressed like a common street bum. Weeks told them he had just dropped off two checks but he would have more the next day.

By the time he left the meeting, Weeks had slipped Dave his telephone number to call him later. For some reason, he felt he could get a better price for the checks from Dave than from Scooter. Our guy told Weeks he was only going to be in town a few days but one of his boys own a store in Toledo and could probably use all the checks he could provide. Weeks fell for the story hook, line, and sinker. Now the undercover agent's goal was to cut out Scooter and deal with Weeks directly. Week's greed set in and he was ready to deal with us and not with Scooter.

Now Scooter's new role was to keep bugging Weeks like he needed the checks pretty bad, although he was not supposed to have any more contact with stolen checks. Weeks continued to put Scooter off over the next few days by constantly telling him he was going to get back with him on the checks some time later. Our Chicago undercover agent told Weeks he would get in touch with him a little later because he had to collect some money. Throughout the month of July our undercover agent met with Weeks several times and baited him for the August checks that were soon to be delivered to recipients. Our undercover agent had convinced Weeks over the next several days that he should watch Scooter because he was on paper (parole). Weeks agreed and eventually cut all contact with Scooter by the middle of July.

During the last week of July I had my first meeting with Weeks and our undercover agent. Our Chicago undercover agent was now tasked with further distancing Scooter by introducing one more person to the scheme. I was later introduced to Don Weeks as Carl Taylor, the new money source from Toledo. I had worked undercover in Toledo so many times that I knew the layout and could talk the talk if Weeks mentioned something about the area. It was a perfect fit. I told Weeks I was part owner of a small market in Toledo and we cash checks for a few people in the neighborhood. I told him if we knew the people, we didn't require any identification, which was perfect for Weeks. I told Weeks, "We have to keep everything between us. I don't want anyone watching me that close." He appeared greedier than I thought and ready to do business.

By the last week of July our Chicago undercover agent saw less and less of Weeks. We had completely eliminated Scooter from the picture and Weeks was convinced that my Toledo market would be the outlet he needed for his stolen checks. I met with Weeks briefly a few times near the latter part of July. I'd just tell him, "Hey everything is straight but I've got to handle some business

Oath of Office

downtown. I'll get back to you a little later." Scooter's name was never mentioned again and Weeks was convinced Dave and I had better dollars than Scooter. In order to keep the bait out front, we let Weeks see us constantly with a big bankroll of cash. After a few meetings he thought we were high rollers from outside Detroit. After the first month of contact with us, Don Weeks only saw dollar signs and big business. We were cautious not to ask him too many questions but to just let him think we were his new check-cashing outlet. Dave told him, "We don't care where the checks come from as long as you can produce volume." Weeks just continued to brag about what he could produce after the first of the month.

Our surveillance team started covering Weeks a little closer. On August 1, Don Weeks reported to work at his usual time and began his mail delivery route along Grand Boulevard. We had already sent teams of agents to about six nursing homes on his route and determined that about seven residents had expired during the month of July. We knew at least seven more social security checks would be arriving at the home and should be returned to the post office at the end of Week's shift. He was scheduled to meet me at the Church's Chicken on Gratiot at 5:00 that evening. Scooter continued to call as instructed and was turned down by Weeks each time. His instructions were to stay away from him until after we get our paper from him. So far he seemed to be following our instructions.

Our surveillance team took Weeks from work to his home on the east side of Detroit and directly to us by 5:00 that evening. That afternoon we had six units set up around the Church's Chicken parking lot. This time I had another undercover agent with me just to make things look normal. By now I was trying to distance Dave from the undercover operation. The new undercover agent was my excuse for visiting Detroit since I was from Toledo. All of us were eating chicken and blending in the area like we belonged in Detroit. As we waited for Weeks to drive into the parking lot, I was sitting in my car eating a two-piece with fries. Every once in a while, I'd throw a small piece of my chicken to the stray dogs hanging around the lot. Sometimes, I'd drop a fry or two as an added treat. I assumed if I were eating, Weeks wouldn't ask me to get out of my car. My car was now wired for audio while the Special Operations Group (SOG) took pictures from across the street.

Weeks arrived on time and walked to the driver side window with a large brown envelope. He was happy to see me and never questioned the presence of the new undercover agent with me. He told us, "Man I hit the jackpot. Those old folks are really dying on my route. I've got ten checks." I looked inside the envelope and discovered they were all from his route on Grand Boulevard. All of the checks he showed us ranged from around $300.00 to $800.00 each.

I told Weeks I didn't want all of them because I have to slowly turn them in for deposit with the bank. I took seven checks from the stack and held $500.00 in my hand. I asked Weeks, "How much for the checks I'm holding?" Weeks said, "The total of those is about $2100.00. Give me $900.00 for all of them." I told him I didn't have that much spare cash on me. We bartered back and forth and he decided to take a $300.00 check out of the stack and we settled for $400.00 for $1800.00 in stolen checks. He told us he would have more in a few days but we told him to hang on to them until he hear from us. The entire transaction was audio taped and photographed by our surveillance team from across the street.

Our surveillance team followed Weeks home and we returned to the office to log the checks into evidence. In addition, Weeks didn't know it but he had taken two marked one hundred dollar bills from us. The next day we presented the case to the United States Attorney for prosecution. We first verified the recipients of the checks were deceased, that the checks had been stolen from the United States mail, and sold to us for $400.00. The federal prosecutor got on this case right away in order for us to stop Weeks before he put too many other checks into the wrong hands. That same day a complaint was sworn out against Donald C. Weeks and an arrest warrant was issued for the Eastern District of Michigan. We had a squad meeting that afternoon and prepared to arrest Weeks the next morning.

Although we told Scooter to maintain his distance from Weeks, he called us before we left the office and told us Weeks was bragging about his sale to us. He was planning to get more checks later in the week and planned to continue doing business with his new outlet from Toledo. We knew we had to get him off the streets as soon as possible. Our plans were to arrest Weeks early the next day, before he left for work. Since Weeks' reporting time was 8:00 a.m., we planned to arrest him at his home at 6:00 a.m.

We assembled our arrest team at the office at 5:00 a.m. and were armed with both the arrest warrant and the complaint on Weeks. Our surveillance team had followed Weeks from home so many times that we knew the neighborhood inside and out. As the sun started to rise early that morning, residents were taking their daily walks and others were leaving for work. The quiet Detroit middle class neighborhood was well maintained. We saw Weeks' car parked in the driveway of his home, which too, was a neat and tidy structure. As yet, Weeks had no idea anything was unusual about his sale of $1800.00 in stolen checks.

We slowly approached Weeks' home, wearing clearly marked FBI ballistics vests. We surrounded the house and covered all exits of the two-story building. So far, we hadn't drawn any attention from the neighbors or anyone inside the house. As I approached the door, I said my silent prayer to Him to deliver us safely back to our families that evening. Three of us ran to the front door and two more ran to the side door. I knocked hard and waited for a response from someone on the inside. Nothing happened and we didn't hear any noise coming from the inside of the house. I knocked hard the second time and heard a noise coming from the inside near the front door. A voice from inside the house said, "Who are you and what y'all want here?"

One of the members on my arrest team was fresh out of the academy. He was a young white guy from a small town in Vermont and a former military infantry officer. Although the east side of Detroit was foreign territory to him, he was tough and in excellent physical condition. Being a new agent, many of them purchased a new pair of heavy wing tip dress shoes while still at the training academy. Young John O'Malley was wearing a shiny new pair of bureau wing tips and ready for action. This was going to be his first arrest.

John responded, "FBI, open the door!!" Just that moment, we heard movement from behind the door near where we stood. Movement in a situation of this nature normally indicates the person behind the door is preparing to mount a defense against us. We didn't want to take a chance on Weeks grabbing a weapon so I looked at John and said, "Kick it!" O'Malley quickly moved to the front of the door, spun around with a karate move, and planted his new wing tips firmly on the side of the door plate on the front door. The rest of us were poised at the side of the door with our weapons drawn. The door sprung open as if it had been blasted with a twenty-pound sledgehammer. O'Malley recovered, drew his weapon, and pointed to the inside the house.

Standing about ten feet inside the room was Weeks, naked from head to toe, and holding a baseball bat, as if he was ready to hit a home run. I had no idea what he was doing before he came to the door but the bat was ready for action and so was Weeks' private part. Weeks seemed happy and his business was standing straight out.

He still hadn't recognized me, since the sun was in face. We all wore FBI raid jackets so it was clear we were law enforcement officers. We kept our guns trained on Weeks and one agent shouted, "Drop the bat or I'll shoot your d--k off!" Weeks slowly lowered the bat and his business slowly moved in the same motion; from pointing to the opposite wall to hanging to the floor. Weeks surrendered the baseball bat and put his hands high in the air without a fight. He then recognized me as the undercover agent he had sold stolen checks to earlier.

At that moment Weeks' wife came running down the steps sporting her complete birthday suit. We now knew why Weeks was so happy. Before the slightly pudgy woman got completely in view, she turned to run back up stairs, but not before one of our female agents shouted, "Stop!! FBI!!" She turned around and stood on the steps with her hands in the air. She shouted to us, "I don't have any clothes on!" She was ordered downstairs by the female agent and was told to sit on the couch next to Weeks. A small child was asleep in a bedroom upstairs and was not disturbed. The rest of the arrest team cleared the house and insured it was safe for us to begin our interview. After Weeks and his wife were handcuffed, and it was determined that they no longer posed a threat to us, they were provided blankets to cover themselves.

After recognizing me from numerous meetings over the past month, Weeks sat with his head down, with a disgusted look on his face. The home was secured and he signed Consent to Search form. He decided it was best, since we could easily contact the court and get a search warrant based on the evidence we had on hand. He told us exactly where to find more stolen checks in his house. We recovered an additional twenty-two stolen social security checks from several places around Weeks' house. Weeks and his wife were later allowed to dress and he was transported to the Detroit United States Marshall office in downtown Detroit. His wife was not arrested. She told us she would notify Weeks' boss that he wouldn't be coming to work that day. Little did Weeks know, his boss already knew he wouldn't be at work that day or any time soon, for that matter.

This case concluded with a plea on Donald C. Weeks' part and a pat on the back for Scooter. Scooter received one "get out of jail free" card from us for his efforts. He'd probably need it sooner or later.

****

During my long time in the Detroit Division I encountered dozens of incidents when I figured I should have had my head examined. Many close calls were nothing more than Him looking over us and protecting us because we were too stupid to do it ourselves. The fact that a subject decided not to use his gun or practice his karate expertise on us was nothing that we did, but Him holding that person's hands close to his side.

One Saturday afternoon, six of us joined Special Agent Victor Boles, a street wise fugitive chaser, to execute an arrest warrant on the east side of Detroit. Boles was a street savvy former homicide cop from Pittsburgh. He was fairly new to Detroit at the time but we knew he could be counted on in a pinch. Our warrant indicated that Thomas Jennings was wanted on a murder warrant from Chicago, and it had the dreaded caption "Armed and Dangerous" on the front page. Jennings had shot the boyfriend of an ex-girlfriend, six times in front of her family. He apparently didn't take their breakup too well and wanted to teach her new boyfriend a lesson. Jennings taught him too well in this case. Jennings trademark was his signature sawed off shotgun, which he always kept close to him. Rumor had it that Jennings spared no expense using the shotgun to teach others a lesson. He had rumors all over Chicago that anyone coming after him would meet their maker.

Special Agent Boles called me one Saturday afternoon and asked me and four other young agents to meet him at the Churches' Chicken on Kerchaval in Detroit. He told me on the telephone, "Don't forget your vest, Jennings has already put the word out that he ain't coming without a fight." That was not the message I wanted to hear on a Saturday afternoon when I preferred to spend time with my kids. Besides, if we had to fight with Jennings, I only hoped his trip to the hospital would be fast and I'd be able to get back to my kids in time to see a movie later in the evening. I was in no mood to bargain that day. Jennings was not going to mess up my Saturday afternoon.

Boles told us he had an informant that swears Jennings was living at a house on Conner Street in Detroit. The informant met us at the parking lot and appeared to be the class act junkie. He was dirty and scratching as if lice were crawling all over his body. In addition, he smoked one cigarette after another. The guy called himself Rick and swore over and over saying, "Boles, I know he's in the grey house, I was just there about an hour ago. We were together comping a bag this morning on the west side." Boles asked him, "Are you sure and what's he driving?" Rick said, "Man he's still driving his black Mercedes with the Illinois plates. It's the same car he's had for the last two years. That car is his pride and joy." I was still reserved about believing anything Rick said, but he was Boles informant. Boles said, "Stay here with the guy and I'll be back in just a few. I'll just take a peek at the house since we're so close."

About ten minutes later Boles returned with Special Agent Dennis Tyler and said, "Well fellas suit up. The car's at our target's house and we don't have long 'cause it's getting dark. Take off Rick I'll call you later." Rick left the area walking and we made our final arrest plans with Agent Boles. Boles made it clear that according to information from the Chicago office, Jennings owned a sawed off shotgun and it was used in the murder of his last victim. He told us,

"According to Rick and another reliable source, Jennings answers the door with the shotgun in his hands. He knows he has outstanding warrants and has told several people he's not giving up without a fight." Tyler said, "Well boss, why don't we just wait until he leaves the house? We can't get him out if he's not coming on his own. We're just going to cause a gun fight." I knew Boles was streetwise and smart but this arrest seemed to be puzzling him. He knew, just as we did, that Jennings could be inside the house for the next several days if we waited and all of us wanted to get away before the sun went down that evening. Besides, it was not a good idea to try to arrest someone like Jennings at night. We waited for Boles next move to devise a plan to take Jennings without bloodshed. None of us figured that could happen and we just prepared for the worse possible outcome.

Boles said, "This will be our plan. I know Jennings has his shotgun next to the door, he always answers the door with it in his arms. But he also cherishes his shiny black Mercedes. I want two of you at the rear door just in case he decides to bolt out of the rear. The other three of you I want at the sides of his door on the front porch." Willis said, "Man, what the hell are you saying? How are we going to get this guy out of house without his shotgun?" Boles said, "I'm glad you asked that question. I'm going to drive up to his black Mercedes at an angle and wedge the front bumper as if I hit his car by accident. When I touch it, I'll slap the side of my door to sound like a bump. I'm going to then start blowing my horn to get Jennings attention. When he comes to the front door I'll tell him I've accidentally hit his car and I want to give him my name and insurance information. When he steps out on the porch, grab him. By then I would have walked toward the steps with my revolver drawn to assist taking him down. If he has his shot gun and raises it, light him up!" We all stood with our mouths open. I thought to myself, that it sound simple enough but I'd better say my prayers, as usual before we get started. Besides, even with the best plans, something always goes wrong at the last minute. I said, "Boles your plan sounds good but who do you want to grab Jennings first?" He said, "You. Any questions? Let's go, follow me."

We all took one drive by the old dilapidated gray house on Conner, to get a good look at it. The neighborhood only had a few people out that afternoon so we didn't draw much attention. We all met about a block away, checked our radios, put on our vests, and moved into position. The last thing we did was took a final look at Jennings' photograph. Two guys drove to the rear alley and signaled they were in place and ready to move. Myself and two others quickly ran to the sides of the house and radioed for Boles to move his car in place. By now, it was starting to become dusk and we knew our time was short. We all made sure our vests were pulled high over the shoulders and low to the waist, covering our stomachs. Many law enforcement officers have sustained fatal wounds when bullets have entered below a ballistics vest that was riding too high on the shoulders. We also checked one another to insure the large, gold "FBI" lettering could be seen by anyone in the area.

As Boles slowly rolled down the street, the three of us drew our service revolvers and positioned ourselves on both sides of Jennings front door. Boles slowly inched forward and slapped his car door loudly as if he had hit the front end of Jennings shiny black Mercedes. Boles started blowing his horn over and over until someone opened the door about six inches. Boles shouted, "Hey man, I'm sorry I hit your car and I want to give you my name and insurance information. I won't move the car until you can see it. O.K.?" The guy answering the door never stepped out into the open, he only said, "Wait a minute man. I'll be there." He closed the door leaving us on the porch alone. By now everyone's heart was racing a mile a minute. Boles was now moving toward the steps of the house and the three of us on the porch were poised waiting to move but Jennings hadn't surfaced. I only imagined Jennings strapping on a pistol to meet Boles at his car or maybe putting his shotgun under his coat and walking out to the car. We still didn't know if Jennings had someone inside covering him as he walked out. Regardless of Jennings plan, I was planning to get home that evening and hug my kids....Jennings was not going to stand in the way of my evening with my kids.

Suddenly, the front door started opening and I could see Boles hand behind his back holding his service revolver. I could clearly see one of Jennings hands coming out of the door and that was good enough for me. In an instant I moved in and grabbed Jennings right arm, which was empty and pulled him outside toward me. He was hit from the rear by Ramirez and tripped to the floor by me. With two blows, Jennings was on the porch, face down with his hands behind his back. The only words he heard were, "FBI!!" Before he could look up, Boles and one other agent ran past him and insured no one was following Jennings outside. I quickly cuffed Jennings told him to stay face down on the porch. He complied without saying a word. Within seconds all six of us stood over Jennings. Boles was holding a sawed off shotgun in his arms. He said, "Look what I found behind the front door guys." Jennings said, "You m..... f...... are lucky. I always answer my door ready for m..... f...... just like you." Boles said, "Jennings, if you had done that, we'd be calling a hearse as we speak." Jennings was home alone that evening and was transported to 1300 Beaubien to be held until the following Monday morning. I made it home in one piece and just in time to take my kids to the movies that Saturday evening.

Thanks to Him, it just wasn't my time that day.........

Chapter Ten

- THE BURGLARS AND DRUG DEALERS -

Sometimes law enforcement officers go to the wrong side and have to be investigated just as any common street criminal. Sometimes, if they are convicted, they are sent to jail and join the ranks of the criminals... unfortunately, most of them don't handle jail very well. As a member of the Technical Operations Group, I found myself on an assignment investigating a group of cops who had moved to the wrong side. The Technical Operations Group was a unique squad of FBI agents that had earned the prestigious title of burglars. All of the members of the squad were specially trained technicians who prided themselves on being experts in installing audio wires, video traps, and devices in the homes and cars of suspects. Obviously, we worked under court order and we possessed some unique technical skills that most FBI agents envied. We had been known to dress down wearing street clothes, construction company hardhats, and tool belts in order to perform our work. We'd perform our installations posing as anything from deliverymen to utility company workers.

At the time I was chosen to join the squad, there were only a small number of FBI agents with the TA (technical agent) designation behind his name. It was a label that we wore proudly, due to the unique training we had to endure to arrive at that designation. Moreover, I was proud because there were less than 20 FBI agents, Bureau wide, with the TA designation that looked like me. To be called a burglar was an honor in the squad room. Our qualifying in-service training was five long weeks of academic brutality. For that reason, most field offices were extremely particular selecting agents to join the squad. Moreover, no SAC wanted to lose a slot to someone who might flunk out. To flunk out of the program was considered a slap in the face to the field office that sent the agent for the grueling technical training.

Some tech agents or burglars would be tasked with entering a subject's home, defeat his alarms, while others would go to work installing the court ordered wiretaps. We'd sometimes have to take a drug dealer's car from under his nose, wire it for audio, and return it to him without him knowing it. At times we'd enter a hotel room where a drug exchange was to take place and discreetly install video and audio equipment for evidence in court at a later date. Often we'd really be surprised of their activities prior to drug deals in the hotel rooms. A regular task we engaged in was sweeping a federal courtroom or a witness' personal office to insure no bugs or wires were planted. Who would be better suited to detect planted wires and traps than an FBI burglar?

One day an FBI division came in contact with an informant who decided he would do whatever he could to lessen his time in jail. The informant, in this case, was also a Columbian national and was faced with a 20-year sentence for drug distribution in the United States. Lucky for me, I was not the agent strapped with debriefing and controlling this person. However, his story was interesting and his motive very clear—he wanted to be free from prison. Even if he had delivered the six major dealers he had promised us, he still had plenty time remaining on his sentence.

According to the guy I only knew as Hector, he had worked with a narcotics operation for several years before the Drug Enforcement Administration finally caught him. He said it was just a fluke that the same police department that had protected dozens of cocaine shipments from South America caught him. He was still pretty angry with the cops and vowed to pay them back for making him the sacrificial lamb for the multi-million dollar narcotics operation. Hector told us the drug loads were flown into the local airport based on a pre-set schedule. He said one sergeant would control the police officers that would be involved with providing protection. Hector told us the police sergeant would insure no one from outside their group was anywhere near the airport when the shipment arrived.

At the time the drugs were off loaded, the police officers would personally handle any inspections and paperwork to clear the shipment as soon as possible. The corrupt police officers would be notified in advance of the drop, the route to escort the shipment out of town, and ultimately to a neighboring location for the switch. Hector said that all the arrangements would be made in advance by a guy he only knew as Joe, who was a police sergeant in the district near the airport. He said every time he met Joe, he was out of uniform but he'd always have his gun on his side. He was completely in charge of the operation and would be the one to accept the payments for escorting the shipments to the neighboring town. Joe would drive his personal car and would travel all the way to the meeting location with the shipment.

Hector said Joe was present during all the meetings to make arrangements when the shipment was due to arrive in town. Hector said he knew Joe well and was still angry that Joe sat in court throughout his entire trial and never attempted to come to his rescue. Hector felt he was sacrificed and left alone to take the rap for the operation. He wanted revenge and rewards for his efforts. He vowed to do whatever he could to get revenge. While Hector talked, the officer involved listened attentively, but didn't make any promises or deals. He told him his story would be checked out and someone would get back to him. Hector provided a full description of Joe and told us he could be identified by a white Cadillac Allante he drove. This was his trademark. Hector said Joe paid for it in cash from the money earned from his drug protection business.

What Hector didn't know was the federal prosecutor knew he had more knowledge than he admitted to during the trial. It was absolutely no way he could have been involved with a major operation and know so little about the inner workings of the ring. The prosecutor felt a few years in federal prison would be enough to jog Hector's memory and bring him on the side of the government. Hector provided the name of an informant that might be in a position to put the FBI in close vicinity to Joe. A check of our intelligence base confirmed the informant might be a good source for the government.

For the next several weeks, FBI agents spent time reviewing informant bases and trying to determine the true identity of Joe. After about four weeks, Joe was determined to be Joe Hamilton, from the metropolitan police department. It took several days to check out Hector's story but he filled in some details that were omitted during his trial. Our next move was to locate the informant that could put us with the Columbian drug connection and Joe Hamilton. The FBI decided we wouldn't let Hector in on our plans, besides he was in the federal prison, and wasn't going anywhere soon. However, we lucked out and finally put an agent in touch with Pedro Talon, the other informant.

The Drug Enforcement Administration had operated with Pedro for several years before he disappeared. He apparently decided he wanted to change his life and quit providing useful information to the government. But in reality, we really thought the money wasn't good enough for him and he started selling information to another agency. However, an FBI undercover agent finally located Pedro and gave him an offer too good to refuse for his cooperation.

At the time the case was being put together, I was one of four agents assigned to the elite technical operations squad and we were dispatched to a city to utilize our expertise. Our first task was to find a white Cadillac Allante, similar to the one owned by Joe Hamilton. According to the case agent, Joe traveled to meetings in his car and never let it out of his sight. The FBI had secured a federal court order to place an electronic listening device in Joe's car to assist us in the investigation. Our job was to take Joe's car from him, install the listening device, and return it to him without his knowledge. Once the device was installed, the case agent would be in a position to monitor Joe's conversations while he traveled in his car. The device per court order could only be turned on to monitor pertinent conversations while Joe was inside the car. For that reason, we would install a remote switch, which could be activated by the case agent following the target vehicle. This device hadn't been used very often but our team was confident we could handle the job.

Because the Cadillac Allante was a relatively new vehicle on the market, most of the local rental car companies did not have many on their rental lots. It was even more difficult finding a white Allante that we could switch for Joe's car. But we finally located the perfect one. The task was to secure the key code and a duplicate key for Joe's car. Although difficult, this was not the toughest part of the tech operations job in this case. We knew our toughest job would be to take Joe's car from under his nose and to install a listening device without him noticing it was gone.

The Special Operations Group followed Pedro for several days to track his actions in order to see if he could be trusted. He passed all his tests with flying colors. We were now ready to pull the rip off of the century on Joe Hamilton. My partner at the time, Al Miner, and I were given the task of taking Joe's car and installing the bug within 30 minutes. We considered our two man team the best at what we did—installing electronic listening devices. To prepare for the rip off and installation, we practiced the switching of the cars and installation of the device for about a week, anticipating every possible trouble scenario.

Finally, on a Wednesday afternoon, Pedro was tasked with meeting Joe Hamilton for lunch at a fancy restaurant away from the city. Joe always preferred his business meetings at locations far away from the city, in the event someone saw him with undesirables. He was careful to maintain a clean reputation so that his narcotics connections would not be discovered within the law enforcement community. Pedro arrived on time and Joe soon pulled up in his shiny, white Cadillac Allante. Pedro was already seated in the restaurant when Joe arrived for lunch. By Pedro arriving early and sitting facing the parking lot, Joe had to sit on the opposite side of the table with his back to the parking lot. Unfortunately for us, Joe found a parking spot about six slots from the end of the main aisle, which created problems for us. His parking spot was unusually close to the front door of the restaurant. This meant that Joe could possibly turn around in his seat and look at his car at any time.

One of our tech operations agents notified Al that we were ready to pull onto the parking lot as soon as Joe and Pedro arrived at the restaurant. The next agent from our team put the key into the door of Joe's Cadillac Allante and jumped in. The key fit like a glove and he started the engine right away. As soon as he pulled out of the parking spot, Al pulled an identical car into the same spot and jumped out only to be picked up by another agent within seconds. The entire vehicle switch took less than fifteen seconds, less than the time we had practiced the switch earlier. Although Pedro was facing the window, he followed our instructions by pretending not to notice anything at all outside the window. He kept up his front by pretending he was glad to see Joe and enjoying the free lunch.

We had two other agents inside the restaurant who were listening to Pedro's conversation by an audio listening device. Pedro's instruction was to insure things were moving slowly in order to give us time to install the device in Joe's car.

Al and I had found a small garage three minutes from the restaurant to start the job of installing the court ordered listening device in the Cadillac. We were under pressure because we knew this guy was just having lunch as a favor to our informant. But we had all the angles covered to keep Joe busy. We had placed an agent inside the restaurant as a timekeeper for Pedro. As long as the guy was eating with his left hand, Pedro knew things were not completed with our assignment. He didn't quite know what we were doing but he knew he had to keep Joe busy with conversation. Pedro had his instructions that when the FBI agent switched to his right hand, Joe was free to go. Pedro knew nothing more than those few facts.

To be safe, the waiter was also on our side. He knew to keep Joe inside the restaurant until the agent gave him a signal that it was time to let him go. The waiter knew to delay his bill, his food, or to spill food on him if he had to keep him there. He knew to do whatever it took to delay the guy because his federal cheese depended on how well he did his job. He too, had no idea why he had to keep him busy, except that he had a few bucks coming from an FBI agent for his trouble.

Meanwhile, Al and I went to work on Joe's Cadillac Allante in record speed. We had worked as a team so many times we knew the moves of the other like clockwork. Our first job was to take a Polaroid photo of the inside of the car and the trunk. We knew we'd have to pull everything out of the trunk in order to hide the device. The last thing we wanted to do was not to put things back exactly as we found them. The photos were our map to replace all the junk he had inside the car and trunk in its exact location. The car was unusually junky for a luxury car owner but that worked to our advantage.

While Al rigged the device and tested it, I laid the wires, and neatly hid them beneath the carpet liners. I was careful not to fluff the carpet or leave a hump anywhere along the linings. Sometimes these guys get suspicious and look to see if their car has been bagged by pros like us. Al and I had batted one thousand so far and we didn't plan to get discovered. The device tested perfect for remote switching and the connection wires were ready to be fused. We tested the device from several distances and decided we were ready to return Joe's car to the restaurant parking lot. We sent out word to the surveillance teams inside and outside, that we were finished and returning the car in a few moments. Pedro knew his role as we returned.....keep Joe's eyes away from the window. We also had coordinated two vehicles to drive past the restaurant and obstruct the view as we made our switch.

We took great pains to insure everything was placed exactly as the photo had them before we tore Joe's car apart. Al got into the car and headed back to the restaurant parking lot. The signal was given to the agents on the lot to get ready for the switch. The two obstruction cars moved into position while two more agents walked past the restaurant for further cover. The two vehicles were switched with precision and without anyone noticing anything. As I picked up Al on the far end of the parking lot, he looked at me and said, "My screwdriver!! Where's my screwdriver?" I knew then something had gone wrong. Al was referring to his fifteen-inch screwdriver he used to place the device into the trunk. We then realized he had left it in inside Joe's car. We immediately sent the signal to the inside surveillance that something went wrong and we had to re-steal Joe's car to look for the missing tool. If Joe found the screwdriver, it could completely blow the entire case.

Our surveillance told us Joe was almost finished eating lunch. We knew we had to alert our inside guy to get the waiter to slow down his service. We met two blocks away and told our team we needed to buy ten more minutes. Al said, "I need ten minutes more with the car, we'll have to steal it back." This part was not rehearsed in our practice runs but we considered ourselves "born again burglars." We quickly rallied and waited for the signal to switch the cars again without being noticed. We got the move signal from the surveillance team and pulled the car out of the parking spot again. We made the second switch with precision within seconds with the help of the two obstruction cars.

We drove like hell and this time we only drove three blocks away from the restaurant and parked the car. I looked in the rear seat and then opened the trunk. Al went straight to his screwdriver that was in the middle of the trunk, next to some papers. We called back to the surveillance team leader and alerted the inside agents we were on our way back for the final switch. By now, we knew we were on borrowed time and that Joe Hamilton was getting restless. We later learned Pedro was faking a stomach sickness to keep Joe's attention and his eyes off the parking lot. He was earning his money like a pro, which was his job. He never knew our paid waiter also had contingency instructions and was also ready to swing into action. He was told that as last resort to stall Joe, to spill a plate of food on the table letting some of it hit Joe.

The switch was timed again and we waited for our signal to move the cars into position. Al and I were sweating like hell but we were still composed. This time I was driving the Cadillac Allante. I listened to my radio and suddenly the team leader said, "Switch!" I rolled onto the parking lot and one agent quickly jumped into the cloned rental car. The switch was again executed flawlessly. We had successfully re-stole the car and got it back to the lot for the second time. This ordeal later became the talk of the office. We had certainly earned our burglar bars that day.

By the time the inside agent started using his right hand, Pedro was about to faint. He too had earned his pay that day. Joe had no idea why Pedro was sweating and breathing deeply but he performed well under pressure. When Joe pulled off the parking lot in his car, he was fully wired and ready to be monitored. The surveillance team followed Joe home that afternoon and tested the remote switch several times. Our work was perfect. Everything worked just fine.

Over the next three weeks the surveillance team monitored numerous conversations between Joe Hamilton and his drug associates. This was all due to the successful placement of the remote switching device. We finally got word that he was meeting with a Columbian drug connection at a hotel near the airport. We went into our burglar mode once again. This time, our entire burglar squad converged on the hotel. Our informant was in charge of renting the rooms for the out of town guests. The FBI had close connections with the hotel managers who politely let us pick our rooms, which were adjacent rooms on both sides of the target rooms.

We arrived the day prior to our Columbian guests and completely wired the entire hotel room for video and audio monitoring. By the time we finished, a major television production could have been filmed in the hotel room, courtesy of the FBI burglar squad. The four of us on the tech squad worked feverishly to ensure all the cameras were in place and no wires were exposed. Jim, our team leader, was a perfectionist and stickler for details. Fortunately for us, our joint attention to detail made us good at what we did for a living.

After all the wires and devices were installed, two of us were volunteered to remain in the adjacent room to make sure nothing was moved or disturbed before our show the next day. We couldn't take a chance on the hotel cleaning staff being bought off by the drug dealers. Besides, the agents staying overnight were on per diem, which meant food and drinks on the bureau.

The meeting for the next day was scheduled for 2:00 p.m. at our admin room on the third floor of the hotel. We made sure the admin room was on a floor away from the meeting room. We made certain we were ready to meet our subjects two hours later at the hotel. The Columbian nationals arrived on time at the local airport and were picked up by the FBI surveillance teams. Joe Hamilton was spotted by the surveillance team waiting for his friends in the main lobby of the airport. They apparently held a brief meeting at the airport and all climbed into Joe's white Cadillac Allante. He was followed closely by a patrol car, as directed to by the surveillance team leader.

We knew following them to the hotel meeting location would be difficult and this time was no exception. Joe was an expert at shaking a surveillance team. His usual method to determine if he was being followed was to use erratic driving tactics. The team reported Joe drove the wrong way on three one-way streets four times in order to be sure no one was following him. He was closely followed by two patrol cars as his cover. When he was certain no one was following him, he got on the highway and drove south out of the city. The FBI was one step ahead of him because our primary surveillance was conducted on Joe from one mile in the air by our twin-engine aircraft.

When the carload of visitors arrived at the hotel, their first recorded meeting lasted only about an hour. The Columbian's had arrived in the city only for the meeting and nothing more. They provided us all the information we needed to wait for the major shipment four days away. Pedro wasn't allowed in the meeting, which was good so he couldn't be accused of leaking information about their plans. He performed according to schedule by staying on the fringes of the operation. He didn't ask too many questions and showed little interest in what they had to say while they all were together. Joe, nor the Columbian's would ever suspect Pedro was on two payrolls. Pedro handled all the details for them and also paid the hotel bill for the room. This was Joe's idea to keep his name completely out of any paper trails. The consensual monitoring continued on Joe's wired Allante. All preparations were made for the large shipment to arrive in a few days.

Over the next few days, we attempted to find out which police officers Joe was planning to use to escort his next drug shipment. We discovered through personnel records he was using eight hand-selected officers from his district. Those officers he felt he couldn't trust were assigned patrol duties on the opposite side of the district sector. Just as before, Al and I were assigned to wire the hotel room for video and audio and wait for the show to begin: thanks to Pedro, we knew the exact room. We rented the rooms on both sides of the target room and waited again. This time the entire SWAT team would be available because we expected several more people to be involved on this trip and there would be large sums of money exchanging hands. In addition, if it was determined that the subjects exchanged drugs, the United States' Attorney had issued arrest warrants for Joe and anyone else in the meeting. Although our job was to electronically secure the room, the arrest of police officers is extremely dangerous because guns are always involved. In addition, drug arrests usually present a special problem of their own. Often drug dealers travel with their own security that are instructed to shoot it out rather than risk arrest or rip off by rival gangs. We were depending on our informant and surveillance to keep us advised prior to the scheduled meeting. As the meeting time neared, things were tense in the FBI major case room. Pedro followed instructions and stayed on the fringes of any plans, not asking any questions and pretending to only be a driver. Pedro knew nothing about the operation and just to keep him honest was

Oath of Office

never told about our arrest plans. He only needed his instructions, nothing more.

The shipment arrived on time at 4:15 p.m. and our surveillance team clearly identified the patrol units involved. Joe seemed to be in charge and was seen shaking hands with his Columbian friends as they met in the terminal. He was not wearing a uniform and appeared to be off duty. Again, he drove his wired Cadillac Allante and talked freely about the upcoming meeting and exchange of drugs and money. The three of them carried six bags. Joe smiled and greeted all the airport workers who knew him personally. Because he was familiar to everyone, no one questioned him or stopped them to check their bags. Joe was the ideal person to meet the Columbian dealers and they felt comfortable with him.

The three of them were observed by surveillance climbing into Joe's Cadillac. They were flanked by two local police squad cars and led out of the airport. Our air surveillance units reported all of Joe's movements and as usual he was extremely cautious and calculating. He didn't want anything to go wrong with the huge drug shipment in the trunk of his car. He drove slowly and was escorted through every neighborhood by a pre-arranged scout car. Again, several times he drove the wrong way on one-way streets to determine if he was being followed. He was being followed all right, but from the air by the twin-engine aircraft. When Joe finally felt it was safe, he headed south on highway 75 to the meeting location.

Air surveillance alerted us our target was on the way to the hotel with the Columbians and with what appeared to be the drug package. Pedro had done his part by renting the hotel room and leaving a key at the desk as he was instructed. As far as Pedro was to know, Joe only needed a room, nothing more.

By now Joe was less than 15 minutes away from the hotel where he would soon be greeted by a huge SWAT team and arrested. As far as the burglars were concerned, the major part of our job was over. Since this arrest could be dangerous, everyone including the burglars had a role in effecting the eventual arrest. At 6:06 p.m. outside surveillance informed us that Joe and two big Columbian men had just driven onto the hotel parking lot and were on the way inside the lobby with six bags. The video cameras began rolling in their adjacent hotel room. As they entered the room we watched and listened to their meeting on our monitors and headsets, trying desperately to minimize any noise interference. As the group entered the room, they congratulated each other with "high fives". They proceeded to open their luggage; one piece was filled with bags of cocaine and another with bundles of wrapped money. The taller of the Columbians pulled out a bottle of scotch and poured three drinks. They then sat back and relaxed from what they thought was a successful trip: the exchange of drugs and cash. The Assistant United States Attorney was contacted by telephone and advised of the transactions as they occurred. He concurred that the transaction was complete and there appeared to be sufficient evidence for an arrest to be made on the subjects involved.

The SWAT team leader was alerted from the other room and gave the signal to start the count down for the arrest. As always, I braced myself and said a silent prayer as the count down began from ten to one. At the count of ten, the three were attacked from two doors of the adjacent hotel rooms. The sudden confusion and shouting caught everyone in the room completely off guard. If the subjects wanted to draw weapons, they were helpless due to the surprise attack. Within seconds, all three men were on the floor, none of them had time to reach for anything. As the three of them lay on the floor in a state of surprise, they looked at one another and wondered where they went wrong. I remained on standby just in case the Columbians pretended not to understand English. The money and drugs were confiscated as evidence and each of them

Oath of Office

was swiftly searched and taken out of the room. They were each transported to the United States Marshall Service in separate cars.

While two of our team members stripped the hotel room of the electronic monitoring equipment, Al and I drove Joe's car to a remote location and stripped it of the remote monitoring package installed a few weeks earlier. We laughed after we finished the car and I asked Al, "Hey man, let me use your screwdriver." This time we could care less if he knew the fed's had bugged his car. There would be no need to monitor Joe any longer.

Joe, seven local police officers, and the two Columbians appeared in court several times over the next two years. Eventually each of them pled guilty and was given assorted tours in federal penitentiary. The burglar team soon changed faces due to transfers, promotions, and the desire to do something newer and exciting for the bureau. Shortly after this case concluded, I was transferred to San Juan, Puerto Rico as their newest burglar.

CHAPTER ELEVEN
- THE HOUSE OF JUDAH -

During the mid 1980s the Detroit Division of the FBI had realized a record number of black special agents. It wasn't because something earth shattering was happening in recruitment but we just happened to all end up where we were needed—in the urban jungles of Detroit. All 14 of us soon realized our combined skills as investigators would soon be put to a test and everyone was watching us to see if we would fail. Also unprecedented was Detroit's first black Special Agent in Charge. This was a first and it wouldn't happen again for a long time. In other words he was being watched as close as we were being watched. We needed to make one another look good for our own survival and success in the FBI. If any one of us screwed up, the shadow would be cast over the fourteen of us as a group.

One afternoon Mr. Duncan called 10 black special agents to the main conference room for a meeting. We all knew that any meeting with the Special Agent in Charge was serious because Detroit was classified as a top 10 office. When we arrived we knew something was about to happen that might affect us as a group. If one of us had bitten the dirt, we'd all get a taste of it. As a young agent I just figured if something really had gotten screwed up and we were all fired, I was still young enough to take my Master's degree and go somewhere else. I had no idea what in the world Mr. Duncan wanted with us at one time. Each one of us could only speculate what would be the topic of this unprecedented gathering. I thought that perhaps he was going to fire all of us. What else could he want? I started to think about the all back alley, sleazy things my informants had done and maybe it had all caught up to me. I thought about something my informant Jokester may have done but he had been in jail for two months.

I looked around and no one had their credentials and gun sitting on the conference table. That alone was a good sign and let me know if we were going to be fired, it wasn't at this meeting. No one's personnel file was sitting on the conference table and that too was a good sign. Most of all, I didn't see any informant files so I assumed my informants had at least escaped getting locked up for now. I did wonder about how long it would take Hubcap to get caught doing something he shouldn't have done. But I didn't see his file on the table so I just waited with the others to hear our fate.

Mr. Duncan began the meeting by thanking us for taking time to come to the meeting. He said, "We have all been asked to take an assignment that will be watched by the entire Bureau. This is high profile but I feel you are the best agents I have to get this done." I said to myself, "You gotta be kiddin. Does the bureau know we're brothers? Have things changed that much since Hoover died?" But I listened just the same as my co-workers.

Mr. Duncan told us he eventually planned to use all of us for this assignment but so far the agents from the Grand Rapids office were attempting to handle this case full-time. Unfortunately, no one had gotten to square one, including the officers from the Michigan State Police. According to the information Mr. Duncan had been provided, a twelve-year-old boy had been killed in a ritualistic ceremony in Allegan County, Michigan. The deceased child and his mother were

Oath of Office

members of a religious sect known as the House of Judah. The members were all black people and a man who called himself the Lord and Master ran it.

Since the group could only be described as a cult, it put us in the mindset of the Jim Jones Cult in Georgetown, Guyana. The House of Judah consisted primarily of women and minor children. The leadership council of this sect was seven men including the self-appointed leader, Wilson Links, aka Lord and Master. Links had two sons who were the enforcers of the sect and they had been rumored to rule the group with an iron fist. According to the intelligence provided their rules were based on religious teachings and were followed to the letter by the cult members. Links required the members of this group to live within the compound in Allegan County and forbade them to speak against Links or any of his teachings.

The residents of the House of Judah were required to sign a doctrine before entering the camp that they would obey his teachings. If they were to fall astray of his teachings, the resident would be punished severely. If any of their children were to go astray of the council's teachings including misbehaving or acting out, the parent would pay a severe personal price. In addition members were required to attend worship services each day of the week, which were led by Links. The attendee was required to contribute financially and they must have all their children in attendance with them during the service. If they were to fall outside of this commitment, they would be punished severely and fined by the governing council.

Mr. Duncan provided us with a copy of the doctrine that governed the House of Judah. The document read like a script from a crazy house. It was hard to believe anyone would agree to live by a doctrine that promised to beat them for "acting up or talking back". Every aspect of the covenant placed Lord and Master in total control of the member's lives and their family. This guy was crazier than Jim Jones.

We sat in the conference room in awe because no one could believe that diminished mentality still existed. Mr. Duncan explained the camp was financed by the public assistance checks, which the women residents received monthly from Illinois, Indiana, and Michigan. The residents of the camp had pledged by contract to relinquish their financial support to Links and the governing council of the House of Judah. To further enslave the women and children, Links operated a store within the compound whereby he sold everything needed by the single parent families. Of course if the meager amount of money the families had left weren't sufficient to purchase needed goods, the good preacher would extend credit until their checks arrived later in the month.

The residents of the House of Judah were brainwashed and totally dependent upon Wilson Links for survival. Needless to say Links was the owner of the ground where the camp was located and he also owned the trailers that he leased to the camp residents. Mr. Duncan said, "This guy has the residents so terrified, no one will say a word about how the young boy died. That's why I called each of you to do your best to break this case. In addition to being excellent investigators, each of you also have children at home and may find it easier to relate to the youngsters."

Mr. Duncan went on to say the only fact they knew for sure was the child was taken to the local hospital with a blunt force injury and he died shortly after arriving. Mr. Duncan said, "We were told by a parent that the injury occurred in a ritualistic discipline ceremony. No one, including the parents, is saying anything and that's why I need each of you to solve this one. The parents are so terrified; they won't talk to anyone outside the camp, black or white. This one is tough." As he looked over the conference room, we all had the same thing in mind—what next?

As with any major case, there generally is a cloak of secrecy over the investigation. Mr. Duncan asked us to keep the details under our hat and to clear out our caseloads for the foreseeable future. We'd all be expected in Grand Rapids for a briefing on Thursday morning. No one talked about the briefing as the meeting adjourned; at least not until choir practice later in the evening at the Golden Gauntlet, our local watering hole.

When we arrived in Grand Rapids on the following Thursday morning, we sat in the briefing room with about a dozen Michigan state troopers and the Grand Rapids agents. Glenn Deberry, the resident agent in charge at Grand Rapids, began the meeting with the usual thanks to everyone who was in attendance. His briefing was just as vague as the one Mr. Duncan had provided two days earlier. I still had no idea why this case hadn't got any further than it had at the time. Deberry said, "I don't know what it is but no one in the camp, including the children will say anything to any investigator. It's as if they have been programmed against anyone outside the camp." Deberry explained that during each interview, the members including the children clammed up and said nothing.

When I walked into the briefing room, all of the officers in the room were stern looking, white males. Some were older, a few were younger, but they certainly didn't look like the people inside the camp. And if the residents had been brainwashed in any way, they certainly weren't talking to any of those guys. But I withheld my opinions just as Pablo Ramirez, my assigned partner and training school classmate. Although we didn't say it out loud, we both had the same assumptions. If any of those stiff guys approached any young black child, they would get nothing but quiet stares. Mr. Duncan had the right idea by giving this case one final attempt by using black agents. We planned to give the interviews a 110 % effort before we abandoned the case.

Ramirez and I had been scheduled to attempt an interview with a five and seven year old brother and sister who had been removed from the camp. All the children had been in the custody of the

Michigan Department of Social Services for about a week. The children had been placed with foster families until the case could be resolved. This meant they hadn't seen their parents in several days and probably wouldn't be very thrilled about seeing us. According to the profile of the children, no one really knew exactly how long they had been at the House of Judah. The social worker, who had met with the kids, simply stated that the children appeared to be traumatized by being removed from their birth mothers. We were told the birth mothers remained at the camp along with about 20 other female residents. I knew this was not going to be easy but we had given Mr. Duncan our assurance we would do our best. We just didn't know we were being placed in a seemingly hopeless situation.

Special Agent Deberry had the game plan laid out with the exception of the magic to get the kids to talk about the murder of James Yardley, the twelve-year-old victim. We felt that someone among the camp residents knew some of the details of his death. However, our first group assignment was a trip to view the camp prior to going to the homes where the children were being housed. We were told up front that because we didn't have formal search warrants we didn't have the authority to enter the camp. However, we could view it from the outside on the main road. That part really confused me. Because we were the FBI, I just assumed we'd do what we always did when people didn't want us inside—go in anyway. I'm sure someone inside the camp had outstanding warrants or stolen property which could justify us entering the grounds. But we were told this would be by the book until something concrete was found out about the murder of the boy. This case was beginning to be anything but a typical FBI investigation.

When Ramirez and I arrived at the camp it was as if someone had placed us in another time zone. The camp consisted primarily of trailers and three or four small wooden structures. Everywhere you looked, there were large signs in blue on a white background. The signs, which had bible verses written on them, appeared to be painted very crudely by free hand. It would have been impossible to go anywhere in the camp and not be inundated with some biblical verse in front of you. Every verse related to obedience to a creator. Wilson Links had dubbed himself the "Lord and Master" so the verses basically related to himself. The camp resembled a monument of brainwashing. Anyone reading those verses day after day and listening to Links could lose his mind within a short time. According to the briefing report, that's exactly what Links had accomplished with practically all the women and children in the camp.

As we stood outside the perimeter of the camp we saw a few ladies who were going about their daily chores. None of them looked our way or paid us any attention to us. There were a few media members parked outside the gate that got more attention than us. Our thoughts were if the children were as brainwashed as adults, our job was going to be tough.

Ramirez and I found our way to the home in Grand Rapids where Denna and Robert Hines had been placed. The neighborhood was extremely neat and well kept as was the small home where they were temporarily living. We arrived somewhat early even though we knew we had to wait for the social worker before we got started with the interview. We had no idea how we were going to relate to the two children or what we were going to say to them. Hopefully we could wear the kids down and get to the bottom of this investigation within a reasonable amount of time. We had about seven hours to get through this interview before the 5:30 p.m. briefing later that evening. The social worker, Ms. Perkins, arrived at the home about ten minutes after us. Ramirez and I introduced ourselves to her and to Mrs. Denny, the foster mother.

In the meantime, no less than ten other teams fanned out over Grand Rapids to interview other youngsters from the camp. Most of the teams consisted of salt and pepper teams assembled by Special Agent Deberry. They learned very quickly that absent a miracle, no one was going to figure out what had happened inside the camp to cause the death of the 12 year old boy. The kids were not gong to talk to salt and pepper teams of investigators. They soon found out the children had been well programmed against anyone outside the camp. The briefing meeting with the teams of investigators was even more interesting later that evening. Deberry went from group to group with the same results. No one had gotten anything but stares and total frustration from the children. That evening, FBI agents and Michigan State Police officers milled around the outside of the briefing room swapping stories of how tough and stern the children were during their interviews. Everyone looked frustrated and worn from a long day of accomplishing absolutely nothing.

Deberry called the evening briefing to order. He began by saying, "I'd like to thank each of you for coming here this week and giving the Grand Rapids office a hand. I've talked to a few of you outside and I know this has been a terribly frustrating ordeal. For the record, we need to go around the room and see if we have enough to piece together any facts that we can use for a search warrant or anything to move forward from here."

Deberry began to go around the room and get a briefing from each team leader. Every team leader began by saying, "This has been the damnedest thing I have ever seen. The children wouldn't even give us their names. They wouldn't look at us in the face. They all looked at us as if we had two heads." Deberry said in each instance, "Thanks a lot but don't feel all alone." Deberry went around the entire room and I think he purposely left Ramirez and me until last. For some reason, I assumed he thought our story would be equally as frustrating and brief because after all, what in the hell could two rookie agents get that veteran FBI agents and Michigan State police officers couldn't? By the time he got to us the stories were all the same. We heard the words "brainwashed and in a trance" so many times we were certain the kids must have all been zombies. Deberry and the veteran officers knew by now they would have to go back to the drawing board and try something new to further the investigation. Besides the media was parked outside the briefing room and waiting for a statement from Special Agent Deberry about the progress of the case. He had already prepared a statement saying that nothing had been accomplished and the teams were still investigating. In fact the Detroit office had been called during the briefing and told it was still hopeless. By the time Deberry got to us, most of them were talking among themselves about their next move on these tough, brainwashed kids.

Deberry said, "Gentleman, let's try to hold it down in the back. We've still got to hear from our last team consisting of Special Agents Ramirez and Thornton from our Detroit office. Gentlemen, did you get anything?" Ramirez stood up and said, "We got everything we went after. Did you guys interview the kids from the House of Judah camp?" By now you could hear a pin drop. Deberry said, "They talked to you?" I said, "Yes and they told us about the boy." By now everyone listened to what we had to say.

Ramirez began by explaining that we first sat down with the five-year-old girl. She was as cute as a button and reminded us of our daughters. The child had thick brown hair and eyes like a baby deer. She was certainly attached to her older brother and with every question she looked toward him for approval. For the first two hours during the initial stages of the interview, we took turns talking to both of them but they said nothing, just looked at each other. In fact they wouldn't give us their names or anything about themselves. All the information we initially learned came from the social worker who also hadn't gotten either of them to speak to her.

We kept pressing the little girl to tell us about James Yardley, the twelve-year-old boy, and how did he get hurt. Each time, she looked toward her older brother. We told her that her big brother would someday be James Yardley's age. We kept telling her that James would have really wanted someone to help him if he was being hurt. After a while, we could see that this tactic working. We figured Yardley was one of their playmates and she was starting to think about him as we spoke about his fate. After about two hours the little girl broke her silence and said, "James Yardley was a bad boy......Lord and Master said he had to be whipped by Big Mac because he was a bad boy". She repeated this phrase over and over and over... that Lord and Master said James Yardley was a bad boy... Lord and Master said he had to be whipped by Big Mac.

Deberry interrupted Ramirez and asked, "What is Big Mac?" I said, "Did you guys read the same briefing material we got earlier?" I held up a photograph that we had been provided with. It showed a big bat that was taped from the mid section to the top. The bat had been removed from the camp at the same time the children had been taken from the custody of their parents. I told the investigators, "No one knew what this thing was until the two children told us about it. The bat is called Big Mac by Links. The children told us Links use the bat to discipline children in the camp." Deberry said, "They told you guys all of that?" I said, "Let us continue."

I went on to explain that the younger child repeated this phrase so many times, she sounded like a programmed robot. By now Ramirez and I knew we'd have to use some skills that the FBI doesn't teach in the academy in order to get the children to talk to us. We decided to take a break and devise a new plan of attack to reach the little girl and her brother. It was an excellent time for a break since the little girl had to use the bathroom. The little girl was tough but Ramirez and I were a lot tougher than a child and determined to get the facts.

Before we resumed with the interview, we decided to separate the children and play with them as we would our own children.

Pretty soon they began to warm up to us. The girl told us her name was Denna and her brother's name was Robert. We had gotten this information from the Social Worker but wanted to get it from the children themselves. Little Denna liked to play patty cakes and Robert liked playing hand slaps. We decided we wouldn't push any more questions on them for a while. After about 20 minutes we were just like any other visitor who had come to play with the kids. Ramirez was sitting on one end of the floor with the boy and I was on the other with the little girl. Ramirez had a small set of rings, which they tossed back and forth for about an hour. While they tossed the rings they talked and laughed. We noticed as Denna laughed and talked to me this time, she stopped looking at her brother for approval. She soon began acting like any normal four-year-old. Denna reminded me of my daughter Christy, who was also four years old at the time. She too was playful and could be easily distracted if she was having fun.

Ramirez and I switched kids and I played with her older brother by tossing a small ball back and forth to him. We talked about baseball. I told him that I had a little boy about his age. I told him my son played soccer on the local recreation center team. The little boy was soon acting like any normal little seven-year-old boy. As we played with the two kids, we slowly began asking questions about James Yardley and the fact that he would probably be having fun playing if he were here with them. After a while, the children were having such a good time we noticed that both of them had quit reciting the brainwashing phrases that Lord and Master had taught them to say. They said nothing more about James Yardley being a bad boy and began talking about him as their friend. We decided to take a lunch break and relax from further questions.

The foster mother had cooked a really nice lunch for us. We sat down with the children and ate lunch with them. They now began to talk about everything under the sun, just like other children do.

We covered everything from school to learning numbers and writing. Both children had hearty appetites. We were slowly breaking down the wall of distrust that Links had built up in them for so long. By 2:00 p.m., it had been well over four hours, and neither child had repeated anything about Lord and Master. Ramirez and I nodded at each other. We felt it was time to get back to the interview, but take it slowly.

Deberry interrupted and said with utter disbelief, "2:00? You guys had been there since 9:00 that morning." I said, "Sometimes it takes a while to get what you need."

Ramirez explained that when he pulled out a photograph of Big Mac and asked the little girl if she had ever seen it before. She jumped up crying and ran to her big brother's arms. It was as if the photograph of the bat rekindled a bad thought in her little mind. They both began to cry hysterically to a point where the foster mother had to get tissue for each of them. Ramirez picked up the little girl and sat her on his lap. I sat the little boy on my knee and we both told them to relax. Ramirez was having trouble calming the little girl. Then he said to her, "Don't cry baby, we've got Big Mac. He can't hurt you anymore." She looked up at her big brother who by now had ceased crying and was being comforted by me. Robert asked me, "Are you sure you have it, because he can whip us again if he gets it." I noticed, this time, he had referred to Links as he and not as Lord and Master. This was the first big break through we noticed. We took them both off our knees and let them hug one another to dry their tears. Ramirez told them again, "You don't have to worry anymore. We've got Big Mac." Robert made us promise that we wouldn't let big Mac nor the Lord and Master hurt him or his sister again. We said in unison, "We promise." They whispered to one another and continued to hug each other. I asked little Denna again, "Can you tell us what happened to James Yardley?" She looked toward her big brother who was now standing holding Ramirez's

Oath of Office

leg. He nodded to her. From that point on she and her brother told us the entire story about the camp. Every few phrases they spoke, they would ask us again if we could keep Lord and Master and Big Mac from hurting them again. We told them each time in unison, "We promise," and they would continue with their story.

They told us they had been at church service on Saturday afternoon and James had been acting up all week. Robert said when they act up, Lord and Master would whip them in the yard after church service. I asked Denna, "Where are your mothers when Lord and Master whip you?" She said the mothers are supposed to stand there and watch you get a whipping. The mothers are not supposed to do anything but watch and make you be good next time. Robert said, "Lord and Master whips us with big Mac" and pointed to the picture of the bat. He said, "I've been whipped by big Mac but my sister is still too little. He will be whipping her soon, when she's bad". Ramirez and I still couldn't believe our ears but we let them talk, since they had finally started to provide us with useful information. As they talked they held one another for comfort. By now they had both stopped crying and seemed confident they no longer had to worry about Links and Big Mac. As we looked in the corner of the living room, the social worker was crying as she listened to the children tell their story about the perils at the House of Judah.

Robert then returned to the story about James Yardley. He said James had been bad, and that Saturday afternoon after church, Lord and Master had whipped him. He said he couldn't remember if anyone else had whipped James but Lord and Master whipped him for a long time with Big Mac. He said, "After the whipping, James was supposed to clean the leaves out of the trailer because Lord and Master said he was a bad boy. Robert told us, "James just went to the trailer and laid down all night. Lord and Master told his mama to leave him there until he did his work." I asked Robert, "What happened to James after that afternoon?" He said, "I don't know.

Somebody said he got sick and they took him somewhere. Nobody told us anymore about him." Then Robert asked us again, "Are you sure Big Mac won't hurt us again?" We said, "We promise..."

We then asked Robert if Lord and Master had ever come to their house. He looked at Denna before answering, then said, "Yes, but we were always told to go in the back and not to come out when he was there. He would come by to talk to my mama sometimes." I asked him, "How long would Lord and Master stay at your house?" The child said, "We don't know, he would make us go to bed and if we came out, he would say we were acting bad and would whip us. I didn't wanna get a whipping so me and Denna would stay in bed." Denna started to cry again and I hugged her until she stopped. By now it was 5:00 and we were exhausted. The two children made us promise we'd come back to see them again. We said, "We promise."

Before we left the home, Robert asked me, "Do you think I can get on a soccer team like your boy?" I said, "Of course." The social worker nodded her head in agreement.

No one in the briefing room could believe his ears. Deberry said, "Somebody get Mr. Duncan on the telephone and call those guys back in the room. This case is far from over." Within moments, Ramirez and I were swamped with officers and agents asking us about our day with the two children. The next day Ramirez and I had to meet with the social worker to continue debriefing the two children. We had become heroes in the eyes of Mr. Duncan by delivering exactly what he knew we could do in the face of tough circumstances. We didn't get a chance to speak to him but our interview made his call to headquarters a lot easier. Ramirez and I had cracked the link to getting this case resolved. But we still had a lot of work to do.

Everyone was surprised that Ramirez and I had gone through so much in order to get the children to talk to us. Our success really came down to being parents and understanding children. Although we explained to Deberry later that this was probably one of the toughest interviews we'd ever had, we knew that most kids are basically the same. The two little ones were seriously brainwashed as much as the adults at the camp, but they were still just children. The situation of the children was sadder than that of the adults at the camp. Even with our assuring them that Lord and Master would never hurt them again, they were still afraid that somehow, Lord and Master would find them and whip them with Big Mac.

Our next task was to develop prosecutable charges against Links and his ruling council. We felt that since we had finally loosened the kids up to us, as far as we were concerned, the toughest part was over.

Our next interview with our two new friends was a lot smoother than the first. Ramirez and I had made a trip to Toys R Us and bought a couple of gifts for Denna and Robert. This time, when we arrived they were both glad to see us. They greeted us with big smiles. They were overjoyed when they saw the gifts in our arms. We bought Denna the prettiest little chocolate baby doll we could find in the store. We bought a soccer ball for Robert. We could see they hadn't been given any real gifts in quite some time. We decided to let them play with their new gifts before we got back into our questioning. Robert and I talked about my son, Cary III, who also played soccer.

We started with some small talk with Mrs. Denny and the social worker assigned to the case. Not surprisingly, they told us the children were now a lot more talkative and behaving like normal children. In fact they had started to smile and seemed a lot happier. Apparently it appeared a big weight had been lifted from the children since they no longer had to worry about Big Mac or Lord and Master.

Mrs. Denny said she had been really worried about the children because they had been so withdrawn. Since meeting us the day earlier, they hadn't recited any of the pre-programmed phrases and smiled a lot more. Everyone could clearly see things were beginning to turn around with the kids since their revelations to us about the camp. Mrs. Denny thought that perhaps some of their joy might have been due to a pending visit with their mother later in the day. Whatever the case we had several hours to capitalize on their relaxed demeanors and to find out more about the inner workings of the camp. Our goal that day was to find out the level of child abuse prevalent inside the camp and who was responsible for it.

We began by again sitting on the floor while we talked to the children. I told Denna and Robert that we came to visit them again because we needed to know more about the camp and if any other children were ever harmed. I looked at Denna and said, "Do you think its right for big people to hit children with big sticks?" Little Denna shyly shook her head, indicating no. When she did this she looked at her brother who also indicated it was not right. I asked Robert, "Can you tell me who Lord and Master beat with Big Mac?" He hesitated and looked and Ramirez very shyly and said, "He whipped most of us because he said we had been bad. But he hadn't beat my little sister yet because she is still too little and he may hurt her." At that time Denna started to cry slowly but I hugged her and told her Lord and Master would never beat her.

The little girl wiped her eyes and asked me, "Can you promise to keep Lord and Master from hurting my big brother too?" I said, "He will never hurt any child again but you've both got to help us by talking about the things that went on inside the camp." They both agreed and we found out some remarkable things about the inner workings of the camp from the two children. They told us that Lord and Master and the other men beat most of the people inside the camp. They said that one time they beat one of the men because he was talking mean to Lord and Master's wife. Robert said, "They beat him with Big Mac and it was nothing he could do." Denna said that one day Lord and Master got angry with her mother and was going to whip her but she was too sick. Robert said, "We could hear him shouting at her but we couldn't come out of the back room. I'm going to get Lord and Master when I get big." Ramirez told the children that as much as Lord and Master may need to be punished, let us do it. Robert shook his head in agreement.

They went on to tell us that from time to time Lord and Master would allow them go into the city to buy things but he would check their bags and if the things were too worldly, he would take them away. Little Denna said, "My Mommy bought me a baby doll but Lord and Master said I couldn't have it. I cried but he still didn't give it back."

Throughout the afternoon we learned a lot about the abuse that had occurred at the House of Judah. The camp was run with a stern hand and Links was the ruler. We took good notes and finally felt we had enough to get started on a search warrant against Links and his ruling counsel. It was determined that each one of Links ruling members was guilty of serious abuses against the women and children at the camp. By the end of the day, we had enough information to supply sufficient prosecutable information according to Deberry and the United States Attorney. The other investigators and officers continued a close surveillance on the members of the camp including Links and his close followers. Although they were not yet charged with any crimes, nothing prevented law enforcement from keeping a close surveillance on each one of them.

By the end of our third day we had assembled our investigative notes and presented them to Deberry and the United States Attorney for review. Ramirez and I returned to Detroit to allow the attorney's handle the prosecution phase of this case. We had been away from our homes for several days and we were anxious to see our families. However we had both been affected by the sad condition in which we had found the two little children. It was still hard to believe the

C. Lee Thornton

level of brain washing the children had endured at the hands of William Links.

As we talked about the condition of the children, we couldn't help but think about our own children who were about the same ages as Robert and Denna. Little Denna was nearly the same age as my daughter and I couldn't help but think about the sadness Denna had experienced in her short life. Although Ramirez and I had provided the crucial interviews to prosecute the case, Denna and Robert's personal situations were far from being settled and their futures were still quite uncertain.

Ramirez and I still hadn't met the children's mother and from what we learned from the social worker, she was quite dependent upon Links for survival. She had been with the House of Judah for the past four years or as long as Denna had been alive. Denna's records with the Michigan Department of Social Services made no mention of where her father resided or his identity. The social worker advised us she had met with most of the children from the camp and all of their records reflected the same information about biological father's—unidentified. She told us she wasn't going to make any assumptions but after we meet Links and his ruling counsel, we could draw our own conclusions.

After thinking about the sadness and hopelessness of the two little kids during the three-hour drive back to Detroit, I couldn't wait to see my own children. When I arrived home in Oak Park, my children were standing at the door waiting for me with big smiles. Their grins somehow reminded me of the smiles Ramirez and I had gotten from Denna and Robert when we gave them their gifts. The first thing I did was to give each of them a big hug and to thank God they had a better chance at life than Denna and Robert. Somehow I couldn't forget about the tough circumstances they had to live under despite all we had done for them. In spite of it all, life was not going to be much easier for the two children. I couldn't help but think that they are going to have some rainy days ahead of them. Somehow they have got to prepare for the rain because it will come.

When we returned to the Detroit office a few days later, our first meeting with Mr. Duncan was interesting. He called Ramirez and me to his office and thanked us for developing the key information to keep the case alive. He said with some luck the United States Attorney could assemble enough information for an indictment within the next several weeks against Links and his rulers. We had a long conversation with Mr. Duncan that afternoon and left satisfied we had done an excellent job. He told us he knew and appreciated the real work was done by brick agents in the trenches. He let us know the information retrieved from the two children was invaluable and crucial. He said, "Those of you in the trenches make it possible for the bureau to be what it is. The real work is not done not by managers but by your hardcore brick agents. Thanks for everything and you have my support." We simply said, "Thank you." We had been around the FBI long enough to know that the brick agent (the investigator on the street) is the backbone of the FBI. He wasn't telling us anything we didn't already know. We've always been and will always be so.......

Mr. Duncan said that at the present time no one had been held accountable for the death of the twelve year old boy. For the present time Ramirez and I knew our portion of the investigation was completed. We had provided the investigators in Grand Rapids with enough to get the case off the ground. Because our two little ones had talked to us, they provided the leads the other investigators needed get started. Mr. Duncan told us he wanted Ramirez and me to return to Allegan County later and assist in the arrests of Links and his so-called governing counsel.

Despite the unusually bizarre behavior of the two little children, we still hadn't seen the even stranger behavior of the adults at the camp. The worst was yet to come.

Each time I thought about the brainwashed little Denna and Robert, I hugged my children and said a silent prayer.

About two weeks later enough evidence had been assembled to execute a search warrant at the House of Judah in Allegan County. The investigators still assigned to the case had taken records and strange looking wooden contraptions from the camp. Among the items seized were a birthing stool and a whipping post. Through later interviews we found out the birthing stool was used to deliver babies by the camp appointed midwife, Miriam Jackson. The birthing stool was wooden and similar to those used a hundred years ago in the south. According to one of the young women who lived at the camp, the pregnant lady would deliver her child while seated upright on the stool and assisted by the midwife. Incidentally, the camp appointed midwife, Miriam Jackson, was the common law wife of Wilson Links.

Not only was she the midwife and had delivered most of the children born at the camp but also the self appointed camp doctor. Just as any other services provided by Links and the House of Judah, the pregnant lady would be obligated to pay for so-called medical services in cash to Links. By the time the mothers purchased food and supplies from his "camp store", the members of the camp would be in serious debt to Links. And of course the person who was responsible for the operation of the camp store was Miriam Jackson.

Our later interviews determined the camp counsel, to discipline those who "talked back or got out of line", used the whipping post. By covenant the camp member agreed to be disciplined by Links or his counsel for "talking back or getting out of line". In a later interview with little Robert he told us children under eight years old were normally not put in the whipping post. He said, "The little kids were too small and would slip out of the whipping post. The Lord and Master would make their mamas hold them while he beat them with

Oath of Office

Big Mac." Robert told us he was glad his little sister didn't have to look forward to being put in the whipping post. The more we talked to the children the more bizarre were the accounts of the camp.

More bizarre than the birthing stool and whipping post was the confiscation of the actual covenant, which governed the House of Judah. The document was laced with religious phrases and brainwashing statements which had to be pledged by the resident. The longer we read the covenant, the stranger it became. But this document would soon become a key piece of evidence in the prosecution of Links and the ruling members of the House of Judah.

Three weeks later Ramirez and I returned to Allegan County to assist the assigned agents with the grand jury preparation. Our input was crucial because we had interviewed the two children who provided the crucial information for the case. The children were spared the ordeal of testifying in grand jury because their statements were stipulated by the court. Our job was to insure the accuracy of what we had been told to us by the youngsters and the information entered into the court record. Each time we read their accounts of the inner workings of the camp, we drew larger crowds of investigators in the major case room. But we were still in for even more bizarre behavior at the Allegan County courthouse when we saw Links and his counsel for the first time.

Security was extremely heavy as was the media on the day Links and his counsel were scheduled to appear before the grand jury. I distinctly recalled the circus atmosphere display when I first observed Links arrive at the courthouse. It was the first time I saw him in person although I had seen dozens of photographs of him. The photos didn't do him a lot of justice. This guy was tall, heavy, and wore a greasy jheri curl hairstyle. He was no less than 250 pounds and resembled a pitted prune in the face. As I took my first glance at him, I wondered how he held such a spell over the women at the House of Judah.

As he entered the Allegan County Courthouse, no less than a dozen men and women surrounded him. Two huge bodyguards entered the building about ten steps ahead of Links. As we stood in the hallway we watched the show unfold. We assumed their job was to clear the way for Links to make sure no one was there to hurt him. I couldn't understand why they thought he was so important that someone was lurking in the building to harm him. He was just a man that had control of the minds of members of the cult. Once these guys assumed the hallway was safe, they motioned for Links to walk inside the building. When they motioned to Links, he started round two of the show.

As Links slowly entered the building, two very large guys on his left and right side flanked him. We assumed their job was to block any attacker on either side of him. This was somewhat of a football play without the football. Bringing up Links rear were three extremely attractive young women. They were well dressed and as they followed him, they repeatedly bowed over and over while saying, "Lord and Master, Lord and Master". It was as if they were in a trance but each one of them was tall, well dressed, and very easy on the eyes. We later learned the ladies were the three of the mothers of children who had been removed from the camp.

The forward body guards walked past us without noticing we were standing in the hallway. I thought about running up to Links and slapping him for what he had done to little Denna and Robert. Needless to say Links bodyguards were only there for the show. The ladies continued to bow and repeat Lord and Master over and over as Links strolled down the hallway of the courthouse. They never made eye contact with anyone in the building other than Links. In fact if he hadn't spoken to them I would have wondered if they could say anything other than Lord and Master.

Oath of Office

As the grand jury convened we waited in the hallway serving as security for the state officials. After about an hour the "Lord and Master" show resumed. Links apparently had to use the potty. Two huge guys ran down the hallway looking for the men's bathroom. Two other guys followed with Links walking hurriedly behind the two of them. Links apparently had to go and bad and was moving pretty fast. The first two guys ran inside to check out the bathroom while two men stood outside to help two other men protect Links. One guy came running out of the men's room and said, "It's clear, let him in." Links was unzipping as he walked in 'cause he was being pushed by nature. I sort of thought they would unzip for him and hold 'em down but he was handling that part on his own.

And as for the ladies, they stood outside the door, bowing and repeating over and over, "Lord and Master, Lord and Master". When a happy but relieved Links surfaced from the men's toilet, you would have thought he was coming home from the war. His entire entourage did everything but kiss his ass. Links walked back to the grand jury room to resume his testimony amid the show of worshippers that followed him. The show was worth the price of admission and a spectacle for everyone in the building.

Links testimony in front of the Allegan County grand jury lasted about three hours that afternoon. When it concluded the show resumed with his entourage in the hallway of the courthouse. The entire cast waited patiently for him in the hallway of the courthouse until he surfaced from his testimony. As Links darkened the doorway, the two larger guys fanned out in two directions to insure the place was safe all over again. The ladies went into their bowing act and began repeating, "Lord and Master, Lord and Master," over and over. Any casual observer could see that Links was eating the attention up. Little did Wilson Links know the worse part of his day had not yet arrived but was only a few hours away.

Later that day the grand jury returned a true bill against Links and four other members of the camp. Officers on the task force later arrested him while he was sitting in his trailer at the House of Judah camp. Unfortunately two of his son's who were also indicted had left the area causing the state of Michigan to issue fugitive warrants against them. As far as the FBI was concerned the investigative portion of this case was completed and trial preparation was ready to begin. Links and his ruling counsel had all been indicted on state charges, which seemed fairly solid. However Links two son's had to be located since they had fled the state of Michigan.

Ramirez and I were later called to the SAC's office on the Monday before Thanksgiving and told we had a federal fugitive warrant to arrest and locate Wilson Links, Jr. Our final instructions from SAC Duncan were to find Links and arrest him before we returned for the Thanksgiving holiday.

Ramirez and I were both busy as hell with our own caseloads but we knew we were deeply involved in the House of Judah matter, which had not yet been resolved. We had been in touch with the agents in Grand Rapids over the past few weeks and we knew the case was far from over. Our interviews with the little Denna and Robert had been the catalyst to get the House of Judah investigation off the ground and everyone was still quite indebted to us. However before things went any further, Wilson Links, Jr. had to be located and arrested. We only knew he was somewhere in the Chicago area.

From the information we had been provided by Mr. Duncan, Links had moved back to the Chicago area and was hiding among some old friends outside the city. The only concrete lead on his whereabouts was from an informant who had been working for a small suburban police department. Our instructions were to meet Sgt. Ron Lasker with the Malden, Illinois Police Department and debrief the informant. Hopefully with the informants help and a small piece of "government

Oath of Office

cheese" we would find Links and get back to Detroit to enjoy the holidays with our families. Ramirez and I got packed, kissed our kids good-bye, and headed for Chicago, Illinois on the Monday before Thanksgiving. The next day would be spent trying to locate Links in order to salvage our Thanksgiving holiday.

Early the next day we got a dose of the "b.s." laid down by a typical informant. It took Sgt. Lasker most of Tuesday morning to contact Mickey Woodson, the informant. The guy had been locked up in Chicago on a car theft charge and had been sprung by Sgt. Lasker's partner. When he was released, his instructions were to immediately contact Sgt. Lasker and help him find Wilson Links, Jr. Like a typical informant he decided to hook up with a couple of his road dogs and resume his old habits. Unfortunately the guy had relapsed into his old drug habits and wasn't changing anytime soon. We contacted Mickey's mom where he lived before he was locked up and sent to prison a few years earlier. She was an older lady who just seemed to be tired of boarding a grown man and supporting his children. She lived in a tidy, well-kept little house in Malden not too far from the south side of Chicago. She was unfortunately burdened with two of Mickey's children because their mother was in drug rehab. The poor lady had taken all she could take from her no good son. She took the opportunity of our visit to finally sit down and talk to us about Mickey. She said, "He stayed here last night but left early this morning. I wish someone could talk to him. He smelled like alcohol and I think he may have been smoking that stuff." She knew if Mickey was smoking dope or hanging out with drug dealers, his parole could be violated. She was secretly trying to get him locked up so that she wouldn't have to worry about what he was doing for a while. Mrs. Woodson said she was sick and tired of being sick and tired.

Our only interest in Mickey was he was a close friend of Wilson Links, Jr. who as far as we knew was our only way to find him.

We had good information that Mickey had seen Links since he had moved back to Chicago a few weeks earlier. According to word on the street, the two of them had been seen hanging out around town. We also had decided attempt to locate Mickey through his parole officer who was also located in Malden. Between the parole officer and Mickey we hoped to find Links before our holiday deadline. After all, Malden was a small town, which only had so many places to hide. The town had two nightclubs and a small strip of stores, which masquerade, as the local mall. To say the town was impoverished was being too kind. It was broke with little hope.

We told Sgt. Lasker we had to work fast because we wanted to arrest Links before the holiday weekend. Of course we knew he could care less about out personal deadlines. However he was willing to do what it took to get Links off of the streets of Malden, Illinois. He had heard about the House of Judah only from the newspaper articles when the case first broke several months earlier. Just like most people in the area, the House of Judah's members were not favored souls. We wasn't sure they were disliked because the reports of abuse of the children or because of the murder of the twelve year old. But we were sure it had something to do with the fact that each of the women had ripped off the welfare systems of Illinois, Indiana, and Michigan and used the money to support Wilson Links.

For the balance of the day Ramirez and I scoured every back alley joint, liquor store, and hole in the wall in Malden, Illinois looking for leads on Wilson Links, Jr. Throughout the day we hoped to get a call from Sgt. Lasker advising us he had located Mickey. The call finally came around 6:30 that evening after we had finally given up for the day. We were just taking an evening break to rest before we hit the clubs late that evening. We had prepared ourselves for a hell of a fistfight with Links because he was a big guy at 6'3" and 250 pounds. Because he ran with a wrecking crew, we knew our work was cut out for us. But we knew we had to find him before the Thanksgiving holiday weekend and if it was a fight he wanted, we planned to win.

Sgt. Lasker told us he was going to meet Mickey at the Texaco station on Main Street at 9:00 later in the evening. Mickey had been hanging out all day with a new lady friend. His Mom woke him up when Sgt. Lasker called him on the telephone. She told Sgt. Lasker his new lady friend was a weed smoker and they had apparently had a party all day. They were both employed at the same place—in the streets. She said he was in bad shape but he promised to meet us at nine.

We arrived a few minutes early along with Sgt. Lasker. We really didn't expect Mickey to be anywhere near on time. At approximately 9:30 p.m., Mickey showed up with his new lady friend. She looked like death warmed over to put it mildly. She was poorly dressed and her hair looked a mess. It was obvious she was still high from her earlier party that day with Mickey. In this case he seemed to be the sober one among the two of them. At least Mickey could walk a straight line and construct a portion of a sentence. But little did Mickey know we had him exactly where we wanted him, at our mercy due to his obvious drug use and his association with a known drug user.

Mickey was on parole and had stern restrictions about his associations with known felons and drug users. He was restricted from being publicly intoxicated and prohibited from using any form of illegal drugs. Mickey walked up to us and said, "Hey Sarg, my Ma said you needed to see me right away." Sgt. Lasker explained to him that we were from the FBI and we needed his help finding someone. Mickey had the nerve to look at us and say, "I might could help y'all but how much ya gonna pay me for my help?" I looked at Mickey and said, "Let me put it to you this way. Your girlfriend is definitely high on something. I'd guess marijuana. Earlier today we know you were high because your mother told us you were sleep and high most of the afternoon." Mickey just stood there with his mouth open and bracing his girlfriend to keep her from failing over.

Ramirez then told him, "We need to find Wilson Links, Jr. right away and because we have an arrest warrant for him. Since you're on parole, we know you don't want to go back to prison. In fact if you go back to prison, who will run around town with your lady friend?" I then explained to Mickey, "I tell you what, you call us early tomorrow with the exact location of Links and we won't report you to your parole officer for violation, agreed?" Mickey dropped his head and said, "But I only had a joint early today. I have been clean up to now." Ramirez said, "Then how about you take a pee test tomorrow morning with your parole officer?" Mickey said, "I'll call y'all in the morning, just don't call my p.o. I'll find him, you keep up your end, I'll keep up mine."

I had dealt with informants long enough to know when they planned to take us for a ride. He looked just like a drug informant I once handled that played a regular game of cat and mouse with us. He would promise us results in few days and would be too happy to leave our company. This was especially true when he knew we had deadlines. Our big problem was that Sgt. Lasker was this guy's handler and not the FBI. He owed his allegiance to Lasker and not us.

But what Mickey didn't know was that our hammers over him were heavier than Lasker's. Lasker had just driven away in the other direction away from us so we decided to circle the block and let Mickey know our trump cards were just a little tougher than he was accustomed. We met Mickey at the next corner near the liquor store. We had no doubt Lasker had mentioned to him we needed Links pretty bad. Mickey was smart enough to know since we were from Detroit and the Thanksgiving holiday was just around the corner, we had no intention of spending Thanksgiving in Malden, Illinois. For some reason I sensed Mickey was either planning to play us for a heavy piece of government cheese or to see if he could use us as leverage with his parole officer. I wanted to insure he knew the ball was in our court and he was at our mercy.

Mickey didn't know we knew he had been locked up two days ago for a scuffle with a local drug dealer. The fight was more of a prelude to his homicide and he got the worse end of the whipping. In fact the only reason he was arrested was to get him of the streets for a few hours because the dealer had a few of his boys still on the hunt for him. This information along with the threat of his parole officer gave us the leverage over Mickey. We knew there were not a lot of places he could hide in Malden and he couldn't leave town because of his parole. More than anything, Mickey hated prison with a passion and we knew it. He barely lived through the five years he recently completed. I knew we had him but we had to let him know it.

Just as Mickey turned the corner near the liquor store we rolled up him. He had just picked up his daily six-pack and was heading back to his mother's house. From the direction he was walking he had planned to enter through the rear door and go straight to his basement roost. His mother didn't like him drinking or smoking in the house but he did it anyway. The nice, church lady said she wasn't more than one minute away from throwing him out of the house but she felt sorry for him. A felon with no residence would certainly be sent back to Joliet State Prison.

I said, "Hey Mickey, over here!!" He looked at us and said, "What's up guys, I thought I was through with y'all." Ramirez motioned for him to get in the back seat. As much as we knew he wanted to ignore us and take off, he reluctantly climbed in and in the midst of our silence he said, "What? What y'all want with me? You know it ain't cool for me to be seen in a fed car, it could be bad for my rep you know." We just sat there and let him ramble on and on.

When we felt he could no longer take the silence Ramirez said, "Listen because you won't hear this again until it's too late for you. And don't think for one minute you've got us over a barrel." Mickey interrupted and said, "You guys are trying to sweat me. I told you I'm going to try to find Links in the morning. I can't do anymore. Why you tryin' to sweat me? I'm gonna call Lasker." We just listened and let some silence fill the air.

Now it was my turn to give Mickey the facts of life. I told him, "Look Mister, we really don't care that Duke Man is still looking for you. In fact we talked to a few of his boys earlier today." He interrupted and said, "You didn't tell them you saw me did ya? Those dudes could kill me!!" I said, "Maybe they will, maybe they won't......we don't care and no one else cares either. Your mother is sick of you, your parole officer is ready to violate you, and Duke Man still wants his money. Quite frankly, we're your only friends and if you don't put us on top of Links tomorrow, you won't have us." Ramirez interrupted and said, "Look man, we don't really have a dog in the fight in this little one horse town but we want Links no later than tomorrow. If you think you're going to take us for chumps, we'll give Duke Man and his boys your address. In fact maybe we'll just drop you off on Main Street near the club." Mickey started sweating like a stuck pig because he never knew we had so much on him. He started to look around because he didn't want to be seen sitting in our car too long. Most informants know it is the kiss of death being seen climbing out of a cop's car. By now Mickey was really sweating and literally begging for his life. The last thing he needed was to run into Duke Man or any of his posse before his parole was cleared. His plans were to lay low and quietly leave town in a few months when his parole was completed.

We let Mickey ramble for about two to three minutes about how bad we were treating him and we decided to let him know our bottom line with him. I said, "Listen buddy, this is our deal. You put us up on Links tomorrow and we stay away from your parole office and Duke Man. If you don't you may as well go to the top the insurance building and jump. Just tell us you understand and get the hell out of this car." Ramirez said, "If not.....see ya." Mickey just held his head down and said, "Okay, keep your end of the deal and I'll call y'all 'round noon." He held his head down and slowly walked down the street. Mickey didn't seem to care if anyone saw him climb out of our car or not. He seemed to feel his life was over either way. Ramirez and I had dinner and went back to the hotel to plan what we felt should be our last day in Malden.

Later that evening we both called home as a reminder to ourselves why we make our living in a profession wreaking with vermin and disgust. We knew if we arrested Links, the last of the House of Judah leadership would be behind bars. I couldn't help but recall over and over the horrible effect Links and his council had on little Denna and Robert. I only hoped his arrest would assure no other child would ever have to suffer the brainwashing which the children of the House of Judah had suffered.

My children at the time were still very young and I'm not sure they understood my work or what an FBI agent actually did for a living. I only hoped they would remain innocent and never have to understand the feelings of little Denna and Robert. I just told them Daddy loved them and I planned to be home by Thursday, one way or the other. I was going to use everything I had to insure Mickey got on his job and not spoil Thanksgiving for my family. They may not have understood my job but they understood Thanksgiving dinner.

Early the next morning Ramirez and I were awakened by an early telephone call from Sgt. Lasker. He told us he tried to reach Mickey at his mom's place but she told him he had left the house before 8:00 that morning. She thought she heard him on the telephone talking to someone before he left home. But he told her to give Lasker a message that he should hear from him by noon without fail. Lasker told us he could always count on Mickey when he tells him he has information. He said he's sure Mickey will call him at the time he promised. We have no reason to doubt Sgt. Lasker but it seemed he had more faith in his informant than we had in him. We never told him we had to strong arm the guy the night earlier but we're sure Mickey would tell him as soon as he got a chance. Quite frankly, we really didn't care.....we only needed Links before the end of the day. If Mickey was smart, he was on the case as we spoke.

Our next contact with Sgt. Lasker was about 12:30 and he had good news for us. Lasker wanted us to meet him at the super market on 8th Street at 3:00. The parking lot was large and we could see if anyone was watching us from any angle. According to Lasker, Mickey had been in contact with someone who knew where Links had been hiding. Mickey thought Links was on the run and planning to leave town in a few days. We've dealt with dozens of guys just like Mickey for years and knew to never get too excited over an informant's promise. Ramirez said to Lasker, "You really seem trusting of old Mickey. Are you sure you can count on anything he says?" Lasker responded with, "Sure can. He knows I have something that can send him away for quite a while. He wouldn't dare stuff on me." Ramirez said, "Well see you at 3:00 on the lot."

The next few hours were fairly uneventful so we just cruised through the streets of Malden looking for our friend, Wilson Links, Jr. We were dressed in old clothes and driving a four-year-old car so no one really noticed us. Ramirez wore an old leather jacket and a hat and I wore my old army field jacket. We blended in like locals in need of a drink. In fact we just stood on the corner for a while and shot the breeze with a few locals. We just pretended we had just gotten fired from the labor pool office for being just a little late the past morning. Everyone seemed equally as ticked with that office as we were and each one of them it seemed had his own story about

Oath of Office

the labor pool. We knew from the streets of Detroit that everyone who was no one could be found at the labor pool office at one time or another. In this case we were no different from every other guy in town who needed day labor and a few quick dollars.

To our surprise when we got to the supermarket parking lot Mickey was sitting in Lasker's car and nervous as hell. Mickey was shaking like a leaf and somehow seemed glad to see us. As soon as we got in the car Mickey said, "Look guys. I'm holding up my end of the deal. Links will be at his sister's place at 8:00 tonight. It's her birthday and they're having a party for her. She's a little older so they're starting early 'cause she don't wanna be up late. She lives on St. Louis Avenue. I don't know the address but I can show you the house."

Lasker said, "Is that the house where we picked you up last week?" Mickey said, "Yeah, that's his sister's place, the small grey house." Our instructions to Mickey was to stay out of sight until we give him a call later tonight, hopefully after we have Links bagged up. We told him we don't want him anywhere near St. Louis Avenue and not to speak to anyone. Ramirez told him, "Look my man, let me give you the facts of life. If we get as much of a hint that you dropped a dime on Links and we miss him, you'll wish you never were born, understand?" Mickey looked at us and said, "Man I want y'all to find that guy and never have to see me again. Damn, Lask, where did you find these crazy dudes?" He climbed out of the back seat and walked down the street toward his mom's house. He went back into his nicotine fit and lit a cigarette as he walked.

Ramirez and I met Lasker back at the precinct to begin planning for Links arrest. We had never seen him in person so we only knew him by the photo and the description provided by the Illinois Secretary of State's Office. As we sat in the briefing with the SWAT team, it seemed that time just wouldn't pass fast enough. The SWAT guys were dressed in their traditional dark ninja uniforms, complete with automatic weapons. Most of these guys are normally pretty pumped up when it's time to rock and roll. As for Ramirez and I we just sat back and watched these guys get ready to attack the little house at 2330 St. Louis Avenue. When they finally settled down Ramirez and I got suited up in our ballistics vests. Ramirez and I began our briefing with the SWAT team to remove Links off the streets. We only hoped this would be the only time we had to go through this ordeal. The only thing we had in mind was bagging the guy and heading back to Detroit to enjoy the Thanksgiving holiday. However we knew better than to get too optimistic or to get too preoccupied with our personal issues. We knew that getting too happy was dangerous precedent to set.

Ramirez began with passing out the briefing forms and photographs of Links to the officers in the room. Lucky for us one guy said he recognized Links from around town. He let us know our description of his height was somewhat off. The SWAT guy told us he was closer to 6'0" and well over 220 pounds. We had driven past the house earlier and could give a good description of the building. Most of the SWAT guys were a lot more familiar with the neighborhood than us and didn't really feel there would be any problems with the arrest. After the team briefing we let the SWAT commander handle the details of the arrest. We all agreed our jump off time would be 7:00 p.m. According to Mickey, the only informant we had, Links was arriving early because he planned to leave town later in the evening. We still didn't know how he got his facts but we had nothing else to go on.

We all positioned ourselves in the neighborhood around 7:15 and had a lookout for the green Buick Regal Mickey told us that Links had been driving for the past week. That's the only fact that actually checked out from the information provided by Mickey. The used car dealer in Lincoln, Illinois confirmed Links had purchased had the car two weeks ago for $900.00 cash. It was still a mystery where Links had gotten $900.00 since he was no longer pimping the unfortunate women and kids at the House of Judah.

At about 7:45 p.m. we got a radio call from a patrol car that was on patrol near the St. Louis Avenue address. He alerted the SWAT van and the rest of the cars involved that the green Buick Regal had been seen driving toward the house on St. Louis Avenue. Although Ramirez didn't say anything I could sense he was getting excited about seeing his children for the Thanksgiving holiday. All I could think about was wrestling with my son on the floor when I walked into the door. But we knew we couldn't get distracted and it was still early. Experience taught us that even the most routine arrest could go deadly wrong at the last minute.

We had decided to let the SWAT team do their thing and secure the perimeter of the house. As the surveillance car trailed the green Buick Regal, everyone got into position. The alternate plan was to grab Links before he got into the house because we didn't know who inside might assist him or cause us trouble. Ramirez and I had positioned ourselves near the front of the house and the SWAT team had already secured the rear and both sides of the house. As Links car slowly rolled down the street, it was as if he was checking the neighborhoods for anyone looking for him. We made sure we sat low in the seats of our car and the darkness made it easy for us to stay concealed. Everyone stayed out of sight and waited for Links car to appear on St. Louis Avenue.

As with any arrest our minds constantly reviewed all the possible bad scenarios before we execute our plans. Since our information only confirmed one person in the car, I knew we had to check it to be sure he was alone. Was there anyone in the car or was there a car following him as protection and were they armed? What if he had a gun and did he plan to use it? Was anyone inside the house going to come out to his rescue? Were any of the SWAT guys going to be mistaken for local thugs or stick-up men? What if Links took off running? Would he use his car as a weapon? Would a child come running of the house and into the line of fire? Would any of the SWAT guys over react and cause a shot to be fired? Since it was already dark would Links take advantage of the cover of darkness and try something? As always you could "what if" yourself into doing nothing at all.........

Just then we saw the Buick Regal turn the corner. Everyone got into position. I said to myself, "Hell with the what if's. I plan to be home for Thanksgiving. My kids are waiting for me." Besides this was the last person in a long list of subjects and he wasn't getting away. Ramirez looked at me and said, "Let get him and go home..." and we moved toward Links with the swiftness of jaguars. The element of surprise was on our side. The SWAT guys moved in from all angles and all Links could see were automatic rifles and pistols pointed in his direction. Links could clearly see the gold FBI letters on our raid vests. By now the flashing lights were all over the street and within seconds Links was on the ground and being searched. His Mother appeared at the front door and screamed, "Junior!! What are they doing to you Junior!!?" He laid on the ground and said nothing.

Just then two small children appeared on the front steps and began screaming and crying for Links. By now the neighbors we coming out to see what was going on and the crowds had started to gather on the streets. Just as fast as we grabbed Links, we had him in the back of our car and ready to be transported to the U.S. Marshal's lockup in downtown Chicago. Before we pulled off we thanked the SWAT commander and Sgt. Lasker for their help. Ramirez told Lasker, "Tell Mickey his slate is clean with us." Lasker said, "I'll tell him." We headed north on I-55 and within twenty minutes we had arrived at the U.S. Marshal's Service. We dropped off the still dazed, Wilson Links and headed to Detroit to enjoy the holiday. We called SAC Duncan to let him know we had arrested Links and he was already with the U.S. Marshal in Chicago. We had made arrangements with agents in the Chicago office to handle Links initial appearance and removal hearing on the day after Thanksgiving. SAC Duncan's only words to us were, "Good job guys and have a good Thanksgiving with your family." That's exactly what we had planned to do.

As far as we were concerned, the House of Judah was history.....

****

Chapter Twelve

- MISSING FROM OAK PARK -

In life things always seem to go bad at the very time when we think we have it all under control. My good friends James and Pam Grimes found themselves in that position a few years ago. Their kids were finally meeting the mark they had set for them in school and although they had endured some rough times, life was good and showing promise. That was until their daughter Misty started spending time with a new group of friends that her parents didn't approve of. Neither James nor his wife felt comfortable with her new friends but they felt their parenting and religious upbringing would hopefully guide her actions.

One Friday afternoon, Misty and her mother had a heated disagreement over her grades dropping at school. This was not at all uncommon for an eighth grader who was starting to realize she was soon going to be a young woman. However, this argument was different. It seemed to be a little more explosive than past ones. This disagreement was so troubling to Ms. Grimes that she called one of the leaders in their church and discussed what was happening. They all agreed it was a phase Misty was entering and it would soon pass. In retaliation towards the family, Misty left the house without telling James, Pam, or her little brother that she was leaving. This was highly uncharacteristic for Misty and especially disturbing after an argument.

James and Pam tried not to worry about Misty and assumed she had gone to visit a friend and hopefully not one that they had disagreed over. The entire Friday evening after that incident was hell for the entire family. It was soon 8:00 p.m. and no one had heard from Misty. She received the usual telephone calls from friends looking for her but they all were told Misty was not home. By 10:00 p.m. Misty hadn't returned home and she still had not called as she had done dozens of times before. Worry replaced anger and the family virtually went into shock and only thought about the worst possible scenarios.

Pam Grimes called every one of Misty's friends to try to locate Misty. Unfortunately she called those friends whom she was familiar and none of the new group. The only ones Pam knew closely were her school and church friends. James had met one young man whom he thought was a little too mature for Misty but he couldn't recall his name nor did he have any way to contact him. By midnight the entire family was in an extreme state of fear that something serious may have happened to Misty. They called the Oak Park Police Department for help.

An officer responded within minutes and took some information about Misty. At the time she had only been missing for about 8 hours and the family wasn't sure if she was missing or hiding. The officer told them until she had been missing for 48 hours; no formal report or investigation could take place. He assured them they would investigate her disappearance but guidelines had to be followed in this case. He advised them to contact her close friends and hopefully one of them may have information about Misty. At the time he left the family was completely distraught.

During the week this event was unfolding, I had spent the week at the training academy in Quantico, Virginia. I was a technical agent at the time and was completing an update on some new equipment. When I arrived home on Friday evening I was so tired I neglected to check my answering machine. Unfortunately, I didn't check the machine until the next Saturday afternoon.

Most of my messages were fairly routine, i.e., call me when you get home. This was with the exception of the message from Jim and Pam Grimes. It had been received early in the morning and I sensed from their tone of voice something was seriously wrong. Although Jim spoke, I could hear distress in Pam's voice in the background. She was clearly crying and very upset. Jim only asked that I call them as soon as possible because something serious has happened with Misty. I returned their call and told them I was coming over right away.

Jim and Pam lived only about five minutes from me in a small bungalow. When I arrived Pam met me at the side door and Jim sat at the kitchen table with his head in his hands. They explained that Misty had been missing since Friday afternoon and they have had no contact with her. Pam cried while she explained Misty had an argument with her over her new friends. Jim cried while he explained they've called all of her friends and no one had seen or heard from her. As I listened and took notes and they cried as they told me the Oak Park Police could not begin anything formal until she has been missing for 48 hours. Forty-eight hours would not be reached until Sunday afternoon.

Jim and Pam begged me to ask the FBI to help them because something terrible may have happened to Misty. I explained to them we have to try to establish some sort of federal nexus for the FBI to formally enter into the case. I told them from what they've explained it seemed that Misty might have run away and may be hiding. I assured them I would do everything I could to find Misty because 48 hours is a long time for a minor to wander the streets of Detroit. I sensed a sigh of relief in each of them but I told them we've got to work together and not to assume anything.

I asked them to show me Misty's room and asked them to let me go through the room alone. I needed time to completely focus on whatever type of lifestyle Misty led based on how I read her room. I asked Jim to stay near and try not to be too upset over anything I found. I explained to him I had dealt with dozens of kids in the past and I've never been surprised as to what I've discovered in their rooms.

Jim and Pam told me they had gone through Misty's room but had found nothing of value. In fact they had called friends from her telephone book and none of them had seen her or have talked to her since early Friday morning. Pam did emphasize she had spoken with each of Misty's friends at least twice but she got nothing from them. I told her, "I'll explain the disadvantage of talking to kids later, but let me look around the room alone for a few minutes." Both of them left me alone in the room.

I first looked under the throw rugs in the room for any scraps of paper with telephone numbers she may have wanted to hide from her parents. It was obvious she hadn't taken many clothes with her if she had run away. Her closet was still full but I had problems with the few obvious gaps in her closet. I made a note to ask Jim and Pam later about what could have been in the gaps. It seemed to me that Misty may have collected some clothes before she took off. In addition it seemed that Misty's room was too neat for anyone to have been in it in the past few days. Either she cleaned it and made her bed before she left or Pam had cleaned it. It was just too neat for a teenager who had planned to run away.

The pockets of Misty's jackets had several spent books of matches. This seemed to be another aspect of Misty's life that she had kept from her family. I was convinced after finding several books of matches in her clothes she was a smoker. Her family had no idea she smoked cigarettes at the age of 14. I sensed the odor of cigarette smoke in her closet, which I knew would be a surprise to her parents. I decided to look under the mattress on her bed. The bed was neatly made and it didn't seem as if it had been slept in for some time. As I lifted the mattress, I discovered another aspect of Misty's life that her family was not aware.

In the middle of her box spring laid two marijuana clips, cigarette paper, and a condom. Next to these things was a telephone book that I knew the family had no idea of the names within it. This last discovery would be the key to locating Misty. Although I knew it would be difficult, I called Jim into the room. I asked Pam to remain outside and I'd share my theory with her later. I had moved nothing and left the findings for Jim to examine. As he walked into the room, he glanced toward the bed and began to cry. He said he had no idea his daughter knew anything about drugs and sex. He cried uncontrollably. I tried to comfort him and told him I had some things to work on but I'd need his help.

I told him it was up to him if he wanted to let Pam see the condom and drug paraphernalia. She was pretty upset and I needed her to do a few things too. Jim put the items away and we took the telephone book to Pam to go over some of the names.

When she looked at the telephone book she only recognized one name. She recalled the name of Delmar Banks as the young man that had been spending time with Misty. Pam said he was one of Misty's new friends whom she did not approve. Pam only knew he lived in Detroit and calls all the time. He had never come to the home to visit which really worried Jim and Pam. I asked Pam if this young man had called in the past two days. Pam slowly sat down on the couch and simply said, "No." Now we had a telephone number for him.

Pam recalled Misty told her that Delmar was a good boy and worked part-time at Red Lobster. She would never say which Red

Lobster because there were a number of them in the metro area. Pam said Misty didn't want to provide too much information about this boy for some reason. Jim now felt he knew why she was so secretive. It was now about 9:00 p.m. and Misty had not been heard from in more than 24 hours.

    I asked Pam if she could remember what Misty was last wearing and she walked to her closet. Pam slowly dried her eyes and said, "She was wearing a green top with jeans but her black leather jacket is missing," as she pointed to the closet. Pam realized several of Misty's favorite outfits were also missing from her closet. This time she and Jim cried together. Jim still hadn't shared the information about the drugs and condom under Misty's mattress.

    I asked Pam and Jim if they had any emergency money around the house. Jim told me they generally kept about $400.00 in the house for groceries and emergencies. I asked Pam to check to make sure the money was still where she left it. She returned to the room in a state of stupor and said, "The $400.00 in our bedroom is gone." She and Jim lost all composure and comforted one another. I had quite a few leads to work on and I knew I needed Jim to be one hundred percent focused.

    I told them we were going to let the Oak Park Police handle this case but first I was going to do everything I could to find her before the 48-hour time limit kicked in. I asked Pam to contact Misty's friends again and this time, ask to speak to the parents. I asked her to explain the seriousness of the matter and ask the parents to call with any information they might have at any time. I said, "Ask the parents not to alert the kids because they often will cover for one another if there is a parent dispute." Secondly, I called the Oak Park Police and spoke to a commander. I told the commander what I had found out about Misty and her dad and I were trying to locate her. He told me they would file a formal request for an investigation if Misty was not found within the 48 hour time period. They told me they'd provide whatever assistance they could to get the young lady back home as soon as possible.

I said to Jim, "Hold yourself together and I'll meet you in an hour. Dress down because we may have to travel to some not so nice areas of Detroit." I called the office and asked the on duty clerk to find anything they could on Delmar Banks. The fact that he was possibly a juvenile meant it would be hard to find any valuable information unless he had been involved with a serious felony. We started our hunt on the east side of Detroit.

I met Jim at his home and I sensed he was ready for just about anything he had to do to get Misty back home. I told Jim, "Look Buddy, we're going to some of the sleaziest areas of Detroit and hopefully Misty has nothing to do with those areas of town or the people in them. Some of the things you're about to see may be troubling. Unfortunately if we're going to find Misty, we've got to deal with some nasty people. That's how the streets work." Jim just dropped his head and nodded yes.

I told Jim the first thing we had to do was to find Delmar Banks. All we knew about him was a telephone number and the fact that he worked at a Red Lobster somewhere in the Detroit area. I found the telephone number was no good and we were taking a chance that he was still working at Red Lobster. We're also hoping he was someone who would direct us to Misty. It was a long shot but we had nothing else to go on at the time. Jim knew we were reaching for straws but I assured him I was willing to go as long as it took to get Misty back home to her family.

Jim and I sat down with Yellow Pages and found a Red Lobster restaurant on Chene in Detroit. I was only assuming that if he worked at Red Lobster it would be one that was not too far from where he lived. Jim kissed Pam good-bye and we left to find Delmar Banks.

The restaurant sat on the eastside of Detroit on a fairly busy street for a Saturday night. It was nearly 11:00 p.m. and Misty still hadn't been seen in over 24 hours. At this time no law enforcement agency had entered into the case. This was much too long for Jim's comfort. He wanted Misty home right away.

As we approached the restaurant I told Jim to let me do the talking and it may come to a point when I'd have to ask him to go back to the car. He said he understood. I knew because this was not an open FBI investigation I had to be careful about doing anything under the guise of the FBI. Not only could this harm any investigation by the Oak Park Police Department but might also get my rear end into a sling with my front office. I knew if anyone could help me it would be the manager and not until he knew I was an FBI agent. I entered the front door and asked the waitress if the manager was available to speak to me. I showed her my badge and she summoned him right away.

He approached me much quicker than I expected and said, "Hello, I'm Dan Kelly the manager, what can I do for you?" As I showed him my FBI badge and said, "Hello I'm sorry to bother you at such a busy time but I really need your help." I explained the timetable we were facing and the fact that we really needed to locate a minor whom we felt was somewhere in Detroit tonight. He understood as I emphasized Detroit and the word tonight. Although it was unspoken, we both knew she was in a hell of a spot. He could see the anguish in Jim's face after I introduced him as Misty's father.

I'm not sure if I continued to make small talk to avoid asking critical questions about Delmar Banks or if I just didn't want to hear he had never heard of the kid. After we talked about kids and the problems parents have with raising them I finally decided to tell him how he could help us. I said, "We've got to speak to a young man we think may work here named Delmar Banks." I then held my breath and waited for his response.

Mr. Kelley then said, "Yes I know Delmar, he's working tonight." Jim almost passed out. He knew we had reached our first milestone. He said, "I'll go get him for you."

I told Jim not to get hostile or pressure the guy. I told Jim, "Remember at this point he's in the driver's seat because we don't know what he knows." Jim simply said, "O.K., I'll be cool but it won't be easy." I told him, "We don't have a choice."

Within a few minutes a young guy wearing an apron walked out and said, "Are you the FBI agent who wanted to see me?" Jim stood next to me and I could see it was all he could do to keep his composure. He was young and extremely cocky but he had the trump card. I had to play my card and pull the best hand. I showed him my credentials and said, "I really need your help son. But first how old are you?" Delmar said, "I'm 16 years old and what do you want with me?"

I thought I'd really need to be careful interviewing this kid because if there is a felony involved, nothing he says can be used against him without an attorney and parent present. I knew he was streetwise enough to know he didn't have to tell us anything. I decided to try one more tactic.

I said to him, "Delmar when is your birthday?" He said, "I'll be 17 on Wednesday, why?" I smiled and thought to myself; bingo I've got him. I know Delmar was wondering what I was thinking about so I just let him wonder for a minute. I could see he was squirming and I felt I had to reduce his cockiness with some hard facts of life. I said, "Delmar are you familiar with the juvenile laws in the state of Michigan?" I watched him while he tried to compose himself and collect a series of street terms he thought would stump me. He said, "Man, I'm a juvie and ain't nothing anybody can do to me 'cause I'm 16." Now his attitude was starting to get on my nerves. I decided to burst his bubble.

I then explained, "Look Delmar although you are only 16 today, if anything tragic happens to Misty, as of next Wednesday you can be treated as an adult. Have you ever heard of the Michigan State Prison in Jackson? Have you got any idea how hot a 17-year-old boy would be among hardened lifers? And remember you're a little guy and a bit too small to fight off too many 300 pounders. You'll make somebody a nice boyfriend. Now Delmar or should I start calling you Della, where is Misty?" His face dropped like a rock. He lost the cockiness the minute I called him Della.

That was a trick we always used on the young wannabe tough ones. Although he was 16, if his defense attorney could prove any harm to the girl happened when he was 16, he would still be treated as a minor unless it was a serious felony. But I knew he didn't want to take that chance or maybe he was just too stupid to know I was pulling one over on him. Whatever the case, it worked. I sensed the look of worry on Delmar's face and his entire attitude changed to one of "they may make a punk outta me". He was now ready to talk.

Delmar looked at me and then glanced toward Jim and said, "I'll talk to you but I won't say anything in front of him." I knew Jim wanted to hear every horrid detail but I diplomatically asked him to wait in my car. He reluctantly agreed and walked away. I said, "Delmar, I can only protect you so far. If anything has happened to Misty you better do your best to find her before you turn 17 in few days. They just are too hard on teens in Jackson and I really don't think you can make it there. I wish they'd change the system Della, I mean Delmar." He nodded his head in agreement but he knew why I accidentally called him Della. He seemed to get more nervous by the minute. I knew by now my method had worked like a charm. The last thing he wanted to see was a prison cell at the age of seventeen. Della, or should I say Delmar, knew that would be fatal for him.

Oath of Office

    Delmar said that Misty had called him yesterday as soon as she left her house. She had told him she was angry with her mom because she didn't want her to see him any longer. Delmar said, "Misty's mom called me an eastside street thug. Man I ain't no thug." He said they wanted to run away but they decided to take off a little later when he could get a little more money. Delmar said they didn't have anywhere to go so he called his cousin to get them a room for the night. Delmar said, "Misty had about $400.00 that she took from her folks and I had my paycheck but I hadn't cashed it yet."

    I told Delmar to slow down because I had some questions for him. I asked Delmar, "First of all how did Misty get to your house, who is your cousin, and how did your cousin take you to a room? If you start lying to me I'm going to personally order you a cell with a 300 pound gay roommate." Delmar explained that Misty came to his house in a taxicab. He said it was about 10:00 p.m. when she got to his house. He explained his father worked at night and she knew it was always clear in the evening. They had to get a room because his father got home early in the morning. He sometimes came home early and they didn't want to be caught.

    Delmar said his cousin had a car and they knew he was old enough to get them a room at a place on Eight Mile Road. He said the three of them stayed at the motel all night and left about 9:00 in the morning. Delmar said they had breakfast at Denny's and she had his cousin drop her at the airport before noon. Misty said she was going to New York because she was tired of her folks and sick of Detroit. Delmar said, "I swear I left Misty at noon and haven't seen her since then. I swear that's all I know." He swore over and over and I finally said, "Shut up man. We've got work to do." He kept saying he wanted her found before Wednesday and hoped she was fine. Delmar said, "Man I ain't going to jail for nobody." He really seemed worried about meeting the roommate that I had promised him.

I just stared at Delmar without saying a word. I wanted to give him a chance to recant his statement before I cut him up. He just kept saying, "I hope she's o.k. I didn't hurt her. We go together." I asked him, "Who is your cousin and how old is he?" Delmar said his cousin was 21 but he didn't want to give his name because he was on parole. He said, "Besides, Misty was with me, he didn't do anything but get us the room and sleep."

I decided to make a deal with Delmar. I said if we found Misty unharmed I won't press for his cousin's name but she better not be hurt. But I told him the cousin's biggest problem might be the guy standing next to the car. I pointed to Jim. Delmar said he understood and proceeded to describe the hotel where they spent the last night together. I told him I was going to check out every detail of his story and if I found any lies, his new roommate would be waiting with flowers and candy.

I told Delmar he'd better call me as soon as he heard from Misty no matter what the time of day or night. I also thought I'd cover myself by getting Delmar's home telephone number and I told him I was going to call his father the next day. I had no allegiance to Delmar nor had I promised him any confidentiality. However I knew if I shared certain parts of his story with Jim before we pulled off the parking lot, it might prove hazardous to Delmar. I decided to talk as we pulled off the lot. I told Jim we were going to check out some leads on Eight Mile Road. I just told him Delmar said Misty might have stayed at a motel on Eight Mile Road the day earlier. I said he didn't know the name of the motel but I was going to check out his story.

We headed to Eight Mile Road on a quest to find out where Misty might have stayed last night and hoping she may be somewhere near. I went over Delmar's information over and over in my mind—an attempt to pick out any inconsistencies. In addition to digesting his information I had to decide how to break the lewd details to Jim.

I said, "Look Jim, you know the business I'm in and it often has a crazy side and sometimes what I find isn't so pleasant." Jim just listened and finally said, "Go ahead I think I can take it. I know Delmar wanted me outta sight for a reason, right?"

I figured while he was in the mood I may as well let him know what we'd be looking for on Eight Mile Road. After all Eight Mile Road on a Saturday night in Detroit wasn't the most pleasant place to be. The streets were lined with hustlers and streetwalkers and everyone was out to make a buck on some poor soul. The hustlers looked like they could sell you the stink out of dog crap if you stood long enough and listened to their story. The hookers were just looking for any john that looked like he was in a fix for their sleazy services. In the midst of all this crap we were looking for Misty in a nasty, grimy three-hour motel. Jim was ready for the worst so I let him have it and I decided to pull no punches.

When I finished giving him the horrid facts of life that he didn't know Misty ever had experienced, I decided the best thing to do was to lean on the motel owners to find out what Misty did the last night she was seen. We followed Delmar's directions to the letter and found ourselves at the American Motel. It was exactly as he described it and open for business just as any Saturday night. Some of the truckers were walking into the rooms with two girls at a time. The stench of liquor and urine was all over the parking lot. None of them seemed to care about the stench or even the two of us for that moment because love was in the air—at least for the next three hours.

Jim and I went to the manager's window and I held my gold badge up where the East Indian manager could see it clearly. He came out apologizing if I had to wait and said, "Good evening officer, I hope there is no problem. I run a good business here." I looked over in the corner and a nasty looking hooker had fallen asleep on the couch in the small lobby. She seemed to be a bit worn out and even though the night was young. I said, "Spare me the details but if I don't get some information on this young lady, your operating days will be numbered." I handed him a picture of Misty.

He said, "I think I remember her from last night. She was with two young men last night in room 43." I said, "Let me see any records on who rented the room and how it was paid." The guy went behind the counter and returned with a card that said Herman Jackson signed it and he paid $43.00 cash when he checked out on that morning. Jackson was the person Delmar was trying to keep hidden from us. After getting a description of Jackson from the manager, he appeared to be in his early twenties. Delmar knew a convicted felon in a motel room all night with a minor wouldn't set well with a parole officer. But our job was to first find Misty and return her home safely.

Of course Jackson didn't leave any locator information that we could use to track him down. If Delmar was telling the truth, all Jackson did was sleep and dropped them off the next day at his house. At least it seemed a portion of Delmar's story was accurate. Now because I didn't have an open case with the bureau, I had no way to verify if she actually left Detroit for New York through the airport. A street wise young lady with $400.00 cash could travel a long way from Detroit.

I took Jim home and told him and his wife to get some rest and I was going to get started early the next day running some leads on Jackson. In the meantime I told Jim to contact any relatives he may have that Misty may be close to in New York and ask them to look out for her if she shows up. He said she had visited some cousins last summer and really fell in love with the Big Apple. It was a long shot but I had to assume Delmar was being straight with me up to now. When I left Jim and Pam they were still crying in one another's arms because Misty had not retuned home.

My parting words were, "Don't worry, I'm going to find her and bring her back to you one way or the other." They both were still holding one another as I drove away.

I got up early on Sunday morning and I knew this day I'd be far from church. Sunday was normally the day I reserved for filling my spiritual gas tank. After a week in the sewers of Detroit I knew I certainly didn't make the journey on my own. Although I professed to be far from a preacher, whenever Jim's wife would ask me if I knew my savior, I'd just look at her and smile. Little did she know I was saying to myself, save it for someone who needs it. Needless to say Misty was from a very religious family.

I had been delivered from so many deathbeds in Detroit that I felt I was on borrowed time. But for whatever reason He saw fit to bring me home time after time. To this day I know I'm not worthy but I still thank Him everyday. But this day would be different. I had made a promise and I intended to keep it. I think the Lord would understand I had work to do—finding Misty.

My first task was to call the office and get an address on Herman Jackson. The weekend clerk answered and I immediately recognized his voice. He knew I wanted something because I started to shoot the bull with him about getting stuck working a Sunday morning. I said, "Enough of the small talk. I've got only a name of Herman Jackson and I know he's around 20 to 25 years old. He lives on the eastside and he's a recently released ex-con. I know that's not much but call me with anything positive you can find. I'll be home for about two hours this morning." There was a pause and I could tell the guy was writing. He said, "I know this is male but is he Black or White?" I laughed and said, "How long have you been a clerk? Do you ever plan to get in the academy asking questions like that? Run him both ways and call me" and I hung up the telephone.

About two hours later I got a call with the information I wanted on Jackson. Herman Jackson lived on the eastside on Chene. Rather than calling Jim, I decided to drive over on my own and see if I could find this guy. Besides Jim and Pam needed time to rest and regroup. Because this was not an open bureau case yet, I worked it on my own as if there were no rules. By the time Oak Park or anyone else decided to enter this investigation, Misty could be almost anywhere and hopefully still alive. I didn't have the luxury to wait as the local police suggested. Somehow I still wanted to believe she was still in town.

As I drove down the street toward the address on Chene, I looked for the old Green Chevy that the motel owner described. It was nowhere to be found. The neighborhood looked like a gutted out bomb crater and the locals were mugging me like I had two heads. But I knew the way around them was to play equally as nuts—mug'em back. I parked my car, stared at the guys on the front porch where I was going, and walked up to the first one I saw. I used one of those "I'll bite your nose off looks" and put my gold badge in his face. I said, "Where's Herman Jackson? He's not in any trouble yet but I've got to talk to him right away." The younger of the two guys stood up and said, "He ain't been here all weekend. I think he's with his lady on the Westside somewhere."

Of course after further questioning no one had any idea where she lived or what was her name. I wrote my pager number on a piece of paper and asked them to give the number to Herman. Although they said they'd tell him, I was born at night but not last night. As I walked back to my car about six more guys came out of the house and sat on the front steps. They seemed to be coming out like roaches and trying to mug me again. Everyone had something to say about the Fed looking for Herman. I just continued my "I'm crazier than you" look at each of them and stared. Although I didn't a have photograph of Jackson, the description I had cleared all of the guys on the porch. By now they just assumed I was a nut to walk on a porch with eight guys mugging me. I guess my bluff was bigger than theirs.

As I drove away I made sure I could see each of them in my mirror until I was out of sight. It was not uncommon for jitterbugs like them to throw a brick after you drove off. I had made up my mind if one of them tried something stupid, I would be obligated to go back and check the clown who was willing to throw away his life. They were just chumps because they each had something to say under his breath after I got into my car. If I had walked back to them, they would have all probably wet their pants. They were just chumps.

I decided to call Jim and Pam to see if they'd heard anything from Misty. I could hear Pam crying in the background before I gave them any information. It really didn't make any sense getting their hopes up because it was just too early.

I called Delmar and told him I was on the way over to talk to him and his father. I could tell by his voice he didn't want to see me but I felt if I could keep him on his toes my chances of finding Misty would be greater.

I found Delmar's house with no problem. He was situated on the eastside in a working class neighborhood. I could tell his Dad was a hard working guy by the looks of the house. It was obvious the owner didn't have lot of time to invest in landscaping or yard work. The home didn't show any signs of a woman's touch on the outside.

Delmar opened the door and invited me inside right away. He didn't want anyone to see me on his porch and mistake him for being associated with the police. Although I didn't think I was dressed like a Fed, Delmar didn't want any mistakes or assumptions pointing to him. It just wasn't cool dealing with the police in his neighborhood. Delmar and I had small talk while he waited for his Dad to come out of the bedroom. The poor guy had worked all night and I know he was tired. But this was important and I wanted Delmar to catch any wrath his dad had to deliver.

The inside of the house also showed no signs of a female presence. It was drab and rather disarrayed. Delmar explained to me he was an only child and his Dad was a single parent. Although Delmar told me he was a junior in high school, he had no idea what he wanted to do when he graduated from high school. He said his only goal was to get a job. I just assumed he had planned to graduate one day by virtue of completing four years of attendance. Delmar said to me several times, "School just ain't my thing. I rather work and get paid." I figured to try to counsel this guy on career education and college was a bit fruitless at the time. It was clear he wasn't listening and cared less about what I had to say.

Delmar's dad walked into the living room and said, "Sorry I took so long, I worked overtime until seven this morning." I said, "I'm sorry to disturb your rest but let me explain the problem we have." I explained to him the seriousness of Misty's disappearance especially in light of Delmar turning 17 in a few days. I told him we really hoped she came back safely and returned home as soon as possible. After showing him the picture of Misty he said, "I've seen her. Hey Delmar, why didn't you tell me this was the person that's missing?" Delmar said, "I didn't know she was missing 'til last night. I don't know where she is."

Mr. Bank's said, "Boy I know you've been sneaking that girl in this house while I'm working!! And why have you been missing school?" I thought Mr. Bank's was going to slap Delmar to the ground. I intervened and said, "Look Delmar, we've got to find this child. You've got a lot of problems but your worse problem is Misty being found dead or hurt. You don't want to know how a 17-year-old kid is treated in a prison. Let's find this kid and now!!" Delmar said over and over he didn't know where she was but she mentioned

Oath of Office

going to New York. Mr. Banks was still on fire and was seconds off of Delmar's rear end.

Mr. Banks thanked me for alerting him about Misty and Delmar promised to page me the moment he heard from her. He said they generally talk everyday but she has not called him since they parted on Saturday morning. He now said they dropped her at a restaurant somewhere on the Westside. He claimed he couldn't remember the street but it was one of those Coney Island places.

I wasn't sure how safe Delmar was after I left the house but realistically he needed a good dose of tough love. His poor dad really had it tough with a "wanna be" gangster, near dropout son. A good butt kicking by his angry dad would be mild compared to what would be waiting for Delmar in a maximum-security prison. I called Jim and Pam just to let them know I was still following up a few leads. I later went back to Herman Jackson's place to see if he had showed up. His boys were still holding down the porch and said he hadn't come back yet. They claimed they would tell him as soon as he came back. I really believed their sincerity.

I spent the balance of the afternoon at the office checking files for any information I could get on Herman Jackson. I really hoped I could have found an outstanding warrant on him. Lucky for him his most recent case had just been cleared a few days earlier. I received a page from Delmar at 7:30 that evening. Before then, I was running into a stone wall. It was my first break in the case.

I found a pay telephone as quick as I could and dialed Delmar on his cellular telephone. I remember thinking how ironic it was that he owned a personal cellular telephone and I didn't. I was the one who went to work everyday. It was obvious as much as Delmar's dad preached; he still spoiled the hell out of him. It was probably just his way of making up for having him grow up without a mom in the house. I knew the call was important because Delmar answered it on one ring and he seemed excited. His first words were, "Agent

Thornton, I've got Misty on the other line. She's in New York." I said, "Keep her on the telephone as long as you can. I'm only about ten minutes from your house and I'm on the way!!"

I still found it hard to believe she was really on the telephone and talking to Delmar. Nonetheless I raced down Eight Mile Road at 50 miles per hour to get to the eastside as soon as possible. I had my credentials in my hand just in case I was stopped by a Detroit squad car. This was one time I had planned to badge my way out of a jam and keep rolling. I made it to Delmar's house in less than the 10 minutes and he was still holding her on the line. Delmar was waiting for me at the door

Delmar quickly motioned for me to pick up the second line to listen to Misty as she talked to him. I could sense from her voice that she was frightened and sounded as if she was crying. I wrote a note to Delmar to tell her someone wanted to speak to her. I decided if I just broke into the conversation it may frighten her and she'd hang up the telephone. That would put us back to square one all over again. Delmar said to Misty, "Look I understand where you're coming from but I got someone here who needs to talk to you real bad. No it's not your father. You've gotta understand if you don't get back here unharmed, it's gonna be bad for me. I'm turning 17 on Wednesday." Delmar knew Misty was angry with her parent's and one of them on the telephone would cause her to hang up the telephone. He then handed me the telephone with Misty on the other end.

I could hear her crying throughout her conversation with Delmar. I said in a calm voice, "Hi Misty, this is Cary Thornton, a friend of your Mom and Dad. Do you remember me?" She continued to cry and said, "Yeah, you're the FBI agent, right?" I said, "That's right and your parents are really worried about you." I knew the next few moments with her was going to be critical because I still wasn't sure she wanted to be found. I could still hear her crying as she tried to talk to me. She was crying as much as her mom and dad had cried all weekend since she had been missing.

I said, "Misty, where are you and are you alright?" I took great pains not to mention her parents at this point. I didn't want to say anything that was going to cause stress or make her want to hang up the telephone. Her next statement frightened me more than anything she said to me. Misty said, "I'm in New York City and I'm scared." She paused and continued crying. I could hear the noise of the subway in the background and what seemed to be men arguing in the background. Misty said she was in a subway station in Manhattan and didn't see anyone she knew. She just kept crying and speaking slowly into the telephone. I knew this was going to be delicate because I had no idea exactly where she was in Manhattan. A fourteen year old was dead meat in that environment.

I calmly said, "Listen to me Misty. I can get you to a safe place but you've got to be strong and listen to me carefully. Do you think you can follow my instructions closely?" Misty shyly said, "Yes but you've got to hurry, I'm really scared down here." I listened to the noise of the trains and the streets of New York in the background. It didn't take a genius to realize Misty was not in a friendly place. I said, "Misty can you see any street signs to let me know where you might be?" She said she couldn't see anything but a bunch of men hanging around the subway station. She explained to me she went down into the below ground station because she was cold and had gotten confused. I told her that was no problem but keep talking to me until we get someone to her. She agreed that she would stay on the telephone and keep talking to me.

Although I had a thousand questions for her beginning with what the hell was she doing in New York? I refrained from any inquisition and passed a note to have Delmar to call Jim at home. I told him not to explain anything but have him get over here right away, alone. I covered the telephone and said, "Tell him not to bring Pam with him this time but get over here as soon as possible."

I told Misty to keep talking to me until she sees a uniform police officer. I said, "When you see him, get his attention, tell him your name, and that you're 14 years old. Give him the telephone and let me talk to him." Just at that time I could hear her say, "Officer!! I need help!!" Within moments I heard him say, "Hello this is Officer Delaney." We exchanged greetings and I quickly told him the position Misty was in and that she was a 14-year-old runaway from Detroit.

I gave the officer the pertinent information about Misty and her family in Detroit. It seemed that only moments had passed when Jim walked into the room. He was still crying like a baby. I asked Jim if he had any close relatives near Manhattan. He said he had a sister in New York but he had her telephone number at home. I asked the officer to take her to the nearest precinct and I'd have her aunt pick her up within the hour. We exchanged telephone numbers and I asked to speak to Misty before he hung up. I said, "Misty, Officer Delaney is going to take you with him and we'll have your aunt pick you up later. I want you to promise you'll call your Mom as soon as you get to the police station. Will you promise me you'll call her?" By now Misty and had ceased crying and simply replied, "I will."

Jim had already called Pam and alerted her to call his sister in New York. He said she was so happy she couldn't stop crying but she said she'd make the call right away. I told Delmar I wanted to talk to him and his father tomorrow but I just said to him, "Get ready for school tomorrow" and I left the house with Jim.

Pam was waiting for us as we pulled up to their small home. They embraced one another in tears and then both turned the hugs to me. I'm not sure they were just squeezing the breath out of me or drowning me in tears. Either way, they were happy Misty was safe. We all went into the house to make plans to get Misty back to Detroit. Pam had already spoken to Misty and said she was doing fine. Her sister-in-law had been called and was on the way to the Manhattan precinct to get Misty. While I sat drinking a hot tea, the telephone rang again. It was Jim's sister from New York who was with the police officers and Misty. The two of them took turns speaking to the officers, his sister, and Misty. They both told me thank you a thousand times that evening. Each time they said it, the words sounded better. Although I didn't show it outwardly, I was as happy as they were that Misty was safe and coming home. I felt the same emotion that they were showing but my ego wouldn't let me do anything but show my tough exterior. After all, I was an FBI agent.

I soon told them I had to go to the office early the next morning and I went home. I knew although they had gone through some tough times, they had some making up to do. I told them I'd see them later in the day when Misty returns home. Pam had already checked the airline schedule and was planning to get Misty home during the late afternoon. I wasn't sure if Jim's sister in New York was waiting on some answers as to how Misty ended up in a New York subway station on a cold Sunday night in December. I was not going to volunteer any information. In fact I decided to spare Jim the horrid details of my encounters on the eastside. The both of them had gone through enough for one weekend. I decided I would let Misty's homecoming be a private affair with her family. I planned to just tell Jim and Pam I got tied up at the office the next afternoon.

The next day I called my contact at the Oak Park Police Department and told him that Misty was safe and returning home. Again I spared them the grimy details and thanked them for their assistance and concern. Around 2:00 in the afternoon I got a call to come to the front lobby for a package. Normally when anyone gets a package the clerk just calls and tells you to come and get it. This time she said, "Hey you've got a package and I know you want to get this before your boys see it." I just played it off and walked up front like nothing was going on. If it was something embarrassing I didn't want to draw any attention to myself.

When I got to the lobby a florist had delivered the biggest plant and card I had seen in a long time. It was complete with ribbons, balloons, and bows. To my surprise our legal counsel was standing there as I walked into the lobby. I read the card out loud so that Special Agent Blabbermouth could report back to the squad area. It read, "Thanks for Finding Misty. Our Family Loves You. Jim and Pam Grimes." I turned to him and said, "Do you need any more explanation?" He turned and said, "The card says it all. Good work," and walked out as fast as he walked in. I suppose he didn't have anything newsworthy to report after all.

Although I never received one "ataboy" from my office or the Oak Park Police for locating Misty, the plant and card from the Grimes family meant more to me than any award or plaque. The satisfaction of the Grimes family being united again was enough for me. Delmar was happy that the spotlight shone away from him for a while and the sheer thought of him spending time in jail was motivation to get him moving.

****

Chapter Thirteen

-TERROR AT METRO AIRPORT -

Terrorism in the United States was somewhat of a foreign concept prior to the events September 11, 2001. Although the Detroit FBI office sometimes received calls of possible terrorist threats, the response to those threats was not nearly as dramatic as they are today. A telephone threat to an airport today would literally paralyze a city whereas during the 1980s it would interrupt the normal flow of business for a few hours and would often never make the evening news. This was the case with a young man we investigated named Bradley Brenner.

During the spring of 1985 a major airline located at the Detroit Metro Airport received a call from a sick individual who told the customer representative, "There's a bomb on the incoming Flight 111. You've gotta do something fast." The caller hung up as fast as he called and left no more information. The manager of the airline office immediately contacted the local police, the airport authorities, and then the FBI. Flight 111 was put on alert and all the emergency authorities braced for the worse. All the emergency measures were implemented and everyone waited for the flight to land at the airport. Luckily the flight landed without an incident.

The caller was apparently familiar with the airline schedule because he gave the flight number to the inbound flight correctly. This fact alone gave creditability to his threat and a reason for the airlines to be worried. To say the least, his call created pandemonium at the airport and serious disruption to travelers. Ironically the caller had chosen one of the busiest times of the day to make his threat, a Friday afternoon prior to the Memorial Day weekend. Lucky for us the call turned out to be a hoax. We surmised this person was one who liked the excitement and confusion at the airport.

Fortunately for the FBI the call was tape-recorded by the airline, which allowed me to compile a composite for the FBI Behavioral Science Unit in Quantico. The Criminal Profiling Unit was in its very early stages and had already been tested to the maximum. The agents in this unit specialized in examining evidence and drawing conclusions on criminals involved in various types of criminal activities. Based on the voice of the person on the tape, the Behavioral Science Unit told us we should look for a Middle Eastern man, approximately 30 to 39 years old, and somewhat of a loner. Unfortunately that was not a lot of information to go on with the caller who now had begun calling Detroit Metro Airport with threats practically every weekend from May through July of that year. With thousands of possible suspects in the area, I didn't have very much information to begin my investigation.

After an investigative meeting with my supervisor, we decided we would have to get innovative if this person was going to be stopped. The dollars losses for the airlines were starting to mount to astronomical levels. With the loss and delay in flight times due to the caller's antics, the airlines were doing everything within their power to minimize the excitement and disruption to their customers.

Although the Behavioral Unit told us the caller was most likely a Middle Eastern male, our search area could practically start anywhere in the metropolitan area. The area where we lived and worked comprised the largest population of Middle Easterners in the United States. The vast majority of them were law abiding citizens that wouldn't dream of such tactics that our caller was practicing. We were starting to get tremendous pressure to solve this case because of the disruption it was causing in air traffic around the Detroit Metropolitan area. I decided to go outside normal investigative procedures and become creative. My office gave me the green light after being involved with this case for about two weeks. It became obvious airport surveillances, constantly interviewing likely suspects, and rousting informants wasn't working. This seemed to be an impossible task although failure was not an option for the FBI.

Because I had a composite of approximately ten taped phone conversations, I requested and was granted permission to open an 800 call-in line for the general public. We went to the local media to air our case and ask the public to call an 800-telephone number and to listen to the voice of the caller. If the citizen recognized the voice they were asked to contact the FBI immediately. As soon as the story was aired and the line released, our office began receiving dozens of possible leads. Unfortunately as we ran down lead after lead, we found ourselves no farther ahead and no suspects identified. None of the leads proved to be positive and no one had given us anything more to follow-up. We found many persons just liked to call the office to talk to FBI agents. The mounting threatening calls and disruption of local air service continued in Detroit with the July 4th weekend approaching.

After several weeks we found ourselves in the same position as before and without a viable suspect. As the case agent, it was not a comfortable position to be in with the Special Agent in Charge pushing for me to locate and arrest a suspect. It seemed the caller had us at his mercy and continued to call the airlines with the threat of bombs loaded on incoming aircraft. The only factor in our favor was by now it seemed the threat was a hoax in each case. However each call to the airline had to be taken seriously. We had expended a tremendous amount of manpower. The caller continued to threaten inbound aircraft and never once an outbound aircraft. This fact told me the caller was most likely someone calling from the Detroit area and most likely from the vicinity of the airport.

SAC Wallers called my supervisor and me into his office for a briefing on our progress. He was not happy we had no suspects and turned up the pressure to get the case resolved. Both he and the United States Attorney's Office had started to receive pressure from the airlines and local citizens to arrest a suspect. The pressure started rolling downhill and rested in my lap. I decide to revert back to good old common street sense that I had developed growing up in north St. Louis.

By growing up in the streets we always knew that people who did bizarre things were generally classed as weird or just plain crazy. Whoever was this caller, he seemed to fit somewhere into that category. He liked the bizarre and got a charge out of watching us scramble whenever his calls landed at the airline switchboard. I surmised he may have been watching while air traffic and personnel were disrupted at the airport. I developed my own scenario regarding where a weird person of this magnitude might spend his time.

I self-profiled this person based on his voice, which was the same thing the Behavioral Science unit had done earlier. I concluded the caller was definitely not a black man. However the airport and vicinity was full of white guys who go about their business on a daily basis and are seldom noticed. I told my supervisor that the person we were most likely searching for was probably not a minority but perhaps a young, delusional, white male. He most likely would not be noticed if he frequented the airport or the vicinity of the airport. Because of the mix of residents in areas close to the airport he would possibly not be noticed at local restaurants or loitering inside hotel lobbies. I decided to concentrate my search on hotels, restaurants,

Oath of Office

and public facilities near the airport. These places had to be within view of the Detroit Metro Airport so that the person could visually watch the confusion unfold. I drew a matrix and began visiting work sites and managers in the suspect facilities. Reverting back to street corner intelligence, I knew this person probably was a mental case so I included in the matrix local mental health facilities and out patient adult day care units. My supervisor reminded me that my assessment and that of the FBI Behavioral Science Unit were far apart. I told him, "I'm going with my assessment because those guys are hundreds of miles away and most of them haven't interviewed one suspect or informant in years."

For several days I met scores of employees and managers and asked them to listen to the taped voice. No one could identify the voice. Although I knew it was a long shot, I was confident our person had to frequent an area near the airport. I exhausted my list of hotels and restaurants and began visiting local mental health and adult day care sites near the Inkster and Romulus, Michigan areas. In each instance I met with facility managers in their staff meetings. The managers played the tape for their staff and caseworkers on numerous occasions without success until one afternoon in July.

During my search through Wayne County health facilities, I met Ms. Barbara Olsen, who was the director of an adult day care center. I had known her for years and she was an extremely competent mental health professional. She told me many centers care for adults who are mentally challenged during the day and the families take them home in the evening. Her facility was one of several similar units in Wayne County. The lady gave me a tour of her facility as we waited for several of her staff members to come to her office and listen to the mysterious voice on the tape. As we walked from room to room she would turn around and lock the doors behind her. Being curious, I asked her for the reason she locked the doors on the sprawling campus.

Ms. Olsen explained that although most of the residents aren't dangerous, the majority of them are adults and they have social needs. She said if they allowed the rooms to remain unlocked, some residents would enter the rooms and engage in sex. Pregnancies among the mentally challenged population create tremendous problems that many families aren't equipped to handle. Ms. Olsen stated, "We have two residents that are blind and have been caught engaging in sex in the patio behind the building during the mid afternoon. They thought that since they couldn't see one another, no one could see them either." Unfortunately, Ms. Olsen's staff couldn't help us locate the caller but directed us to a nearby facility. Ms. Olsen assured me my theory on the caller seemed plausible and I should pursue the mental health angle.

I continued my search to another facility recommended by Ms. Olsen. That facility was also in the vicinity of Detroit Metro Airport. It housed mentally challenged adults during the day hours as well as offered counseling services for patients and families at all hours. The facility manager called her staff to the conference room to listen to the tape, just as the other manager's had done in other locations. She said her staff generally handled about 200 mentally challenged adult men and women a week. Many of them are self-sufficient and some hold part-time jobs in the community. She said others spend the day at the center while their parents and family work during the day.

The manager said they had all categories of patients attending the large facility. She explained that many were not harmful but they displayed unusual behavior and had to be monitored the entire time they were at the site. The patients at this mental health facility were all nationalities and races. We took a chance that someone within her staff of counselors may recognize the caller's voice.

To our surprise as soon as one counselor heard the voice on the tape, she stood up and said, "That's Brad!!" Her manager asked her if she was sure. She said, "I'm positive, that's Bradley Brenner. I've counseled him for over two years." The manager asked another counselor to come to the room and listen to the taped voice. He also said without hesitation, "I know that voice, that's Bradley Brenner. Bradley has been coming here for some time now. What has he done?" Finally my street corner hunch seemed to pay dividends. They said that Bradley came in regularly for counseling but he lived with his mother in Romulus, not very far from the airport. I immediately contacted the Detroit Special Agent in Charge to let him know I've finally gotten a break in the case.

Our squad immediately began a background work up on Bradley Brenner. According to his caseworker at the Wayne County Center, Mr. Brenner reported to their site twice a week with his mother. Although he was not considered a fully independent adult, he had a part-time job delivering mail from Willow Run Airport to Detroit Metro Airport daily. The two airports are several miles apart in Wayne County, Michigan.

Bradley's normal working hours were midnight to 5:00 a.m. Our hunch was right in that the caller was probably free in the afternoon hours and able to watch the excitement unfold at the airport in the afternoon. In addition, Mr. Brenner's exposure to the airport would provide him knowledge of the airline flight schedules. Mr. Hawkins, Bradley's counselor, assured us Bradley was not violent but just a troubled young man. He was 21 years old but had the mental capacity of a 12-year-old child. We were provided the home and work addresses of Mr. Brenner by the facility.

We immediately drove to Willow Run Airport to contact Mr. Brenner's employer. We thought it was good idea to speak with his employer first to confirm his working hours and to ask him to verify Bradley's voice on the tape one final time. We arrived at Willow Run Airport at approximately 10:30 a.m. and George Perkins, the facility manager, met us in his office. The mental health facility had alerted him that we needed to speak to him about Bradley right away. He and another manager took us to a private room and listened to the voice recording. They both looked at one another and agreed the voice sounded like Bradley Brenner. To confirm their suspicions, they asked another manager to listen to the tape and he said, "Hey, that's Bradley. What has he done?"

We called the United States Attorney's Office who concurred that we should interview Bradley Brenner as soon as possible. According to Mr. Perkins, Bradley had worked earlier in the morning and should be at home with his mother. He said, "Bradley normally sleeps in the morning when he gets off work. He is generally a quiet kid. He's harmless." In view of the Bradley's diminished mental capacity, we didn't feel he posed a threat of violence therefore additional agents wouldn't be necessary to meet us at the home.

We drove to the quiet neighborhood in Romulus and located the home as described by Bradley's mental health counselor. The license plate on the vehicle matched that provided by the center so we knew we had the right location. The two of us approached the door to the home and knocked several times. Within moments a small unassuming older lady answered the door and we politely introduced ourselves. I said, "Good morning. We're with the FBI and we'd like to speak to you about your son Bradley." She said, "Bradley? Is he in some sort of trouble?" Ken said, "We can talk about that." Mrs. Brenner was somewhat nervous but extremely kind. She asked us to step inside and offered us coffee, which we refused. The small neat bungalow had numerous pictures throughout the living room area, one of which we noticed was a young man we assumed was Bradley. Without delay we explained the reason for our visit and asked her if we could speak to her son. She became extremely upset but we assured her that we wouldn't arrest him after our interview. We allowed her to listen to our tape and she said, "Yes, that's my son's voice."

Oath of Office

She said, "I'll have to wake him because he has been asleep since he got off work this morning. Of course you know that Bradley is mentally challenged. He's had that problem since he fell as a small child." I said, "Yes, we understand he has developmental problems. But we still need to speak to him and we'd like you to stay with him while we talk."

Ms. Brenner apologized over and over for Bradley's actions and told us several times he wasn't a bad person but sometimes he does childish things. She explained although he was an adult, he has the mental capacity of a much younger person. Ms. Brenner was really upset and asked us several times if Bradley was going to go to jail. Unfortunately we couldn't provide an answer but assured her if he told the truth and cooperated, it would be to his advantage later.

Mrs. Brenner went upstairs alone and later led Bradley into the living room area where I sat with my partner. We stood as Bradley walked to us in a very shy demeanor. He looked as if he had just been awakened from a deep sleep. He quietly sat next to his mother and said very little. Mrs. Brenner was still upset but we assured her everything would be fine.

Bradley was about five feet six inches tall and somewhat pudgy around the middle. He wore glasses and a stripped red, white, and black shirt. With his withdrawn demeanor, he seemed to resemble an overgrown child. I interviewed Bradley and got as much background information as I could but it soon became evident that he had a very diminished capacity to understand details or to comprehend what he had done. In covering the specific events Bradley really didn't appear to understand dates, times, or events that he had caused at the airport. However Bradley said, "I really enjoy watching the flashing red lights and fire trucks race down the runways at the airport. I didn't mean any harm to anybody but I like to see the lights and excitement."

Bradley told us he got an airline schedule from the ticket counters when he delivered mail to the airport. He said he would pick out a flight that was scheduled to arrive in the late afternoon and he would stand in the lobby of the airport as the excitement unfolded. He said he could stand there and watch everything on the runway from the lobby window. He said, "When the excitement was over and no more lights were flashing, I'd drive home." Bradley added he would make the calls to the airlines from the pay telephones at the airport so he could be there when the lights started flashing.

When we completed our interview with Bradley, we called SAC Wallers at the Detroit field office. He was pleased we had brought this case to a conclusion but was concerned because of the nature of the subject involved. He felt that most likely there would be no prosecution but certainly a stern warning to Bradley and his mother.

He instructed us to have Bradley's mother bring him to our office at 8:00 a.m. the following morning for processing. We were told not to tell them what was happening beyond that time because we had to present the facts to the United States Attorney's Office. Mrs. Brenner assured us they would be there on time and thanked us for not arresting Bradley as we had promised. She and Bradley stood in the doorway and hugged as we drove away. She was still crying when we left the home.

Just as expected, Mrs. Brenner and Bradley were waiting in our lobby as the doors opened the next morning. Bradley was dressed more like a 12-year-old child rather than a 21-year old man. Quite frankly I think his adolescent style of dress may have been more for sympathy than anything else. However I asked Mrs. Brenner to wait in the lobby while I processed Bradley in our office. I led him inside the office to the fingerprinting and photograph area. He was processed as any other arrested felon. Throughout the entire ordeal he was meek as a lamb and said very little. I waited for

Oath of Office

Bradley to explode in any moment but he remained quiet and humble throughout. We knew it was senseless to take a signed statement from him because he really didn't understand much beyond the flashing red lights on the emergency trucks.

SAC Wallers had already spoken to the United States Attorney's Office who had declined any form of prosecution due to the mental capacity of Bradley. However SAC Waller asked us to bring him into his office when we finished processing him. The office of the Special Agent in Charge is a place no one wants to visit when he's in trouble. It was an uncertain walk where you don't know what is going to happen when you get there. You don't know if it's terminal or if you'll get one more try at life. And Mr. Wallers didn't make it any easier with his stares. He would stand tall with his custom-made suits and every hair on his head in place, and just look down on you. He was very unpredictable and Bradley could sense that as he walked into his office and sat down in front of SAC Waller's desk. Mr. Wallers sat at his desk and just stared at Bradley for no less than three minutes. I stood behind Bradley near the door of the office. Bradley still said very little and had no idea what was going to happen to him.

About five minutes had now passed and no one had said a word in the office. I could clearly see Bradley start to squirm in his seat. Mr. Wallers just sat and stared at him and suddenly got up walked over to Bradley. He asked Bradley, "Do you know the trouble you have caused the citizens of Detroit over the past several weeks?" Bradley looked down at the floor, shrugged his shoulders and said, "I think so." Although Mr. Wallers stood directly over Bradley he refused to look anywhere but at the floor. It was clear Bradley had a diminished ability to understand but he sensed he was in big trouble. Mr. Wallers got silent again but said to Bradley, "Look at me!!" Very reluctantly, Bradley looked up in his direction. Mr. Wallers said, "Bradley, only because of your mother you aren't going to jail. But if we ever have to pick you up again for anything, you're going so deep in jail they'll have to pump sunshine up your ass. Do you understand me, son?" Bradley looked up at Mr. Wallers and shyly said, "Yes sir," and looked back to the floor. He resembled a child being scolded by his teacher but I think Bradley got the point of this scolding.

I escorted Bradley out of the office and explained the no prosecution decision to Mrs. Brenner. She thanked me and again assured me that Bradley was not a bad person but just curious like any child. They left the Detroit FBI office and the threat calls to the airport ceased.

On this one occasion in my career, my street corner hunches and experience paid off and were more accurate than the FBI Behavioral Science Unit in Quantico.

****

Chapter Fourteen

- WELCOME TO PUERTO RICO -

My transfer to San Juan came about the time I was ready for a change of scenery. Although I had many friends in Detroit and it was more of a home to me than St. Louis, I was ready to get away from the deep snow and frigid cold winters. Puerto Rico represented a new start in life for me. A tropical paradise seemed to be the ideal place to begin anew. However, the idea of a move almost two thousand miles away didn't set so well with Pop. He was finally starting to accept the idea that I was an FBI agent and now they were transferring me to the middle of the Atlantic Ocean.

I remember Pop hitting the ceiling when I told him I was being transferred to San Juan. I called Pop on the telephone and gave him and Moms the news about my new assignment. He said, "San Juan!! Why the hell do they wanna send you there?" I said, "Pop it's going to be a good assignment. I'll get a chance to use my Spanish everyday and things will be fine for Elsie and me. You and Moms can visit as soon as we get settled in the house." Pop wasted no time responding to the idea of flying to San Juan. He said, "I'm not getting in no airplane. I haven't flown since World War II and I didn't like it then. I always knew those folks that Hoover left behind had a plan to try to get rid of you. You better watch yourself down there. I don't like, I don't like it."

I'm not sure Pop ever bought the idea of me living in Puerto Rico and he held fast to his commitment not to fly. However he did talk Moms into visiting. She had never flown that far, but flew down anyway. She was bragging to anyone who'd listen about her son the FBI agent. She finally accepted the idea about the Bureau and said, "The hell with Hoover, he's dead anyway."

The San Juan Division is the one place many FBI agents spend an entire career dodging. It ranked at the top of the most undesirable places to be stationed, right along with New York and Newark. No one wanted to be sent to San Juan, including most native Spanish speaking agents. San Juan was the place with all the rumors of horror stories of home invasions, robberies, and daily muggings. Agents talked about the horrible traffic problems and the hurricanes that devastated homes whenever they arrived and all of it was true. However if you survived an assignment in San Juan, you were considered a "real" FBI agent.

The one question for anyone going there was, "Why would any sane person want to go there?" Although I was transferred to the San Juan Division, I would have been eventually drafted and probably at a time that I felt was inconvenient for me and my family. I knew that I'd someday have to repay the Bureau for all my Spanish language training and this was the best time for me in my career. In addition to being language trained, I was a certified technical agent, and San Juan was in need of a Spanish-speaking tech agent. My draft was around the corner anyway unless something drastic happened to prevent it.

Moreover a move to San Juan represented a boost on the Office of Preference list. The Office of Preference (OP) is the one thing many agents work an entire career to achieve. It means you finally get a chance to choose where you're assigned rather than being told to go somewhere. An OP transfer means you finally beat the system, but in the case of San Juan, the FBI beats you first. The reward for a San Juan tour is the elusive OP transfer but only after a five-year tour. By the time your five years are over, you deserve anything you ask for from the bureau.

San Juan was a very interesting place to live and work. The people, both male and female, were unusually friendly and sometimes reminded me of Southerners in the states with their hospitality. I remember the first day I stepped into the U.S. Federal Building and Courthouse in Hato Rey, Puerto Rico. I found the guards were unusually helpful and seemed interested in getting me to my destination. They weren't the usual cold guards I had become accustomed to in the federal buildings in the states. I just assumed their hospitality was due to my dapper attire I wore that first day.

I recall walking onto the elevator and immediately six very stunning ladies all looked at me and smiled. Each one of them said, "Buenas dias Senor," in unison. I was flattered and stunned by their beauty to say the least. I assumed they noticed someone new in the building and each of the stunning ladies was trying to outshine the other. I returned the smile and said, "Buenas dias."

My ego was at an all time high because each of the ladies looked as if they were preparing for a fashion magazine shoot. Each was prettier than the other with their caramel toned skin and tight short skirts. To think they'd go out of their way to speak to a stranger from Detroit really pumped me up. But then I noticed as the elevator reached each floor, everyone got the same greeting and smile from the group of ladies. In fact as each person stepped off the elevator, he also got a "Buenas dias Y adios" from everyone on the elevator. I realized to speak to everyone on the elevator was more of a custom than a matter of flirting. Nonetheless it still was good for the ego to be spoken to by such pretty ladies. In that States that same courtesy would be considered flirting and definitely inappropriate.

I also noticed the same cordiality was extended at the main cafeteria in the federal building and in most restaurants. Whenever I sat in the cafeteria or any public place for that matter, I was never alone. If I found myself sitting alone at a table for four, it was not uncommon for two strangers to walk up to my table and say, "Por favor, puedo sentar?" (May I please sit with you?) In keeping with the courtesy and custom, you always said, "Si, por cierto" (of course) and returned the smile. If this happened in a large urban city in the United States, especially with two strange ladies, you'd think they were hitting on you. This practice is very common in the Puerto Rican culture and no one thought anything about it.

Regardless of your command of the Spanish language, it was always customary to attempt to exchange greetings and courtesies in the native language. To attempt to exchange even the most basic greeting was a sign of respect and admiration for the culture. It generally does not take a visitor to the island very long to catch on to this aspect of the culture.

Early during my tenure in San Juan I noticed a guy walking toward me in the hallway of the U.S. Federal Building in Hato Rey. He was tall, dark complexion, and had somewhat of a bounce in his walk. I initially assumed he was a dark skinned Puerto Rican but his walk was a little distinctive. As we neared one another we walked slower to see exactly what was different about the other. I couldn't figure it out but something was unusual about this guy. After we passed one another he stopped at the same time I stopped and we both repeated in English, "Are you from the States?" He smiled and said, "Yeah, I'm from Boston." I said, "I'm from Detroit." Just then I realized and so did my new friend that some people from the States stand out because their unique style of walking and the manner in which they carry themselves. It is a little different from the native Puerto Ricans. We became good friends for the remainder of my tour in San Juan.

Although I had a fairly good command of the Spanish language prior to arriving in Puerto Rico, the first people I heard speaking the language was at the airport. I thought they were speaking something other than Spanish. In fact, the manner in which they spoke, I could hardly pick up a word for some time. It was over a month before I could listen to a radio newscast and understand an entire story. I found out in short time that textbook Spanish and the everyday spoken language are as different as night and day. I really thought my Spanish was excellent until I started traveling around the city of San Juan and venturing into some of the rural areas. I listened to groups of people talking at shopping areas but I really didn't pay them very much attention. People spoke so fast I couldn't understand a word they said. I once asked my wife, "What language are they speaking?" She listened and said, "I don't know, but it may be something similar to Spanish, maybe Portuguese. That couldn't be Spanish, it's too fast." It went down hill from there. I found spoken Spanish in San Juan to be rapid fire fast and initially very difficult to understand.

After some time I could finally listen to a news broadcasts and television in Spanish and not be totally confused. Even the newscasters spoke fast. They would normally slow down to take a breath but to only give the time and temperature. For the first three months all I understood on the radio was the time and temperature.

One of my hobbies in Michigan was officiating high school and collegiate baseball. I figured one of the best methods to stay abreast of the language and baseball was to join an officials association in Puerto Rico. Early during my tour I met an official and became involved in officiating A and AA baseball around the island. The competition was excellent and I discovered it was the perfect vehicle to learn the various vernaculars around the island. Especially since all the games were officiated in Spanish.

C. Lee Thornton

It didn't take me long to realize that local slang and Spanish words varied by area of the island. My new officials association scheduled games throughout the island in both rural and urban areas. There were times I'd officiate in small towns where my wife and I were the only persons in town who spoke English. And regardless of the economic area, even the poorest towns had immaculate baseball stadiums. Their stadiums sometimes resembled mini-Tiger Stadiums and were sometimes the main recreation from Friday afternoons to Sunday nights during the baseball season. For town rivalries the small stadiums would have upwards of a thousand paying spectators.

My most memorable game was held in a small town called Cieba near the city of Caugus. The game was a Saturday afternoon rivalry between the towns of Cieba and Canovanas. I was umpiring behind home plate, which was situated approximately twenty yards from the nearest spectator seat. I only had my wife to talk with between innings because I didn't know anyone from the town. Throughout the game I could hear about four guys arguing in the seats directly behind home plate where I worked. I could only hear them saying, *"Esta Dominicano! No el es Cruzan! Cinco dolares! Deme cinco dolares!"* (He is Dominican! No he is from St. Croix! Five Dollars! Give me five dollars!") Because I was calling the game in Spanish and no one was complaining about my calls, I just ignored the men arguing for more than three innings behind me.

I knew they were talking about the Dominican Republic and St. Croix, U.S. Virgin Islands. I had recently been given a history lesson about St. Croix from an older gentleman. He told me that during World War II many families in St. Croix sent their sons to the Dominican Republic to live so that they wouldn't get drafted in the military and die fighting in Europe. He said for that reason many dark complexioned Cruzan's have large families in the Dominican Republic. He said that most of the darker complexioned Hispanics are thought to be from either St. Croix or the Dominican Republic. In addition he said that many Puerto Ricans feel that Dominicans and Cruzans speak the worst grade of Spanish.

As the game continued the small group of men argued constantly, not about the game but they kept saying, *"El es Dominicano!! No, senor esta Cruzan!!"* (He is Dominican!! No sir, he is Cruzan!!) I continued to call the game until the fifth inning when they called out to me. Between innings one of them stood up and motioned to me. He said, *"Arbitro!! Mira Arbitro! Ven qui por favor."* (Umpire! Umpire! Come over here please.) I walked over and said, *"Ola, que tal amigos?"* (Hello, what's up friends?) As a rule I generally never address anyone in the stands during the game because spectators frequently want to argue the strike zone and calls. That's always a distraction for the balance of the game but I was curious to see what in the world had these guys arguing and passing money since the first inning. I knew my accent was much different from a native Puerto Rican but I also knew my Spanish was more than adequate and I felt my strike zone was right on the money.

One of the three guys said, *"Mira, deme amigo. Es usted Cruzan o Dominicano?"* (Look, tell me. Are you Cruzan or Dominicano?) He had a fist full of one-dollar bills and looked at the other two as they anxiously awaited my answer. I looked at them and in English I responded, "Hell man I'm from Detroit!!" They changed to a sobering look on their faces and one guy laughed and snatched the fist full of dollars. I learned after a short time on the island that to be mistaken for a Dominican was not a compliment.

As I finally started getting accustomed to the spoken language and living in the Caribbean, I realized that the Caribbean culture was much different from that in the United States. People are generally very friendly, similar to people from small towns in the south. From time to time we would find ourselves in the midst of a fugitive hunt for a dangerous suspect. Unlike in the States, once you locate a family member or relative, you immediately get down to business and get all the information you can about the person's whereabouts. Getting that same information from a family in San Juan was a little different and took some tact on the part of the agent.

Practically all the homes on the island were encased in *rejas* or steel bars. The bars around the homes in San Juan would make any home in Detroit seem virtually a fortress. Every conceivable opening of the structure of private homes had steel bars covering the contents. Every home was the equivalent of a steel and concrete cage. Depending upon the location of the home and the size of the backyards, the home may have steel bars covering the tops of play areas. This was sometimes prevalent on private homes located near public housing areas. One co-worker told me the enclosed cage was to prevent intruders from jumping the fence and climbing onto his property. He said, "To be safe we just encased the entire yard for the sake of my kids."

Whenever a federal agent was transferred to the San Juan Division, if his home didn't have existing *rejas* (steel bars) already on the home, the government would pay to have them installed for him. We also had burglar alarms installed on our personal vehicles and homes provided at the expense of the United States government. The emphasis was on protecting U.S. citizens but it didn't make you feel any better. Even as a native of St. Louis I realized early that security was a very serious matter in San Juan, Puerto Rico.

It didn't take long for me to figure out that driving in San Juan was also a hazardous task. It sometimes seemed that practically no one obeyed traffic laws and you took your life in your hands simply by driving to work. I lived in an area called Borinquin Gardens, which was in the south sector of Rio Piedras, Puerto Rico. From my home to the office was exactly 6.1 miles door to door. However with the horrible traffic and with most motorists ignoring the traffic laws, my morning drive to work averaged about an hour.

The traffic on the highway was always outrageous to put it mildly. The entry lane onto the highway was as any other highway entry ramp with one lane for on coming traffic. However it was no less than two to three cars deep trying to get on to the three lane main highway every morning. Everyone decided to make his own entry lane for the highway every single day. The congestion was awful and no one bothered to yield for the other driver. On a tough day it would sometimes take no less than thirty minutes to get onto the highway from my home, which was exactly 800 yards from my door.

My daily challenge wouldn't begin until after I've pushed my way on to the three-lane highway. I found out my first day after driving from home, that the three-lane interstate became five lanes during rush hour traffic in the morning. The shoulder became a driving lane and so did the center emergency lane. In addition if there were no barriers in the center of the interstate, motorists would drive on the grassy area between the highways. On any random morning a normal three-lane interstate could be as many as six lanes of total confusion. To top off the confusion, motorists constantly honked their horns to signal their intentions, which generally went un-noticed by even observant drivers.

During my early days in San Juan I realized that in order to receive English-speaking television you had to buy cable service. It generally averaged about $60.00 per month. This allowed you to receive stations out of New York, Atlanta, Chicago, and Miami. However the bulk of your commercials were the same as in the United States but in Spanish. They were the same product advertising you get in the United States in most cases but advertised to a Spanish audience. It was a strange story how I found out about cable television service.

I had just moved to Borinquin Gardens when I noticed a guy parked beneath an overpass with his trunk opened. The area was fairly abandoned which seemed strange but he had a sign on top of his old car which read *"Cable de Television Servicio"* (Cable Television Service). I noticed the sign right away and pulled over since I was in the market for cable service. I had assumed there was a local company where residents went to buy cable service.

The guy was very casually dressed and spoke very little English. However he told me he was the local representative for General Cable Service of San Juan. I couldn't believe a cable salesman would be selling cable service from the trunk of his car beneath a freeway. I asked him, *"Tiene identificacion?"* (Do you have identification?) To my surprise he produced documents stating he represented Cable Television of Puerto. He was the local representative and he said he sold at that location because the road was in a busy section of town. The salesman showed me a contract and explained the terms of the installation. He told me the installation guy would be at my home on Wednesday between 12:00 and 4:00 p.m. My final point of business was to give this guy a check for $56.00. Under normal circumstances there would be no way I would have given the guy a check but I thought if he was phony, I could always cancel the check. After I left the area I started to think I needed my head examined for giving a stranger beneath a freeway a check for $56.00, even if it was made out to General Cable Service of San Juan. I kept telling myself that this was Puerto Rico and things were different here.

However I spoke to a few co-workers and was told that cable is sold by independent vendors and there was nothing to worry about. I took off work on the following Wednesday and the cable guy showed up a 3:45 p.m. I had ordered two cable boxes but the guy only brought one box with him. He installed the one cable box downstairs and left in about one hour. I took my tech equipment home the next day and wired the upstairs in my house for cable television and it worked fine. I realized that things are done a little different in Puerto Rico.

I wasn't as lucky with telephone service installation. The telephone company told me the installation man would be at my home between noon and 4:00 p.m. on a Wednesday afternoon. I took off work and waited for the guy to arrive. He arrived at 3:45 p.m. The installer, who didn't speak English explained to me had had been tied up on another installation and of course he said, "*Lo siento Senor.*" (I'm sorry, Sir) He was no different than any other installer; he was late and sorry about it. I told the guy where to place my three telephones and he went to work drilling and laying telephone wire around my house. Suddenly his pager went off and he went outside to his truck. I assumed he was going to be outside for a few minutes since he had wires and staples all over two floors of my house. I looked outside ten minutes later and the installer had driven away. I waited until approximately 6:00 p.m. and I convinced myself he was gone for the day. I later called the telephone company and they told me that installers were independent contractors and they had no control over their work schedules.

The following Friday afternoon I was home from work and out of nowhere came the same installer for an unscheduled visit. He asked me if he could finish my telephone installation. He said he was sorry but his cousin had gotten hurt the past week and he had to help him. The guy said he tried to get back but it was too late in the day. I told him to finish my telephone because I was using the pay telephone to make calls back to Detroit. The installer went back to work since I hadn't removed any of his equipment. Again the installer's pager sounded and he began to walk back to his truck. I stopped him and asked him if he could turn on my service to the rear at the house before he answers his page. The guy agreed and walked back to his truck. Ten minutes later the installer had left the area with the work unfinished. However this time I had service in the rear of the house.

The next day I took home my tech operations bag and tools. I had wired bugs and traps dozens of times for the bad guys so I knew I could install my own telephone service. Within 20 minutes I had finished the job of installing my telephone service at my home. I called the General Telephone Company service number and after about two hours, I was given a telephone number to my home. My service worked flawlessly from that day on with no help from the telephone service installer.

About two weeks later I saw the same installer working at the junction box in my housing area. I drove up to him and said, *"Senor, me recuerde?"* (Mister, do you remember me?) He looked at me for a few moments and said, *"Si senor. Como esta su telefono?"* (Yes sir. How is your telephone?) I just looked at him and said, *"Esta bien."* (It's fine.) I didn't think it would have done any good to ask him where the hell he had been for two weeks.

****

I was initially assigned to the Domestic Terrorism Squad as its technical agent and I soon learned the local traffic had a tremendous effect on the effectiveness of our job performance. This couldn't have been more evident than during the celebration of the Grand Regatta during the summer of 1992. The Domestic Terrorism squad was responsible for monitoring and insuring acts of terrorism didn't occur in Puerto Rico during this event. The Grand Regatta brought thousands of visitors to the island and tremendous security concerns for the FBI. The island unfortunately had a history and tradition of anti-American activities during large-scale public events.

Some past anti-American activities, although not widely known in the United States, included bombings and physical assaults against Americans. One of the more noted incidents involved the firing of a military style rocket at the U.S. Federal Building in Hato Rey. Fortunately there were no injuries because of the time the projectile struck the building. Our job as a squad was to ensure no terrorist incidents occurred during the Grand Regatta and to gather as much intelligence as possible to thwart any planned incidents.

Based on the rocket event and others, our jobs were extremely perilous and the gathering of anti-American intelligence became critical. We knew that major events, which drew large crowds, represented an ideal opportunity for Anti-American terrorist to strike and to make their existence known worldwide.

The Celebration of the Grand Regatta was a large group of ships that traveled the east coast of the United States and the Caribbean displaying ships from around the world. This could have potentially been a domestic terrorism nightmare had anything serious occurred on the island. The main celebration took place in Old San Juan and the Mirimar areas of the island. Geographically this was directly west of the main airport and the main primary where passenger cruise ships arrive in San Juan. All of the federal agencies had prepared contingency plans to implement in the event of a terrorist action. The entire venue was placed under electronic surveillance by our team of technically trained agents, which we monitored from several command posts including the FBI office.

One of the first problems we encountered during the Grand Regatta was a clash of culture between a group of French sailors and some citizens of Puerto Rico. Because the FBI was responsible for any international incidents we generally received the first telephone calls when foreign visitors got into any type of trouble. The first call received by the FBI was from the Police of Puerto Rico concerning seven French sailors who had been arrested on the second day of the regatta. We couldn't understand the nature of the arrests because each country had been briefed by their respective embassies about the proper conduct while on the island.

The Police of Puerto Rico told us they had arrested the seven sailors for groping and improperly fondling a group of ladies during a gathering in the Old San Juan area. The incident occurred at one of the main venues where the Grand Regatta celebrations were taking place. The soldiers, when arrested, were not intoxicated and seemed confused as to why they had been arrested. Unfortunately none of them could speak either Spanish or English and were sitting in the local lockup when we received the telephone call. The police couldn't communicate with the French sailors and could not explain to them why they had been arrested or why they were detained.

Fortunately our office in San Juan had two agents who spoke French, Spanish, and English and were sent to the central cuartel *(precinct)* to assist with the arrested French sailors. One agent was also dispatched to contact the French counsel about the pending international incident. Special Agent Juan Maldonito, a former marine officer, spoke French and interviewed the sailors in the lockup. He began his interview with the senior officer of the group to try to understand why they were groping the ladies. He was only at the cuartel about 15 minutes and returned to the office laughing as we waited to update the French counsel general.

Special Agent Maldonito said it seemed the French sailors were confused because they thought they were just being friendly by pinching the rear ends of the young women in Old San Juan. They told Maldonito that in France it is a sign of innocent flirting for young men to publicly pinch the rear ends of women. The French sailors thought the young Puerto Rican women were flirting with them by wearing their short, tight skirts, and smiling as they encountered the young sailors. They said when the police arrived and arrested them they had no idea they had done anything wrong and went willingly with the officers.

After the incident was explained to the French counsel, the young sailors were released with their promise to keep their hands to themselves during their remaining days in San Juan. To be safe, the counsel confined the young French sailors to their ship for the balance of their visit on the island. They agreed and enjoyed the remainder of the time in San Juan. We averted the only potential international incident during the festival.

****

I had only been in San Juan about six weeks when I was involved in my first automobile accident on the service road along Interstate 26, the main interstate freeway. Agent Ramon Garza and I were driving east on the service drive to meet an informant who had information on one of our fugitives. Agent Garza and I had worked together in Detroit several years earlier and were again partners in San Juan. I felt comfortable working with him in San Juan since he had been assigned there about three years.

It was about 1:00 p.m. when we approached an intersection near the Llorenz Torres Public Housing Projects. I was driving and had stopped at a stop sign, having made a complete stop. As we moved forward a vehicle approached us from a side street at rapid rate of speed. The car completely ignored the stop sign and hit our right front end with a huge impact. Our vehicle tipped on two wheels and we went over the embankment into the main section of Interstate 26. Lucky for us the traffic had cleared and our sudden entry on to the highway didn't cause another collision.

When we gained our composure we noticed the driver had driven back on the service road and was leaving the scene. We drove back over the embankment in our damaged car and pursued the escaping disabled car. It was difficult to determine if the occupants had been injured but they were slowly hobbling down the service road in the disabled car. It only took us a few moments to catch the escaping car. Garza and I managed to pull in front of the car and stop it. We drew our revolvers and shouted, *"Pone sus manos en avista."* (Put your hands in sight). Neither person in the car spoke English. We told them to exit the car slowly and keep their hands in sight.

C. Lee Thornton

Because of the terrorist climate on the island we didn't know if this was a deliberate attempted hit on us or just a random accident. However we were not in a position to second-guess the escaping driver or the passenger.

It only took a few moments to see the driver and passenger were only teenagers and frightened by our badges and guns aimed at them. This didn't preclude the two of them from being members of an anti-American group but we weren't taking any chances. We took the names and addresses of the two and discovered the driver had no driver's license or identification on him. Agent Garza was still not convinced the driver hadn't been sent by an anti-American group to try to eliminate two FBI agents.

We couldn't assume we had good information from either of them in light of the prevailing political climate in Puerto Rico. While I covered both of them with my revolver, Ramon called the information to the office to check their backgrounds. In addition we asked the switchboard to contact the Police of Puerto Rico to report the accident. We let them know there were no injuries but the driver didn't have a driver's license and he was only 16 years old. The office let us know the driver didn't have any warrants but we should detain him until the local police arrived. So we waited and waited and waited in the 90-degree heat for the Police of Puerto Rico to arrive.

After about 20 minutes we called the office again and asked them if they had made contact with the local police. It seemed the longer we waited the hotter the sun became as it shined on us that afternoon. After about 30 more minutes we heard sirens screaming in our direction from west of us on the freeway. We didn't pay it very much attention because it was a busy highway. We started to wonder when the two patrol cars got on to the service road and appeared to be coming directly toward us.

Suddenly the two cars stopped on the opposite corner from us and three of the eight officers exited their cars with M16 automatic rifles and ran in our direction. None of them spoke English but they seemed terribly excited and spoke rapid fast Spanish. I could only understand about every third word but they told us when they got the call they realized we were in a hot zone and had to call SWAT. They told us whenever they respond to any incident in the Llorenz Torres public housing area, they respond with a SWAT team and no less than four officers. The officers told us the public housing projects, which were directly across the street from us, is one of the most dangerous public housing areas on the island of Puerto Rico. They said when automobile accidents occur in the area, thieves and muggers from the public housing area, generally swarm down and rob the motorists before the police can arrive. They said we were lucky to have been in the spot so long with no one approaching us.

As they talked the SWAT officers stood over us and waved the M16s like they were ready to attack the housing projects. They told us when they got the call that two FBI agents had an accident in Llorenz Torres they just assumed the worse. They thought we were trapped and pinned down so they summoned a SWAT unit. I wondered if that was the case, why did it take them so long to arrive? If we were in a tough spot, we would have been in sad shape with almost a one hour response time.

The driver was ticketed but they let him drive the disabled car home—still with no driver's license. Sometimes being ignorant of the true facts is the best defense against fear.

****

One of my earlier assignments in the San Juan Division of the FBI was the supervisor of the Special Operations Group (SOG). This elite team of agents was responsible for the physical surveillance of every type of criminal from drug dealers to extortionists. The team consisted of pilots, photographers, and technical agents. Sometimes I felt as if I was in charge of the United Nations. In terms of nationalities we had FBI agents with origins from Mexico, Argentina, Cuba, and Puerto Rico. From the United States we had Mormon, Catholics, one American Indian, and of course me, the one African American.

Unfortunately sometimes they didn't all see eye to eye on things. It was especially strange for me because I felt like the lone outsider who really thought all Hispanics were in one accord. On one occasion two pilots got into a shouting match while in the cockpit of the single engine aircraft. I grounded both of them after the incident.

Sometimes the arguments were as petty as one agent criticizing the other's Spanish. I found out shortly after taking over the squad that every nationality spoke a slightly different version of Spanish. The varying versions of Spanish were no different than the many versions of English spoken in the United States. The Mormon agents often spoke an impeccable grade of Spanish because of their intense academic training and participation in missions as youngsters. I found when FBI agents were scored by the Department of Defense language test, many Mormon agents generally scored higher than native-born Puerto Ricans agents. The mere level of test scores sometimes brought dissention in the squad areas among the different groups of agents.

In addition, dissention sometimes developed between the Mexican and Puerto Rican agents because one couldn't understand the spoken Spanish of the other. They would accuse the other of using incorrect tenses and slang and argue constantly over who was correct. Each thought his version of Spanish was better than the other although I used the Mormon agent's as my standard. The lone American Indian and I would normally stay out of the disputes.

Although the longer I remained in Puerto Rico, the more I realized the Mormon agents were right most of the time.

During one period in the early 1990s, the Special Operations Group provided around the clock surveillance for the San Juan Division narcotics squad. The narcotics squad had several operations going at the same time and required us to have around the clock surveillance on roughly six major drug dealers. Most of them operated near the Isla Verde and in the Old San Juan areas. This increased the need for our services and caused us to rotate agents from the States for over a two-year period for temporary assignments. Fortunately, we had no shortage of volunteers to work 30-day tours in San Juan during the winter or summer.

Those agents, who were fortunate enough to draw a 30-day San Juan tour during the summer, often used it as a family vacation. We provided a furnished apartment at the El San Juan Tower Hotel and at least one four-day free period. During the summer the daily per diem was around 170.00 per day. During the winter months the per diem could be over $200.00 per day. Most of the guys used the four-day break to visit one of the many islands in the Caribbean chain. This assignment amounted to a Caribbean summer vacation at the FBI's expense.

The first point of business when the new temporary duty (TDY) agent arrived on the island was a mandatory security briefing, which I conducted. Although the island was beautiful, it was far different and much more dangerous than most cities in the United States. The pristine, white beaches represented a great opportunity for muggers to prey on unsuspecting tourists and people who didn't pay very much attention to where they were going. One unfortunate downfall was because most male tourists became so involved while watching the stunning, half naked women parading on the beach; they would completely let their guards down. The scenery was often so breath taking for most men, they sometimes became easy targets.

C. Lee Thornton

My first briefing would include a list of places to be avoided both night and day. Off limits places included a group of strip bars in Mirimar, which had been known to be tourist targets. I warned agents to avoid most areas of Isla Verde or Condado after dark whenever they were alone. These were two of the most popular tourist areas in San Juan but they could be dangerous when isolated after dark. Agents were warned to stay in at least pairs and to avoid dressing too "touristy". This generally meant to avoid the white shoes, white shirts, and leave the expensive cameras in the hotel rooms after dark. Most agents didn't have to be told not to flash too much money because they normally didn't have very much anyway.

And of course newly arriving TDY agents were warned about the spread of the AIDS epidemic in the Caribbean and not to take anything home they didn't bring with them. Most of the agents were married but I included the warning anyway in the event they became weak. The standard phrase was "If you go to war, put a helmet on the soldier." Everyone, both male and female, received the same standard briefing. There was generally no need to dwell on that issue.

My biggest problem was the agents who were chosen for the assignment who happened to be heavy drinkers. They also got a warning about their activities. One night I was awakened by a telephone call about a group of FBI agents who had gotten drunk and jumped into the swimming pool at the El San Juan Hotel. They were escorted out of the pool and banned from the hotel for the balance of their tour. For this reason alone, I preferred some of the Mormon temporary duty agents to those who were good workers and had reputations as partiers. I never had to worry about receiving after hour calls about the behavior of the Mormon agents. They always avoided the off limits places, were in the hotel at night, and drank nothing stronger than soft drinks. The Mormon guys were never any trouble to manage and enjoyed their time on the island.

One night I received a call from the Police of Puerto Rico at approximately 1:00 a.m. They told me in Spanish they had arrested an FBI agent who was involved in a serious traffic accident on Interstate 26. They said the guy did not speak Spanish and he was seriously intoxicated. I asked the officer his name and he said, *"El nombre esta James Grover Y dice el esta un agente de FBI de Nuevo York."* (His name is James Grover and he says he is an FBI agent from New York.) I couldn't believe my ears because Grover had just arrived on the island less than 24 hours earlier and he had sat in my briefing the afternoon prior. I called the Assistant Agent in Charge at home and asked him to meet me at the *cuartel* (precinct).

In one day Grover became one of my worse nightmares. He had completely ignored my briefing about things he shouldn't do while on the island. According to the officer at the *cuartel*, Grover had been involved in a head on collision on Interstate 26 about two hours earlier. Agent Grover, who apparently was intoxicated, had gotten turned around and entered the freeway in the wrong direction. He had only been on the highway a moment when he collided with another motorist. His rental car was completely totaled and so was the other car.

The other driver was in the local hospital and his condition was unknown at the time. Even though Grover was very drunk, he only received a small bump on his forehead, which was treated at the scene by emergency personnel before he was arrested. Grover had been in Puerto Rico less than 24 hours and was under arrest for DWI. Unfortunately, a supervisor's worse day begins when one of his agents gets arrested.

It seemed obvious Grover had ignored all the warnings during the briefing. We later learned that Agent Grover spent his first evening in San Juan at the Pink Slipper, one of the largest strip bars in Mirimar. Mirimar was one of the off limit places all the new arrivals were warned to avoid. According to information received, Grover had spent the entire evening drinking shots of Puerto Rican rum with two *"mujeres de la noche"* (women of the night). We found out he had spent over $200.00 on drinks alone not including the cash he spent on the ladies doing whatever. At the time we reached Grover he sat in a drunken stupor in a Puerto Rican jail cell.

The San Juan Division Assistant Special Agent in Charge was briefed about Grover prior to meeting him in the lockup. We're not sure what strings were pulled but Grover was released to us and placed under house arrest by the ASAC. Grover smelled like a huge whiskey still and although still drunk, he was glad to be out of the jail cell. We assigned two agents to Grover while we waited for advice from our legal counsel the next day. When we finally got settled it was not yet 5:00 a.m. and Grover had upset the entire San Juan Division. He still had not worked one day in the San Juan Division.

Early the next day the Assistant United States Attorney and our office received a report that the other motorist would be fine and had been released from the hospital. After a "backroom meeting" we were told to take Grover to the airport and send him back to New York immediately. The worse of his problems were yet to come during his Office of Professional Responsibility (OPR) investigation. I'm not sure how Grover avoided getting fired but I was glad he was no longer my problem and out of San Juan. I later heard Grover miraculously was not fired but only given some time off without pay. The rumor mill around the Bureau said that he had contacts with someone in high places that elected to salvage his career. Realistically, the only way he could have survived were high level hooks, no one ever speculated whom was his savior......

****

The primary investigative priority for FBI in Puerto Rico was domestic terrorism matters. Because of the unstable political situation many groups on the island were adamant in their distrust and dislike of some Americans. However every four years the general election was just as important for Puerto Ricans as it was to Americans. Political campaigns were alive and well all over the island and unlike any of those in the United States, they sometimes became violent. For that reason federal workers from the United States were encouraged not to become involved in local politics. For those who chose to become involved, they were clearly identified and marked for all to see. The neighborhood where I lived was a mixed bag of political ideologies and everyone appeared to be adamant about their personal political convictions. Because we were Americans we didn't discuss politics or display political signs of any type that identified our party preferences. I lived between two distinctly politically different neighbors who professed different political views. Strangely enough although they didn't speak to one another very much, they somehow both felt comfortable talking with me. I guess they viewed me as politically neutral and one who would not argue their ideologies.

One neighbor, Willey, considered himself aligned with the Partido Independentistas or Independent Party. Willey felt Puerto Rico should be an independent country and completely separate from the United States. From Willey's point of view the United States was tampering with the sovereign business of Puerto Rico and should go home. Willey's party, whose colors were green and white, were allegedly responsible for some of the terrorism on the island against United States interests. This party was also the party of many of the FBI's fugitives on the island. According to United States government records some members of this party were responsible for past bombings and anti-government activities on the island. Although my neighbor later found out I worked for the FBI, he had no problems displaying his flag. My personal opinion was there was only a small

C. Lee Thornton

group of persons responsible for the terrorist acts and the entire party had been labeled as responsible parties.

I could never understand how Willey felt Puerto Rico could survive without the millions of dollars in government aid spent on the island. The United States aid was in the form of roads, education, medical, public assistance, infrastructure, and courts. Every imaginable government program offered in the United States was also afforded the citizens of the commonwealth of Puerto Rico, irrespective of their political affiliation. Many Americans felt it would be no problem if the United States just kept the several billion dollars in aid and used it at home. My neighbor seemed to think the idea of an independent Puerto Rico was fine with him and definitely overdue.

However, my neighbor on the other side, Lupe, was a member of the Partido Progresivo or Statehood Party. His political view advocated Puerto Rico becoming the fifty-first state of the United States. Lupe's political party welcomed any benefits bestowed upon the island but they wanted to vote for the United States president and to have representatives in the congress. I've never heard him say anything about being willing paying federal taxes like any U.S. citizen but we all assumed that went along with the right to vote and receive federal benefits. In addition, if Puerto Rico became the fifty-first state of the United States, they would have to also continue to pay Puerto Rico's commonwealth tax, which was similar to any state tax. However the commonwealth tax was a lot higher percentage of income than any state tax I had ever known levied in the United States.

The total amount of taxes a Puerto Rican citizen would have to pay, if they became a U.S. state, would raise anyone's eyebrow. However my neighbor continued to display his blue and white colors proudly.

My neighbor Rosa, who lived directly across the street, always displayed the red and white colors of the Commonwealth Party of

Puerto Rico. The Commonwealth Party advocated keeping everything just as they were in Puerto Rico. It was what many citizens considered "the best of all worlds." The citizens of Puerto Rico received all the benefits of any United States citizen and were obligated to pay no United States federal taxes. Although the benefits afforded Puerto Rican citizens were sometimes only slightly less than citizens of the United States, they still had roads, healthcare, housing, and any benefits afforded citizens of the United States. The only luxury the Puerto Rican citizens didn't have was voting for the United States president and having representatives in congress

In other words, I lived in a tremendously political diverse area and I kept my opinion of politics to myself. The multitudes of different flags displayed during the campaigns were interesting and they made the neighborhood quite colorful.

During my five years in Puerto Rico I lived through two major political campaigns. They were unlike any major election period I had ever experienced in the United States. November of every fourth year was just as important in Puerto Rico as in the United States. While in the United States the citizens were selecting a president and congressional representatives, a governor and many local officials are being selected in Puerto Rico. Unlike in the states, political campaigns and marches are conducted when they could get the most attention or be the most disruptive.

One Tuesday morning as I was making my six mile, one hour drive to the office, the Commonwealth Party was in the midst of a political rally. The rally was being held in the main business district in Hato Rey. Avenida Roosevelt was generally as busy as any main street in New York during the early morning. A political rally at 8:00 a.m. on any weekday morning can create a horrible disruption for traffic in practically any business district. Even the casual motorist knows the campaign is in progress and can feel the stress by the time he gets to work. The rally is as loud and colorful as any rally conducted on any Saturday afternoon.

But on the same day the Progressive Party decided to have its rally on the same busy street at 5:00 p.m. that evening. The same traffic that was disrupted in the morning was disrupted that evening. The afternoon political rally was complete with floats, marching bands, and signs to attract the most attention. Political campaigns were designed to draw attention and to create confusion, which they did very well.

Later during the weekend two of the parties squared off to make their point and to create disruption on the main interstate highway. This time the political parade took place on one of the main highways leading into San Juan from the south. Interstate 18 was a three lane, divided highway just like any major interstate in the United States. The first time I saw one of these political events up close I had no idea what was occurring. It was a sunny Sunday afternoon when Elsie and I found ourselves driving north on Interstate 18, enroute to the Condado beach area of the island. The traffic seemed to come to a complete stop about a mile north of Borinquen Gardens where we lived. We just assumed there had been an accident and the traffic was being funneled into one single lane.

As we got closer, I could see the commotion was occurring on both sides of the interstate and the traffic had stopped on both sides. It was clear the traffic was being funneled to one center lane on both sides of the interstate, which was unusual for a traffic accident. As we drove into the commotion, we found there was a large group on one side of the freeway wearing red and white and waving flags. The northbound lane had hundreds of people all over the freeway wearing green and white and waving flags. Two lanes on both sides of the highway were full of people shouting at one another and on the verge of violence. By the time we worked our way to the single open lane moving north, people started to stare closer at us to determine if we displayed any sort of flags representing a particular political party. This is the one reason during our initial briefing we were told not to align ourselves with any political faction.

Those persons with the wrong flags displayed and moving into the slowed traffic quickly became involved in shouting matches with the crowds. These folks took elections very seriously, sometimes becoming violent. As we slowly drove into the single northbound lane, we saw only a few police officers who were struggling to keep the peace due to the size of the crowds. By the time we got to the center of the highway protest, we could clearly see objects being tossed across the highway from one group to the other. This was the one time I felt overwhelmed because if things had gotten bad, I was seriously outnumbered by protestors on both sides of the interstate. I drove slowly and took great pains not to address any of the shouting protestors. When I finally saw the crowd thinning, I drove like hell to get away from the two opposing groups.

As I looked in my rear view mirror I could see motorists who just happened to display the wrong flag and driving on the wrong side of the interstate. They were arguing with those who were attempting to obstruct the only open lane of the freeway. While the protests and shouting was occurring, the local police stood by and watched the activity. I'm not too sure the police hadn't aligned themselves with one party or the other and refused to carry out their law enforcement function. Political alignment was a subject never discussed with me prior to my transfer to Puerto Rico.

Second only to our mission to combat domestic terrorism was the FBI's mission to eliminate drug trafficking in Puerto Rico. The island of Puerto Rico was considered a trans-shipment point for drugs traveling from South America or the Dominican Republic into the United States. The major undercover operations targeted drug dealers who operated around the island and also the United States Virgin Islands. From our surveillance we learned that the majority of major narcotics dealers were good family men. Some were even active in their local churches. Our surveillance teams would frequently follow these guys as they took their children to private school and sometimes to shopping centers with their families.

The one factor we found surprising was many major drug dealers would cease or slow down their movement of narcotics from mid November through the end of January every year. This practice seemed to be because of the many religious holidays celebrated from November through January. Of all the religious holidays celebrated with the families, the largest religious holiday celebration was on January 6th of every year. This day is called Three Kings Day and is by far the biggest holiday of the year in Puerto Rico. Many of our major narcotics targets could be found at home with their families on Three Kings Day and the two months prior. Our drug surveillances reduced to home surveillances during the November to January period for obvious reasons. Our targets became homebodies with their families and nothing could vary that schedule. But on February 1st it was business as usual and shipments generally resumed.

When federal agents arrive at a home to conduct business, there are generally no doorbells; just huge bars and razor wire around the exterior of most homes on the island. You'd always have to stand outside the home, tap the bars, and shout, *"Buenos Dias...Buenos Dias!!"* until someone acknowledged your presence. If the resident answered the door, your first task is to explain the purpose of your visit before being invited inside. The Caribbean culture is very cordial, therefore you would never begin business with the household immediately.

If there was a senior family member in the home, it was considered highly disrespectful to begin asking questions without first seeking the approval or acknowledging the senior member of the household. Without that senior's approval or acknowledgement, information could not be exchanged and your visit to the home might become fruitless.

Even FBI agents from the States realized that some customs had to be adhered to in order to exchange information with citizens. It didn't take very long for agents to learn that no information could be exchanged without first showing respect to the household and acknowledging something attractive or interesting in the home being visited. Whether or not the visit was adversarial, it was always customary to comment on something in the home in the midst of small talk. Sometimes to comment on a child's' photograph or the arrangement of flowers on a table was a sufficient courtesy in order to get the business underway. However when admiring something about the home, you had to be careful not to admire small moveable objects because the home owner would feel obligated to give that item to you.

As a new San Juan agent I realized that another area of cultural difference was to be courteous when the family offered us something to eat or drink while visiting the home. It was never recommended to sit down and have dinner with the family regardless of the purpose of the visit. However it was considered rude to not accept something to drink. When offered something to consume by the family, courtesy should always be kept in mind in order not to offend the family members. I would generally say, *"Agua, por favor Y gracias"* (Water please and thank you). To not accept anything was the equivalent of saying the home is too dirty to consume anything and that was considered an insult to the household. This was one of the worse insults a person could bestow upon a family's home. After all, most Americans were generally not viewed with a favorable image because of their arrogance. I'd always recommend a new agent ask for water even if you only took a sip—and always let them see you take a sip.

American agents would sometimes run into cultural difference problems when executing search warrants in private homes. Court ordered search warrants could not be conducted in the same manner in Puerto Rico as they generally were handled in the United States. Many Hispanic households are practicing Catholics and they display numerous religious relics throughout their homes. Another insult a law enforcement officer might commit is to disrespect religious relics and symbols during the execution of a search warrant. The agent had to be careful not to move these objects and especially to take care and not damage them. If they were to be moved, it was respectful to ask the matriarch of the family to assist you if at all possible.

Some of our agents from the States found out the hard way that when conducting a search of a residence, no matter how heinous the subject may have been, you should always show respect for religious items in the home. Throwing the objects around the home is the best way to get a bad reputation in a local community and to shut the door for any future cooperation from the family. After a social blunder of disrespect occurs, your intelligence base goes to zero in that area of town.

****

My early weeks in Puerto Rico immersed me directly into the culture with the search for a fugitive in Rio Piedras. On any Friday evening in the area of Rio Piedras, the traffic is bumper to bumper, and one could probably walk from place to place faster than driving. However on this particular hot, sticky evening, I was summoned to a huge multi-story apartment building to assist my co-workers. By the time I arrived the traffic was at a complete standstill. I could see FBI agents and police officers with their weapons drawn holding the traffic back. Despite the heat, everyone was wearing a ballistics vest as required on any major arrest situation. I'm not so sure the drivers were angry because we were Americans or because we had interrupted traffic at 6:00 in the evening. Motorists were calling us some mean names in two languages and waving their fists at the officers. I had never seen a traffic stop involving drawn weapons before and I sort of understood why they were so angry with the law enforcement officers. I was simply responding to a call by my office to assist some agents in trouble. I had no idea what I was walking into on that treacherous evening in Rio Piedras.

My supervisor grabbed me and told me to relieve one guy holding traffic at the end of the busy street. As a far as I could see there were angry people in cars shouting and blowing their horns at us. I thought I was about to melt from the 90 degree heat with my ballistics vest against my chest. I tried my best to ignore the shouting but to watch the motorists and the windows of the 16-story, high-rise apartment building. Somewhere inside the building was the fugitive the FBI had searched for over the past several months.

Citizens were hanging out of practically every window of the apartment building and shouting names at us. It resembled an out-of-control circus. Dogs were barking as well as few goats made noises in our direction. No less than a dozen people in that area had been stopped by the FBI and the Police of Puerto Rico and were being detained from carrying out their normal business. Of course everyone got angry because we couldn't tell them who we were looking to arrest. But I kept my eyes open for a flash from the windows that were the familiar sign of gunfire. I had been in Detroit long enough to know what to do when I heard that crack and flash of light anywhere in my vicinity. I only prayed the first shot would miss and I'd hear it soon enough to take cover. My other eye stayed trained on the dozens of people trying to breach the sealed off area to get a closer look. I never took my eyes off of anyone with his hands in his pockets. If his hands stayed in his pockets too long, we pulled him out of the crowd and searched him for our own comfort and protection.

The FBI SWAT team finally arrived along with the Police of Puerto Rico Tactical Squad and stormed the eighth-floor apartment where the suspect was alleged to be hiding. Within a few minutes they signaled that it was a dry hole—no one was home. That was the best sound I had heard since I had arrived at the scene of uncontrolled commotion. I heard my supervisor shout, "Release the traffic!! It's a dry hole!!" Now we could let the angry, rush hour motorists through the secured area, and we didn't have to listen to any shouting and name calling any longer. I was still not too familiar with some of the street jargon but I was called a bucket of local, dirty street names that night.

****

Chapter Fifteen

- BANK ROBBERY PUERTO RICO STYLE –

I had been in the San Juan Division for less than eight months by the summer of 1992. I was still learning my way around the island and beginning to understand the culture. Listening to Spanish most of the day was finally starting to sound normal to my ears although I doubted if the slang would ever sink in to my brain. English was fairly common around the office but that was about the extent of my English exposure. I was still in the *"Hablar despacio por favor"* (speak slowly please) stage of things with regard to Spanish. On this particular day I had planned to leave the office early because my daughter, Carmon, had come to visit me with her new husband. I decided to walk to the break room to get a donut before I left the building that afternoon.

When I arrived at the break room a supervisor grabbed me and asked if I was an *agente certificado technico* (certified technical agent). I told him yes and I sensed something was on the horizon and waiting for me. He told me to meet a group of agents in downtown Hato Rey who had responded to a bank robbery. He told me I'd be briefed at the scene but I was instructed to take the triangulator equipment with me.

C. Lee Thornton

The triangulator is an electronic device used to track a computer chip placed inside money packages during bank robberies. A bank teller is generally instructed to include this pack of bills with the bank robbery money. The responding agents can trace the money to a particular area by following an electronic signal emitted by the bait package. However an FBI with technical expertise has to be available to locate the signal.

The problem using the equipment is the operator is completely exposed to the elements, which often are hostile during a bank robbery. If the bank robber is anywhere in the vicinity of the package and decides to take a shot, he can see the technical agent first. Unfortunately for me, the other two technically trained agents were off the island. This left me to be the guinea pig for the afternoon bank robbery. This was one of my first bank robbery responses since arriving in Puerto Rico as a technical agent and I was not looking forward to being the target out front. As always, as I gathered my equipment I said my silent prayers and asked Him to look over me just as He had many time before. I was now starting to wonder if He answered requests in Puerto Rico but I knew I was about to see for myself.

I started to think about Pop's warning to me when I first told him I was being transferred to Puerto Rico. He had always been suspicious of the FBI and definitely of foreign assignments with the FBI. He said, "Puerto Rico? What the hell do they want with you down there? Boy you better look out 'cause I told you they would cook up some way to get rid of all the black guys. What ever happened to your buddy I met here in St. Louis?" I said, "You mean Julius? He was sent to D.C." Pop said, "See there I told you, they're just trying to get you. Julius was sent to a safer place. Boy you better look out down there 'cause Puerto Rico in nothing to play with. They will pretend they don't understand your Spanish and try something. You better sleep with your pistol ready!" Mom held her

Oath of Office

head down and said, "Lord please take care of that boy." I began to wonder if Pop knew something that I didn't that afternoon.

I arrived at the crime scene, which was about three miles from the office. The site was a large housing project area with about a hundred people milling around in the streets. We had about 15 FBI agents waiting for me and no less than 30 police officers from the Police of Puerto Rico (POPR) standing at the entrance of the housing project. I couldn't believe so many people were loitering in the midst of a bank robbery investigation. I met the case agent for my initial briefing and I immediately began testing my equipment. The electronic chip signal gave me the worst possible scenario. The bait package signal seemed to be coming from the middle of the huge public housing area directly in the front of us. This was not the scenario I had hoped to find myself but I had an oath to uphold. I gathered my team members and told them we were moving forward to locate our package and hopefully the subject in the midst of the confusion.

As I started down the alley following the electronic chip signal, six FBI SWAT agents flanked me with their weapons drawn in the ready position. Behind them were about 10 officers from POPR, three cameramen from the local television stations, three stray dogs, a goat, and no less than forty local citizens including children. It was a huge production that I had never seen before in my law enforcement career.

When I noticed all the people behind me, I stopped and asked the case agent, "Hey man, can you hold the crowd back and out of the way?" He told me, "No way buddy. The media laws are different here in Puerto Rico. The public has access to anywhere that law enforcement wants to go. The media could also go anywhere. Look, we're strapped with 'em. Let's go." One SWAT agent said, "Let's go, this ain't the States." The stray dogs were starting to get restless; they started to bark repeatedly. They too, wanted to see some action.

I recalled walking between two large public housing buildings with hundreds of people looking out of their windows and shouting at us. It goes without saying that law enforcement officers, especially the FBI, were not welcome in Puerto Rican public housing areas. This time we had brought a huge production that was drawing a lot of attention. In past situations citizens were known to assist the drug dealers when the police showed up. Sometimes drug dealers would pay kids to stand atop the tall buildings and throw bottles and rocks at the police. Then there would be the familiar crack of a shot to scatter everyone. I tried stay focused but I kept recalling my conversation and warning from Pop.

Unfortunately for me, I was in the front of the parade and it was nothing I could do about it. I decided I was going to find that stolen money package as soon as possible and get the hell out of the war zone. I adjusted my ballistics vest just in case I heard gunshots. I knew any shots would probably be aimed at me because I was in front of the parade. That was not a good feeling but I knew most of the time they couldn't shoot straight and I stood a chance to grab cover if I heard the shot soon enough. I continued to have the flashbacks of Pop's warning before I left the states.

By now I had completely blocked out the noises of the crowd behind me and I focused solely on the windows of the high rise apartments on both sides of me. It seemed that the FBI was an enemy of everyone in Puerto Rico that afternoon. I only watched the indicator needle on my equipment and any early sounds of a round racking inside a weapon. My days in Detroit and St. Louis had taught me to hear that "two step" racking noise a mile away. I knew my ability to distinguish that noise would be my ticket home safely.

Up to this time most of my neighbors had no idea where I worked or what I did for a living. They only saw me switch cars every few weeks and leave home early in the morning. I tried to keep things quiet because I was not sure how I'd be accepted because of the anti-American sentiment in some parts of the island. Although my neighbors seemed cordial, I didn't want to test their allegiance by announcing that a federal agent lived among them. My neighborhood was several miles in the interior of Puerto Rico and quite a distance from the tourist area. In fact I lived closer to the city of Caugus, which was definitely not an American tourist trap.

In addition most of my neighbors were fair-complexioned Puerto Ricans. Most of my neighbors employed maids who were darker complexioned Puerto Ricans or Dominican. Because my wife had a dark complexion, they assumed I also had a maid who kept my house during the day while I worked. They would see her in the yard, washing clothes, and sometimes taking the trash out during the day. Many of my neighbors, with the exception of those on both sides of me, had never held a conversation with either of us. They didn't know if I spoke Spanish or not and had never bothered to ask. However, because they saw me leaving for work everyday they assumed I made a living somewhere that allowed me the luxury of having a housemaid. They only waived and nodded at me in the morning. I think they assumed that I was a Dominican because I have a dark complexion and seemed to know my way around. The last thing they assumed was we were American because Americans generally only lived around other Americans. This was an all Puerto Rican area and fairly upper class.

My electronic chip signal started getting stronger and more intense as I ventured into the interior of the Hato Rey public housing area. The electronic signal pointed to an abandoned building in the center of the large public housing project. I patted my pistol to make sure it was still there because I kept imagining the bank robbers hiding inside the old building and surprising us as we entered. I imagined them preparing to fight it out with the dozens of police officers and FBI agents who were approaching the area. I knew this situation could get worse but I had taken all precautions and I was focused on my assignment.

I gathered the SWAT guys and told them where I thought the package might be located in the old building. We devised a plan to approach the old, abandoned building from the rear. Three guys covered each side of the opening of the abandoned building as my heart raced twice its normal speed. Because there was no gate at the rear, two guys handed me their M-16's and jumped the fence. The television cameras were rolling and the crowd was growing in size. I took great pains to stay away from the sight of the television cameramen.

I handed the SWAT agents their guns and then handed them my equipment before I jumped the fence. When I landed over the fence, a television cameraman reached over the fence and handed me a huge camera. I asked the case agent, "What the hell is this?" Before I knew it the camera was in my arms. The case agent said, "They can do that here." The cameraman jumped the fence, reached for his camera, and politely said, *"Gracias Senor"* and continued to film.

The signal took us to the lower level and rear of the abandoned building. It was a perfect recipe for disaster. The SWAT guys secured the entrance and told me the room was clear. They had completely lighted the area with flood lights as I entered the small room and watched the signal get stronger and stronger on my equipment. I was not sure the building was unoccupied and I feared being bitten by a large rat or perhaps a dog living inside the structure. I moved slowly through the building as I instructed the SWAT team which rooms to clear next. I asked myself if I needed my head examined because I should have been at home with my daughter and family. I heard Pop over and over in my head saying, "Boy, what the hell do they want with you in Puerto Rico? You better watch your back."

Suddenly, the signal pointed to the area of the building, which had to be accessed from the outside. The basement was darker than the rest of the building. No less than 10 people were following me around this old, smelly, abandoned structure. I crawled through the basement opening and pointed my flashlight toward the position where the signal peaked. I slowly handed my equipment to an agent and lifted a large piece of metal siding that had been left on the basement floor. Before I could get my flashlight into the darkened corner, a television cameraman pointed his camera between my legs, placed a big spotlight on the huge package of bank robbery money, and shouted into his speaker, *"Vivo a las cinco!!"* (Live at Five!!) This guy videoed our discovery before we had a chance to examine it. It turned out to be $8,000.00 in cash that had been taken from Banco Popular two hours earlier.

I confirmed the package and examined the electronic chip inside the bait money. I handed everything over to the case agent on site and got out of the nasty smelling structure. As I surfaced from the basement I was sweaty and smelling just like the building. There were no less than 30 local residents, media personnel, cops, dogs, cats, and two goats standing at the front of the building cheering as I surfaced. Everyone was talking so fast I could only make out that they were wondering if I was *Dominicano* because of my dark skin.

I told the agent in charge of the scene the place was out of control. I didn't see how we could ever operate in this environment. He said, "Don't worry, we manage." I had found the stolen money but not without the assistance of a local television crew and dozens of residents of the public housing area following me. I turned off my equipment and went back to the office. My job was finished for the day and I went home.

By the time I arrived home, my next-door neighbor, Willey excitedly greeted me. He was a little more anxious than when I normally see him on most evenings. Since I had moved to the neighborhood, he was trying to learn English. He would use me to practice a few phrases that he had learned everyday. On this day Willey seemed a little more excited than usual for some reason. I just assumed he had learned a few new words to practice and was little more excited. I parked in my *maquisina* (garage area) and walked over to him as I always do when I arrive home.

I said to him, *"Ola, que tal Willey?"* (Hello, how are you Willey?") He said, *"Senor, Senor, canal cuartro...canal cuarto!!"* My wife came out and said, "You're all over the evening news." My neighbor then said, *"Usted FBI en canal cuartro!!"* ("You're the FBI on Channel Four!!) The entire story of the bank robbery was on the Channel Four Evening News with my face all over the screen. From that day on none of my neighbors had to wave and wonder where I worked or what I did for a living. Now they all knew an FBI agent lived in the neighborhood. I really didn't know if this was good or bad at the time. The fact that the Independentista's Party was still active on the island could have presented problems for me; however no one approached me about party affiliation or the FBI while I lived there.

However, my neighbors still thought my wife was the maid. After my television appearance they just assumed she was the maid to the FBI agent living in the neighborhood.

****

An interesting experience for an urban trained FBI agent, newly arriving on the island of Puerto Rico, is hunting for fugitives in the El Yunque Tropical Rain Forest. The rain forest presented an ideal hiding ground for fugitives because of the dense vegetation and constant rain. These factors alone presented unusual obstacles for local and federal law enforcement to track and surveil criminals. The rain forest is one of the only natural rain forests in the United States.

I had to constantly keep in mind that Puerto Rico is a territory of the United States.

One of my first encounters with a Puerto Rican fugitive took me to a small town near the base of the El Yunque Mountains during 1992. The only instruction my domestic terrorism squad was given was to arrest Jose Pablon Rios. Pablon Rios had recently been indicted for acts of terrorism against the United States and was alleged to be living in the El Yunque Mountains. According to the indictment Pablon Rios was considered armed and dangerous based on his involvement with the bombing at a United States Post office building near San Juan. The bomb exploded at the doorsteps of the post office at 2:00 a.m. No one was injured but the group made a point—they didn't like the United States and they could strike at will. Pablon Rios was a member of a subversive group that purported to be anti-United States and was not beyond acts of terrorism against other United States targets and interests.

When I first read the indictment I had no idea acts of that nature still occurred in the United States or any of its territories. As we discussed the indictment and arrest plans with our squad, our supervisor reminded us that only a short time ago a rocket was fired at the federal building, as one of the groups' biggest acts of terrorism. He said, "The rocket was fired at the FBI office but fell short by a floor and hit the United States Attorney's office. Fortunately, the terrorist group fired the rocket at 2:00 a.m. and no one was obviously in the office. Their intent was to get attention and they were successful." We all knew the Puerto Rican terrorists had a propensity for violence and the density of the rain forest gave Pablon Rios all the cover he needed to see us long before we saw him. We decided to take all 10 members of the squad plus four SWAT guys to the small town near the base of El Yunque to arrest Pablon Rios. Our plans would put us there at 5:00 a.m. and hopefully in time to arrest Pablon Rios before he went to work in Canovanas, Puerto Rico.

According to all the intelligence we had on Pablon Rios, he still held a job and generally drove down the mountain to Canovanas where he worked as a cook in a small diner. The informant only described Pablon Rios as a mean person with a bad attitude. He had no idea he had been indicted and he thought his involvement with the domestic terrorism group was inconspicuous to the FBI. Unfortunately for him our network of informants had identified Pablon Rios and six others involved in the bombing.

Just as any arrest, we made all our detailed plans and assigned every member of the squad a specific job. Included in our arrest plans was the location of the nearest hospital, which was quite a distance away from the El Yunque rain forest. Because I was the new man on the squad, I was given a job to secure the outer perimeter of the house along with Ricardo Garza. Garza and I had worked together in Detroit and we knew one another's moves like brothers. We had been together quite a lot since my arrival on the island and Garza knew his way around Puerto Rico.

As we drove to the location it was still dark and our only job was to arrive at the house before Pablon Rios left for work. The last thing we wanted to do was to pursue Pablon Rios along one of the dark, winding roads leading through the tropical rain forest. As the convoy of FBI agents approached the small town, it was unusually foggy and began to rain heavily as we drove up the mountain range. It was terribly uncomfortable wearing ballistics vests and especially since the rain caused the humidity to rise as we drove up the mountain. The lead vehicle was about 1500 yards ahead of our vehicle, which was last in the team of agents pursuing Pablon Rios. Suddenly the lead vehicle called out saying, "Attention squad six, attention squad six. Surveillance just advised Pablon Rios has just left his residence and is driving down the mountain toward your convoy!! Stop him immediately and affect the arrest!! Remember the subject is armed and dangerous!!"

My vehicle was the last of six and we pulled over to get ready for a defensive stop of the blue 1986 Toyota Corolla. Lucky for us there were only a few cars traveling down the road that morning. We only had a photo of Pablon Rios and a description of his car but the heavy rain, high vegetation on both sides of the road, and the darkness of the morning represented a difficult arrest waiting to happen. Pablon Rios's vehicle was less than a mile ahead of us as the rain continued to pound on our windshield. My decision would have been to meet Pablon Rios at his place of employment rather than attempting to arrest him on a dark, winding, rainy road. Garza and I followed instructions and pulled to the side of the road and looked out for the oncoming blue Toyota, which would soon be approaching. The heavy rain continued to pound on our windshield as we prepared for the worse.

All the FBI vehicles got into position and radioed to the lead car that they were in position for the traffic stop and arrest. Suddenly, the lead vehicle, which was parked on the side of the northbound lane, radioed that they had spotted Pablon Rios's car and was following it in our direction. Everyone's heart began to pound, anticipating disaster and a possible shoot out with our armed and dangerous suspect. As we heard the events unfold on the radio, Garza and I knew we'd be the last vehicle available to stop Pablon Rios in the event he decided to ignore the first five cars and speed down the mountain away from the arrest team.

All of a sudden we heard the team leader say, "Squad six, the subject car has been spotted. All agents converge on the location and assist with the arrest. Agents Garza and Marti vehicles are to get into position and block any oncoming traffic until the subject is in custody, move!!" Garza pulled onto the road and sped up the mountain toward the flashing lights of our cars. The heavy rain continued through the dark of the early morning. I only thought to myself that I was about to use my federal agent's liability insurance but I just wasn't sure it would be effective in Puerto Rico. I could sense that Garza was thinking just as myself, he looked at me and said, "Man how in the hell are they going to be able to stop a car on this dark narrow rode? How are we going to be sure we have the right car?" I said, "Man we think alike. This does not look good. Tighten up you vest and let's move slowly. We're the last car if he gets through."

At that time I started to combine my St. Louis–Detroit street training with good old common sense. The plan the case agent had put together didn't fit in anywhere as far as I could see. I told Garza, "Look man, since we're the last car let's hold back. If he gets past all of the lead cars, we'll let him think he's free before we approach him. We won't turn on our blue light but let's lay back. If he breaks through, we'll follow him into town where he works and grab him after he thinks no one is following. Besides this old car won't attract any attention." Garza said, "We think alike." We turned the car around in the same direction Pablon Rios would have been heading and drove down the mountain. We wanted to appear as if we were not a part of the arrest team if Pablon Rios drove upon us. We both listened for the next response from the radio, which seemed an eternity. The heavy rain continued to beat on our vehicle and the sun was slowly starting to peak through the heavy vegetation on both sides of us in the rain forest. Nonetheless, it was still tough spotting any vehicle driving down the mountain range and we knew it. Garza and I could only hear our heavy breathing beneath the sounds of the heavy rain in the rain forest. The radio remained silent as we waited.

The next sounds we heard through the heavy rain and our breathing was our team leader who said, "Squad six, squad six, the subject is in custody. Proceed in this direction. We've got a search warrant to execute." We again had been spared disaster and no one was injured. Garza turned our car around and headed toward the flashing lights about a mile ahead in the road. By the time we arrived at the scene Pablon Rios was dripping wet, handcuffed, and sitting in the rear seat of an FBI vehicle. He said nothing but sheepishly held his head down. I think everyone was as relieved as us because this could have been a bloody arrest if He had not intervened and calmed Pablon Rios. Although no one said anything out loud, I'm sure all were saying prayers of thanks.

Garza and I were dispatched to the home of Pablon Rios to assist with the search warrant to locate any weapons. The small mountain home was in a heavy vegetated area surrounded by a high steel fence. The sounds of the tropical birds chirping continued as the sunrise approached that morning. I still had not grown accustomed to the strange sounds which were much different from the urban noise of Detroit, Michigan.

A team of FBI agents and I cautiously approached the front gate of Pablon Rios's small concrete house. Just as I had been accustomed in Detroit, I trusted no one and took nothing for granted. I expected the worse possible scenario and did not assume the lady was going to cooperate with us simply because we were FBI agents. I constantly scanned the heavy vegetation for any signs of an accomplice of Pablon Rios. After we shouted out, *"Buenas dias!!"* (Good Morning), a lady appeared at the front door and walked slowly toward our cars. I closely watched both of her hands and the front windows of the house as she approached us. My outstretched left arm held my steel framed flashlight, which I aimed directly at her face. The light blinded my exact location behind my car. The other agents trained their heavy lights on the front door and windows of the house. Nothing was taken as safe until we could prove it to be so. The tropical birds continued to sing through the sunrise. The rain, although not stopped, dripped slowly through the slowly rising morning light.

Pablon Rios's wife Marissa, a somewhat heavy lady of short stature, politely unlocked the front gate and acknowledged the agents standing with a search warrant in hand. It was almost as if she was waiting for us to arrive. Without hesitation she escorted us through the front yard and opened the door of her home to us. I watched the sides of the rural house for any signs of dogs used for protection. Ms. Pablon Rios was very unassuming but quickly obliged and escorted us through the small tidy house. The one small child in the house stood next to Ms. Pablon Rios while three agents searched for weapons and ammunition, which were listed in the search warrant. Within the next hour the search was completed without any weapons or ammunition being located. Throughout the search, agents were careful not to disturb the many religious relics neatly placed throughout the home. The search turned up dry and we left the home. Ms. Pablon Rios was provided a number she could call to contact her husband later in the morning. I was really surprised by her demeanor because I've seen spouses become very irate and violent during search warrants. Sometimes the spouse would wind up getting arrested along with the main subject. Surprisingly, this was not the case. We thanked Ms. Pablon Rios for her cooperation and left.

By now the sun had peaked through the heavy forest and the morning fog was heavy in the El Yunque Mountains of Puerto Rico. As my partner Ricardo Garza and I drove down the mountain toward San Juan, we realized that we had been spared again to work another day in the tropical paradise of Puerto Rico. The sun had risen brightly while the tropical birds sang their morning songs to us. The traffic was as usual heavy with the morning commuters, as we drove through Rio Grande and ultimately past the San Juan International Airport.

****

Oath of Office

Although most of us in the United States make a science out of complaining, we have absolutely nothing to complain about compared to most people in the Caribbean. I was surprised the first time I visited a small town called Louisa, Puerto Rico. The town was virtually all black and with the exception of everyone speaking Spanish, a casual observer would think he was in any small town in Tennessee. The kids walked down the roads barefoot, dogs and goats roamed freely in the streets, and the people were as friendly as in any small town in Mississippi. It seemed that everyone went out of his way to speak to us, although they spoke in Spanish.

Power outages are common occurrences on the island of Puerto Rico. When you live in the United States, if your town experiences a power shortage, they simply draw power from another area or grid. Normally you never know there is a problem and your life is not interrupted. When you live on an island like Puerto Rico, when the power is out, it's gone. There were times when my wife and I were having dinner when the power went out and we just continued eating in the dark. In most cases you never let a power outage interrupt your business at hand, you simply do it in the darkness. The homes were so close you could hear your neighbors talking at the dinner table. If the power went out they never quit talking. In most cases you never know when it will return so you deal with it.

It was senseless calling the power company during an outage. In fact, what am I going to tell them that they don't already know? If you reach the power company, officials simply say to you, *"Lo sentemos senor"* (We're very sorry, Sir) and hang up the telephone. That is if they ever answered the call at all. For that reason we always kept plenty of batteries and emergency supplies on hand at home.

On any random morning I'd awake at six in the morning and find we have no water. The water may return that day and it may only be out for a few hours. To prepare for water emergencies we kept several full camp showers at home. The problem then becomes camp showers are cold early in the morning and you only have five gallons. However you just get used to the cold emergency camp showers and used them when necessary. Another option most agents used was to install gravity-fed water tanks on the roof of their homes to use during water outages for emergencies; or the cheaper method was to buy a 30-gallon trash can and keep them filled for emergencies. Of course you had to keep a lid on the drum so that mosquitoes didn't breed on the water.

I was transferred back to the United States at the end of 1996 for my final assignment and second assignment in St. Louis. Both Pop and Moms were getting up in age and had been very sick over the past several years. In addition, Elsie's Dad had passed away and her mom was also getting along in years. After five years in a non-continental assignment, the FBI let me choose my next assignment. My wife Elsie decided our final assignment would be in St. Louis, where I had grown up. Besides, after spending thousands of dollars on airlines over the past five years, it was time to move a little closer to family

Life in Puerto Rico was interesting for someone who grew up "up south" in St. Louis. However Pop's marching orders, Mr. Jeff's history lessons, and Moms advice for the rainy day were just as useful in Puerto Rico as they were growing up as small child. And as in the Unites States and everywhere else I had ever lived, He delivered me safely back home.

****

Chapter Sixteen

- NORTH COUNTY DRUG TASK FORCE -

My final assignment with the FBI was in the St. Louis Division. Pop was in his 80s and in poor health and Moms was not far behind and not doing well either. Elsie's father had passed while we were living in the Caribbean and her mom also was in poor health. When I completed my tour in San Juan I welcomed the chance to live closer to family.

My first assignment after arriving in the St. Louis Division was with the North County Drug Task Force. The undercover drug operation focused on determining the source of narcotics distributed in the St. Louis North County area. The team was interesting because of the characters we used as informants. I recalled from my first assignment in St. Louis the suburbs were considered the safe havens of the "well off" and they didn't have to worry about major narcotics and drug traffickers. However when I was told to meet with the North County Task Force and to provide the federal nexus to their investigations, I approached the assignment with enthusiasm. Returning to St. Louis after being away a number of years was much different than it was during the 1970s. Drugs and everything they brought with them had arrived in volume.

C. Lee Thornton

I first met the undercover drug team at a remote location in St. Louis County. It was so far out the way that it provided a perfect location to confuse any informants taken to the site. The site looked like a typical police undercover drug hideout. There were pictures of skuzzy looking subjects on the walls, recovered pornography items in boxes waiting to be logged into evidence, girlie magazines, and the officers wore beards and old clothes. Most of the officers really looked like rejects from a rock band; but they fit the role of typical narcotics agents.

We initially discussed several common narcotics subjects the FBI and the task force had an interest. One subject, whose name repeatedly surfaced, was Derrick Jones, a drug dealer who frequented the Berkley, Missouri area of North County. Jones had numerous narcotics arrests and always traveled with outstanding warrants under his belt. It never made much sense for the local police to arrest him too early because if he were followed, he'd lead you to the big stash. The FBI was certain Jones had a large out-of-state supplier that provided his narcotics and he was only a small portion of a major drug network.

On the day I arrived at the off site, an informant waited in the rear room to be debriefed about his knowledge of Jones and his operation in North County. He sat in the back room all alone and looked as nervous as a first time felon. The guy was dirty, tattooed, and smoking Camel cigarettes one after another. He dropped ash after ash on the floor and desk as he shook like a leaf on a tree. He did his best to aim at the overfilled ashtray but never succeeded.

When I walked into the room with the two undercover officers, he glanced up at me and continued to shake like hell while he puffed on a cigarette. They introduced me to the guy as an FBI agent that was also interested in Jones and that I was on their side. He reached out his grimy, shaking hand to shake my hand. He said to me, "Hey man, they only call me Bit around here." As a matter of respect, I

Oath of Office

shook his hand but took great pains not to touch anything else until I got to the washroom. I said, "Hey, what's happening?"

The informant had been handled by one of the county drug officers for the past two years but was somewhat out of control. I generally made it a habit not to get to know informants too well and this guy would be no different. This would be a business relationship. I found over the years that once informants found out you were federal, they would try to sell information to you rather than the local officers. I'm sure someone told them that the feds paid more money for information and generally paid a lot faster. However in more than 20 years I can still count on one hand the number of times I'd ever paid an informant a dime of federal money. I'd always strike an agreement with them to talk to the prosecutors or local cops if they got in a pinch. For some crazy reason they felt our word would be much more valuable when they got in trouble than money. Most of them always got into trouble and really needed a hand sooner or later.

What they really didn't know was sooner or later they would be cut loose anyway for the petty crimes they often committed. Generally the court has a set schedule to clear the jails for the next round of prisoner's everyday but my informants never knew that schedule. I'd take advantage of their lack of knowledge of the system and get as much useful information possible in the process.

In most cases the court would always cut the weekend prisoners loose by 10:00 a.m. on Mondays anyway. Generally if they were locked up over the weekend for being drunk in the public or fighting, the local jails wouldn't have to feed them lunch if they got them out before noon on Monday. The taxpayers would save money and the prisoner would be happy to be free. If the case was not that strong against them, they would be free in 20 hours anyway. As usual I'd always make it my business to be close to the door when they were freed around 10:00 a.m. on Monday mornings. I'd let them see me talking to one of the cops and always shaking their hands.

Without saying a word they would always thank me and pledge their continued flow of information in my direction. My words were always, "Now you really owe me." This was always the best way to handle informants—paperless and moneyless. I tried my best to keep the best informants in the "hip pocket"; that is off official paper.

I planned to work with Bit the same way I've always worked with most informants—from a distance. I found they called this guy Bit because they could only use bits and pieces of whatever he provided them. But he was no different from any informant. You could never take all of his information to the bank. Informants would tell you where you might find a stash of stolen goods but he would make sure he had taken his share before you got there. Or they would tell several agencies where to find a fugitive and would later try to collect money from each agency. Some would hang around and later try to hit on the fugitive's lady after he was in jail. He had money now and could buy her nice things like cigarettes and Pampers.

Anyway Bit told us he had the line on the biggest heroin dealer in North County. Bit gave us the description of the guy who turned out to be Derrick Jones. When I heard the name I was cool and showed Bit no emotion. If an informant knows you want someone pretty bad or was excited about his information, you had given him a license to pimp you. But Derrick Jones was one of the biggest dealers in the food chain and we wanted him in order to move up the line to his out-of-state supplier.

Bit rattled off about his connections with Jones and the people Jones sold drugs to around town. He swore to us that although he never bought anything from Jones, he was close enough to make a big score if he was provided the money. Of course Bit never admitted to buying anything because he was smart enough not to admit to a felony in front of three cops and a federal agent. Bit knew how to think on his feet.

I assumed Bit was a common hype and really was not that close to Jones from his conversation. Bit had his share of tracks under his tattoos, which confirmed he was a user. Because he didn't have a regular source of income, he was probably more of a drug hype than a confidant of Jones. In other words Bit and my old informant Gee from Detroit were one and the same. I had been around long enough to know what was coming up next. Bit was leading up to the "Give me some cash and I'll bring back your dope". I told him, "Sorry Buddy but my money don't get out of my sight. Besides if you've never bought anything from Jones, why would he all of a sudden sell you volume?" Bit stared and looked confused. He had no answer.

I stood over Bit, pointed at his face, and explained to him how the deal would be handled with Jones. I told him I wanted a recorded telephone conversation with Jones agreeing to meet him and sell a half-ounce of heroin. I told Bit he would be wired and we'd watch his every move during the buy. I finally told Bit, "Look, if things go bad you're the first one to be shot. I guarantee it, I'll do that myself." Bit looked at me in shock and told the officers, "That guy wanna kill me man!!" I told him, "You're right, in the worse way."

But Bit knew the federal money would be good if he delivered Jones, so he said he'd make it his business to get him for us. Although Bit proclaimed he was a good friend of Jones, the federal money was a better friend. Bit took his final puff on his disappearing cigarette and asked for another. I stood up over him, looked at him in the eye and said, "Man, do I look like I smoke?" The officer gave him another cigarette and he continued puffing.

I walked to the corner of the room and overheard Bit say to the officer that the federal guy was crazy and he didn't know if I was going to go off. That's the exact impression I wanted Bit to have

C. Lee Thornton

of me, so when I started kicking him in his butt, he wouldn't be surprised. I told Bit to get out, handle his business, and not to call me until he could deliver Jones. He told us he'd get to work and when Jones was ready, he would let us know. Bit said he planned to get Jones to their usual location in the park in Kinloch.

Over the next several days we had several false alarms from Bit. Jones was ready to deal, then he wasn't. Bit's back and forth alarms happened for about a week after my initial meeting with him. All of a sudden I got a call from the Task Force alerting me to get ready because the deal was finally going to happen. When I arrived at the remote offsite, Bit was in his usual form, puffing and shaking like a leaf. I could see Bit was getting ready to do something out of character but he knew if he was successful he would be set for a while.

He told us Jones had agreed to meet him at the park on Third and Jefferson at 3:00 that afternoon. The officers played a tape of the conversation, which was somewhat unclear, but the part about the 3:00 meeting was clear. I told Bit we'd talk about his money when the package was on the table. He took another puff on the cigarette and said, "Cool. Let's get going."

The lead officer came back to the room and told us they had run low on cash from an earlier buy and the plans would have to change. Bit got nervous as hell and started shaking. He said, "Man I told him I wanted a half ounce. What am I gonna do with no money?" I told them we'd change the plans and still pull it off at 3:00.

I gathered the officers and Bit and I said, "This is the plan guys. Bit you can still meet him at 3:00 in the park. I want you guys on foot and walking in the area of the park. Bit when you walk up to his car, tell him your cousin is coming in a few minutes with the money he owes you. Don't get in the car with him, stand outside and stay cool. Don't seem nervous, just shoot the breeze with him, and we'll do the rest. And remember, you'll be wired so if you pull anything funny, you're first to fall. Got it?" Bit looked at me shaking like a leaf. He was taken out of the room.

The other officers stood there confused. I told them, "We will post in six different spots around the park. We'll each have an eyeball on Bit and Jones while covering both ends of the street. When Jones drive up the street and Bit let us know he has seen the package, we'll send a squad car down the street on routine patrol, but checking license plates. Jones always has bad plates on his car. We also know Jones has outstanding warrants. That's enough for the officers to get him out of the car and search him. When he's out of the car, he'll be handcuffed, the other uniformed officer will search the car, and bingo. We'll have the dope and Jones and it won't cost us a dime. The squad cars will handle everything; Jones and Bit will never see us." I told them after Jones is taken away in one of the squad cars, we'll roll in and finish searching his car and impound it later.

The lead officer said, "But how do we clear Bit? We don't want to burn him." I told them, "That's simple, he won't have any identification on him so they'll take him away with Jones to I.D. him at the station. Bit will be cut loose in few hours after he is identified and that will have nothing to do with Jones. Let's leave Bit in the lockup for a few hours just in case Jones get wind of Bit being cut loose too early. In addition, let's be sure to put them in separate cells. Any questions guys?" Everyone agreed the plan would be simple enough; Bit was wired and only told what he needed to know.

I knew that when I'd show up after Bit was cut loose, he'd thank me for getting him out again. Bit's outstanding warrants will be his ticket to freedom and I'll look like his hero. Besides his failure to appear warrants are more of a nuisance than anything else. I might work something out with the judge later, but for now, I think I'll just let them remain outstanding.

Bit seemed to be nervous as the undercover officer wired him and gave him his final instructions. I walked over to him and told him not to screw this one up and to just relax. Bit said, "I'm cool but give me another cigarette".

The officers and Bit left the site in the dusty old truck that Bit was driven to the site in. As usual, he was told to lie down in the seat and not to look up until he was told to do so. The last thing the undercover officers needed was to have Bit in a position to find his way back to the undercover drug site. It was a good break-in spot because drugs and money are sometimes stored at the site. Bit took one more puff and I saw his head disappear in the rear of the old truck.

We all arrived at the park around 2:30 p.m., just to survey the general area. Bit was held about a mile away and waited to be dropped off near the park. We told them to hang on until we called them on the radio.

The afternoon was warm and the park was full of kids playing. It was spring break for the local schools and the park was the neighborhood playground. Four undercover vehicles strategically took their places around the park, insuring the main street where Bit would meet Jones, would be blocked on both ends. The call was made to drop Bit off near the park and let him start walking. Just to check his wire reception, we told Bit to sing until he saw a car flash its headlights. He would then know we had him covered.

As Bit arrived at the park he was singing Marvin Gaye's song, "Let's Get it On." No one would notice a grimy looking guy wearing dirty, tattered clothes and singing a song. We all checked our radios and I gave one car the signal to flash its lights at Bit. Now we have him covered, he could relax. Bit had his instructions and knew exactly what to say when he saw the package of drugs. He only had to say, "Cool". He knew all he had to do was stall for a moment until his make believe cousin showed up. He had no idea he was going to be searched and locked up along with Jones. I figured the less he knew, the madder he would become, and the more believable he would be to Jones.

By 3:00 p.m. nothing had happened and Bit was pacing the street like a mad man. One of the undercover officers, dressed like Bit, walked past him and told him to quit acting so nervous. Bit was smoking like a chimney and shaking like a leaf as he waited for Jones to arrive. I told the guys to expect the worse because our guy was too obvious with his actions.

Around 3:24 p.m., a shiny black, Pontiac Grand Am approached the park from the Jefferson Avenue end of Kinloch Park. Everyone held their breath and hoped the car contained our target, Derrick Jones. Suddenly Bit quit pacing and waved to the car to come over to him. Our target was about to land. We only hoped Bit wouldn't screw up as he displayed his obvious nervousness. We all opened our ears and listened to his conversation on the wire.

"What up Dog? Nothin' man, you ready to cook? Straight up Dog, you got the stuff. Show me my cheese Dog. Lookie here, Lil' Ron is on the way with my package, he just walked to my gal 'round the corner. Give me two minutes." Bit was doing his thing but never said he saw the package as instructed. He was totally engulfed in idle street corner chatter that wouldn't do us any good. The last thing we wanted to do was to search Jones' car and get nothing. Sometimes dealers show up dry and pick up the stuff from someone waiting a few blocks away. We needed confirmation and Bit was not providing it as instructed.

While Bit continued to shoot the breeze, a St. Louis County Police squad car rolled south on Gardner Street, as if it were on routine patrol. Jones' conversation with Bit suddenly stopped. Bit said, "Be cool man." As the squad car made a slow right onto Third Street at the park, Jones slammed his car into reverse and hit the car parked behind him. He then slammed into drive, but realized another squad car was making a left in front of him onto Third Street, blocking his exit. He was heard to say, "Oh shit!!" into Bit's body wire. With no room to escape, Jones drove over the curb and into the crowded park full of playing kids. This was the proverbial, if something can go wrong, it will, scenario. The plan had gone all wrong and this guy was scared and speeding his car across a crowded park full of children.

Two undercover officers stationed in the park, stood directly in front of Jones' charging car and pushed several small children out of his path. They dove out of Jones' way, just in time; the front bumper missed them by a fraction of an inch. As Jones weaved around the park, kids scrambled to get out of his way. Amid screaming parents and kids, you could hear the shouts of "Police! Halt!" Kids and parents in the park screamed louder than the officers to their kids. As Jones drove across the park trying to get away, he had no less than 10 automatic pistols aimed directly at his head. The 10 included my pistol. My vehicle was no more than 20 yards to the right of Jones. At this time, I had a clear aim, away from the children in the park. In an instant I shouted, "Stop!!" But Jones continued to drive like crazy to avoid capture. Just as I took aim and prepared to squeeze the trigger, a small figure appeared in my sights. It was that of one of the children, I had to back off. By now, Jones had managed to reach the opposite side of the park. He drove onto the street and sped south on Gardner. I realized I had hesitated one second too long and the driving maniac had gotten away from the drug team. I began to have flashbacks about the child who ran into my sights.

As Jones sped up Gardner in a mad rush, a St. Louis County Police squad was close on his heels with the lights on and siren blasting. We all ran to the children to assist anyone that may have been hurt while running out of the path of Jones. Luckily, no one was injured, only shaken by the trauma. As Jones continued through Berkley, we monitored the chase from the county police radios. We continued to check the children to make sure no one was hurt and to assure the parents we were concerned about the children's safety.

As we monitored the police radio, we heard Jones had reached Hanley Road, with the police car close on his heels. We then realized Jones had made it to Highway 70. We couldn't believe he was driving so crazy in the midst of rush hour traffic. We braced for the worse and prayed no one would be hurt.

We continued to listen to the radio and suddenly heard a great deal of commotion on the police radio. The officer said he was near the intersection of Bermuda Road and Interstate 70. He said Jones was still driving frantically, only now he was on the right shoulder of the Interstate. This was particularly frightening, because although Berkley and Kinloch schools were out, Normandy schools were on a different schedule and their buses, filled with students, were probably on the highway at this time of day.

All of a sudden, the officer shouted, "He hit the school bus and kept going!!" We knew Jones was deranged and would stop at nothing to avoid being arrested. Jones had hit the school bus, pulled around the shoulder of the freeway, and escaped through Jennings, Missouri. The Normandy school bus was incapacitated. Thankfully, none of the students on the bus were injured. Derrick Jones had managed to escape the pursuing officer.

However, thanks to Bit, he played his role like a pro. He was locked up according to our plans, I was there when he got released, and waiting for my thanks. Bit thanked me like I was his savior. He didn't do jail very well.

Bit got his marching orders to find Jones for us later that afternoon. I bought him a meal, which was more than any of his handlers had done for him lately. After discovering Jones' car at his girlfriend's house in Jennings, Bit gave us a call. The task force officers responded right away and arrested Jones before he could escape. From then on, I was the best friend Bit thought he ever had...

Chapter Seventeen

-YOU KNOW WHEN IT'S TIME... -

After more than 20 years of drugs raids and dealing with the worse elements in the world, little by little it begins to wear you down. The one case that started to finally get to me involved a young lady by the name of Roshana Norton. Roshana came to our attention quite by accident as does many of our regular "customers". The snow was finally starting to melt in St. Louis and I realized I couldn't comfortably wear my ballistics vest all day. Nonetheless, it still provided me the protection I needed if I just happened to be unlucky enough to block a small caliber round. The local drug dealers were starting to use .22 and .25 caliber pistols because they were small and easier to conceal. Although we always wore ballistic vests, any federal agent knows they are only a false sense of security. We knew the young ballers (drug dealers) were starting to take head shots while they ran from the police. It was a dangerous environment to operate and we had to think about our personal safety.

I was completing a six-month tour on the North County Drug Task Force when we got a call from an informant working for the task force. The informant, like most of them we used for information, was working off a favor for being sprung from the lockup. The informant decided to turn us on to a local "drug Kmart." A drug Kmart was the term we used when the dealers set up shop in a hotel room and sold what we called blue light specials all weekends. A blue light special is an endless supply of drugs sold by the dealers. Dealers generally set up shop in local hotels and motels to secure their personal property. If the police raided the rooms, they wouldn't lose anything except what they have on them and whatever was in the rooms. We had cracked open a number of drug houses in North County and we were starting to hit the weekend Kmarts. Our source was good at identifying the good ones according to the local police.

Local North County police called the source Ice Pick and he had a beef against Roshana Norton and her new boyfriend, Wilber "T-Man" Thomas. Ice Pick had a narcotics record and had done time in prison. He was on parole and should not have been associating with known felons. Roshana and T-Man had done time for drug distribution and they had planned to be a little more careful this time around. According to the source they generally would build up their drug stash during the week and would rent a motel room from Friday through Monday. Roshana and T-Man would put their pager number in the streets as a means of contact for buyers. They would normally pick and choose their customers after they decided to contact the callers. The two would move from motel to motel every week in order to throw off any potential stick-up men or police raids. T-Man would generally only return calls to regular customers in order to keep their location a secret from potential stick-up men. They generally had a large assortment of everything from marijuana to heroin for their regular customers. The business was all cash and carry.

T-Man had been involved in the drug business for quite a while and generally preferred to use hotels located near interstate highways. Drug dealers chose the freeway locations because they offered good escape routes for their customers. T-Man and Roshana set up operations at the Comet Inn off Interstate 270 and were open for business during the second week of April in 1999. Ice Pick felt he could work off some bad debts with the county by dropping a dime on Roshana and T-Man. He was somewhat of a con artist but nonetheless better than average informant. We met Ice Pick at the Hazelwood Police Department to prepare to shut down T-Man's operation that weekend.

During the meeting in a rear room at the police department, Ice Pick told us he was certain T-Man and his girl was open for business that weekend. He said, "Man I saw them check into the hotel on 270. They are open for business. People are rolling in and out like mad." Whenever an informant comes forward with a case, he's generally got an angle. He wants money or he has a beef against someone. It was our job to figure out what he wanted in this case.

We knew Ice Pick had a pending case and he wanted someone to talk to the prosecutor. His preliminary examination was pending and his girlfriend had just had a baby. To say Ice Pick had personal problems was putting it mildly. In other words we knew Ice Pick needed money and help with his case but we didn't know what else he wanted. However we decided to take a chance on Ice Pick's information and put him to work for the task force. However before we'd take a chance on Ice Pick we decided to give him our standard federal warning. We asked the police officers to give us a few moments alone with Ice Pick before we got started. They obliged, walked out, and closed the door behind them.

Bill Severts and I sat on both sides of Ice Pick and said nothing for about two minutes. After a long pause of silence Ice Pick said, "What? What y'all want me to do?" Bill said, "Listen because we'll only tell you this one time. Your job is to go in the room, find out what they're selling, and let us know if there are any guns in the room. Nothing more. Do you understand?" Ice Pick said, "Yeah, I can do that." We gave Ice Pick some more silence and when he couldn't take it anymore I said, "Listen up. You got one chance to screw this up. If you do all bets are off and your case will take a serious wrong turn. We'll make sure you redefine the phrase "hard time." And if things go bad, you get it first. Understand?"

Ice Pick looked at me as if he was thinking, "What the hell is wrong with that crazy guy?" That's exactly the impression I wanted to leave with him. I let Ice Pick know I wasn't his friend. We then called the officers back into the room and told them we were ready for business.

Ice Pick was given his instructions again and $200.00 flash money (money to only show and not to spend). He was sent walking over to the Comet to meet with Roshana and T-Man. Our role now was to wait for Ice Pick to return and evaluate the information. We went to grab a late afternoon sandwich and had planned to meet at the squad room in two hours. Ice Pick had our pager numbers and instructions to call us as soon as he made contact with T-Man and Roshana.

About 3:30 in the afternoon Detective Lindsey paged us and said he had some good information and to meet him at the squad room as soon as possible. When we got to the squad room Ice Pick was sitting in a chair, smoking a cigarette, and smiling like a cheshire cat. He told us he met with our subjects and verified they were open for business just as he had told us earlier. He said they had a large supply of marijuana and at least a quarter ounce of black tar heroin in the room. He said he wasn't sure but Roshana had some pills but he didn't know the type. According to Ice Pick the customers were rolling in like they were the only supplier in town. He couldn't verify if there were any guns in the room but he didn't see any.

Detective Lindsey was in the process of preparing the search warrant. He based everything on the fact that Ice Pick had been reliable in the past and it was no reason to think he would lead us in this wrong direction.

Oath of Office

The surveillance team maintained an eye on the hotel room and all the customers leaving were stopped after they cleared the area. Prior to executing the search warrant, seven customers of T-Man and Roshana had been arrested and their drugs had been confiscated. It was no doubt they had a full-fledged Kmart set up at the Comet Inn. In a couple hours the warrant was signed and ready to be executed. We were set to close their shop for the weekend.

As usual we prepared detailed arrest plans to cover all possible known areas of trouble. Our surveillance team confirmed there were only two people in the hotel room and they hadn't served any customers in about 30 minutes. Just as we left the department squad room, the surveillance team told us the two occupants had walked downstairs to the restaurant and apparently having dinner. By the time we arrived on the hotel lot, the officers had arrested them before they entered the restaurant. They were both caught by surprise and were quickly put on the ground and searched for weapons. Fortunately neither was armed and was easily taken into custody.

I noticed both of them staring at my FBI raid jacket as I arrived at the scene. T-Man and Roshana looked at us as if we had two heads and I'm sure they couldn't understand why the FBI and local police would be interested in them. T-Man looked at me and said, "Hey man, what do you want with me? I didn't do anything." My partner said, "Well let's walk back to your room and see if you're open for business." T-Man looked down and said nothing. He gave a quick glance to Roshana who was being searched by a female officer and saying nothing in her defense.

We found exactly what we expected when we got to room 203 in the hotel. The room was trashy as we expected with clothes and pizza boxes all over the place. I leaned over to T-Man and said, "It looks like you got some nice stuff in here and if you don't want these guys to throw it all over the place, you'd be smart to just tell us where you're hiding any guns and drugs." He looked up and said, "The box in the bottom of the closet." I motioned to the officer to go to the bottom of the closet and he pulled out a large brown shoebox. It was full of his supply for the weekend. It contained marijuana, heroin, and crack cocaine.

I know these guys never operate without protectors or guns close by. They have to protect their stash at all costs. So I said to him, "And the gun?" He said, "It's in the top of the closet." We found a 9-millimeter Beretta, loaded with a nine round clip. I thought about how easily he surrendered in the parking lot because he didn't have his gun on him. In this case we lucked out—no confrontations, no injuries.

Both T-Man and Roshana were arrested and all the drug evidence was confiscated. Because the case at this time was considered a state prosecution, we returned to our office and allowed the Task Force officers to process the prisoners and the evidence. Under the task force rules, if the heroin or crack amounted to five or more grams, the case would be prosecuted federally. With regard to the marijuana we had to have at least two pounds to pursue federal prosecution. The larger amounts of drugs generally were considered distribution quantities by the federal guidelines and would have greater federal jury appeal. We let the task force do its thing and we waited for the official lab results.

Two days later the task force officers advised us that the heroin was 28 grams, the crack cocaine was 36 grams, and the marijuana was 19 grams. We just assumed the marijuana was for their use over the weekend and they hadn't planned to sell it. By the time the lab reports were confirmed both T-Man and Roshana had made bail and were on the streets again. We knew that now the federal system was prosecuting the case and we would have two fugitives somewhere in the city.

Over the next two weeks I worked with the federal prosecutors preparing indictments for Wilber "T-Man" Thomas and Roshana Norton. Their past arrest records were extensive and both of them had prior convictions for drug distribution. Because T-Man was on parole we knew where to find him every two weeks if he kept his appointments. It wouldn't be so simple with Roshana who had completed her last parole.

Roshana was a single mother with six small children. She left the children under the care of her mother and sometimes with her sister when she went on her drug binges. Unfortunately her sister was also a drug user and had recently served time for drug distribution. The children ranged from nine months to eight years old and had a very difficult life surviving with Roshana being addicted to drugs. Despite her children, we knew she would be tough to locate after her federal indictment and arrest warrant was issued. Nonetheless, Ice Pick went to work to try to locate Roshana for us.

The indictment posed no problems for us and the two arrest warrants were issued for our two drug dealers. By the time the indictment and warrants were issued the weather had changed and St. Louis temperatures were pretty warm.

We immediately began contacting every North County source to locate Roshana and anyone who had contact with her. No one had seen her but all of our intelligence indicated she was still in business and still in St. Louis. All of our sources indicated T-Man had left town. We kept a close watch on Roshana's mother's home, her sister's apartment, all of her hangouts, and the home of every one of her known friends but came up with a blank. A cousin who lived near Velda Village, Missouri was caring for the children. Ice Pick went to work to locate the cousin's home for us. Within a few days Ice Pick provided us an address on 59th Street that he said Roshana had been sleeping but leaving the house early in the morning. We instructed him to keep an eye on the house and to call us right away if she was seen spending time there during the day.

The next day we received a call from Ice Pick about 11:00 a.m. He said he couldn't sit in front of the house too long but he described it as a brown, single-family structure in need of a lot of repairs. Ice Pick said someone dropped Roshana off at the house and he was certain her kids were living there with a relative. He said it was a small house and it would be tough for six small children to live there with the cramped conditions. We're certain the kids weren't living under the best of conditions with Roshana and anytime a stable adult could watch the children, it was a plus for them. We had to take Ice Pick's word that the information was accurate because we had no other leads on Roshana. As for T-Man, we had leads he was in Detroit so we sent leads to our field office to locate him. Our focus at this time was Roshana and salvaging the children.

This time the arrest of Roshana Norton would be by no means a routine arrest. I had participated in dozens of arrests over my career and for some reason I felt this one would be unique. Roshana was desperate and we knew she had a record of violence with a weapon. Unfortunately, the last time she was arrested she used one of her small children as a shield. In addition Roshana was a known drug user so her actions were never predictable. By the time I got to this stage in my career, I knew I was getting to the end of my rope handling criminal matters. Drug arrests were no longer routine and were becoming increasingly dangerous.

According to Ice Pick's information, Roshana was hiding in the house in Velda Village on 59th Street. We only had a description, which had to be sufficient in this case. Because we had no more information and a strong desire to take a drug dealer off the street, we had to move and fast.

When we received the most recent information on Roshana, most of our agents were out of the office and handling other matters. I

Oath of Office

grabbed two young rookie agents and headed out to meet with Ice Pick to confirm his information and to arrest Roshana. We met Ice Pick at the McDonald's on Lucas Hunt Road and Natural Bridge. He was waiting for us when we arrived and not because he was anxious to give us an update on Roshana. Ice Pick was hungry and it was a few hours past noon. He always liked to meet us at McDonald's because he knew we'd buy him a Big Mac meal with a super-sized coke. That was his favorite combination and he'd do anything to get it including lie about information.

Ice Pick said, "Hey fellas what's up? Look Roshana is living at the house I gave you on 59th Street. I saw her go in about an hour ago and she should still be there. She lays there during the day with three of her kids." I said, "Are you sure you saw her or are you just lying to get us to feed you?" He said, "I swear man, she's there now. I swear." By now the young agent had gone inside and got the Big Mac meal for Ice Pick.

We told Ice pick to wait at the McDonald's and we headed to 59th Street to locate the house and to arrest Roshana. We had two cars and we decided to park several doors away from the house where we thought Roshana would be hiding. We walked onto the porch while one of the young agents watched the side of the house. After two knocks a teenager opened the door and immediately saw my blue and gold FBI raid jacket. The child was so use to police raids at the house he knew to step back and let us inside. The child, who was no older than 12, called to the younger ones to get in the corner of the living room. One little girl about seven years old grabbed three younger ones and they all huddled in the corner. The baby whom was about two years old screamed and cried while the older child comforted her. The seven-year-old, who seemed to know the duties of law enforcement, was calming them all. They all huddled together in the corner of the living room and cried. Each of the children looked at us. It was really a sad situation to see such young children hugging one another and crying at the sight of law enforcement. It seemed that they had gone through this ordeal before and had built up distaste for law enforcement officers.

In the midst of the commotion and crying I said to the oldest child, "We're from the FBI. Where is Roshana?" He looked at me and said nothing. I asked again, "Do you understand? Where is Roshana?" He just stared at me and said nothing. In the meantime one of the young agents was trying to assure the children that no one was going to be hurt and we had to find Roshana. The children kept looking toward the basement door in the rear of the house. I was convinced the 12-year-old was not going to tell us anything so Agent Hill and I began to secure the home while Agent Severts watched the children. The younger children just continued to scream and cry uncontrollably. Agent Severts was not having any luck calming the children. It was really a sad situation watching the fear in the children's faces.

They were very pretty children and I assumed they belonged to Roshana. There were three girls and a boy. They all had the biggest brown eyes and smooth chocolate brown skin. As we cleared the house room by room for our own safety, I wished I knew what they were thinking.

Within a few moments Hill and I had cleared the upper level of the house and we still hadn't located Roshana. I really hoped we'd find her upstairs for two reasons. One reason was to hopefully quiet the hysterical children and the other was to avoid having to go into the basement of the home. Searching a basement is an agent's worse assignment. It is a dangerous and uncertain place to have to search for a hiding fugitive. Despite your training, you can never predict the outcome. In this case we knew Roshana was known to have used a weapon and she had a felony record. She had been on the run and we knew she was desperate to stay out of jail. In addition, Roshana was a drug user and none of her actions were predictable. Knowing what we knew about Roshana, Agent Hill and I slowly entered the dark basement.

We entered the dark stairwell and could hear the growl of a dog somewhere in the dark. Hill had his automatic pistol drawn and said, "Hit the light switch." I said, "Sorry buddy, it doesn't work. We're down to our flashlights." I was the first to reach the bottom of the stairwell. It was totally dark except for the glow from my flashlight. We could still hear the dog growling but we couldn't determine where it was hiding. I thought to myself that after 20 years, I'm not supposed to be risking my life chasing fugitives. Hill and I could still hear the children crying upstairs while Agent Severts tried to comfort them. The house was in total chaos but we had to locate and arrest Roshana before we left. I was convinced that in addition to the growling dog, Roshana was somewhere hiding in the dark basement. At that point we hadn't found Roshana or the growling dog.

Hill covered the north end of the basement while my flashlight pointed to the opposite end of the basement. The south end of the basement seemed to be where the growling was coming from.... it seemed to be coming from a small room with a door that was shut. I opened one door and searched for Roshana while Hill looked around and covered the other end of the basement. Thoughts of "I should have my head examined" continued to flash through my head as I walked through the basement area. The growling continued from my end of the basement. When I peeped into the small room a dog moved away from the door. My flashlight seemed to startle the dog that was more bark than bite. I covered the entire room with my flashlight and found a light switch in the center of the dark basement. After I was convinced the dog didn't want any trouble and that Roshana wasn't inside the small side room, I turned on the light. Unfortunately the dim light was only enough to light the small room. I managed to keep the small dog inside the room and closed the door.

Hill and I headed to the opposite end of the basement convinced our fugitive was hiding somewhere out of our sight. We listened while Severts tried to keep the children calm upstairs. The children cried louder and louder while we could hear the older child trying to comfort the baby. The two youngest children screamed "Mama," over and over. This convinced us Roshana was somewhere in the house and still hiding. We just didn't know how desperate Roshana was or to what length she would go to stay free. She had spent time in a room where guns had been recovered and was probably familiar with weapons. We really had no idea what to expect from her but we had to find her since we had gone so far. The children continued to cry, "Mama, Mama," over and over so long that it became annoying. The entire situation was a sad, sad affair.

We heard someone knocking at the door upstairs and listened while Agent Severts told them they had to wait to come inside. The upstairs had turned into pandemonium but Severts was keeping it under control.

One section of the basement had huge stacks of old furniture piled in a corner. Hill was convinced Roshana was hiding somewhere within the stacks of furniture. I shined my flashlight over the huge stack while Hill unloaded the mound of furniture one piece at a time. The stack contained everything from old chairs to cardboard boxes loaded with paper. I watched closely for any movement as he slowly unloaded the cartons. My first hope was there weren't any rats nesting under all that stuff. A mad mama rat will fight like hell if she thought the babies would be harmed. She's being no different than any mother protecting her young from intruders. My second hope was if Roshana was hiding beneath that stuff, we'd get the jump on her before one of us got it first. By this time both Hill and I were breathing pretty deep and we were sure Roshana heard us coming closer to her. Hill continued to peel the stack down while I held the flashlight and my automatic in the ready position.

I called upstairs to see if Severts needed help but the crying was all we heard. We had worked together long enough to know if he was in trouble he would let us know. Hills said, "Man I'm at the bottom and I know she's down here somewhere." I said, "Quiet...I think I hear some noise." We did our best to silence our heavy breathing and could faintly hear breathing from the opposite corner from where we were standing. Hill pointed his automatic in the opposite corner from me and we both pointed our flashlights in that direction. By now we paid no attention to the dog that was again growling at us. There was one small wooden closet in that corner of the basement with the door shut. It appeared to be full of trash and boxes...we both moved slowly to that area with our automatic pistols drawn.

We shined our flashlights all over the wooden closet and saw nothing but a huge stack of plastic and boxes. The closet was full of debris and only allowed enough room for one of us to enter. Hill started pulling boxes out one at a time while I held my automatic pistol and flashlight on the rubbish. Hill moved cautiously as he unloaded box by box. The screaming continued upstairs from the children. By now we could hear banging at the door that we knew was not law enforcement but either neighbors or friends. Suddenly I saw what appeared to be a hand under a stack of loose plastic. Hill shouted, "Keep your hands in sight or die!!" On the concrete floor of the closet laid Roshana Norton, who slowly surrendered to us without a struggle.

Because we still were in a dark basement, our fear now became focused on anyone else who may still be hiding in the basement. We had assumed the basement was safe but in a dark area with a prisoner found hiding from us, we could never be too sure. We quickly handcuffed Roshana with her hands behind her back and I asked her, "Is there anyone else in this basement?" She shook her head and responded, "No." Roshana was very unkempt and was wearing dirty, soiled, and smelly clothes. She was a heavy woman and the clothes she wore were ill fitting and torn. It seemed as if she might have been in a struggle prior to hiding from us in the basement. She had all the signs of a drug addict who needed serious help as soon as she could get it.

Hill kept his flashlight pointed around the dark basement as we led Roshana upstairs to the ongoing pandemonium. I held Roshana in front of me just in case I had a need to shield myself. From upstairs, the younger children were still crying and screaming, "Mama, Mama." Agent Severts still had his automatic pistol out and standing to the side of the front door. There seemed to be at least two people on the front porch as we made our way to the living room area. When the children saw Roshana handcuffed, the youngest child screamed uncontrollably and ran to her side. Someone was still knocking hard on the front door demanding to get inside.

The oldest child said the lady at the door was their Aunt Ruby. The children continued to scream at the sight of Roshana dirty and handcuffed in the living room. I took control and told the two younger agents to stay inside while I confirm the aunt's identity. I walked out on the front porch and asked the two men standing on the lawn to step away as I held my credential case in view. A small crowd had gathered in the street in front of the house and each one of them had a lot to say about what seemed to be going on at the house. I showed the lady my credentials and said, "Hello ma'am I am from the FBI and may I help you?" The lady said, "Young man my name is Ruby Jackson and I am the aunt of these younger children. Can you tell me what's going on here?" I asked to see her driver's license and she complied with no problem. I said, "Ma'am we have an arrest warrant for Roshana based on a narcotics indictment. I'm sorry we couldn't let you inside right away but she was hiding in the basement. While we were looking for her we couldn't have the home full of people we couldn't identify." Ms. Jackson said, "I understand

Oath of Office

but my niece needs help with her drug habit and we're all trying to help her with the children but it's hard." I said, "I understand but we have to leave the children with a responsible adult or we'll have to notify the Missouri Department of Social Services." She told me she'd be responsible and would call her sister to help watch them. Ms. Jackson then broke down crying and said, "Jesus what are we going to do with her six children. I'll just put it all in the hands of the Lord."

From the living room, both of us could clearly hear the children screaming and crying. I knew what I had to say next Ms. Jackson would not like but it was necessary. I said, "Ms. Jackson I apologize but for the safety of the agents inside I'll have to look inside your purse before I allow you inside." In the midst of all the confusion, some guy standing in front of the house shouted out, "Ruby you ain't under arrest, you don't have to do s--t for him!!" I could see he had nothing in his hands and I ignored him. I said, "Ma'am could you please open your purse?" She looked at me, then at the guy in front of the house, and slowly opened her purse for me to look inside. She said, "I understand officer" and walked inside to the children. She simply glanced at the guy in front of the home who was then gathering with a small crowd across the street. It seemed they all had an opinion about what was going on in the house. Each of them seemed to be loud, intoxicated, and nosy.

I walked inside to the loud screaming of the children. The older child, who seemed to be no older than seven or eight years old, was crouched in the corner of the living hugging two younger children. One finally stops crying when the aunt walked inside the room. The baby continued to bellow louder and louder at Roshana's feet. It was a sad, sad affair to see the aunt pick up the youngest child as we prepared to take Roshana with us. The child screamed to a point I thought she would be sick. The children all walked to Roshana at one time to hug her as we led her away. By the time we left the room everyone inside including Ms. Jackson was crying.

I stepped onto the front porch first to make sure the "peanut gallery" hadn't decided to get a closer look. However by now the "peanut gallery" had grown to about six bummy looking, intoxicated men standing near our car across the street. Several neighbors were now standing on their porches trying to get a closer look as Roshana was led out of the house in handcuffs. I'm certain everyone in the neighborhood could hear the screaming children, especially the one child standing on the porch screaming, "Let my mama go, let my mama go!!" One of the peanut gallery shouted, "Y'all let her go, she ain't done nothing!!" The two young agents held tightly to Roshana as we walked to our car. One of the "peanut gallery" walked toward our car and I pointed my steel flashlight in his direction and said, "One more step and you're coming with us." He slowly backed away and rejoined his buddies.

By the time we got Roshana to the car and belted in the rear seat, there must have been a dozen neighbors standing at the front of the house. Three of the small children were screaming and Ms. Jackson was standing on the porch holding the baby who continued to cry. As we slowly drove away I kept an eye on the "peanut gallery" to make sure they wouldn't try something stupid like throwing a bottle at the car. In many neighborhoods, it was not uncommon to collect a few bottles as we drove away from an arrest of a subject. I stared at the "ring leader" until we completely got out of sight and I made sure he knew he was being watched.

This day turned out to be one sad, hot, summer day. I'll never forget the screams and the looks on the children faces as Roshana Norton was led away from the house in Velda Village. We took her to the U.S. Magistrate where her bond was set at over $500,000.00. Roshana never made bail and it probably was best that she wasn't released to the same drug culture, which had imprisoned her for a number of years. At least while Roshana was in jail, her children had a drug free mother. Roshana's children didn't have to fear someone coming to their door in the middle of the night and possibly hurting one of them over an unpaid drug debt. While Roshana was locked up the six children didn't have to worry about her having a drug induced fit and throwing objects around the house in a fit of rage. Roshana was a threat to her children as long as she was around them using and selling drugs. Roshana Norton's arrest was a blessing for her family and especially her children.

Roshana later pled guilty to distribution of narcotics and sentenced to 48 months incarceration. We later learned the six children were distributed among relatives and hopefully, now had hope for a better future.

The arrest of Roshana Norton was one of the saddest days I've ever spent with the FBI. Unfortunately drugs have caused the demise and breakup of many, many families in this country. I looked into Randy's eyes and told him, "There is no future in a life of drugs. They may seem glamorous and the things the money might buy may appear exciting. But the excitement is short lived. Just ask yourself when was the last time you saw a drug dealer over thirty-five years old? The lucky one's die and the rest of them are sent to prison long before that age." Randy just stared at me without making a sound. Hopefully he finally got the point I was trying to get across to him.

Wilber "T-Man" Thomas was arrested the next month in Chicago and also pled guilty to federal narcotics charges. T-Man collected 60 months in federal prison for his drug activities. T-Man was not a big guy and somewhat timid in his appearance. I suspect he had a tough time in prison keeping his baggy pants up…….

****

- EPILOGUE -

As I look back over my career with the FBI and my life I realize that He has blessed me beyond belief, more than any one person deserves. My children are all healthy and have never done anything to make me wish they had never been born. My children have been obedient and have shown me respect as their parent throughout their entire lives unlike many I've encountered during my career in the FBI. Although they may not have done everything I've always wanted them to do, they have fared well and have become good citizens and productive adults. He saw to it that I have never had to visit them in a jail or at a hospital emergency room as a result of urban violence. I've never had a visit from a police officer or social worker delivering bad news as a result of any of their actions. I thank Him for providing that blessing in my life.

I also thank Him for steering my children away from the influences of those similar to Jimmie Pierce. Although kids like Jimmie were all over their schools and neighborhoods, they did not influence them in a negative manner. I thank Him for looking over my family while I made a living as an FBI agent in some of the most dangerous, despicable environments imaginable.

Many times during my life total strangers, whose profession I suppose, has been to profess religion and to save the world, have approached me. I guess when they first saw me they felt that I could use some saving. I have been approached numerous times by people with the traditional, "Pardon me Sir but I'd like to know if you know your Savior? If you don't mind I'd like to talk to you for a moment." The last time that happened to me I had to collect myself before I spoke. But I always revert back to my upbringing by Pop and do my best to show respect despite how ridiculous the request is for my personal information.

With regard to the person who questions my knowledge of my Savior, I'd always mentally collect a few thoughts about the many, many times in my life, had it not been for Him I wouldn't be here. After 50 plus years of life and nearly 22 years as an FBI agent, I'm not sure I've met anyone that has had as many breaks from Him as me. In my life I've survived race riots, denial of medical service, gang fights, a house fire, and poverty to the worst degree possible. Despite all of this I have never been seriously hurt and have never visited a hospital emergency room as a result of my employment as an FBI agent. Many law enforcement officers have been seriously injured and some have died as a result of doing some of the same things I've done routinely many times.

He made it possible for me to successfully out run bigots and homeboys in north St. Louis and live to tell about it. I know many, many people that were not as fortunate as me. During my tour with the FBI I have participated in scores of dangerous narcotics arrests, search warrants, foot races, and I have never received one scratch to my body. I've arrested people that have pledged to kill anyone related to law enforcement and He, for some reason, saw fit to calm the person while I handcuffed them. Despite entering many dark basements with hiding fugitives and barking dogs, I have never been surprised and injured in their pursuit. During my career I have never been hurt while working undercover in the sewers from Detroit to Cleveland to New York to Chicago to St. Louis just to name a few.

For some reason as I look back over my career I realize I've taken chances far beyond the call of duty and due to my "Oath of Office" and His grace, I have been more than blessed. I could say when you look up the word "risk" in the dictionary, you should see my picture. I feel I've redefined that word over the course of my vast career in the urban jungles of this country and Puerto Rico. I know Him so well that I followed the commandment to Honor thy Mother and Father more than anything I've ever read. I thank Moms and Pop for constantly preaching my marching orders, whipping my behind, and teaching me to respect adults.

As a child I was always taught to listen to my parents and to never question anything they told me to do. I had enough faith in Him and Pop to believe after I was denied medical treatment in 1959, that I would still be fine. Although I cried and winced because I could hardly breathe, I just didn't think it was the end of the road for me. I understood faith at the age of eight, just as I believe and understand it today.

Each time I entered a dark alley or a dingy back room of a narcotics den, I always said a silent prayer to Him before I entered. I'd ask Him to get me out of the place in one piece and to deliver me back to my family safely. I often think back to my five-year tour in Puerto Rico and the many flights I've taken to the states. Not once have I ever boarded a shaky or near collision flight that has caused me consternation. Of all the times I've flown between San Juan and the U.S. Virgin Islands in a small single engine aircraft, I've never experienced an emergency landing or a mechanical problem. I'd like to tell the street corner preachers about a few times when I thought the drug dealers knew I was wearing a wire and that I was an undercover FBI agent. I'd like to tell of the times when I sat inside jail cells or stood on street corners trying to extract information from criminals while working as an undercover agent. Thanks to Him and my obedience to Pop's rules, I have never been discovered or hurt as a result of my actions.

I often try to recall the first time He blessed me or simply took care of me because I was too naive to do it on my own. Every time I think of something stupid that I did and came out unscathed, I think of some event that happened earlier and I have to simply say, "Thank you Father". The earliest blessing I can recall receiving and understanding was when I was about five years old. At the time, we were living in an upstairs three-room apartment at 2825 Stoddard in downtown St. Louis. Earlier, my parents had tried to get an apartment in the Pruitt Igoe Public Housing Projects but couldn't get on the list. The public housing projects were just being built in the late 1950s and were not originally intended for poor people. In fact I remember standing across the street on Jefferson watching them being constructed. I distinctly recalled asking Pop, "Hey Pop do you think we can get a place over there? I would really like to play on those swings." He said, "No son, those apartments are for people with money." I saw white children on the swings in the play areas and thought about how much fun it would be to play on them one day. We also heard the projects had little dials on the walls which allowed you to get heat in the winter months without making a fire in the furnace. At the time, that concept was just too hard for me to imagine—heat without making a fire in a furnace.

One summer afternoon, my brothers and I were playing in the hallway when we heard a loud boom and noticed smoke coming from beneath the first floor door of the apartment. It was about 2:00 in the afternoon and no one was home in the downstairs unit. Two of us ran to Moms and told her something had just happened downstairs and we saw smoke coming from beneath the doors. She screamed to us to run outside while she looked for my middle brother. She also called the fire department on the one two-party line telephone we had in the house. Luckily the other family was not using the telephone at the time. When we got outside all three of us stood in front of the house as the crowd gathered behind the fire trucks that had just arrived. The first floor was engulfed in flames as the firemen poured water through the windows.

Suddenly the three of us boys, ages five, six, and seven realized that Moms was not with us and we sensed something was wrong. All three of us struggled free from the grasp of the firemen and charged back into the burning house. Although the fire hadn't reached the second floor where we lived, the entire house was thick with heavy black smoke. I remember there were people screaming in the streets for us to come back but we all cried, "Mama, mama!!" as we ran into the burning building. I recalled all three of us running through the entire second floor which was only three rooms screaming for Moms. The smoke was thick and smelly but for some reason our breathing wasn't affected at all. My oldest brother, who was only seven years old at the time, gathered us at the top of the steps crying and said, "Mama ain't here". We all slid down the banister, which had always been our quickest way down the steps. When we surfaced outside we were all crying and said over and over to the firemen, "We can't find our mama, we can't find our mama!!" Throughout our crying the firemen continued to pour water through the first floor windows to extinguish the flames.

One of the neighbors comforted the three of us, but we all continued to cry and feel all alone. After a few minutes of crying uncontrollably on one another's shoulders, we heard a lady say, "There's your mother walking up the street." We ran up the street and hugged Moms while we all cried. It seemed Moms thought we were still in the house and had gotten trapped upstairs by the heavy smoke. Because she couldn't get down the steps to the front door, she used a hammer and broke the lock on the rear door. She told us she went down the rear steps before the flames got too heavy from the first floor windows.

In our neighborhood locks were important and because we didn't have a good rear lock, the door was practically nailed shut. It was nearly fatal for Moms who had to climb the rear fence and walk around the block to the front of our house. She was crying when she met us because she thought we had perished in the fire. She cried and said, "Thank you Jesus", over and over until we were all calmed down. As she hugged me I felt a warm feeling of security overcome me. I think this was the earliest blessing I can remember. He saved Moms, my brothers, and me. Somehow as many persons as I've heard about being overcome with smoke and perishing in house fires, the smoke filled house didn't affect us at all as we searched for our mother.

Pop was called home from work to comfort us and help clean up our smoke filled apartment. None of our belongings were burned but everything we owned was smoke filled and smelly. But we had one another and no one was hurt. It was later determined that a gas stove had somehow exploded. We were lucky, or might I say blessed, to have heard it in time to get out of the house to safety. Shortly after the fire Pop said, "Get me the For Rent For Colored Section and start packing." We found another three-room apartment in a four family flat on Temple Place on the west side of the city. And that was a three-room apartment, not three bedrooms.

I realized over the years that although most of my co-workers and I came from far different backgrounds, we were similar in some respect. All of us had endured the rigors of the FBI Academy and we had unique life experiences. Those experiences were the basis that guided us through our careers. None of us were fond of criminals and drug dealers because of the harm they caused society. However we detested them for different reasons. During choir practice after a search warrant or mass arrest, cops and federal agents had a tendency to let out those thoughts and views that were eating their insides. They would say things like, "That scum needs to be in jail for the rest of his life, look what he's done to his family."

My view of that same person was somewhat different. True the criminal's life of drugs may have caused serious irreparable harm to his family but I'd say he was a lot different from "common scum". I viewed many of them as victims of society, due to their lack of faith, poor, and possibly no parenting, and no knowledge of Him. These unfortunate victims had allowed themselves to fall into the trappings of money and drugs as the only way out of their conditions. Sometimes I wished I could have grabbed them just to say, "Have you any idea how tough it was for me to survive growing up "up south" and living in a tenement apartment? Do you realize people have died so that you could have the opportunity to go to school? Have you any hope for the future of your family?" I often thought many criminals both black and white found themselves in their positions because they had no faith, no hope for the future, and no knowledge of their own history. Those that had even a slight knowledge of their history probably wouldn't fall prey to such crap in life. But most of all they didn't have Pop.

But the societal conditions that put that person in the life of crime and drugs were not all his fault. That person's ancestors didn't ask to be kidnapped and brought to this country. Nor did their grandparents ask to be beaten and run out of Mississippi in the middle of the night, during the 1930's. That guy's father didn't ask to become victim of educational and job inequity that caused him to give up on school at an early age and drop out. As I looked at many of those I've arrested over the years, I found most of them to be no different than me. We went to school under the same conditions but I went to school because Pop said it would make my life better.

I used to look at some of the guys I had arrested and saw them wearing the same clothes I used to wear. When they became the topic of discussion during choir practice, I'd just listen to my co-workers. Sure the guy was dirty. I was dirty at one time, too. The guy was also unemployed. We were all one step from being just like him at one time.

My first history teachers were Moms, Pop, Mr. Jeff, and Aunt Ida. As a youngster I used to wonder if they all grew up in the same neighborhood because they all preached the same stories to us over and over. I later realized that they felt that by constantly repeating our history to us, we would never forget it. They all had the same passion for our history and would tell us that we had life laid in front of us because the price had been paid. I really didn't understand that concept until I was an adult. Although they had many different experiences in life, their history was the same. They displayed the same passion, the same anger, and preached the same sermon. Mr. Jeff once said, "I only wished I coulda gone to school and learnt' to read like young folks today. I'd be in class everyday and learning all I could. But plantation owners only let us work those fields. I paid for your education with the whippings I took for not working fast enough, and I was only a boy. Don't waste my whipping...don't you dare waste my whipping." Pop and even Aunt Ida used to get all worked up and emotional over education because they paid their dues for us to go to schools, too. I also get heated when I think of my experiences on the corner of Riverview and Thekla in north St. Louis when I was thirteen years old. Just as the old folks felt, how in the world can any kid who looks like me, take his history and education so lightly? I'm glad the price has been paid and that I'll continue to preach my history to those who will listen.

I recalled numerous occasions going to a cold residence in Detroit on any random winter morning. Grandma would answer the door and say, "May I help you officer?" I'd show her my credentials and say, "Ma'am I know Jimmy doesn't live here but we have information he is sleeping here from time to time." The elderly lady would look down and say, "Come on in, what has that boy done now?" We'd walk in and see that she is caring for no less than three small children who were sleeping on the floor. She'd explain the children belonged to her daughter, who was having problems with a drug habit. One child was always school aged and Grandma would say, "That girl was supposed to come by and take the child to school this morning. I couldn't leave 'cause the other ones were still sleep."

As we looked in the back room we'd notice Jimmy's bed was unmade. The elderly lady would say he was there that morning but didn't know if he had left the house. I'd look in the closet and would hear a rustling noise in the ceiling area. We'd ask the grandmother to let us look around and one of us would open the trap door in the closet. After shining my flashlight toward the attic I'd see two beady eyes peering out at me. I'd say, "Jimmy, you've got two seconds to give up or we'll put holes in the floor!!" He'd say, "Don't shoot, I'm coming down." Jimmy would climb down and surrender without a fight. He'd be smelly and wearing the stench of liquor on his breath. As we lead him through the house in handcuffs his mother would cry and say, "Lord, I'll just do my best to raise these children they've left here." We'd apologize for any inconvenience and take Jimmy away. The children and grandma would all hug and cry, as we'd lead Jimmy to jail.

But after I thought about it, I could have very easily ended up just like Jimmy, unemployed, broke, and hopeless. Choir practice was just a time to forget but for me never to laugh at the unfortunate. I've heard my co-workers say dozens of times, "The poor children don't stand a chance." This was repeated whether we were in Detroit or a rural area in Missouri; poverty and life's conditions were killing families and producing criminals. We made our living collecting them and sending them to jail.

As I handcuffed many criminals over the years, I realized my upbringing was actually no different from most of those I've arrested. We just made different choices in life. They dropped out of school because they didn't have "Pop" waiting to kick their butts for not going to school. They became bored because they didn't have Pop to constantly preach their history to them and to make them account for their idle time. And perhaps, some gave up because they were given a little too much by a single parent trying to over compensate for the missing parent. In other words, the difference between many of those I've locked up over the years and me was my Pop and my blessings from Him. For that reason, during "choir practice," I never joined in the conversations to castigate the criminals because had it not been for Pop and my belief in Him, I'd also be in handcuffs and the topic of some cops conversation, too.

I've often asked myself how in the world someone with any knowledge of his own history and struggles could ever go wrong and hurt people. And this is my philosophy as to why many of our offsprings have gone so far astray. They have no idea from whence they've come. My belief in Him and my fear of Pop has guided me throughout my life and I only hope I can guide my family in a similar manner.

I spent an entire career in a job that most people in this country envy. I can't recall one day when I didn't want to go to work, because everyday as an FBI agent presented unplanned excitement. Everyday was a challenge that I looked forward to approaching with enthusiasm and pride. Although Moms and Pop have passed away, I know they are smiling down on me and bursting with pride. They're probably saying to St. Peter, "That boy did alright!" I take my Oath of Office, the life lessons learned from my parents, and my belief in Him seriously. Moms and Pop taught me my true history and to prepare for that rainy day with education and common sense. Pop always said, "If you prepare yourself, you won't get wet; if you get wet, you'll soon dry off."

I'm proud to be the son of Carey (Pop) and Elve (Moms) Thornton and to have served in the Federal Bureau of Investigation.

****

"Someday it will rain, but if you are prepared, you can overcome life's obstacles."

Printed in the United States
43225LVS00004B/271-321